What the experts say about the Previous Editions of *The Concealed Handgun Manual*...

"*The Concealed Handgun Manual* is a 'must read' for every serious defensive shooter. Chris Bird's recommendations are firmly grounded in reality, unlike so much of what masquerades as good advice on this subject. Each new edition contains even more timely, useful information. I regularly distribute the *Manual* to my own defensive shooting students." — **Emanuel Kapelsohn, law-enforcement firearms instructor, author, attorney, and expert witness in firearms cases.**

"I'm impressed with the 'street reality' of this book. Chris Bird goes beyond the usual hardware and into the critical software: the ethics, the morality, the emotional and psychological elements of preparation, survival, and aftermath in a way that gives his book the third dimension of depth. I would recommend *The Concealed Handgun Manual* for the library of anyone who goes armed in public." — **Massad Ayoob, author and Director of Lethal Force Institute.**

"Chris Bird's work on concealed carry comes at an appropriate time on this important issue. The book is well written, illustrated, and very informative." — **Clint Smith, director, Thunder Ranch shooting school.**

"An excellent guide to responsible, safe, and lawful exercise of the right to bear arms. Useful for persons who carry licensed firearms for protection, and for persons who want a better understanding of this controversial, important subject." — **Dave Kopel, author and research director, Independence Institute.**

"Mr. Bird has relied on his own years of experience and extensive research to compile an intelligent and well laid-out work. Detailed case studies have been used to validate theories and techniques. Not only does the book cover firearms and their safe and tactical use, *The Concealed Handgun Manual* also offers some interesting and poignant commentary on current societal views. Recommended reading material." — **Louis Awerbuck, president, Yavapai Firearms Academy.**

"Through Chris Bird's significant journalistic talents, the reader 'meets' numerous gun owners, and learns why they carry a defensive firearm. A good number of Bird's anecdotes concern women and how they came to carry a gun. Expect stories about female stalking survivors, women who used cunning and courage to emerge unscathed from home burglaries, survivors of infamous shoot-outs and more." — **Gila Hayes, author of *Effective Defense* and staff instructor of The Firearms Academy of Seattle, in *Women & Guns.***

"After reading *The Concealed Handgun Manual* by Chris Bird, it is apparent that a book has finally been written that teaches the proper techniques needed to safely carry a handgun concealed. The techniques used and applied are both life-saving and practical. Survival is what this manual is about, and for that reason I personally recommend it to everyone who carries a concealed handgun, both civilian and law enforcement. . . . survival is our number one objective, and I believe that Chris Bird's number one objective is the same." — **Jerry D. Lane, law-enforcement firearms instructor.**

"Outstanding! What I like is the anecdotes. It's a really good book for someone who is not sure if they want to carry. It definitely fills a need." — **Jerry Patterson, Texas Land Commissioner and former state senator, who sponsored the Texas Concealed Handgun Law.**

"Each chapter contains real-life accounts of gunfights, often by the persons involved. The reports of the Luby's horror-story, and Gordon Hale's episode which became Texas' 'first-use' incident are worth the price of the book!" — **Craig Palmer, president of the Kentucky Firearms Foundation, Inc.**

"*The Concealed Handgun Manual* is a truly universal manual, covering virtually every conceivable aspect of carrying and using a concealed handgun." — **Tony Fabian, president of the Colorado State Shooting Association.**

*Appears on **Texas Department of Public Safety** list of approved reading for concealed-handgun license holders.*

Reviews of Previous Editions of
The Concealed Handgun Manual...

"The book explores all aspects and ramifications of carrying a concealed firearm. In addition to shooting instruction and guidance as to when it would be necessary to fire a gun in self-defense, the book also recounts many real-life events. This is an extremely useful guide for those who want to learn more about the world of concealed carry." — **Michael O. Humphries in *The American Rifleman*.**

"The fourth edition adds two-hundred pages to the original book. Given the quality of the original the question is what could be added? The answer is, a great deal. The author has not simply fleshed out his basic work; he has provided layers of illustrative detail to owning, carrying, and using firearms for self-defense. The author has conducted an impressive amount of research to gather incidents which illustrate the many aspects of carrying and using firearms in self-defense." — **K.L. Jamison on the website of The Western Missouri Shooters Alliance.**

"This book has made me re-evaluate my life and more importantly, my expectations of myself and the police. I do have the power to avert an attack either subtly or with direct action on my part. I thoroughly enjoyed reading the personal accounts throughout the book from real people who I can identify with." — **Toni Winchester, *Colorado Shooting*.**

"The chapter that I find the most interesting is Chapter Nine, entitled Advanced Shooting: Back Up and Move to Cover. Even experienced instructors can learn something from this chapter."— **John Krull in *Gun Week*.**

"A must for those looking to carry a concealed handgun." — ***The Second Amendment Foundation Reporter*.**

"Bird teaches through illustrative stories of self-defense and survival experienced by moms, laboratory workers, electricians and other everyday people who learned, sometimes the hard way, the value of the self-defense handgun." — **Gila Hayes in** ***Women & Guns.***

"One thing that jumped out at me as I was reading *The Concealed Handgun Manual* was the 'easy-to-read' text layout and the fantastic use of pictures. The photos in this book are top notch. It is imperative to have explanatory photographs in a handgun manual. The quality and quantity of the images used in this book really put it into its own category of professionalism. In addition to these great pictures, the author writes in a very appealing easy-to-read style." – **Timothy J. Schmidt in** ***Concealed Carry Magazine.***

"Carrying a deadly weapon is too serious a matter to go unstudied. Chris Bird's work serves as a fine textbook for those who have made, or are considering making, that commitment." — **Will Cox in** ***Gun Week.***

"Provides useful information on how to keep fender benders from escalating into homicidal nastiness . . . . Far from being 'psychobabble,' this chapter is an honest look at the psychological dynamics of conflicts and how to deal with them." — **Charles M. B. Smith,** ***The Sharpshooter,*** **newsletter of the Oklahoma Rifle Association.**

"I would recommend your book to anyone applying for a concealed carry permit . . . to understand the rights and responsibilities of concealed carry, along with very helpful information for choosing the proper equipment, all in a very readable and interesting form." — **Representative Roy L. Brun, an author of the Louisiana Concealed Handgun Carry Law**

"As a concealed weapon license holder and NRA Personal Protection Instructor for the past ten years, I found a lot of very effective information and answers to questions that I hadn't considered in an enjoyable and easy-to-read format. If you carry or are considering doing so, I strongly recommend this handy and informative resource." – **Ray Walters, editor,** ***Shoot! Magazine.***

THE CONCEALED HANDGUN MANUAL

Fifth Edition

How to Choose, Carry, and Shoot a Gun in Self Defense

THE CONCEALED HANDGUN MANUAL

Fifth Edition

How to Choose, Carry, and Shoot a Gun in Self Defense

Chris Bird

Privateer Publications

San Antonio, Texas

Published by: Privateer Publications • (210) 308-8191
Post Office Box 29427 • San Antonio, TX 78229

Printed in the United States of America.
First Edition 1997; Second Edition 2000; Third Edition 2002; Fourth Edition 2004; Fifth Edition 2008.

Publisher's Cataloging-in-Publication
(Provided by Wordwright Associates)

Bird, Chris.
    The concealed handgun manual : how to choose, carry, and shoot a gun in self defense / Chris Bird. -- 5th ed.
    p. cm.
    Includes bibliographical references and index.
    ISBN: 978-0-9656784-7-6

    1. Pistols.   2. Pistol shooting.   3. Self-defense.
    4. Gun control--United States.   5. Concealment (Criminal law)   I. Title.

    TS537.B48 2004   683.4'3
                      WA-200417

Photo Credits: Kemp Davis Photography, San Antonio; Smith & Wesson; Galco; Beretta; Browning; Colt; Crimson Trace; Dillon; Fobus; Glock; Kahr; Kel-Tec; Kimber; Magnum Research; Manuel Maltos; *NRA News*; North American Arms; Pager Pal; Para-Ordnance; The Safe Outlet; SIG Sauer; Milt Sparks; Springfield Armory; Taurus; Toby Threadgill; Thunder Ranch; and XS Sight Systems.

Warning: Neither the publisher nor the author assumes any responsibility for the use or misuse of any information contained in this book.

Usage Note: Use of the masculine personal pronoun is not intended to be discriminatory.

Trade Names appearing in this book are the property of their respective owners. Products and services are mentioned in this book for reference only. Nothing written or implied should be construed as an endorsement of any product or service.

Printed on recycled paper.

ii

*To Anita, whose idea this was and
who suffered through its completion again and again.*

"Those who give up essential liberties to purchase
a little temporary safety deserve neither liberty nor safety."

—*Benjamin Franklin*

"The constitutions of most of our States assert that all
power is inherent in the people; that . . . it is their right
and duty to be at all times armed."

—*Thomas Jefferson*

"Forewarned, forearmed; to be prepared is half the victory."
—*Miguel Cervantes*

CONTENTS

FOREWORD

Chris Bird and I became friends more than a decade ago, after meeting on a South Texas shooting range. As well as being avid handgun shooters, we shared a firm belief that everyone is ultimately responsible for his or her own safety. I was surprised that someone from England should share my thoughts on this, as I knew that handgun ownership was generally discouraged in that country. It is now prohibited. I have watched Chris adapt to our South Texas culture and notice that some of our colloquialisms have crept into his speech and even his writing style.

At the time Chris and I met in 1990, Texans had not been able to legally carry handguns for self defense for more than a century. A lot has changed since then. We watched with envy as other states passed concealed-carry laws in the early 1990s and experienced frustration when in 1993 our own governor, then Ann Richards, threatened to veto similar legislation here. I like to think that her threat was responsible for the end of her political career. The legislation finally passed in 1995 and was signed into law by our then governor, now president, George W. Bush.

The new law required applicants to complete a ten- to fifteen-hour training course, so qualified course instructors were needed. While I was among the first people qualified to teach the concealed-handgun course, Chris saw a need for a book that would go further than the mandatory course prescribed by the state. The result is *The Concealed Handgun Manual.*

As a long-time handgun shooter and a former crime reporter for a big-city newspaper, Chris is eminently qualified to write on this subject. In a way that no single expert might do, Chris has brought together the philosophies and tactics of many self-defense masters. He has provided a comprehensive overview simple enough for the first-time shooter to understand, and from which even experienced shooters can gain insight. I believe that in reading this book, many shooters can develop a mind-set to keep them out of trouble.

The Concealed Handgun Manual is a must-buy for anyone who considers carrying a concealed handgun for personal protection. Studying the text is a learning experience which will increase your awareness and understanding of the principles of pistolcraft and the mental discipline needed to win a gunfight. The book has valuable and potentially life-saving tips to incorporate into your training and dry-fire sessions. It is an outstanding, enjoyable, and very readable book.

Each chapter contains true-life accounts of actual shootings and events where handguns were used in self defense by private citizens as well as law-enforcement officers. These anecdotes are exciting, educational, and well-researched. They provide examples of how others have faced deadly force and survived.

This is not just a book for those interested in the Texas concealed-handgun license. The text is of vital interest to anyone concerned with armed defense in a violent society. In addition, Chris has provided a summary of the laws and concealed-carry license statistics for each of the thirty-nine states that allow law-abiding citizens to carry guns for protection. This book is for you, regardless of where you live.

The Concealed Handgun Manual ranks with the best publications available for making an educated and informed decision about legally carrying a handgun for personal protection. I highly recommend you add it to your library.

> *Ted Bonnet*
> *Twice World Champion, Standard Division*
> *International Practical Shooting Confederation*

INTRODUCTION TO THE FIFTH EDITION

Since the previous edition of *The Concealed Handgun Manual*, two major incidents have happened that drive home to the concealed-carry-license holder how foolish it is to rely on law enforcement for protection.

The most recent example is the mass shooting at Virginia Tech in April 2007, when a young man with severe mental problems managed to kill thirty-two students and faculty members. Thirty of these murders occurred in an eleven-minute time span on the second floor of a classroom building. For half that time, police officers were outside the building trying to get in. No student or faculty member in the building was armed. During the previous year, the university had lobbied the legislature hard to maintain its status as "a gun-free zone." When the Virginia governor's panel, appointed to investigate the incident, came out with its report, it contained no recommendations about how the victims might have acted differently to save their lives. There was no recommendation that students or faculty members with concealed-carry licenses should be allowed to be armed on campus. The report, as far as the victims were concerned, was an endorsement of the *status quo*.

The other incident was in the aftermath of Hurricane Katrina, when for more than a week, those residents remaining in New Orleans were subjected to a nightmare of looting, shooting, and anarchy. There was no police protection, so residents had to rely on their own firearms for self-defense. After a week, the police chief made the situation worse. He ordered officers under his jurisdiction to confiscate all privately owned firearms. More than a thousand were seized, leaving their owners defenseless against the criminals who still roamed the city. As a result of this outrageous behavior, at least nineteen states and the federal government have passed laws to prevent authorities from confiscating legally owned firearms during periods of crisis. While Hurricane Katrina was a natural disaster, the aftermath was a dress rehearsal and a warning for the conditions that will likely follow a major terrorist attack. I have not gone into great detail about the aftermath of Katrina, as I have given it more attention in my book *Thank God I Had a Gun: True Accounts of Self-Defense.*

In the past two years, two more states have passed laws that enable most law-abiding adults to carry concealed handguns for protection in public. Kansas and Nebraska started issuing permits at the beginning of 2007. They bring to thirty-nine the total number of states where permits are relatively easy to get or are not required. Nine more states have more restricted permit systems, leaving Illinois and Wisconsin with no licensing program for civilians at all. Chapter 13, which contains summaries of concealed-handgun laws, has been extensively updated, particularly concerning reciprocity among states.

In the fifth edition, I have also covered two subjects that were not touched upon in previous editions. Laser sights are becoming better and more popular among civilian gun carriers. Crimson Trace claims that their sights improve law-enforcement officers' hit ratios to 90 percent or more from about 20 percent. This is certainly worthy of note. I have not before addressed the issue of insurance against legal expenses for civilians involved in self-defense shootings. There are numerous examples of people who have defended themselves and have then been prosecuted. Even if they win, the legal costs can be ruinous.

As we head into the 2008 election year, prospects do not look good for gun owners. If one of the front-running Democratic candidates becomes president, we can expect an attempt to return to the so-called assault-weapons ban and a limit on magazine capacity. This at a time when more and more police officers are carrying "assault rifles." Even if a Republican is elected president, several of the front runners have very dubious records regarding gun rights. So we are likely to be in for a fight for our gun rights.

Stay safe and remain undefeated.

Chris Bird

San Antonio, December 2007

ABOUT THE AUTHOR

Chris Bird has been a journalist for twenty-five years and a handgun shooter for more than forty. His love for shooting  has steered him through the bureaucratic red tape of owning handguns in England, Canada, and Australia. As a commissioned officer in the Royal Military Police of the British Army in the 1960s, Bird was stationed in Berlin, West Germany, and Belgium, serving as company weapon-training officer and winning awards for shooting in competition.

An incurable romantic, Chris migrated to Canada after leaving the military, where he worked as a cowboy in British Columbia while shooting and hunting extensively.

Chris became a journalist and worked as a crime and investigative reporter for the *Vancouver Province* and the Canadian Broadcasting Corporation. He has also worked as a salesman, a private investigator, and a shotgun guard for an armored car company. In 1986 Chris competed in the Canadian Practical Pistol Championships.

The call of the sea lured him away from his Canadian career for a two-year voyage from Vancouver, Canada, to Sydney, Australia, aboard British Privateer, a twenty-seven-foot boat that he built himself. He sailed back across the Pacific to take up residence in the U.S.

Married to a native Texan, Chris has adopted the state as his spiritual home. He and his wife, Anita, live in San Antonio, where Chris worked as a reporter for the *Express-News*. As a police reporter, he gleefully claims he has reported on more shootings and killings than Wild Bill Hickok had gunfights.

Given his choice, Chris would never be without a gun at hand. He has shot in practical shooting competition and at one point belonged to so many shooting clubs his wife complained she never saw him. He belongs to the National Rifle Association and the Texas State Rifle Association and is a director of the Texas Concealed Handgun Association.

ACKNOWLEDGMENTS

This book would not have been written without the help and encouragement of many people. First, my wife, Anita, who had the idea, then encouraged, nagged, and supported me until I completed it, while the kitchen counter I had promised to rebuild remained unfixed. Bill McLennan, Greg Ferris, Robert Butler, and Bill Davison unstintingly shared with me their time, skills, and expertise. I cannot thank them enough.

Other experts in the self-defense field provided information and experience. They include Ed Lovette, Michael de Bethencourt, Mas Ayoob, Dean Thompson, Clint Smith, Jerry Lane, Jeff Cooper, Manny Kapelsohn, Terry Kenney, Harry Fleming, David Ham, and Bruce Siddle.

I would particularly like to thank those who shared the stories of incidents in which they were involved: Patricia Konie, Tracy Bridges, Garry Brookman, Susan Gaylord Buxton, Rory Vertigan, John Long, Bill Stroud, Carol Lane, Christi Kincannon, Jennifer Palmer and Hal Diggs, Suzanna Gratia Hupp, Shayne Katzfey, Leo Arredondo, Judy Kuntz, Domingo Moncada, "Joe Archer," Gordon Hale III, Jake Ryker, Joel Myrick, Marguerite Everheart, Laura Poldson, Habib Howard, Jim Eichelberg, Pete Kanakidis, and Ralph Williams.

Others who helped me in this project include Sheriff Wayne Rausch, Blaine Smith of *America's First Freedom* magazine; Greg Crane of Response Options, Dr. Mike McMains, Walt Cleveland, Brandon Brown, Dan Holliday, Ashton O'Dwyer, Marion Hammer, Chip Walker, and Bill Powers of the National Rifle Association; Texas Land Commissioner Jerry Patterson; Ron Wilson and Ray Allen of the Texas Legislature; Candy Ruff of the Kansas Legislature; Eric Croft of the Alaska Legislature; Al Cuellar and C.J. Havrda, formerly of the Texas Rangers; retired Deputy U.S. Marshal Parnell McNamara; Jeff Page, Ray Torres, Joe MacKay, Joery Smittick, Jimmy Holguin, Andy Hernandez, and Al Ballew of the San Antonio Police Department; Detective Kevin Ruggiero; Eliza Sonneland; Rob Davie; Jack Dean; Dennis McElroy; Gordon Hale Jr.; Vincent Perini; David Kopel; Jean Souza; Gary Kleck; John Lott; Ken Jorgensen; Richard Stengel; George Aylesworth; Eugene Cotton; Charlie Wells; Karen Beary; Jay Griffin; Chuck Dewey; Ted Bonnet; Bob Nagel; Denise Griffin; Charlie Johnston; and even Robin Terry. I thank you all.

In addition I want to thank all the manufacturers and their people who provided photographs and information, as well as all the state government employees who were so courteous and helpful in providing the information in Chapter 13.

Finally, I wish to thank my editor and typographer, Susan Hughes, Wordwright Associates; Bruce Hughes, who provided technical support and incorporated changes to the manuscript; Kemp Davis, who took most of the photographs; Tom Hudgins, who designed the cover; Lisa and Luke Ham, who appear in the front-cover photo; and Greg Ferris, Bill McLennan, Bill Davison, James Williams, and Dennis McElroy, who modeled for other photos in the text.

Chapter One

VIRGINIA TECH: IN SEARCH OF ANSWERS

When Seung Hui Cho reached Norris Hall on the campus of Virginia Polytechnic Institute, better known as Virginia Tech, on April 16, 2007, he chained and padlocked the three main entrance doors to the building from the inside. This prevented anyone from entering or leaving. It also delayed the police response and gave him about eleven minutes to murder thirty students and faculty members.

According to the Virginia Tech Incident Review Panel's report, in those eleven minutes Cho fired at least 174 rounds from two semi-automatic handguns—a 9mm Glock and a .22 caliber Walther.

The shooting at Norris Hall was Cho's second assault on the campus of Virginia Tech that day. He started shortly after 7 a.m. by murdering Emily Hilscher and Ryan Clark in West Ambler Johnston student residence. Hilscher was shot in her room on the fourth floor, and police speculated that Clark, whose room was next door, went to her assistance. Both were found in Hilscher's room shot at close range.

Cho apparently escaped from the building without being seen and returned to his room in a nearby student residence. Originally police thought the shooting was a domestic dispute and began searching for Hilscher's boyfriend, who lived in Blacksburg, the location of Virginia Tech. No connection was ever found to link Cho with Hilscher or Clark, and his motive in that shooting remains a mystery.

Cho took the time to change out of his bloody clothes, then went to the Post Office in Blacksburg to mail a package to NBC News in New York. The package included a diatribe of rage and resentment against the university and its students, as well as

1

the infamous video clips of Cho holding guns, which were shown on national television.

The twenty-three year-old Korean-born student returned to Virginia Tech. Sometime between 9:15 and 9:30, he entered Norris Hall. He chained the doors of the main entrances of the three story engineering building then went up to the second floor and poked his head into several rooms where classes were in progress.

The incident review panel's report outlines what happened next. Cho walked into classroom 206, where Professor G.V. Loganathan was teaching Advanced Hydrology engineering. Without warning he shot and killed the professor then turned his guns on the students. He killed nine and wounded two. Only two students in that class were unscathed. Cho made several visits to the four classrooms, shooting some students six times or more.

Students and faculty in nearby classrooms heard the shots but did not immediately realize what they were hearing. Meanwhile Cho crossed the hallway and entered room 207, where Professor Christopher Bishop was teaching a German class. Cho shot Bishop and several students near the door, then walked among the desks shooting others. Bishop and four students died, and six more were wounded. One student tried without success to wrench free the podium that was bolted to the floor to barricade the door.

About two minutes after he left, Cho tried to re-enter room 207, but two wounded students and two who had not been hit managed to hold the door closed with their hands and feet while keeping their bodies away from the center of the door. Cho beat on the door and pushed it open an inch, then fired several shots around the door handle. He eventually gave up.

In room 211 a French class was in progress. The professor, Jocelyne Couture-Nowak, realized that she and her students were hearing gunshots and asked a student to call 9-1-1. The first call reached Virginia Tech Police Department at 9:42 a.m., and the police response started. Other students in the room tried to use the instructor's table to block the door, but Cho pushed his way in and started shooting. He killed Couture-Nowak first and then several students on that first visit but returned several times. In addition to the instructor, he killed eleven students and wounded six. No one escaped unscathed in room 211.

In room 204, Professor Liviu Librescu was teaching solid mechanics. The seventy-six-year-old Romanian Jew was a survivor of the Holocaust and came to the U.S. from Israel in the mid 1980s. When Cho tried to enter the room, Librescu braced himself against the door and yelled for his students to jump out of the window. They responded by pushing out the screens and jumping from the second-floor windows, a drop of nineteen feet to grass and bushes. The smart ones lowered themselves from the windows then dropped about thirteen feet.

While the students were escaping, Cho shot and killed Librescu through the door then got into the classroom and started shooting the students waiting at the windows to escape. Ten students got out of the windows and reached the ground, some breaking bones when they hit the ground. Cho shot four students in Librescue's class, killing one.

The students in room 205 came off best. They were attending a scientific computing class when they heard the shots. They held the door closed with their feet while keeping low to the ground. Cho tried to force his way in, but the students kept him out. He fired through the door but did not hit anyone.

According to the report, police officers started to arrive at Norris Hall three minutes after the university police department received the first call. The officers were slowed by the chained entrances but eventually found a locked door to a maintenance shop. They shot the lock with a shotgun and entered the building. Two police teams entered and ran up the stairs to the second floor where the shots were coming from. They heard the last shot as Cho shot himself in the head, ending the worst massacre by a gunman on a U.S. university campus.

The panel's report estimates that between 9:40 and 9:51, Cho shot and killed twenty-five students and five faculty members in the hallway and in four of the classrooms. He wounded seventeen other students.

Immediately the local and national media were all over the incident like blowflies on a dead cow in August. They concentrated on the victims, on the university and police response, on Cho's obvious mental problems, and that the country obviously needed more gun-control laws. There were comparisons to the shooting in 1999 at Columbine High School in Littleton, Colorado, in which two students killed twelve other students and a teacher before shooting themselves.

They were aided and abetted in calling for more gun-control laws by the usual suspects—the Brady Campaign to Prevent Handgun Violence (Formerly Handgun Control, Inc.), the Violence Policy Center, and other anti-gun and anti-self-defense groups.

Although the media and anti-gun organizations' responses were predictable, the political response was muted. It was interesting and encouraging that after the shooting many politicians kept their mouths shut about gun control, saying it was too early or inappropriate to raise the issue.

Many Democratic politicians have been stung by the party's enthusiasm for disarming law-abiding citizens. After prompting by former President Clinton, they have come to realize that gun control likely cost the Democrats control of Congress and the Presidency. It is an issue they don't want to deal with.

Newsweek noticed the hush from Democrats in the wake of Virginia Tech. Even such rabid anti-gun politicians as Illinois Congressman Rahm Emanuel didn't want to talk about gun control anymore than he wanted to talk about term limits for congressmen. The Democrats recruited some pro-gun politicians to run for Congress in 2006 and were trying the court gun owners, albeit with their fingers crossed.

The response from the pro-gun, pro-self-defense citizens and organizations was also predictable. The feedback I heard again and again from people interested in taking responsibility for their own safety was: "If only one student there had had a gun . . . ."

But Virginia Tech was a "gun-free zone." Even students and faculty members with concealed-handgun licenses were forbidden to take their guns on campus. In 2005 a student with a concealed handgun permit was disciplined for bringing a gun on campus.

For more than two years, the Virginia Citizens Defense League had been trying to get a law passed in the legislature that would prevent public colleges and universities from banning guns from their campuses. The bills were stalled in committee after much lobbying by Virginia Tech and other institutes of higher learning in the state.

Apparently Virginia Tech spokesman Larry Hincker was pleased the bill in 2006 was defeated. He was quoted in *The Roanoke Times* as saying: "I'm sure the university community is appreciative of the General Assembly's actions because this will help parents, students, faculty, and visitors feel safe on our campus."

Right.

In the days and weeks after the Virginia Tech shooting some people spoke in favor of allowing students and faculty members who have concealed-handgun licenses to carry handguns on campus just as they can off campus.

Texas Governor Rick Perry was quoted as saying that Texans with concealed-handgun licenses should be able to carry anywhere. He included college campuses, bars, courthouses, and churches.

Suzanna Gratia Hupp, who saw her parents killed in the mass shooting at Killeen, Texas, in 1991, told a reporter from *Time* magazine that she puts some of the blame for Virginia Tech on politicians. She was angry because the shooting was preventable, she said.

"The politicians haven't figured it out. They have created gun-free zones, and all of the dreadful things that have happened were in these gun-free zones," Hupp told the reporter.

Hupp's story is told in chapter three.

Alan Gottlieb, chairman of the Citizens Committee for the Right to Keep and Bear Arms, agreed. He said every tragic school shooting and some other mass shootings had one thing in common. "They all happened in so-called 'gun-free zones,'" he said. "You can pass all the laws you want, but the only proven way to stop shootings in 'gun-free zones' is an armed response."

Sheriff Wayne Rausch of Latah County, Idaho, favors more law-abiding citizens, including adult students, getting permits to carry concealed handguns. However, he has experienced occasions when permit holders have hindered police while intending to help. In most cases permit holders should use their guns only to defend themselves or their families, he says.

"An active shooter situation is certainly an example of an exception where I would like to see the armed citizen get involved," Rausch said, "because one of the questions that was posed to me by many of the people that called was: 'What could law enforcement have done differently at Virginia Tech?'

"Quite frankly I've spoken to a lot of my fellow sheriffs and chiefs, and we all agree: basically nothing. It's absolutely ludicrous to think that on a huge campus like that, when there is an isolated incident going on that is not only dynamic but changing fast, that somehow or another police are miraculously going to be able to pinpoint the exact location and have immediate response to shut it down before it gets worse. That's just not feasible; that's just not going to happen."

Rausch feels the most reasonable expectation is that law enforcement is probably going to get the information about a shooting from someone calling on a cell phone. When police are alerted, they go there and take care of it as quickly as possible.

"On the other hand, the quickest answer to this obviously is that if you've got a classroom full of students and you are lining them up to shoot them and some of them are armed themselves, there is a possibility this may be shut down much quicker."

He says the deterrent factor of some students being armed should not be discounted.

"It seems to me that there must be some sort of intimidation factor for the bad guy—that if I know I am among an armed populace, I could be picking a fight with someone who is going to kill me."

The University of Idaho, with a student body of ten thousand, is located in Latah County and the city of Moscow. Rausch says the university has a policy of no guns on campus, but the state attorney general was trying to determine whether the policy was legal.

While some colleges and universities have not banned students or faculty with permits from carrying concealed handguns on campus, one state has tackled the issue head on. Utah has fought the battle against such bans in the courts and so far has won.

In 2006, the Utah Supreme Court upheld a law passed by the legislature in 2004 that requires public colleges and universities to honor concealed-handgun permits on campus. No mass shootings have been reported at Utah colleges since the law went into effect.

The Virginia Tech Incident Review Panel's report stated that data on the effect of carrying guns on campus are "incomplete and inconclusive."

"The panel knows of no case in which a shooter in campus homicides has been shot or scared off by a student or faculty member with a weapon."

However, in an appendix that lists school mass shootings, the report notes two cases where this happened.

One of the incidents mentioned happened five years before and only a hundred miles west of the Virginia Tech campus. Another foreign-born student went on a shooting rampage on January 16, 2002, this time at the Appalachian School of Law, near Grundy, Virginia.

When Tracy Bridges and his friends got back to the law school after lunch they were late, so Bridges parked his Chevrolet Tahoe in a faculty spot near one of the exits from the classroom building. He and the friends with him climbed the stairs to the second floor and entered the classroom. About fifteen students were waiting in the room for the professor to arrive.

Bridges, twenty-five, was in his third and final year at the law school. He was also certified as a peace officer in North Carolina and was a deputy with the Buncombe County sheriff's office in the far western part of that state.

The students were talking among themselves when they heard what could have been a shot, Bridges said. One of the students in the class was Ted Besen, another third-year student who had been a law-enforcement officer also in North Carolina.

"We both kinda looked at each other and kinda jokingly said that sounded like a gunshot. And then when we heard the second and third; that's when we knew it was a gunshot," Bridges said.

He and Besen ran into the hallway where they saw Professor Wesley Shinn who, according to Bridges, told them: "Peter's in the building and he's got a gun."

Shinn was referring to Peter Odighizuwa, a forty-three-year-old naturalized U.S. citizen from Nigeria, who had been told he was to be dismissed for failing grades.

"We didn't know what he had done at that point. We didn't know if anybody was hurt or injured," Bridges said.

He and Ted ran back into the classroom and herded all the students out of the room, along the hallway to a back entrance, and down a metal staircase.

"At that point we didn't know where Peter was or anything, so my thinking was: get them outside. At least we have some escape routes if we get them outside."

Many of the students who escaped from the classroom went to a grocery store which is right next to the school, but Bridges had other things on his mind.

"My immediate thought was I needed to get to my vehicle, because I knew that I had a weapon in my vehicle."

It was fortunate that he had parked in a faculty spot, because the vehicle was much closer than it would have been had he parked in the student area. He ran to his Tahoe, unlocked it, and got his gun from its hiding place under the seat. The gun was a Ruger Speed-Six revolver with a 2¾-inch barrel in .357 Magnum caliber that he had received as a gift some years before.

Leaving his vehicle door open in his hurry, Bridges ran towards one of the front entrances where he could see some students milling around where Odighizuwa had come out of the building. He was about twenty yards away when Bridges first saw him and he was holding a small pistol, later identified as a Davis .380, a cheap semi-automatic. He advanced on Odighizuwa, yelling at him to put the gun down and get down on the ground.

"They say you get tunnel vision, but I think I got tunnel sound

Tracy Bridges.

[auditory exclusion], because I don't think I heard anything except for me screaming and yelling."

He did glance to his left at one point during his advance, where he saw Mikael Gross, a first-year student who also was certified as a peace officer in North Carolina. Bridges saw that Gross had a Beretta semi-automatic in his hand.

In training Tracy had been taught that at some point you have to make up your mind that you're ready to pull the trigger. "I had already made that decision; it was a question of when— how I could get the shot off and be safe about it."

As he approached Odighizuwa, he saw that Ted Besen and another student, Todd Ross, were in the way of a clear shot. Besen was in front of the student with the gun while Ross was behind him. Bridges said he could hit Odighizuwa without hitting Besen but he was afraid the hot loads from his .357 Magnum would go clean through the gunman and hit Ross.

Bridges did not shoot, but as he got close, Odighizuwa put his gun down on the ground and moved away from it. The moment for shooting passed.

"It seemed like once Peter turned around and recognized that other people were armed—myself and Mikael …. I'm not sure if he seen Mikael's gun, I'm not sure if he seen mine. There's no way to tell. I think once he noticed that we were armed, he laid his weapon down."

Besen was in front of the gunman, who hit him on the jaw with his fist. Ross grabbed him from behind, and then the others joined in. They wrestled him to the ground, where Bridges got his arm in a lock. He asked Gross if he had any handcuffs. Gross said he did, and ran back to his car to get them. When Gross returned, they handcuffed the gunman and held him until the first police officer arrived.

The police officer asked if anybody had been inside the building, so Bridges went in to check on who had been hurt in the shooting. Several students urged him to check on Dean L. Anthony

Sutin. There was a lot of blood in the front lobby, but Bridges went straight up the stairs to Sutin's office.

"When I went into his office he was lying there on the floor. I checked for vitals and there were none."

It appeared to Bridges that he had been shot several times in the body. The student left Sutin's office and entered the office of Professor Thomas Blackwell. He found Blackwell still sitting in his chair facing his computer with his head down.

"It looked like he had been shot at pretty close range in the back of the neck."

He again checked for signs of life but found none.

Bridges went back downstairs to find Angela Dales, a thirty-three-year-old student, had been shot in the neck. The blood he saw when he first entered the building after capturing the gunman was hers.

Dales was shot beside some couches in a lounge area, but she apparently jumped up and ran towards the door. Although she was somewhat responsive when Bridges got to her, she had lost a lot of blood and died shortly afterwards.

In addition to Dales and the two faculty members, three other students were wounded but recovered.

Dean Sutin was a personal friend of Bridges. He had been a senior official in the U.S. Justice Department under Attorney General Janet Reno during the Clinton administration. He and Bridges were at opposite ends of the political spectrum, but they had an agreement: Bridges would read one of Sutin's left-wing books if the dean would read one of his right-wing books. They traded books frequently, Bridges said.

"He was very open to listening to what I had to say."

Rather than face the death penalty, Odighizuwa accepted a plea bargain of multiple life sentences, which he is now serving.

Afterwards it seemed to Bridges that the pro- and anti-gun people were using the incident to further their own agendas. The anti-gun people were deploring the use of a gun to murder three people and wound another three. The pro-gun faction said that, in this case, having guns on campus saved lives.

In his book, *The Bias Against Guns*, Professor John Lott of the University of Maryland uses this incident to show the media's unwillingness to portray the use of guns by citizens in a positive light. He wrote that he ran a Nexis-Lexis computer search and found 208 stories about the law-school shooting in the week following the incident. However, only four reports mentioned that Gross and Bridges were armed with handguns when they confronted Odighizuwa. Most of the stories stated that the shooter was tackled by the students but failed to mention that any had their own handguns.

The day after the shooting, Bridges was interview by Katie Couric, then co-host of NBC's "Today Show." He got the impression that she didn't want to talk about the fact that he and Gross were armed.

"As soon as I mentioned the weapon, she very quickly said, but we need to mention that you are a law-enforcement officer," he said. This is borne out by the transcript of the show.

Bridges thinks that if students with concealed-handgun permits had been allowed to carry on campus at Virginia Tech, the incident might have ended differently. "I think it would have. That's my personal feeling," he said.

While after Virginia Tech many people railed against the ostrich-like attitude of most educators towards guns on campuses, another more disturbing question was being raised: Why did none of the students in Norris Hall fight back?

The answers varied, but the theme seemed to be that we have produced an emasculated generation of young adults who have been socialized by educators to obey orders and avoid conflict at all costs.

Nationally syndicated radio-talk-show host Neal Boortz opined: "It seems that standing in terror waiting for your turn to be executed was the right thing to do, and any questions as to why twenty-five students didn't try to rush and overpower Cho Seung-Hui are just examples of right-wing maniacal bias. Surrender—comply—adjust."

National Review Online columnist John Derbyshire asked: "Where was the spirit of self-defense here? ... Why didn't anyone rush the guy?"

Syndicated columnist Michelle Malkin stated: "Instead of teaching students to defend their beliefs, American educators shield them from vigorous intellectual debate. Instead of encouraging automony, our higher institutions of learning stoke passivity and conflict-avoidance. And as the erosion of intellectual self-defense goes, so goes the erosion of physical self-defense."

National Review columnist Mark Steyn refers to a "culture of corrosive passivity."

"It's deeply damaging to portray fit, fully-formed adults as children who need to be protected. We should be raising them to understand that there will be moments in life when you need to protect yourself—and, in a 'horrible' world, there may come moments when you have to choose between protecting yourself or others," Steyn wrote.

Michael de Bethencourt of Northeastern Tactical Schools blames television for turning people into passive watchers rather than doers.

"We are conditioning ourselves to sit on our fat, lazy backsides and watch and watch and watch and then click the remote to stop," he says. "And when horrible things happen, we're looking at them and going: 'Oh, that's terrible, that's terrible, that's terrible. How could it happen?'"

The television is there to amuse us and to sell us things. It never interacts with us and the more time we spend watching it, the less we interact with the world, de Bethencourt says.

"We need to deprogram ourselves to get involved with what's going on in the world."

The hero of the Virginia Tech shooting was undoubtedly seventy-six-year-old Professor Liviu Librescu, but he was from a different generation. He sacrificed himself by holding the door while ordering his students to escape through the windows. He understood the responsibilities of leadership—the leader, like the captain of a ship, saves himself last.

Another professor who successfully saved his students and also died was Kevin Granata. His class was on the third floor. He locked his students in a small room then went down to the second floor to investigate. Cho shot and killed him there.

We talk of flight or fight as a response to danger. Flight is a respectable and preferable course of action. Students who jumped from the windows in room 204 followed Librescu's order and saved their lives. Those who tried, some successfully, some unsuccessfully, to block the doors have nothing to be ashamed of. They saw that action was needed and took it.

But if you are trapped, what about the other option: fight? *Time* magazine quoted one student in room 211, who cowered under a desk while other students were being executed around him. He was waiting for it to be his turn. He heard the gunman reload three times, but no one apparently thought to attack him while his gun was out of action.

Another student in the same class who feigned death told *Newsweek*: "Nobody tried to get up and be a hero."

The Incident Review Panel's report states: "Several students, some of whom were injured and others not, successfully played dead amid the carnage around them, and survived. ...This worked for at least some students."

The report made no mention of anyone trying to rush the shooter. Apparently this was fine with the panel. Its recommendations concerned action by police, making sure that exterior doors cannot be chained shut, and that bomb threats should be taken seriously. The focus of the report seems to be to absolve the police and administration of any responsibility, while failing to address how students could save their lives.

There was no recommendation that students should be taught to fight back.

However, students can and should be taught to fight back, even when unarmed, against a classroom shooter, according to Greg Crane of Response Options.

Crane and a partner started Response Options to teach school teachers and students what to do when faced with a gunman such as Cho. Crane has a law-enforcement background and taught high school for two years.

Response Options first came to public attention in October 2006, shortly after a gunman walked into a one-room Amish school in Pennsylvania, murdered five girls, and wounded six before killing himself. People were asking what could be done about such incidents when the Response Options program came to media attention.

For two years the company had been teaching the staff of the Burleson School District, just south of Fort Worth, how to cope with a gunman in a school. In 2006, Crane had a contract to start teaching the students what to do. When the program became national news, the school district administrators said they didn't know Response Options was teaching children to fight back and ended the program. The school district apparently couldn't stand the heat and got out of the kitchen.

However, the Virginia Tech incident opened up a new venue for Response Options. Crane says he is getting enquiries from colleges and universities, as well as schools across the nation, requesting information and training.

"I guess what Virginia Tech did was change some thinking, because now you had a whole building full of young adults who were attacked by one person and he won. The question was: how did this happen?"

Crane's answer is that either the shooter was a highly trained individual or the targets were just too easy. In all these school mass shootings, the shooter was not a highly skilled tactical operator, therefore the targets were too easy.

"A static, passive target just does not require any kind of skill set to win that battle," he says. "Hiding under desks and praying for rescue from professionals is not a recipe for survival."

Crane takes issue with school lock-down policies that keep students and teachers in the target area. They are locked in their classrooms and are not provided with any information that would allow them to escape and survive. Lock-down allows for three things: command, control, and convenience. But not just for police and school administrators, it does the same thing for the bad guy.

"Should the shooter gain access to them (the students), they do exactly what they have been told to do, which is either sit quietly in a corner or cower under their desks, and he gets to just walk amongst them and do whatever he wants to do."

Response Options initially focuses on escape from the area of the threat, but most schools are poorly designed to make this easy. They have long hallways with classrooms off both sides. Each classroom has only one door, only one way in or out. Because of fear of property crimes, if there are windows they are small, high off the ground, and don't open.

"There is no escape from these rooms should you actually be attacked. These kids have no choice, if they're going to survive, they're going to have to fight their way out against the gunman."

Shooting a gun accurately, particularly a handgun, requires skill and concentration. Even trained police officers in a dynamic situation don't hit the target with more than about one shot in five, Crane says. "You've got to interrupt his ability to shoot accurately."

One way to interrupt the gunman's ability to shoot accurately is to throw at his head anything you can get your hands on—books, chairs, pocket change, rulers, etc.

"At a minimum you get a closing of the eyes. Usually what we see is a turning of the head and even a raising of the hands to protect the head," Crane says. "We want to cause mass mayhem and chaos where he is going to have to mentally and physically deal with an environment that he was not expecting—stimuli that he was not expecting. And then we use our numbers to gain back control."

He recommends a swarming technique in which as many students as possible use their numbers and their total body mass to subdue the shooter.

"It doesn't take very many people to overcome one individual if you know how to do it. We're not guaranteeing that there won't be any casualties, but you've got to be proactive."

Crane pointed out that at Virginia Tech, in rooms 205 and 204 where teachers and students were proactive, only two people were killed. Five were killed initially in room 206, but then the students blocked the door preventing Cho from returning, and no one else was killed in the room. In rooms 207 and 211 where the students were not proactive, twenty students and two teachers were killed.

Asked why he thought nobody actually fought back at Virginia Tech, Crane said: "It's because they have been taught since they were little kids that when you are in the school you are passive. We have zero tolerance rules in place now in education."

Even though self-defense is perfectly legal, and you have an absolute right to defend yourself outside school, if a student is attacked in school and fights back, he or she is in as much trouble as the attacker.

"It's now been ingrained in these kids ever since they were little, that they cannot fight back. They need to walk away."

Crane admonishes teachers and administrators, telling them: "You guys are neutering a bunch of people."

One high-school student who did fight back was Jake Ryker. He didn't know he had already been shot in the chest when he charged the shooter in the school cafeteria that Thursday morning, but it probably wouldn't have made any difference if he had.

It was Ryker's seventeenth birthday—May 21, 1998. He was just getting up from a table with his friends at Thurston High School in Springfield, Oregon. It was just before 8 a.m. and the students were getting ready for their first class. Ryker had a history assignment to turn in.

That's when Kip Kinkel walked through the cafeteria door and opened fire on his fellow students with a .22-caliber Ruger semi-automatic rifle with a fifty-round magazine. Kinkel had sawed off the butt of the rifle to make a pistol grip and to make it easier to conceal under his trenchcoat.

Kinkel, fifteen, had already murdered his parents—both teachers—before coming to school. And in the breezeway a few feet from the cafeteria door he had executed Ben Walker with a shot through the head.

At first, Ryker didn't see the gun as Kinkel came in, but he did hear the shots. When Kinkel started shooting at the students around his table from about twenty feet away, Ryker pushed his girlfriend, Jennifer Alldredge, to the ground. That was when he got shot. But he thought as he landed on the ground that the blow was from someone's arm or fist. He was unaware that a bullet had gone through his right lung and broken a rib. He looked up to see Kinkel approaching the end of the table where he and the others had been sitting.

"He grabbed my friend Mike, held him down, and shot him in the head," Ryker said, referring to Mikael Nickolauson. "That's when

Jake Ryker.

I got up and started running. I tripped over this girl Christina and hit the ground. I hit my chin or my forehead or something. I remember my face bouncing off the floor."

Ryker looked up to see Kinkel pointing the rifle to fire again, and he heard the click as the firing pin snapped on an empty chamber.

"I knew when I heard that click that if anybody was going to hit him, now's the time," Ryker said.

Kinkel had fired all fifty rounds in the magazine and struggled to reload the rifle as Ryker came up off the floor and ran at him.

"When he saw me, he started backpedaling."

Ryker, a high-school wrestler six-feet four-inches tall, swept Kinkel's feet from under him in a wrestling tackle and the rifle went flying.

"I hit him hard enough that it knocked him over. His feet went up in the air, and I came down on top of him."

Another teenager picked up the rifle, and several others joined in the attack on the shooter, including Ryker's brother Josh. But Kinkel was not ready to give up. Ryker could see Kinkel was armed with a knife, but he also had a Glock 9mm semi-automatic pistol in his waistband under his trenchcoat.

"When he hit the ground, that's when he started going for that Glock," Ryker said. "I thought he was going for the knife. I put my hand on the knife and grabbed his face, but then he took the gun out. That's when I grabbed the barrel of the gun. By that time, he had it up in my face so I was looking down the barrel."

The previous weekend, Jake Ryker, his fourteen-year-old brother Josh, and their father Robert had been shooting at a local range. They had been shooting a .45-caliber Colt Gold Cup semi-automatic. The pistol is a target version of the .45 semi-automatic that used to be the standard issue for the U.S. military. Robert Ryker, at that time a chief petty officer in the U.S. Navy, knew all about the big pistol. He was explaining the safeties on the .45 to his sons. He told them that if you push on the muzzle or the slide of most semi-automatics they will not fire.

"If you push the slide back an eighth of an inch, it throws it out of battery. I said that if somebody stuck one in your face or pointed one at you, you could push back on the slide and it won't go off," Robert Ryker said. "But then I said, if he's still got his finger on the trigger and you release the slide, it'll shoot because it'll slam back in battery and the hammer will fall."

Jokingly, Robert warned his sons not to try this move except as a last resort. He said he never expected that less than a week later his oldest son would be fighting for his life with someone who had stuck a pistol in his face.

"I was taught that very same thing when I was in the Navy as a gunner's mate, and when I went to gunnery school, they showed us that. Our chief told our class: don't ever try this unless you know you're going to be dead anyway," Robert Ryker added.

When Kinkel stuck the muzzle of the Glock 9mm in Jake Ryker's face, Ryker grabbed the muzzle with his left hand. Remembering his father's advice, he tried to push the slide back out of battery.

"I figured that would be the best thing for me to do with that thing pointed in my face," Jake Ryker said. "If not, I was going to get a bullet between my eyes. So I grabbed the end of it. When I grabbed it, I guess I didn't grip it strongly enough, but I got it away from my face, and it discharged."

The 9mm bullet went through the knuckle of Ryker's left index finger, burned the top of his thumb, ricocheted off the floor, then ripped through another boy's buttocks. But Ryker's grip on the slide prevented the gun from cycling, and it jammed.

By this time several boys, including Adam Walburger and Josh Ryker, had piled on Kinkel and managed to get the Glock away from him.

"Adam was helping Jake, and I grabbed the legs because he was kicking and fighting," Josh Ryker said. "We kept fighting him until we got pulled off by the adults."

"I was beating on him as much as I could. They had to pull me off him," Jake Ryker said.

It wasn't until another boy, Chris, pulled him off Kinkel that Jake Ryker realized he had been wounded. Chris grabbed him where his rib had been broken, and Ryker felt a stab of pain. The boy rolled Ryker over and pressed down on his chest where blood was welling from his chest wound. Ryker noticed blood all over Chris's hands. He noticed his own left index finger hanging by a piece of skin from his hand. Chris told him he had also been shot in the chest.

When he was arrested, police found that, in addition to the .22-caliber rifle and 9mm pistol, Kinkel was also armed with another handgun and had more than a thousand rounds of ammunition on him.

Jake Ryker has been called a hero for his actions in the school cafeteria, but he plays this down, pointing out that he was not the only teen to charge Kinkel, just the one in front. He said he did not have time to be afraid.

"By the time I got to stop and think about what the hell I just did, I was actually in the hospital," he said.

Ryker spent about a week in the hospital. Doctors were able to save his finger, and he was fit enough a year later to survive Marine boot camp. In November 1999, Kinkel was sentenced to one hundred eleven years in prison for murdering his parents and two Thurston students and for wounding more than twenty students.

Robert Ryker is a concealed-handgun license holder and life member of the National Rifle Association. He is proud of his sons' knowledge and ability with firearms. He believes this knowledge enabled Jake to take down the shooter and almost certainly save the lives of more students.

"He knew enough about guns, had been around them enough, so he respects them like anybody should," Robert Ryker said. "But he knew when he could make his move because he was familiar with them."

Jake said he remembers shooting with his grandfather at beer cans with a .22-caliber revolver when he was six or seven years old. "I got my first BB gun for Christmas when I think I was eight," he added.

The country has been plagued by a rash of school shootings, starting in February 1996 in Moses Lake, Washington, when a fourteen-year-old student killed two other students and a teacher, as well as seriously wounding a third student. This was followed about a year later in Bethel, Alaska, when a sixteen-year-old student killed the principal and another student, while wounding two more students.

With these incidents as a warm up, there followed five mass shootings at schools around the country in which seven youths killed twenty-three students and two teachers. They also wounded sixty-eight others.

• October 1, 1997, in Pearl, Mississippi, a sixteen-year-old student murdered his mother at home then went to school, where he killed two students and wounded seven.

• December 1, 1997, in West Paducah, Kentucky, a fourteen-year-old boy killed three students and wounded five.

• March 24, 1998, in Jonesboro, Arkansas, four girls and a teacher were killed when two boys, aged eleven and thirteen, opened fire from ambush with rifles. Ten others were wounded.

• May 21, 1998, in Springfield, Oregon, Kip Kinkel opened fire with a sawed-down rifle, killing two students and wounding twenty-three. He was stopped by Jake Ryker and others. Kinkel killed his parents before starting his rampage at school.

• April 20, 1999, in Littleton, Colorado, two boys, aged seventeen and eighteen, killed twelve students and a teacher at Columbine High School, while wounding another twenty-three. The shooters then committed suicide.

The media frenzy that followed each of these incidents caused widespread paranoia among parents, students, teachers, and school administrators. Some politicians and other public figures were quick to blame these shootings on the "easy availability of guns." They pushed for more government control of both guns and law-abiding gun owners. The administration of President Bill Clinton and Vice President Al Gore, aided and abetted by Attorney General Janet Reno, led this campaign. However, even those who pushed for more gun controls generally admitted that none of the proposed new laws would have prevented any of the school shootings.

The proposals included the FBI's instant check system applied to all gun-show firearms' transactions; limiting gun purchases to one a month; and raising the age for possession of a gun from eighteen to twenty-one. With more than twenty thousand gun laws nationwide, passing more would only have disarmed and inconvenienced law-abiding citizens.

Since the Columbine High School incident, there has been less sensational media coverage of school shootings, partly because, until Virginia Tech, no incident resulted in as many casualties. Two more shootings were covered extensively, however.

On March 21, 2005, Jeff Weise, sixteen, killed his grandfather and the grandfather's woman friend, then went to his high school on the Red Lake Indian Reservation in Minnesota. There he killed a security guard, a teacher, and five students. He also wounded seven other students before killing himself.

At Nickel Mines, Pennsylvania, on October 2, 2006, Charles Carl Roberts, a thirty-two-year-old milk-truck driver, entered an Amish one-room school and cornered a group of girls. He shot and killed five and seriously wounded six before committing suicide.

Blaming the gun for school shootings is like blaming the car for traffic accidents. Guns have been readily available in the United States ever since the country was founded, so this is not anything new. There are still many Americans who can remember taking guns to school. Texas Land Commissioner Jerry Patterson, who, as a state senator, helped push the concealed-handgun law through the Texas Legislature in 1995, is one.

"In 1959, I took a gun to school for show-and-tell, and nobody thought anything of it," he said.

Robert Ryker, Jake's father, said that when he was at school he took a gun to school to work on during shop class.

"In my school annual, there is a picture of a teacher with an actual six-gun on his hip that we shot blanks in. We had a quick-draw contest in the courtyard," he said.

While demonizing guns has been popular with many public figures, other factors are probably more to blame for the school shootings: lack of discipline at home and at school, single-parent families, child abuse, the use of behavior-altering drugs such as Luvox and Ritalin, and the Internet.

Retired Lieutenant Colonel David Grossman and Gloria DeGaetano, authors of *Stop Teaching Our Kids to Kill,* blame violent video games and films. They make a compelling case for blaming violent video games for removing kids' inhibitions against killing and for making them more aggressive.

Many people blame the media for sensationalizing these school-shooting incidents.

Patterson argues that the First Amendment to the Constitution—the amendment that guarantees free speech and freedom of the press—is far more responsible for the shootings than the Second Amendment which guarantees the right to keep and bear arms.

"The press's First Amendment right to report as they see fit has killed children in this country," Patterson said. "It's unequivocal. You can't argue that these copy-cat killings would have happened without the press."

However, he would not support more restrictions on First Amendment rights any more than he would support further erosion of Second Amendment rights, he added.

Robert and Jake Ryker both agree the media is much to blame for the shootings. Jake feels that if the media didn't give so much publicity to the shooters, others would not be encouraged to do it. He also thinks the media made Kip Kinkel into a national hero.

"I received hate mail because of this guy, because there are people who like this guy and think he did the right thing," Jake said. There is an Internet site for Kinkel groupies, he added.

"One of them wanted to know how she could marry him. She was madly in love with him. They're seeking that attention."

Robert Ryker believes the media has a right to report what's happening; he just wishes they wouldn't make so much of it.

"If the media would quit making a circus event out of these shootings, the damn performers would quit coming to the circus," he said.

Media celebrities have not been slow to voice opinions about school shootings, most calling for more restrictions on guns and gun owners. Talk-show personality Rosie O'Donnell said she thought all gun owners should be jailed. She then weighed into Tom Selleck for taking part in ads for the National Rifle Association. Selleck had appeared on her show to promote a movie. He seemed angry and uncomfortable at O'Donnell's attack, later calling her unprofessional.

In May 1999, actress Sharon Stone made a big production of turning in a shotgun and three handguns to the Los Angeles police as a result, she said, of the Columbine High School shooting. Stone said she was surrendering her right to bear arms and urged other gun owners to turn in their guns. This is a woman who has made a lot of money from violent films. In one of her movies, she portrays a character who murders lovers with an ice pick during sex.

While the Second Amendment has come under attack as a result of these shootings, so has the free speech guarantee of the First Amendment. A thirteen-year-old boy in Ponder, Texas, was jailed for five days after writing a scary Halloween story as a class assignment. Christopher Beamon's essay described shooting his teacher, Amanda Henry, and two students. The teacher gave him an "A" and had him read the story aloud in class. Parents named in the story complained, and Principal Chance Allen called police.

When Christopher appeared in front of Denton County Juvenile Court Judge Darlene Whitten, she ordered him imprisoned for ten days. He was set free only after the family's lawyer demanded his release and the district attorney declined to prosecute.

In another incident of bureaucratic stupidity, nine-year-old Vincent Olivarez was almost suspended from Telfair Elementary School in the Los Angeles Unified School District when he was caught with what administrators called "extremely disturbing and offensive" photos. Are we talking porno shots here? No, they were photos of him and his brother shooting guns at a shooting range under the supervision of their aunt, who happened to be a police firearms instructor.

In November 1999, the Chicago public-school system abolished rifle training with air rifles for some nine thousand cadets in the Junior Reserve Officer Training Corps. The move was another paranoid reaction to the school shootings elsewhere in the country. It took prompting from *The Chicago Tribune* to bring this harmless and useful form of training to an end. The newspaper published an article drawing attention to weapon training in Illinois schools, while schools nationwide are pondering how to prevent shootings.

Paul Vallas, speaking for the school district, said it didn't want to send a contradictory message to students, discouraging the use of violence and weapons, and at the same time supporting a marksmanship program. This evisceration of the JROTC is particularly troubling, as there appears to be no reason for it other than a desire by officials to avoid controversy. This action was taken at a time when the media were reporting about plummeting rates of violent youth crime and gun deaths since the early 1990s.

According to the Centers for Disease Control and Prevention the number of gun deaths—homicides, suicides, and accidents—dropped 21 percent between 1993 and 1997, while gunshot wounds dropped 41 percent during the same period. Fatalities dropped from 39,595 in 1993 to 32,436 in 1997 as non-fatal injuries fell to 64,207 from 104,390.

Meanwhile, violent youth crime fell 30 percent from 1994 to 1998, according to Justice Department figures. The arrest rate for juveniles aged ten to seventeen was the lowest for murder, robbery, rape, and aggravated assault since 1988.

However, a report by the National Commission on the Causes and Prevention of Violence found that these rosy assessments tell only part of the story. The report stated that violent crime in the larger cities has risen 40 percent since the 1960s.

It seems these school shootings and other multiple shootings around the country have given the national media, some politicians, and anti-gun activists a wonderful opportunity to brainwash the American people into believing that guns are bad and that the people who have them are evil. Their ultimate aim is the disarmament of America.

The shooting at Columbine High School came at a time very convenient for those to whom guns are an anathema. A bill that would have given law-abiding Colorado residents the right to carry concealed handguns for protection was before the state Legislature. It would most likely have passed had it not been withdrawn in the furor that followed that shooting.

Many people who support the right of civilians to carry concealed handguns for protection seem to be in favor of allowing teachers to be armed. Jesse Ventura, then the colorful governor of Minnesota, spoke for many when he suggested that if someone at Columbine High School had had a concealed-handgun license and been armed, lives would have been saved. He was widely criticized in the media for this statement, but at least he kept his job.

The same cannot be said of John Varis, superintendent of Reading Community Schools in Ohio for thirteen years. Reading is a suburb of Cincinnati. Varis was forced to resign after he suggested at a public meeting that teachers could be armed and trained to respond to a school shooting. He pointed out that guns can be used to save lives as well as kill people. Some parents circulated petitions calling for his removal. Varis said he was discussing school-safety options.

Most of the high-profile school shootings have occurred in states that give ordinary citizens the right to carry concealed handguns for protection. But in each of those states, concealed-handgun-license holders are prevented from carrying guns at schools. Is this an effective policy? Professor John Lott, author of *More Guns, Less Crime: Understanding Crime and Gun Control Laws*, thinks not.

"I understand the motivation behind it—to try to create safe zones—but what I think happens when you do that is, rather than making it safer for the good people, you make it safer for those who are intent on doing the harm," he said.

Lott has studied the effect of concealed-handgun laws on multiple shootings in public places. He concludes that in states where concealed-handgun laws have been passed, such shootings have been reduced more than 80 percent. Where they have occurred in those states, they have been in places—like schools—where concealed-handgun-license holders are not allowed to carry their guns.

"Allowing teachers and other law-abiding adults to carry concealed handguns in schools would not only make it easier to stop shootings in progress. It could also help deter shootings from ever occurring," Lott said.

Probably as a result of the Virginia Tech shooting, a proposal was put forward in Nevada in August 2007 to make volunteer teachers into armed reserve police officers.

A nother high-profile school shooting that was brought to an end by a civilian with a handgun occurred in Pearl, Mississippi, on October 1, 1997.

Shortly after 8 a.m., Joel Myrick, an assistant principal at Pearl High School, was walking back to his office with a cup of coffee in his hand. He was dressed as usual in a pinstripe suit, white shirt, and tie.

He crossed a large area about the size of a basketball court with a high ceiling that was referred to as the Commons. About six hundred students were milling about in this vast area. They had just arrived and were waiting around for the school day to begin. It would be unlike any other school day they had ever experienced.

Joel Myrick.

As Myrick reached his outer office, he heard a loud explosion. Immediately, he set down his coffee and stepped back out into the Commons.

There was another loud boom. Most of the children in the Commons ran for the exits, many of them screaming. As some ran towards Myrick, he held open the door and they flooded into his outer office. After fifteen or twenty children had run past him into his office, Myrick heard the third boom.

He realized someone was shooting. He started moving carefully out into the Commons looking for the source of the gunfire. His view of part of the Commons was blocked by a stairwell. By this time the area was almost empty of students. After moving a few steps, Myrick saw the barrel of a rifle, then as he moved further, a large youth wearing a long coat. He was walking, with the rifle pointed forward and down, towards the center of the common area where there were four columns, each about three feet thick.

As Myrick watched, he saw the shooter lift the barrel of the rifle slightly and fire another shot. Myrick saw chips of concrete fly from one of the columns as two girls fell to the ground. The shooter, later identified as 16-year-old Luke Woodham, kept walking towards one of the columns where several children were trying to hide. But one boy was left exposed.

"He pulled his book bag up to his chest, and he said: 'No, man, no.' And Luke shot him within about four or five feet," Myrick said.

The two other children behind the column turned and ran. Woodham worked the lever of the rifle, chambered another round, and fired at them. The bullet hit the floor behind them and broke up. They were hit by pieces of the bullet and went down. Woodham was walking away from Myrick thumbing rounds into the magazine through the slot in the receiver of the .30-30-caliber Marlin rifle.

"I was contemplating running [at Woodham] but I was scared. Because there was about forty or fifty feet between me and him, and I thought, if I start running and he turns around, I'm dead, because he's killing folks," Myrick said.

The assistant principal said he has been hunting all his life and knows what the .30-30 round will do to a deer.

Woodham turned and started to walk towards one of the halls that lead off the Commons. Myrick sprinted along the side of the Commons towards an exit that lead to where his truck was parked. In the truck he kept his .45-caliber handgun.

"I knew I had to get to my gun, because I was defenseless and I couldn't do anything with him at that point. I knew there was no one else around that could do anything with him at that point," Myrick said. "He was king. He was God of that school, and he could take life whenever he got ready, and he was doing it."

About halfway to the exit, Myrick turned and looked back. "This is the image I'll remember for the rest of my life. I looked, and I saw seven bodies laying around in various positions. I could smell gunpowder," he said.

Woodham was walking away from him down the hall with the rifle held diagonally across his chest. Myrick had his truck key in his hand even before he reached the back door. He sprinted across the parking lot to his pickup, opened it up, and reached under the seat for his gun. The .45-caliber Colt compact semi-automatic was in a soft case. Myrick undid the zipper and took it out. It had a full magazine but no round in the chamber. He paused a moment realizing that he was holding a loaded gun on school property, then he racked the slide, chambering a round, and put on the safety. Myrick said that once he had the gun in his hand he felt "unbelievably safe" during the rest of the incident.

He took off running with the gun pointed up in the air and his finger alongside the trigger guard. He didn't want to enter the building through the door from which he had exited, so he started running clockwise around the building.

Myrick fondly remembers an elderly black custodian named Irene who summed up the whole situation in two words. She was standing in the next entrance with one foot each side of the door so she could run in or out depending on the threat. She looked at Myrick running past with a gun in his hand and she said: "Oh, my."

Myrick turned the corner of the building and ran towards the front door. He figured that was the closest entrance to where he had last seen Woodham. He thought the shooter was probably searching classrooms, closets, and bathrooms looking for more unarmed victims.

When he was about forty yards from the front door, Woodham emerged from it still carrying the rifle. Myrick stopped and settled into a classic Weaver stance, pointing the gun at Woodham, and yelled: "Stop."

Woodham turned his head and looked at Myrick, but kept walking to his car, which was parked at the curb. Behind Woodham cars were leaving the parking lot, and kids were running. Myrick didn't have a clear shot at him, and Woodham didn't point the gun at him.

"I made the decision not to shoot at him at that point. I safed my weapon again, and took off running towards his car."

Before Myrick could reach the car, Woodham had taken off, burning rubber as he accelerated away.

"I remember looking at the white smoke coming off his tires."

Myrick ran as fast as he could to cut Woodham off before he could escape from the parking lot onto the street. Woodham was slowed by traffic at an intersection on school property. Some cars were still bringing students to school, and others were trying to leave the area as fast as they could. A car was stopped in front of Woodham at a stop sign. Woodham backed up and went around the car, but the delay allowed time for Myrick to reach the exit ahead of him.

Myrick was standing with one foot on the road when Woodham turned the corner about thirty yards away. There was nothing on the other side of the road but trees, so this time the assistant principal would have a clear shot.

"I was going to shoot him as he came across my field of fire, because the junior high was right down the road, and that's where my son goes to school," said Myrick. "I don't know where he was heading, but I knew he had just shot up a bunch of folks with a high-powered rifle, and he was getting away. I just figured I needed to stop him."

When Woodham turned the corner and headed straight for him, Myrick took up his position, covering the shooter with the .45 in a two-hand hold. He clicked off the safety. When Woodham saw him, he swerved off the road onto the grass away from Myrick. The grass was wet, and the car spun out, coming to a stop across the road about fifteen feet away from him, Myrick said.

The assistant principal kept Woodham covered and told him not to move. Woodham's knuckles were white from where he was gripping the steering wheel and his glasses were askew on his face, but he didn't move. Still keeping him covered, Myrick walked quickly to the car.

"I knew I had him at that point. I moved right up to the car and held the pistol a couple of feet from the side of his head. I told him: 'If you do anything, I'm going to kill you.' And he never moved. He never said a word. In the seat next to him was the rifle lying muzzle down."

Myrick noticed that Woodham had black electrical tape around both of his hands. He found out later that Woodham had stabbed his mother to death before coming to school and had cut himself.

Myrick got the youth out of the car and made him lie face down on the grass. The assistant principal pulled Woodham's jacket up over his head, partly to immobilize him and partly to see if he had any other weapons on him. Myrick put his foot on the back of Woodham's head to make sure he didn't move, then asked why he had done this.

"Mr. Myrick, the world has wronged me, and I couldn't take it anymore," Woodham replied.

"I didn't think twice, I said: 'My God, wait till you get to Parchman,' which is the state penitentiary," Myrick recalled. A few minutes later a police car pulled up, and the police officer took over, handcuffing Woodham. Myrick cleared his gun then ran back into the school. He found Woodham had killed two girls and wounded seven other students.

Although no one but Woodham knows for sure, Myrick believes he would have continued his murderous rampage if he had not been stopped. He still had two rounds in his rifle and thirty-six rounds on him at the time of his capture. Myrick said, "I truly believe that he would have continued to do what he was doing."

In June 1998, Woodham was sentenced to life in prison for his rampage, which he tried to blame on the leader of a satanic group that he belonged to.

Like Jake Ryker, Joel Myrick has received hate mail. He has received more than twenty letters from around the country from people blaming him for what happened. Some were bizarre enough that he was concerned for his safety.

"The gist of what they were saying was that I was the problem. Luke Woodham was not the problem; that I created Luke Woodham because I'm a big bully that carries a gun."

Myrick has been a hunter and shooter all his life and is a member of the National Rifle Association. He is also an officer in the National Guard. He believes children are being desensitized to killing because of the graphic violence they see in movies and the violence they participate in when playing video games. This is the same sort of indoctrination that soldiers receive to enable them to kill an enemy.

Myrick says kids need to feel a sense of belonging. If there is a common thread to the school shootings, it is that the shooters felt alienated from the student body. "They were really not a part of the mainstream culture," he said. "They were a little bit outside."

In 1999, Myrick moved from Pearl to a job as the principal of a high school in northern Mississippi. He has been working to develop a sense of community in his school, so all students feel that they belong. If he sees a kid sitting alone, he will go and talk to him or her, he said. He also speaks to adult community groups to get them to become involved in the school and its students.

"I've really made a big effort to try to draw kids into the mainstream of the school, so everybody feels like they're part of the school and nobody is just left out."

Myrick is in favor of taking the initiative and trying to head off such incidents before they start. However, in a school situation, once someone has decided to go on an armed rampage, it is not easy to prevent them. "You are not going to stop them by making the school into a prison, although I do believe an armed security guard is a great deterrent, because some of these shooters are cowards," he said.

If these youths knew there was a good chance they would be shot or killed it would deter some, Myrick said. Under the current system, schools proclaim loudly with signs that they are drug- and gun-free zones.

"It's a shooting gallery. What better place to go and shoot than a gun-free zone," he said.

Myrick does not have a concealed-handgun license, though he could easily get one in Mississippi. He said it is legal for him to have a gun in his home and in his vehicle. He is usually not far from one or the other and does not want to carry one on his person.

He believes having teachers carry guns would create a problem. Teachers get jostled by students in crowded hallways. Female teachers with guns in their purses would be vulnerable because they have to put down the purses to teach.

"You're not maintaining a posture of keeping your weapon secured in a crowded hallway. That's why I think that an armed guard would be better."

Myrick did feel that with sufficient training, it would be an advantage to have a teacher or administrator have a gun locked inside the school building.

"I would love to have a gun loaded in my desk, drawer locked. It would be safe there; it would be inaccessible," he said. "It would really be safer than the one in my truck that's there now, because I'm not watching my truck, and if you wanted to take a pipe and knock my window out and snatch my gun, you could."

He acknowledges that if he had had a gun in his desk at Pearl High School he could have reached it a lot quicker and perhaps saved some of the students from being shot. He stressed that whoever was allowed to keep a gun on school premises should receive training and have strict instructions about when it could be used.

Former Texas State Senator Jerry Patterson agrees that allowing teachers to carry guns in school buildings would pose serious security problems.

"I think a teacher who has a license to carry should be able to carry everywhere except in the building. Leave it in your car, like Myrick did," Patterson said.

Although the school shootings have received an enormous amount of publicity, they are quite rare. According to a Justice Policy Institute report in 1998, the chance of a student becoming the victim of a school-associated violent death is slightly less than one in a million.

Meanwhile, another, more terrifying threat looms over U.S. schools. Up to 2007, mass shootings at schools have been carried out by one or two socially isolated and paranoid students and have resulted in less than a dozen people murdered in each incident.

However, according to news reports, Muslim terrorists are setting their sights on American schools. A report in *World Net Daily* on September 20, 2007, states that *al Qaida* terrorists in Afghanistan have practiced attacks on schools issuing commands in English.

Plans of schools in Virginia, New Jersey, and Texas have been found on terrorists captured in Iraq, the report stated.

Retired Lieutenant Colonel David Grossman, author of *On Killing* and co-author of *Stop Teaching Our Kids to Kill*, estimates that U.S. schools are quite unprepared to deal with a terrorist attack. He urges school teachers and administrators to carry firearms.

SCHOOL SAFETY TRAINING

Response Options, 251 S.W. Wilshire Blvd, Ste. 124, #550, Burleson, TX 76028; 877-652-9461; <www.ResponseOptions.com>

Chapter Two

VICTIMS OR SURVIVORS: FIGHTING BACK AGAINST CRIMINALS AND TERRORISTS

One of the most compelling reasons for citizens to keep arms for self-defense became apparent in the aftermath of Hurricane Katrina. On the morning of Monday, August 29, 2005, the Category Four storm roared ashore just east of New Orleans, proving that close is good enough for horseshoes, hand grenades, and hurricanes. The levees that should have protected the city broke in several places, and much of the Crescent City flooded.

In the days that followed, law and order broke down, looting and shooting were rampant, and anarchy reigned. Gangs of armed looters roamed the city and took what they wanted from those who could not defend themselves. Forget calling 9-1-1: some police officers tried to do the best they could, others fled the city, and there were reports of some officers joining in the looting.

Their own firearms were the only protection most residents had, and they needed them. There were many reports of home owners defending their emergency supplies and their very lives with guns. Vinnie Pervel, a forty-nine-year-old renovation contractor, lived in Algiers Point, an area of the city that did not flood.

Before Katrina Pervel couldn't imagine why anyone would want a gun for protection. Immediately after the storm, he was hit in the head and his van hijacked. He went home a convert to gun rights and stood guard on his baloney with a shotgun for several days. He reported hearing frequent shots particularly at night.

"I have no problem with having a gun in my house now," he said.

John Carolan stood guard over his home with a gun, and it was the gun that persuaded a band of looters that they didn't want his generator badly enough to risk dying for it. Some residents banded together in groups to protect their neighborhoods, while predators looted stores and homes that were unprotected.

Many people with boats came to New Orleans to help local police and firefighters in the rescue of people stranded in the top floors and on the roofs of flooded homes. Two days after the storm, Mayor Ray Nagin ordered the city to be evacuated, but not everyone wanted to leave, particularly those in areas that did not flood. Police officers from other jurisdictions as far away as California moved in the help keep the peace.

About ten days after the hurricane swiped the Big Uneasy, Mayor Ray Nagin gave an illegal order to the police that would reverberate during the following two years in legislatures across the country and even in the halls of Congress. According to court documents and reports in the media, he ordered the law enforcement officers under his authority to evict people from their homes and confiscate their lawfully owned firearms. On September 8, television viewers across the United States watched as P. Edwin Compass III, the Superintendent of the New Orleans Police Department, announced all guns belonging to residents would be seized.

"No one will be able to be armed. Guns will be taken. Only law enforcement will be allowed to have guns," he said.

Not a word of criticism emanated from members of the main-stream media, but gun owners nationwide were outraged. The symbol of their outrage was an unlikely victim.

Patricia Konie was a frail, fifty-eight-year-old former bar maid, who happened to have a small revolver only because it was given to her by a friend in 1986, she said, when he went into government-subsidized housing and couldn't take the gun with him. The revolver was a .32 caliber Colt made in

1905. She said she had taken it out of a drawer in her wardrobe after the storm because she thought she might need it for protection. However, it was unloaded, and she had no ammunition for it. Patricia regarded it more as a keepsake than a weapon. She said she didn't know anything about guns and had only cleaned it once, shortly after she got it, with vegetable oil.

Konie moved to New Orleans from Chicago at age fifteen. Her lawyer, Brandon Brown, describes her as "a funny, scrappy survivor."

She lived in a rented house on Magazine Street, about three miles southwest of the French Quarter in the Lower Garden District. The house was undamaged by the hurricane, and the area did not flood. She was well prepared to remain in the house and didn't want to leave. She had enough fresh water and food for several weeks, and she had two dogs—one a Rottweiler-German Shepard cross called Sasha that weighs more than a hundred pounds and looks like "a big bear," according to Konie. One reason she didn't want to leave was because she didn't have cages for the dogs, and she didn't want to leave them. Her "boyfriend," Albert Bolte, then eighty-seven, used to stop by most mornings for coffee. She was part of a group of seven people from the neighborhood who got together most mornings to socialize.

On September 7, people from a nearby restaurant bought Konie more fresh water and two pies—lemon meringue and coconut.

"They had brought me four ten-pound bags of ice and batteries for my battery-operated TV. I had food for three or four months," Konie said.

About 10 a.m. a group of policemen, a Louisiana state trooper, and several from the California Highway Patrol, started banging on her doors. They were being followed around by two television crews, one from San Francisco and one from England. Her dogs started barking.

"I was minding my own business when they came to my side door and were banging on my door, and I said: 'I'm not letting you in,'" she said.

"I was scared to death that they were going to shoot my dogs. That's known to happen," Konie said. She shut the dogs in her back bathroom.

When it became clear that Patricia wasn't going to let them in, the officers asked if the reporters and cameramen could come in. She agreed to let them come in, but made it quite clear she did not want the police officers to enter her home.

The news people came into Konie's kitchen. She started showing them all the food and supplies she had. This was all caught on tape by a cameraman from KTVU-TV, a Fox affiliate in San Francisco. The news story that aired that evening showed Konie waving at her shelves of food. She is casually holding her small revolver in the palm of her hand by the cylinder. She was not holding it in a shooting grip.

"As the cameraman was coming in with all that bulky stuff, he went to close the door and they [the officers] pushed the door open," Konie told me. She said the uniformed policemen who pushed their way in "looked like four linebackers."

Brandon Brown, Konie's lawyer, said the four officers entered her home illegally.

The next shot is of Konie shouting at the police officers: "You're going to have to kill me 'cos I'm not going. I don't want you in here. I don't want you in here period."

Apparently one of the officers suddenly noticed she was holding the gun. He shouted: "Gun, gun," then knocked her down and wrestled her on the ground, taking her empty gun away. The officers twisted her arm and broke her left shoulder, Konie said.

The next shot on the video is of a large police officer on top of Konie. One officer is heard saying that she had a gun. Then an officer can be heard saying: "Relax ma'am, relax ma'am." This is followed by Konie's voice yelling: "You son of a [beep]."

The video shows her being led outside with a burly officer on each side of her holding her arms. She and her dogs were loaded onto a military vehicle.

Konie said she never pointed the gun at the officers or threatened them with it.

The KTVU reporter, Ken Wayne, says she was taken to the Convention Center then flown by helicopter with her dogs to the airport.

When Wayne is talking to the anchorman at the end of his report, he appears as an apologist for the officers in their assault of Konie. "She doesn't appear to be a threat but a gun is a gun," he says.

Konie says the British reporter was "real nice" because she went back into the house and got Patricia's purse and cigarettes. The police officers would not let her back into the house to get them.

Konie and her dogs were flown to South Carolina where they stayed for a month before she was allowed to return. She estimated that the government spend at least $5,000 flying her and the dogs to and from South Carolina and for their food and lodging while they were there.

Her "boyfriend," Albert Bolte, didn't know where she was, and she didn't know what had happened to him. She tried to get the Red Cross to find him, she said.

"I was frantic and he was frantic," Konie said.

D octors found that her shoulder was broken in three places, and she had to have surgery to repair the damage. In June 2007, she suffered a stroke.

Brandon Brown, her lawyer, said Konie had had several surgeries. Her stroke rehabilitation has been complicated by the injury caused by the police attack, he added.

Konie has filed a law suit in federal court against California and Louisiana police officers. She accuses the officers of various civil rights violations, including assault, kidnapping, and illegally disarming her.

If the police officers ever testify in a courtroom, it is likely they will invoke the Adolph Eichmann defense: "I was just following orders."

The video of four burly police officers slamming a frail, fifty-eight-year-old woman to the ground in her own home, disarming her, and forcing her against her will to be evacuated caused not a ripple of complaint from members of the mainstream media. But more than anything else, it outraged and mobilized gun owners. They called the National Rifle Association, which along with the Second Amendment Foundation, filed a law suit in United States District Court for the Eastern District of Louisiana to stop the confiscations and get the guns returned to their owners.

The complaint cited the Louisiana Constitution, which gives citizens the right to keep and bear arms. It cited several rights guaranteed by the U.S. Constitution including the right to keep and bear arms in the Second Amendment, protection from unreasonable search and seizure from the Fourth Amendment, the guarantee of due process of law in the Fourteenth Amendment, and the equal protection clause of the same amendment.

On September 23, 2005, lawyers for all sides agreed to a consent order signed by U.S. District Judge Jay C. Zaney, which ordered the seizures to stop and the seized guns to be returned to their owners. Mayor Ray Nagin, New Orleans Police Superintendent Edwin Compass, and his successor Warren Riley apparently ignored the order. Lawyers for the city and police department initially claimed that no guns had been confiscated.

In February 2006, the NRA and Second Amendment Foundation filed a motion in federal court to have Nagin and Riley held in contempt of court. The memorandum in support of the motion cited several cases, supported by affidavits, of guns being confiscated from law-abiding citizens. These affidavits indicate a pattern of rudeness and arrogance more in keeping with police in countries like China or Zimbabwe than officers in a western democracy who claim to be servants of the public.

One of the affidavits involved Ashton O'Dwyer, the lawyer who first represented Patricia Konie. O'Dwyer stated that he got out of his vehicle at his home in Southport, a "bad" neighborhood. He was lawfully carrying a .38-caliber Smith & Wesson revolver from his vehicle to his house when two New Orleans police officers told him to drop the gun and raise his hands. O'Dwyer complied and was handcuffed and put in a patrol car. He was released, but his gun was not returned, and the officers refused to give him a receipt for it.

After stonewalling for months, the city's lawyer, Joseph Vincent DiRosa, finally admitted that police had seized some guns. He showed NRA lawyers a rental truck containing about a thousand long guns and handguns in deplorable condition. NRA lawyer Dan Holliday said he thought about ten guns had been returned to their owners. The city made it as difficult as possible for people to get their guns back, insisting on receipts for proof of ownership.

One gun owner, I.H. Spurlock, had several long guns seized. He took down their cases, which had their serial numbers written on the inside of each case. This was deemed insufficient proof of ownership, and he was turned away.

The NRA tried to get an inventory of the guns, but the stonewalling continued until in March 2007. Judge Carl J. Barbier cited DiRosa for contempt, calling him wholly unprofessional. He was ordered to pay part of the NRA legal fees.

As of September 2007, lawyers for the NRA and Second Amendment Foundation had little success in getting guns returned to their owners due to the intransigence of New Orleans and its police department. More details of the confiscations are contained in the first chapter of my recent book, *Thank God I Had a Gun: True Accounts of Self-Defense.*

However, gun owners have had some successes. They made it quite clear to their state and federal representatives that what happened in New Orleans must never happen again in this country. In the subsequent two years, nineteen states passed laws making it illegal for governments to confiscate legally owned firearms from citizens during periods of emergency. They are Alaska, California, Florida, Georgia, Idaho, Kentucky, Louisiana, Michigan, Mississippi, Missouri, Montana, Nevada, New Hampshire, Oklahoma, South Carolina, Tennessee, Texas, Virginia, and West Virginia. The federal government has passed similar legislation.

Hurricane Katrina was a natural disaster, but it can also be looked at as a dress rehearsal for a major terrorist attack on a U.S. city. Some gun owners realized that many of the same conditions that prevailed after the storm will occur in the aftermath of a biological, chemical, or nuclear attack. Law and order will break down; gangs of criminals will roam the city raping, robbing, and murdering residents who cannot defend themselves. They will lose their homes, their vehicles, their water, food, and other disaster supplies if they do not have their privately owned guns to protect themselves. This is why legislation that prevents governments from disarming law-abiding citizens in times of crisis is so important.

Meanwhile there are some other lessons to be learned in Louisiana about fighting back against criminals. John Long and his father run what might be called a full-service barbershop in Shreveport, in the northwestern part of the state. They cut hair; they cut keys; they notarize documents; out back, they perform state vehicle inspections; and on the side, they sell used cars. While barbering is not usually on anyone's list of high-

Long's Barbershop on West 70th Street in Shreveport, Louisiana.

risk occupations, Long's shop is located on West 70th Street in a predominately black, high-crime area of the city and is about the only store in the neighborhood that has not been robbed at gunpoint. Long, forty-three, says about three-quarters of his customers are black and many are gang members, but they don't scare him.

"If it were not for the black customers, we would almost have no business. Black people are very free about spending their money. That's just maybe their nature, and gangbangers need notary work, gangbangers need keys made, gangbangers have to have inspection stickers like anybody else, and as long as they come in and do business, we're open for business, but I will not sit there and be intimidated."

For more than a hundred years, Louisiana has allowed its residents to carry handguns openly. After the state passed a concealed-carry law in 1996, Long was one of the first to get a license. Until then, Long and his father kept several handguns hidden, but within easy reach, at the shop. On one occasion, a man aroused Long's suspicions as he approached the door to the barbershop by looking around and crouching before he entered. Long reached into a closet, took out a .32-caliber semi-automatic, and held it behind his back as the man came into the shop. The man looked at his father, who was nearest the door, and then at Long. Long said he could see the outline of a revolver in the man's pocket. Suddenly, his eyes got really big, he made some excuse, and left rather hastily. Long figured out later that the man saw the gun in the mirror behind Long. He moved the mirror.

For several years after getting his concealed-handgun license, Long wore his gun concealed, while at work and elsewhere. That changed after he was involved in a confrontation in January 2000.

He was in a barbershop-chorus singing at a local Lutheran Church. The singers practiced on Monday evenings in the gymnasium of the church, and that night Long was late. His father had kept him late at work, and his wife wanted him home early to help her with some homework.

Usually he would take off his gun and leave it in his van when he reached the church parking lot. This night, he forgot.

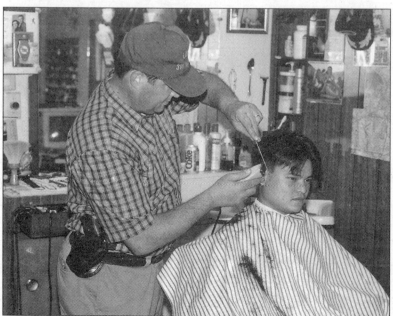

John Long in his Shreveport, Louisiana, barbershop.

"At the time, I was wearing my .38 Rossi concealed in an ankle holster," Long said.

He didn't realize he was still carrying the gun until he was in the gymnasium.

"I was sitting there singing with the chorus when I realized I had forgotten to take it off. So I thought, I will just make sure I don't sit down and cross my legs so someone would notice," Long said.

He left the practice early so he could get home to assist his wife. As he walked towards his van, a man came out of the darkness and asked him for money. The man said he was out of gas and didn't have any food. Long had heard such begging stories repeatedly and told the man he was in a hurry. He said he told the man to leave him alone.

"Suddenly, the man stopped, looking way to his left, then way to his right. He was looking around, making sure nobody's watching. That's a sign. When someone's doing that, they're making sure nobody's gonna see something they're about to do. I yanked up my pant leg, grabbed my gun, and ripped it out," Long said.

The man was about ten feet away as Long brought his gun up. He saw the man pull a knife from under his belt, Long said.

"I was intending to shoot him straight in the face, but as I was coming across in slow motion, he turned and ducked, and I had to hold myself to stop me from shooting 'cause he had suddenly turned his back. In a flash, he was gone."

This was an epiphany for Long: "This was the one day I had forgotten to take it off, and one day I seriously needed it, and I just happened to have it. I swore then I would always carry a gun if I am legally able to, because that is never going to happen to me again. This had a profound effect on me."

He also realized that if he had been wearing a gun openly, the man would never have sought him out as a possible victim. From then on, he determined to wear his gun in the open most of the time and all the time at work.

Doug Stump.

Long started wearing a gun openly. His father was against it at first because he felt the customers would feel threatened. He has since changed his mind. Wearing guns concealed is less likely to deter would-be robbers, his father said. When I interviewed him, Long was wearing a .45-caliber Glock semiautomatic Model 30 in a thumb-break holster on his right hip in full view. His colleague and co-worker, Doug Stump, was wearing a .45-caliber Heckler & Koch USP also exposed on his right hip. While Long's father doesn't usually wear a handgun, he has several within arms' reach in the shop.

Long's father has seen the neighborhood deteriorate over the years. When he opened the barbershop in 1959, there was little crime in the area.

"It used to be that you could walk outside, leave your door open, and nobody bothered nothing, but it's not that way any more," he said. "We almost got robbed a couple of times. We had our guns with us, but they were concealed, and they didn't know we had them until it was almost too late. Since we've had open carry, we've had no problems and haven't had any attempts of anybody robbing us. In fact, everybody in this neighborhood has probably been robbed two to four times but us."

Stump said he used to get a hassle from his wife for going to work wearing a gun. "My wife used to say that I wore a gun so that I could shoot somebody, but I think she's finally come to the realization I wear it so I don't have to shoot somebody," he says.

Long and Stump feel that a gun carried visibly has a deterrent effect on criminals looking for an easy score. This would not be legal in many states, but it is in Louisiana. Although this is a book about concealed carry, the Long's experience with the deterrent effect of wearing a gun in full view should not be ignored. An ounce of deterrence is worth a pound of lead.

"Since we've hung the hardware on the outside, the confrontations have gone down in quantity and aggressiveness quite a bit," Stump says.

Over the years, there were other confrontations where Long persuaded people who may have been planning to rob the business to leave, usually by exposing a gun to view. According to Long, there have been at least half-a-dozen incidents where men have entered the barbershop intending to rob it but changed their minds when they realized that staff members are armed.

Long says he once recognized a would-be robber, who had seen his gun and left the barbershop, as one of two men who went on a test drive with a local used-car dealer, robbed him, then executed him in cold blood.

Long and Stump are very adept at spotting potential robbers. Anyone who is looking around as he approaches the door is immediately under suspicion. Long says criminals intent on robbery tend to give themselves away by their body language. They are usually extremely nervous and antsy, and they look around a lot. In addition to always keeping his eyes open for potential trouble, Long has learned to trust his instincts.

Long's has developed a reputation in the neighborhood, as Stump realized when he overheard a conversation between the driver and the passenger of a car he was inspecting. He was doing the paperwork when he heard the passenger say to the driver: "See, I told you the Longs are gonna treat you right.

They're gonna treat you fair, but you f--- with them, they're gonna kill you."

In a high-crime neighborhood, it's not a bad reputation to have. They have never had to fire a handgun in self defense.

Another incident happened in July 2001. Long was notarizing some documents for a woman when she asked him why he was wearing the gun. Just then, a car pulled up in front of the barbershop, and three young men got out. One of them walked to the back of the car and took a revolver from the trunk. He stuck it in his belt at the back, covering it up with his shirt.

"The woman said: 'Did you see that?' I said: 'Yes, you just go ahead. I'll take care of this,'" Long recalled.

He ushered the woman to her car, and she left while he went out to confront the three men. He was wearing his gun in full view as usual. As he walked towards the men, he called out: "Hey there, can I help you?"

Long says they turned towards him as he kept walking up to them with his hand on his gun, then looked at each other. Long said the nearest was about three steps away, but his focus was on the one behind, whom he had seen stuff the gun in his waistband.

According to Long, one of them said: "We're just lookin' at the cars. I think we'll go somewhere else."

The three men left, but that was not quite the end of the story. Shortly after, the man Long saw take the revolver out of the trunk of the car tried to pull a robbery at the Tool House, a store about a mile from Long's barbershop.

Bill Stroud was a Baptist Youth Minister when he took over the Tool House from his father. In early December 2000, the area suffered from a rash of armed robberies, he said. Although his store wasn't hit, one incident concerned him. He was working behind the counter when a man came in and started talking to one of his employees while standing behind him.

The Tool House on Hearne Avenue, Shreveport, Louisiana.

"I'm not the kind of guy to read people, but I thought that my employee must know the guy 'cause of the way the guy was talking to him," Stroud said.

He saw the employee step to one side and point at the store's video security camera. The man made some excuse about going to get his drill and left. When the employee came over and told him what had happened, Stroud was concerned enough to call the police. The police found the man, who was carrying a .357-caliber revolver and several bags of crack cocaine, Stroud said. They arrested him.

Later Stroud told his father and other family members about the incident, so they would be aware of the possible dangers. He also bought several handguns and hid them in the store with one behind the counter.

Just before Christmas that year, Stroud's second cousin was raped and murdered during a car-jacking incident in southern Louisiana.

"It was a very bad situation that was sort of on the heels of all this. So that's when we got our guns and started being prepared 'cause there were a lot of robberies," he said. "I had guns previously, but now they are stashed where I can get to one."

Several months later, in the early summer of 2001, Stroud had a particularly disturbing dream. He dreamt that he was in his store when a man came in and shot at him. He fired one round in return, and the man shot again.

"In this dream, I saw something fly out of my chest, so I looked down and didn't feel anything, but there was blood coming out of my chest. And I died. I woke up at the point that I died," Stroud said.

The dream upset him so much he told his pastor about it. The pastor suggested that God was trying to tell him something— that perhaps he was going to get robbed, Stroud said.

Nothing happened for about a month, until Friday, July 20, 2001. Shortly before 5 p.m., Stroud was behind the counter working on a report. One employee was also behind the counter, sitting on the floor counting drill bits. Another was over in a corner behind some toolboxes. Stroud said he had just finished talking to Jerry Wilson, a customer and off-duty police officer from nearby Bossier City. Wilson, who was unarmed at the time, was looking at a jointer-planer they had been discussing, Stroud said.

Bill Stroud.

His wife would have been working behind the counter, but they had adopted a baby two weeks before, and she was at home, he said.

A man entered the store. Wilson later described him as a black male, about seventeen years old, five-feet six-inches tall, weighing about 135 pounds. He was wearing a dark blue print shirt and dark blue golfer-type ball cap. He was holding a dark blue or black bandanna or "do-rag" to his face, covering his mouth and nose. Stroud was conscious that a man had entered the store and was making a lot of noise.

"When I'm working, I like tune out the world," Stroud said. "I was doing my work, not paying attention or even looking up for a minute. I was thinking: as soon as I get to where I need to be, I'm gonna see what this loud customer wants."

When finally Stroud did look up, the man was about eight feet away, pointing a .38-caliber snub-nose revolver at him and yelling at him that he wanted the money from the cash register.

"He was obviously on drugs, upset at how I was ignoring him, and about to explode. So when I looked up, he had that gun on me. I thought he was going to shoot us all."

Just under the counter Stroud had an Arminius .357 Magnum caliber revolver loaded with .38 Special +P cartridges. He picked up the gun just as Wilson, the police officer, made a movement. Wilson later told investigators that the would-be robber pointed the gun at him and told him not to move. He said the man yelled at Stroud that, if he didn't give him all the money, he would shoot Wilson. The distraction gave Stroud time to cock the gun and bring it up.

"When I pulled my gun up, he started coming at me, and when he did, I didn't aim or nothing—boom. When I did that, he shot and hit the wall," Stroud said.

He dove down behind the counter on top of the employee who had been counting drill bits. When Stroud got up, it was in time to see the robber running out of the door.

"I shot over his head deliberately, wanting him out of my store," he said. That bullet shattered a window in the front of the store.

At the time, Stroud didn't know whether his first shot had hit the man or not. After he had gone, Stroud did find the revolver the man had dropped in his haste to leave. The robber was later identified as nineteen-year-old Deandre Lias, according to police reports. He was picked up by two friends and driven to Louisiana State University Medical Center, where they dropped him off.

Stroud's bullet had hit him in the center of the chest between his nipples, according to the police report. He died shortly after his arrival at the hospital. His friends told police Lias had been hanging out with them and had gone to get a hamburger. When he didn't return they had gone looking for him. When they found him walking along the street, he was patting his chest with both hands and staggering. One of the friends told police he thought Lias was playing around, but he collapsed into the car and said: "Carry me to the hospital. I been shot, and go get my mama."

Lias was known to several of the police officers involved in the subsequent investigation. At the time of his demise, he was a fugitive, wanted on a warrant for a charge of attempted murder. He was also a suspect in seven armed robberies in the previous month, according to the police report.

The district attorney determined the shooting was a justifiable homicide, and Stroud was not charged.

The day after the shooting, John Long walked into a fast-food restaurant and picked up a newspaper.

"I saw that guy's face on the front page—the one that had the gun—shot and killed trying to rob the Tool House," he said.

Some of the people most at risk for becoming victims of violence in our society are women who are being stalked by estranged husbands or former boyfriends. Despite the passage of anti-stalking laws in many states during the 1990s, police are often unable or unwilling to protect these women. They do not need to be told the police cannot protect them—they know.

Jennifer Palmer met Randy Wiley early in 2000 at a dance hall called Cowboys, located in Arlington, a suburb between Dallas and Fort Worth. She was taking dancing lessons and went to Cowboys to practice every Wednesday evening. Wiley was usually there and, after a couple of months, he asked her out. Some of her friends had known Wiley, then thirty-two, for about ten years. He talked about his daughter and seemed like a gentle kind of man.

"We went out kinda' sporadically," Palmer said later.

As spring turned into summer, the relationship became more serious. They took a trip together to Cancun, a resort city popular with tourists, on the coast of Mexico's Yucatan Peninsula. She found out he was taking lithium, a prescription antidepressant. She also discovered that Randy had been retired from the military with a disability pension because he was bipolar—a manic-depressive disorder caused by a chemical imbalance of the brain.

"I knew about it, I understood it, so it didn't scare me," she said.

At the time, Palmer, who has a degree in medical technology, was working as a microbiologist at Huguley Memorial Medical Center on the south side of Fort Worth.

"Anything that comes out of the human body, falls off the human body, is removed from the human body, we culture it to determine the harmful bacteria," she said.

Towards the end of August, Wiley and Palmer were not getting along well. One of the causes of friction was that Palmer likes pets and had several of them. Wiley didn't like them.

"Things were not working out," she said. "We both decided to not date."

According to Palmer, it was a mutual decision. However, they agreed to remain friends.

At the time, Randy Wiley was living in an apartment that he found too expensive, so Palmer allowed him to move into her house as a lodger while he looked for another place to live. She lived in a house in Burleson, a city of about sixteen thousand people, just across the county line in Johnson County, south of Fort Worth.

They agreed he would stay for September and October and pay rent. While he was staying at her house, two of her three cats mysteriously disappeared, she said.

At the end of October, Wiley said he hadn't found a suitable apartment and refused to move out. It took pressure from Palmer's grandparents, her mother, and sister to get him to move. He finally left near the end of November, taking her photo albums with him.

"It was terribly, terribly embarrassing," she said.

As soon as Wiley left, the phone calls started coming at work and at home. He would leave up to twenty-five messages a day on her answering machine, Palmer said.

"The messages were: 'I love you, I want you back,' nothing threatening," she said.

At the same time, Wiley started following her to work in his white Ford pickup. He would approach her in the parking lot at the hospital and try to start a conversation with her, but she told him to leave and that the relationship was over.

Wiley also used the Internet to get information about Palmer's relatives.

"He invaded my whole family—my uncle and aunt, my cousin, my grandparents, and my mom. He found out all their addresses, where they were at," Palmer said. "At the time, I didn't know this at all. I just know I'm being tracked by somebody who won't give it up."

Wiley got into her e-mail and sent some of the e-mails from her former husband to her relatives in order to embarrass her, she said.

December 2000 started badly. Palmer started to take the situation more seriously when it appeared someone had been in her house and taken spare keys to her house and car. She suspected Wiley but did not report her suspicions to police. She could prove nothing. She had the locks on her house changed. She had no idea what a fateful month December would be.

The following day, December 6, she went out with some friends after work and met Hal Detrick Diggs, then a thirty-five-year-old computer programmer with the Fort Worth Star Telegram.

Diggs attended a Christmas party at his work that evening. He left the party about 9 p.m. and went into a bookstore in downtown Fort Worth. The bookstore was above a nightclub. Diggs was looking for something to read in the science-fiction line when he saw Palmer.

"There was this cute girl standing there looking in the science-fiction section. Being a guy, I just made a comment to her about, 'it's really interesting to find a girl here.' She laughed and we conversed—nothing serious—and then she went about her way," Diggs said.

About an hour later, Diggs went down into the club below the bookstore and met a friend of his. They hadn't been in the club long when three girls walked in. One of them was Palmer.

"You could tell they were on an anti-guy night," Diggs said.

Later in the evening, he asked her to dance, and she agreed. As they walked to the dance floor, they exchanged information about themselves. "In ten minutes we knew everything about each other," Palmer said.

Her companions left, and she offered to drive Diggs to his car a few blocks away. They talked in her car into the early hours of the morning. Palmer mentioned that she had a former boyfriend, but didn't tell Diggs much about the harassing phone calls and the stalking. They exchanged phone numbers, then Palmer drove home. She arrived about 3 a.m. to find her home had been broken into. A miniature Schnauzer she had had for eight years was gone. She called the police, but she didn't tell them about Wiley stalking her.

"I didn't have anything concrete to give them," she said.

She called Diggs on his cell phone. He had given her the number when they parted earlier that evening.

"She was upset because her dog was gone," he said.

Diggs didn't think much about the incident at the time, because he didn't know the whole situation. However, he did encourage her to contact the police about the stalking. At her mother's urging, she contacted the police Victims Assistance Unit. She wanted to know what she could do about the harassment. She was told: "They can't do anything until he hurts you or he breaks into your home." A couple of days later, Palmer had a security system installed in her house.

The relationship between Diggs and Palmer developed rapidly. They had bonded, they said, and were spending a lot of time together.

On Friday, December 15, Diggs invited Palmer to join him for a few drinks during happy hour at a bar where he was going to meet friends after work. She was an hour late.

"When she came in the front door, she was all smiles, but when I put my hand on her arm, she was shaking," Diggs said.

Palmer told him Wiley had been waiting for her to come out of her house. As she drove north on Interstate 35 towards downtown Fort Worth, he followed her in his white Ford F150 pickup and tried to run her off the road. He kept making hand signals and swerving into her lane. "He didn't know where I was going: that's what bothered him," she said.

Diggs followed Palmer home and offered to stay the night on her sofa. She accepted his offer. They set the new alarm and talked late into the evening. They had turned in, Palmer in her bedroom and Diggs on the sofa in the living room, when Wiley made his presence known.

"All of a sudden the door went bam, bam, bam, bam, bam," said Diggs. "I'll tell you what, the skin crawled on my hands."

The rapid hammering on the door was followed by continuous ringing of the doorbell. Diggs jumped up and ran into Palmer's bedroom. He found her on the bed, curled up in a fetal position. He was scared, but he could see she was terrified.

"I knew something [that] had happened before that [had] scared her. She knew what this guy was capable of possibly. On the inside, there was something. He had gotten to her that deeply in her mind," Diggs said.

Palmer's bedroom had two windows in it—one on each side of her bed. Wiley had run around the house and was hammering on the windows, then running back to the front door and repeatedly ringing the doorbell. Diggs was frantically running from door to door, window to window.

"She's sitting there curled up in a ball, and I threw her the telephone. I said, 'Call 9-1-1, and I'll watch him,'" Diggs said. "This guy is screaming and yelling. He's saying: 'Jennifer, I know you have a guy in there, I know you have a guy. Lock him up if you have to, I need to talk to you.'"

Diggs desperately searched the house for a weapon, but he couldn't find anything. She had no gun. Palmer is a black belt in *tae kwon do* and taught martial arts to children for two years.

"I have been trained to defend myself with myself," she said. "Never have a weapon, they teach you in *tae kwon do*, don't have a weapon that can be taken away from you and used against you."

Diggs asked Palmer how big Wiley was, in case he broke in and Diggs had to fight him. Palmer told him not to do anything. Using Diggs's cell phone, she reached the 9-1-1 operator, who told her to stay on the phone.

While the police were on the way, Diggs worried about the psychological effect the incident was having on Palmer. Although she had been taught in martial arts to fight back against an assailant, this man had succeeded in cowing her into a submissive mindset.

Palmer tried to explain it. "You never think you're going to be in that situation. You don't know what you're going to do. If somebody jumped out at me and tried to take my purse, I could defend myself. But here I am, I'm in my home, and I'm tired. This had been going on for a month and a half. My freedom had been taken away."

The police arrived—three patrol cars containing five or six officers. A reassuringly large officer was at the door when they answered it. They had Randy Wiley up against his white truck that was parked in front of the house.

"They had him on the other side of the truck," said Diggs. "One cop was holding him, and he's still yelling: 'Jennifer, Jennifer, I know you want to talk to me. Tell them you want to talk to me.'"

According to Diggs, the officers were rough on Wiley. They frisked him twice and gave him several sobriety tests. They told him he wasn't supposed to be there. The sergeant asked Palmer if Wiley had broken anything or made any threats to her. She said that she honestly couldn't say that he had. He just made a lot of noise and shouted that he wanted to talk to her.

"They said the only thing they can do is give him a warning for trespassing," Palmer said.

The police told her they could drive by her house during the day and at night and make a police report.

"But we can't do anything until he hurts you," she quoted the police as saying. "I heard that so many times."

The police did not arrest Wiley. They gave him a warning and let him go. Diggs could not believe it. By this time, he and

Palmer were beginning to realize that the police could not protect them.

The following day at work, the harassing phone calls continued. Palmer became virtually a prisoner in her own house. The only time she went out was to go to work. Diggs stayed with her most nights, initially on the couch in the living room.

On December 22, a Friday, there was a ring at Palmer's doorbell about midnight. She looked out of the window and saw a box on her front porch. She and Diggs could see the wording on the box. It read: "Merry Christmas, I love you Jennifer." Although they did not see him, they had no doubt it was left there by Wiley. They called police. When the officers arrived, they made Diggs open the box.

"They wouldn't touch it," he said.

In the box were a pair of diamond earrings and two letters. One letter pledged Wiley's undying love for Palmer, and the other was from his daughter.

"She was actually very important to me," Palmer said. "I liked her. She was a pretty little girl—I love kids."

The officers told Palmer she would have to keep the box and its contents. The officers said they couldn't do anything, and when Diggs became angry one of them asked him to leave. Diggs wanted Palmer to make a police report, but she objected, saying she didn't want to be a victim.

"I just grabbed her and I said: 'Right now you are the victim, and this is the only chance we have to get some help to get this guy put away, and we have to establish a paper trail.'" Palmer made the police report.

The following day, Saturday, December 23, Diggs decided to introduce his mother and stepfather to Palmer. They took Diggs's parents to dinner at a restaurant in Fort Worth, then the four of them went downtown to a piano bar. They had just entered the club when a blond-haired, blue-eyed man, about six-feet tall appeared in the doorway.

"As soon as I saw him, I knew who he was," Diggs said.

He watched as Palmer walked up to the man, grabbed him by the shirtfront, and said to him: "Let's not make a scene; let's go talk." She took him around a corner, out of Diggs's sight, while he escorted his mother and stepfather to a table. He didn't want to leave Palmer alone with Wiley, so he went to find them. He wanted to give her time to get rid of him, so he waited a couple of minutes before following them. While he was waiting to see if Palmer would return, he told a waitress that there might be trouble. He added that if the police were called, he was the good guy.

When Diggs found them, he said she was trying to tell him not to buy her things and that she didn't want to see him anymore. Palmer is five-feet two-inches tall and Wiley, at six feet, was towering over her.

"He was doing this controlling guy thing, where he's almost up on his toes to come down on her and get his chest in her face."

Diggs said he tried to get between them, while asking Palmer if she was all right. She assured him that she was, so he decided to give them another couple of minutes to finish. He returned after a few more minutes to find they were making no progress. Wiley was still there and showed no sign of leaving. He and Diggs almost came to blows, when Palmer leaped between them and pushed them apart.

"She jumped right in between us and does one of those arm-spread numbers, because we were getting ready to fight right then and there," Diggs said.

Finally, Wiley agreed to leave and walked out. When they left the club sometime later, there was no sign of Wiley.

The harassing phone calls continued all through the weekend. Wiley would call often between midnight and 1 a.m., trying to make sure Palmer was home.

"He wanted complete control of me, where I was at all times, but he was never ever crazy," Palmer said.

The phone calls dropped off somewhat during Christmas week, but then started picking up on Thursday, December 28. The following day, Friday, Palmer received flowers at work from Wiley. She tried to refuse them, but they were dropped off for her at the front desk. She gave them away at the hospital.

A week after the confrontation in the piano bar, on Saturday, December 30, Palmer went to work at Huguley Memorial Medical Center, arriving at 6 a.m. About 7:30 a.m. she heard the phone ring. On weekends, there was no receptionist so she picked up the receiver. It was Wiley. Palmer doesn't remember what he said, but she does remember telling him she was busy and not to call her. This would be the last of many harassing phone calls from the man who was stalking her.

"I just had this odd feeling," she said.

When she arrived at work in the dark, it was her habit to step outside the hospital when it was light to check on the weather. The odd feeling was not enough to keep her from her usual routine. Wiley knew where Palmer parked her car, which was well away from the main entrance of the hospital. If he was waiting for her, she figured he would stake out her vehicle. However, she was cautious. She looked out, but there were several pillars outside the entrance obstructing her view. She could see nothing wrong, so she took a deep breath and walked out.

She was well outside when she saw the white pickup and a flash of silver that she knew instantly was a gun. She threw up her right arm and stepped sideways as she heard a popping sound. But she was too late. The bullet hit her upper right arm, striking the bone, then ploughed into her chest. Wiley got out of his truck and continued firing. She went down, but her martial arts training served her well.

"I'm going to be a moving target; I was trained to do this. So I'm rolling on the ground, and he's shooting at me on the ground. He did that twice more. So, three bullets in total. At that point, there's a pause.

"I'm still laying on the ground. Bullet one hit me; two hit the ground beside me. I hear a pause. I go over to the side, I kinda crouch. There are six witnesses at this point that are watching us. I crouch, I see the hospital entrance. I zigzag into the hospital entrance.

"The witnesses all say that they didn't know what I was doing. I knew what I was doing. I was not going to be moving in one direction. I hear another bullet, and I'm just praying: please don't let it hit anything. My arm hurt so fiercely, it was on fire, and my chest hurt. I didn't know what it was.

"I hide behind a pillar. Always hide behind a solid object. Some people hide behind windows—no. I hid behind a marble pillar and I crouched. I had heard that fourth bullet—no shattering glass—and I crouched behind a pillar like in a little ball. But all of a sudden the blood was all spurting out on my leg, and I'm like: I can't do any more, dear God, I just can't.

"I lay flat. I applied pressure to my arm, and I waited until somebody walked by, and I said, 'Somebody please help me.' I said, 'Help me.' She didn't know what was going on. I said, 'I've been shot.' And it was a nurse, and she went into the ER. And by that time two other people, a respiratory therapist, a woman that I knew, and another woman from the ER, they all came."

The bullet that hit Palmer in the right arm tore into her chest piercing her right lung before coming to a stop near her spinal column. She was taken into the emergency room, examined, and x-rayed. Her lung had collapsed and was filling with fluid.

"There's blood bubbles in the back of my throat, and I'm like: 'Drugs, please; give me drugs, it hurts,'" Palmer said.

But she is allergic to some painkillers, so they couldn't give her any. Huguley was not equipped to cope with serious bullet wounds, so the doctors decided to send her by ambulance

Jennifer Palmer identifies the entry site of Wiley's bullet.

to Harris Methodist Hospital in Fort Worth. By the time they found the right drugs it was too late, and they operated on her without any anesthetic, she said.

Meanwhile, Wiley had driven off in his truck as soon as Palmer had escaped into the hospital. At both hospitals, police asked her what had happened. She gave them Wiley's name and cellphone number. Officers asked what kind of gun she was shot with. Knowing nothing about guns, she told them it was silver and "had a little turney thing," referring to the cylinder of a revolver. She told them she had been shot at a range of about twelve feet.

Within an hour or so of the shooting, the word had gone out on the police radio that Palmer's boyfriend had shot her. This caused Diggs some discomfort when a Burleson police officer arrived at Palmer's house. It was Saturday and Diggs was not working. He had heard nothing of the shooting.

"The cop knocks on the door, and I'm thinking: a cop, great. So I opened up the door, and he has about as shocked a look on his face as I do on mine. I'm standing there, no shirt on, just pajama bottoms type thing. I go: 'Hey guy, what's up?' and he goes: 'Who are you?' and the first thing out of my mouth is: 'I'm the boyfriend.'

"So now this guy takes about three steps back, puts his hand on his holster and tells me to hold still while he makes a phone call."

Diggs realized something must have happened, and he explains that he is the good guy who was there the last time the police were called.

Wiley was arrested the following day at Osteopathic Medical Center of Texas, where a doctor friend had checked him into a psychiatric ward. He was charged with attempted murder, and bail was set at $50,000. This meant he could be released if he came up with 10 percent or $5,000. On January 2, a judge granted Palmer a ninety-day emergency protective order.

"I finally got my protective order. This is three days after I had been shot," Palmer said. "They said: 'Okay, now you are granted this, if he ever comes around you, contacting you, it would be a violation of the protective order.' Well, if he comes around me, I'm already in trouble. That's just a piece of paper."

Jennifer Palmer and Hal Diggs.

On the day she got the protective order, she and Diggs discussed how they were going to cope with the possibility that Wiley might make bail and get out of jail. They talked about guns, though neither knew much about them. Palmer had never been exposed to guns at all and, while Diggs had been taught to shoot as a kid, he had not done any shooting since he was about fourteen years old. Guns were not an option they had considered until after the shooting. However, Diggs quickly came to the decision that he needed a handgun. They needed protection that the police could not provide. The following day, he searched the Internet and found Tac Pro Shooting Center about sixty miles west of Fort Worth.

Palmer was kept under guard by police until she was released from Harris Methodist Hospital on January 4. She was amazed when, after she was released from the hospital, people from Huguley where she worked turned up with guns for her to borrow.

Diggs borrowed a 9mm Taurus from his stepfather, and one of Palmer's friends lent them a 9mm Ruger.

Two days after Palmer was released from the hospital, she and Diggs attended Ladies' Day at Tac Pro Shooting Center, where they were made welcome among the dozen or so women. Diggs and Palmer saw a variety of different guns, and she recognized a revolver by its cylinder, which she referred to as "the little turncy thing." Palmer was not able to operate a semi-auto because of the wound in her right arm. When I interviewed her at Tac Pro in mid-February 2001, I watched as Bill Davison taught her how to operate a semi-automatic entirely with her left hand.

A year later, Lawrence Randall Wiley Jr. was convicted of attempted murder and sentenced to fifteen years in prison. Palmer still does not have full use of her right hand and has to shoot left-handed.

Initially, Palmer said she had difficulty reconciling carrying a gun with her Christian faith.

"The rationalization that I really did have to come to is: if you look in the Bible, you read that God helps those that help themselves. That's the truth, and I'm not going to sit around and be a victim."

Her biggest issue when I interviewed her six weeks after the shooting was that everybody was trying to portray her as

Bill Davison gives instruction in handling a semi-automatic
to Jennifer Palmer at Tac Pro Shooting Center
about six weeks after she had been shot.

a victim—the police from Burleson, the police in Fort Worth, the district attorney, and even her family. Palmer intends to learn from her mistakes and make sure the same sort of thing never happens again.

"I'm not a victim, I'm a survivor," she said.

When four Arab terrorists took over United Airlines Flight 93 shortly after it left Newark, New Jersey, en route to San Francisco on September 11, 2001, they reckoned without the reaction of passengers and flight crew. News reports indicate that, in particular, they underestimated five American businessmen—Todd Beamer, thirty-two; Mark Bingham, thirty-one; Tom Burnett, thirty-eight; Jeremy Glick, thirty-one; and Lou Nacke, forty-two.

The passengers learned from cell-phone calls that two other airliners had been hijacked and used as missiles to hit the World Trade Center in New York City. They later heard about the third plane that hit the Pentagon. They realized theirs was no ordinary hijacking when passengers are held hostage while negotiations take place with government officials. The hijackers intended to use the Boeing 757 as a flying bomb. Later speculation pointed to the White House or Capitol Hill as the most likely targets.

Some of the men said goodbye to their loved ones. Beamer tried to call his wife, Lisa, but couldn't get through. Bingham called his mother, Glick and Burnett their wives. According to a *Newsweek* report, Burnett, a medical company executive, got through to his wife, Deena. She was busy getting breakfast for their three young daughters at home in the upscale San Francisco Bay area suburb of San Ramon. Burnett called his wife four times, exchanging information with her. He told her that one of the terrorists claimed to have a bomb, but that he thought the man was bluffing. During the last call, he told her that the passengers were "going to do something." She pleaded with him to sit down and not draw attention to himself.

"Wait for the authorities," she urged.

Good advice perhaps under the old customs of hijacking. Deena Burnett still believed in the power of the government to protect its citizens. But the rules had changed. The authorities would protect no one on Flight 93 that day. In fact, if the plane had approached Washington, D.C., all the flight crew and passengers could have expected from their government was a Sidewinder air-to-air missile fired from a National Guard F-16 fighter.

President George W. Bush and Vice President Dick Cheney had already taken the decision that an airliner that threatened the nation's capital would be shot down. The passengers and crew were on their own that September morning. According to news reports in October 2003, the U.S. military practices shooting down commercial airliners three or four times a week, either with fighters or surface-to-air missiles.

Burnett did not take his wife's advice and wait for the government. The passengers had apparently taken a vote and decided they could not let the hijackers use the plane to kill them and perhaps hundreds more people on the ground. They decided to fight back.

The five men, possibly accompanied by others, charged the cockpit where one of the hijackers was flying the plane towards Washington, D.C. The hijackers, wearing red bandannas around their heads, were armed with fanaticism, boxcutters, and ceramic knives, but the five were big men. Bingham was a rugby player, Glick a judo expert, Nacke a weightlifter, and Burnett had been a college quarterback. How the fight went is not known, but moments later United Airlines Flight 93 plunged into a field in southwestern Pennsylvania killing all forty-four people on board. The five men, and probably others, fought back and likely saved the lives of countless others on the ground. They took charge of their fate and refused to be victims. Though they died, they behaved like survivors.

FBI Director Robert Mueller was later quoted in the *New York Times* as saying: "We believe those passengers on this jet were absolute heroes and their actions during this flight were heroic."

For decades, Americans have been brainwashed into taking a passive role in their own survival. "Leave it to the experts," and "Wait for the authorities," we are told in chorus by government officials, politicians, and the media. "Don't fight back. Give them what they want, and the government will save you."

In public schools, our children have been subjected to zero tolerance for violence. This means that, if a child fights back against a bully, he or she is as guilty as the bully and faces suspension or expulsion. As adults, we are taught not to resist criminal attack. Many police departments issue leaflets offering advice about what to do if attacked or robbed. Mostly, the advice seems to amount to: give them what they want, and don't resist, because you might get hurt. I have yet to see a leaflet that recommends buying and carrying a gun—the most effective defense against attack. Give the criminals what they want. Be a victim, we are encouraged. Luckily, the brainwashing didn't take, at least with the passengers of Flight 93.

The most important lesson Americans learned on September 11 was that the government could not protect them.

In the weeks that followed the attack, the government arrested hundreds of Arabs in the country and attempted to improve security at the nation's airports and on its airliners. According to undercover tests carried out by the Transportation Department's inspector general and reported in *USA Today*, airport security was abysmal. Flying was no longer a pleasure, but an unpleasant ordeal. Thousands of passengers were inconvenienced by extended lines and airport evacuations. Many were embarrassed or humiliated by intrusive searches. Seventy-five-year-old U.S. Representative John Dingell was subjected to a strip search when his metal hip joint and leg brace set off metal detectors. Thousands of passengers had personal items such as nail files and nail clippers seized by screeners in an orgy of government theft.

According to the Federal Aviation Administration, between October 30, 2001, and March 7, 2002, the government evacuated airport terminals fifty-nine times causing 2,456 flights to be delayed or cancelled. On another 734 flights, passengers were forced to leave their seats and go through the screening process a second time.

Despite all this security pantomime, undercover auditors managed to smuggle guns past the screeners in 30 percent of tests. With knives, it was 70 percent, and for simulated explosives, 60 percent. Not a happy or reassuring record. The tests were carried out between November 2001 and February 2002 when security was supposed to be at its height.

What was perhaps worse, auditors managed to secretly board aircraft or gain access to the tarmac almost half the times they conducted such tests. When I first heard about the hijackings, but before I learned that the hijackers were armed with only knives and boxcutters, I assumed aircraft cleaners had probably smuggled guns aboard the planes and taped them under seats or hidden them in the bathrooms. Apparently that was still a viable option more than two years after September 11.

After the terrorist attacks on the World Trade Center and the Pentagon, some pilots told their passengers they were the first line of defense against hijackers. A headline in *USA Today* on October 17 warned: "Passengers turning into air police: Board a jet today and you might be asked to help subdue terrorists." The story quoted a US Airways pilot encouraging his passengers to "beat the snot" out of any potential hijacker. Obviously the pilot no longer believed in following the hijackers' orders and waiting for the government to ride to the rescue.

On several occasions, passengers, sometimes assisted by flight crew, subdued crazy people considered a threat to the safety of the plane. In one case, passengers overcame a suspected Muslim terrorist before he could destroy the aircraft. On December 22, 2001, Richard Reid, a British citizen on a flight from Paris to Miami, was attacked and overpowered by passengers and crewmembers before he could light a fuse to the explosives packed in his shoes.

The Administration's answer to further terrorist threats was the creation of a massive new bureaucracy, the Transportation Security Administration. The TSA came under the Department of Homeland Security, which grouped together most of the federal bureaucracies that would be engaged in the so-called "War on Terrorism." The TSA took responsibility for screening airline passengers out of the hands of private contractors, but security apparently has not improved. The new bureaucracy hired thousands of screeners, including many with serious criminal records. At the same time, according to news reports, it did little to improve security on the back sides of airports where aircraft are serviced. Baggage handlers, maintenance workers, and catering staff, including many illegal immigrants and convicted criminals, were still allowed easy access to airliners.

In September 2003, Nathaniel Heatwole, a twenty-year-old student from Maryland, smuggled box cutters, bleach, and other forbidden items aboard two Southwest Airlines planes. He then e-mailed the TSA to let the agency know what he had done. Heatwole stated that he did it to draw attention to weaknesses in airport security. The e-mail was not turned over to the FBI until a month later.

Meanwhile, according to news reports, investigators for the inspector general of the Department of Homeland Security smuggled knives, a gun, and a bomb past screeners at Logan International Airport in Boston without being caught. The planes that were hijacked and flown into the World Trade Center both took off from Logan.

Until September 11, airline pilots were taught to cooperate with hijackers. Follow the orders of the terrorists, do not fight back, and the government will rescue you. And even after the terrorist hijackings, federal legislators and government officials refused to allow commercial pilots the only really effective defense against hijackers and terrorists—firearms. By refusing to allow pilots or passengers to be armed, the authorities ensured that commercial aircraft continued to be killing zones for terrorists.

If there is one group of people who should be allowed to carry concealed handguns, it is our commercial pilots. Every time we fly, we put our lives in their hands, and yet the government does not trust them with firearms to defend themselves or their aircraft.

The TSA has increased the number of armed air marshals from a few hundred to a few thousand. However, according to news reports in August 2002, the air marshal program was suffering significant problems with marshals leaving due to broken promises about working conditions and lowering of training standards. Meanwhile the agency has done everything possible to discourage pilots from carrying guns, according to the Airline Pilots' Security Alliance. More than a year after Congress passed legislation to arm and train volunteer pilots only a few hundred have been trained and qualified to fly armed.

First Officer Rob Davie, a board member of the Airline Pilots' Security Alliance, says commercial pilots nationwide were polled before the training program was put into effect. The poll showed that 87 percent or more than 87,000 were "strongly in favor" of pilots carrying handguns.

"We would have expected a very high number of volunteers," Davie said. "What we've been finding is that we haven't been getting those volunteer numbers, and this can be directly attributed to the TSA and the tactics that the TSA has used to avoid performing properly under the mandate of Congress and the people."

The program, which lasts a week, qualifies pilots as Federal Flight Deck Officers. Davie says the TSA delayed putting the program into operation and has made it onerous to the point that pilots are declining to participate. After holding the first class or two in Georgia, where it was reasonably accessible, the TSA moved the training to a remote area of New Mexico, which was much more difficult for pilots on tight schedules to reach.

The program includes what Davie describes as an overly rigorous psychological test designed by a woman who set up testing for the Postal Service. Davie says current and former federal law enforcement officers have told the Airline Pilots' Security Alliance that pilots who apply for this program get more intrusive psychological testing and questioning than people going into the FBI. Pilots are afraid that if they fail the psychological test and this is reported to the Federal Aviation Administration, they may get their pilots' licenses yanked.

"That's a psychological risk to the pilots, promoted by the program and TSA's onerous requirements," Davie said.

Pilots also object to TSA rules regarding how they are required to transport and handle their handguns after becoming qualified as Federal Flight Deck Officers. TSA requires pilots to carry their guns locked in a hard-sided container at all times except when they are in the cockpit of the aircraft. Many pilots travel on commercial aircraft between where they live and where the planes they pilot are located. They commute by air to work. Davie would like pilots to carry concealed handguns while they are traveling as passengers in the same way as federal law enforcement officers.

If pilots and perhaps passengers with concealed-handgun licenses had been armed on September 11, there would have been few casualties in the air and none on the ground. Three thousand or so lives would have been saved. But the anti-self-defense people don't believe that pilots and ordinary citizens can be trusted to do the right thing. Tell that to the passengers of Flight 93.

There is at least one documented case where a pilot shot and killed a would-be hijacker who threatened him with a handgun. It happened on July 6, 1954, aboard an American Airlines DC-6 that was waiting for take-off from Cleveland, bound for Mexico City with a full load of passengers. According to news reports, a large young man pointed a gun at the pilot, Captain William Bonnell, and demanded he fly the plane to Mexico. At first Bonnell thought the man was joking, but it soon became obvious he was serious.

The captain retrieved a handgun from his flight bag and shot the man before he could endanger the passengers. In those days, pilots were required to be armed when carrying U.S. mail. Pilots were prohibited from carrying firearms by Federal Aviation Administration regulations sometime in the 1980s.

Meanwhile, one thing concealed-carry license holders can do is take our guns with us when we fly. Most of the time when Texas Land Commissioner Jerry Patterson flies around the state on commercial aircraft, he takes a handgun with him, and he advises others with concealed-handgun licenses to do the same.

"Whenever I travel by air, unless I'm really, really in a time crunch and every little minute is a factor, I always carry my handgun," Patterson says.

"I always do that because, if you don't, it will be considered unusual. And unusual things that are done by few people are those things that are first in jeopardy by some bureaucrat or some airline that says: 'We don't want to do this anymore.'"

Patterson was the state senator who sponsored the Texas Concealed Handgun law when it was passed by the Legislature in 1995.

"It's a good thing to exercise that right to travel with a firearm," he says.

Patterson takes his handgun, unloaded, in a locked, hard-sided container, to the ticket counter and checks it with his checked baggage for the flight. He is careful to comply with the regulations of the Transportation Security Administration which can be found in Chapter 13 and on the TSA web site at <www.tsa.gov/public/>. He also urges people to check with their air carrier because airlines have slightly differing regulations regarding the transportation of firearms and ammunition.

Patterson said he has had trouble a couple of times with TSA screeners who are unfamiliar with the regulations. He has printed the regulations from the TSA web site and carries a copy in the hard-sided container in which he transports his handgun.

One effect of the terrorist attacks of September 11 was that, to the horror of the anti-self-defense crowd, Americans rushed to arm themselves. They swept the shelves of gun stores clean of handguns. The FBI reported a 20 percent surge in the number of instant background checks they conducted on gun buyers in October.

The reaction of some members of the gun-control crew was scathing and sarcastic. "What are they going to do—shoot down an airliner with a handgun before it hits a skyscraper?"

No. The gun buyers were smart enough to realize that the next attack is unlikely to be on commercial aircraft—been there, done that. It is more likely to be a chemical or biological hazard. This is likely to be coupled with a breakdown of law and order as people flee from a new ground zero. It is likely to be a time when clean air, clean water, and uncontaminated food are at a premium. And if you have them, you had better be able to defend them.

The head-in-the-sand attitude towards firearms displayed by the TSA is apparent elsewhere in the U.S. Department of Homeland Security. The list of emergency equipment and supplies recommended by the department on its web site <www.ready.gov> includes a first-aid kit, but you may never get to use it if you don't add one piece of equipment not on that list—a gun.

It is all very well to stockpile food, water, and duct tape in case of a chemical, biological, or even nuclear attack, but unless you have the means to defend them, you are likely to lose them in the panic that will follow. To quote NRA Executive Vice President Wayne LaPierre: "Remember New Orleans."

When then homeland security honcho Tom Ridge issued advice to Americans about what to expect in case of an attack by terrorists with weapons of mass destruction, he omitted any reference to firearms. There was no suggestion that people would need to defend themselves and their emergency supplies. However, following such an attack, there is likely to be a breakdown in law and order. When a jury found three police officers not guilty in the beating of Rodney King, riots erupted in Los Angeles. In some areas, the only stores not looted by rioters were those defended by business owners with guns. In the breakdown of law and order likely to follow a major terrorist attack, police will be far too busy supervising evacuations to be able to defend individual residents from opportunistic criminals or just ordinary people caught in the grip of fear. Remember New Orleans.

Ridge suggested civilians prepare two emergency kits, one for the home in case they stay put and the other for the vehicle if they need to evacuate. Residents who stay home in the aftermath of an attack had better be prepared for home invasions. People who are being evacuated are likely to have their vehicles hijacked at gunpoint. Remember New Orleans.

In states where it is legal, citizens should prepare for terrorist attack by getting concealed-handgun licenses and arming themselves. It is encouraging that many are.

"What I'm hearing is that a lot of the buyers are first-time gun buyers," says Smith & Wesson's Ken Jorgensen. "I think it gives people a sense of security and control over their lives."

There were also reports out of Washington, D.C., that some anti-self-defense politicians were buying handguns and seeking training in their use. Unfortunately, no one named the names of the hypocrites in the reports.

Americans filled handgun-training courses and applied for concealed-carry licenses in record numbers. In some states, applications for licenses doubled in the weeks after the terrorist attacks. In Texas, the Department of Public Safety sent out 21,604 application packages for concealed-handgun licenses in the ten weeks after September 11, more than double the 10,164 sent out in the ten weeks before the terrorist attacks. In Arizona, the Department of Public Safety received 2,457 applications for licenses in October and November 2001 compared with 1,294 in the same two months in 2000.

In Oklahoma, the increase was even more dramatic: the State Bureau of Investigation noted a 145 percent increase in new license applications in the two months following September 2001 compared with the two months prior. In October and

November 1,181 new applications were received, up from 482 in July and August. Considerable increases in applications for licenses were reported in other states. In Alaska, one official said she noticed more young women and members of minority groups were applying for licenses.

B ill Davison, owner of Tac Pro Shooting Center in Texas, has fought terrorists in Northern Ireland as a member of the Royal Marine Special Boat Service, the British equivalent of the U.S. Navy SEALs. He believes people armed themselves after September 11 because they felt vulnerable.

"There could be a feel-good factor in there, but it's an absolute fact that if they are armed, they've got a chance [against terrorists]. If they're not armed, they have no chance at all," Davison said.

He emphasized that when people buy a gun, they also need training in how to use it. He likened it to buying a car and learning to drive.

Many Americans were learning that the government could not protect them from terrorist fanatics bent on martyrdom and using a commercial aircraft as a missile anymore than it could protect a woman being stalked by a former boyfriend or a storeowner from an armed robber.

T he aim of this book is to provide advice and information that will lower the odds of your becoming a victim and encourage you to be a survivor.

Chapter Three

WHY CARRY A GUN?
THE POLICE CAN'T PROTECT YOU

It was a sunny fall day in central Texas when Dr. Suzanna Gratia walked into the Luby's Cafeteria in Killeen, Texas, with her mother and father. As they entered the restaurant, Gratia had no inkling that she would be the only one of them to leave there alive.

October 16, 1991, was Bosses' Day, and the cafeteria was packed with employees taking their employers to lunch. Gratia, then 32, was a chiropractor in nearby Copperas Cove. She and her parents were waiting for her friend, the restaurant manager, to return to their table. They had just finished eating and were dawdling over coffee.

The pleasant atmosphere was shattered when a pickup truck burst through the window into the restaurant, smashing into customers and showering them with broken glass.

Suzanna Gratia Hupp.

At first, Gratia thought it was an accident. She started to go over to help the people knocked down by the pickup.

Then she heard a flurry of gunshots.

Immediately, Gratia and her father tipped over their table and, with her mother, took cover behind it. Gratia decided it must be a robbery, but the shooting continued. Then she thought maybe it was a hit. Perhaps someone important was in the restaurant because it was Bosses' Day.

But the driver of the pickup was walking unhurriedly from one person to another shooting them.

"It took a good forty-five seconds, which is a long time, to figure out that the guy was just going to walk around and shoot people," Gratia said. "You kept waiting for him to stop and give some sort of explanation, but he didn't."

By this time, the gunman, later identified as George Hennard, was standing at the right-front fender of his truck, about fifteen feet from Gratia, still shooting people.

"I thought, I got this turkey. I reached for my purse. I had a perfect place to prop my arm; everybody in the restaurant was down; he was up. Then I realized that a few months earlier I had made the stupidest decision of my life. My gun was one hundred yards away, in my car, completely useless to me. I had made the decision to begin leaving it in my car because I was concerned about losing my license to practice chiropractic."

In 1991 Texas had no concealed-handgun carry law. Only law-enforcement officers could carry concealed handguns legally in the state.

Gratia was appalled. She groped for something to do to stop the carnage. She thought about throwing her purse at the gunman. She eyed the sugar container and the butter knife, but Hennard had two semi-automatic handguns and was in complete control of the situation. Any attack would be suicide.

Meanwhile, Gratia's father, Al Gratia, was getting increasingly frustrated.

"I've got to do something. I've got to do something. He's going to kill everybody in here," Gratia remembers her father saying, as he started to rise to his feet.

Suzanna grabbed him by the shirt collar and jerked him down, cursing at him and saying: "If you go at him, he's going to kill you, too." But he shook her off and, when he thought he had a chance, tried to rush Hennard.

"I remember ducking down because I already knew what was going to happen. He didn't have a chance. The guy could see him coming a mile away. Dad probably covered half the space, and the guy turned and shot him in the chest. My dad went down in the aisle. He was still alive and still semi-conscious, but he was maybe eight feet from me. I saw the wound and, as horrible as it sounds, I basically wrote him off at that point."

After shooting Gratia's father, Hennard changed direction away from her and her mother. For the first time she looked at the gunman's face.

"You think the stupidest things. I remember looking at this guy, thinking, this is a good-looking guy—with a new truck. What could possibly be so wrong in this guy's life that he's doing this?"

Hennard reached the wall and fortunately turned away from Gratia. She and her mother were in the front part of the restaurant and were trapped until somebody broke a window near the back. Her first thought on hearing the crash of the breaking glass was that Hennard was not alone. Perhaps it was a terrorist attack. But she saw people escaping through the broken window and knew it was their only chance to get out.

Gratia kept peeking around the table, where she and her mother were crouched, until she saw an opportunity. She stood up with her back to Hennard who was still shooting people, expecting at any moment to be shot.

"I remember standing with my back to the guy, and I kept hearing the gunshots. I kept waiting to feel the impact. I remember feeling that so vividly."

Gratia grabbed her mother by the shirt, pulling her to her feet. "Come on, come on, we've got to run; we've got to get out of here," she urged.

Her feet grew wings and she ran, not stopping until she was through the window and outside in the sunshine. The restaurant manager, Mark Kopenhafer, met her outside and asked if she was all right.

"I said, 'Yeah, but Dad's been shot.' And I turned around to say something about Mom or something to Mom, and she wasn't there."

Her mother had not followed her out of the restaurant. Gratia learned afterwards from the police what had happened. When they arrived on the scene, the officers knew a man was inside the restaurant shooting people. Earlier, while Hennard had been systematically executing people, everybody was hugging the floor, and it was quiet except for the sound of the gunshots. But when the police arrived, people were scrambling to get out, and pandemonium reigned. The officers could not see who was doing the shooting.

"My mother, according to them, had crawled out into the open where my father was and was cradling him until the gunman got back around to her.

"According to the one cop, he didn't realize who the man was at that point, and he saw the guy look down at my Mom. He said, she looked up at him, put her head down, and then he put the gun to her head and pulled the trigger.

"My parents had had their forty-seventh wedding anniversary a week and a half before, and she just wasn't going anywhere."

Hennard killed twenty-three people and wounded another thirty-three before he put one of his pistols to his own head and pulled the trigger.

Since that day, Suzanna Gratia, now Suzanna Gratia Hupp since her marriage, has testified before Congress and numerous state legislatures, urging law-makers to allow law-abiding citizens to carry guns for self defense. She is acknowledged to be one of the most compelling witnesses in the gun-control debate. Hupp has been elected to the Texas Legislature and as a politician is a champion of gun rights.

"I'm not a crack shot, but I can definitely hit what I'm pointing at," she says.

When legislators ask her what would have happened if she had shot at Hennard and missed, she answers: "It's possible, but if nothing else, it sure would have changed the odds, wouldn't it? Because, as it was, I can't begin to get across to you or anybody else what it's like to sit there and wait for it to be your turn. I get very angry right now even thinking about that. Can you imagine not being able to fight back?"

Hupp's testimony in February 1995 before the Texas Senate committee looking at a proposed concealed-handgun carry law undoubtedly helped sway lawmakers to the reality that the police and the justice system cannot protect people. Although the justice system is supposed to deter crime, it hasn't been doing a very good job. While patrolling police officers do deter some crime, it is difficult to determine how much. Most often they take reports of crimes after they happen and then try to catch the perpetrators.

Retired U.S. Deputy Marshal Parnell McNamara is a strong supporter of the Texas concealed-handgun law. He believes that the Luby's massacre would have turned out differently had some of the citizens been armed.

"What if four or five good citizens had been in there with nine millimeters: they probably would have killed that sorry rat really quick, or at least he wouldn't have got as many people," McNamara says.

He has talked to many law-enforcement officers who don't think civilians should be able to carry handguns. He usually tries to change their minds and personally is "100 percent in favor" of honest citizens carrying handguns.

"I talk it up every chance I get," he says.

Another retired law-enforcement officer who believes in an armed citizenry is Bill McLennan. He retired as a detective and chief firearms instructor for the San Antonio Police Department.

"I think you're living in Wonderland if you think the police are going to protect you," McLennan says. "If anything, we're going to be there in the aftermath. Rarely will we be there to prevent anything."

Even when police catch the offender, the punishment seldom fits the crime. In the early 1990s, Texans were told that on average a convict spent less than one month in prison for each year to which he was sentenced. Convicts serve more of their sentences now, thanks to a prison-building program.

In the mid-1990s, when discipline at home and at school, as well as self discipline, seemed at an all-time low among teenagers, people were being killed at a high rate for fun and profit. No one seemed to be successfully attacking the root causes.

Former Attorney General Janet Reno was quoted in November 1995 as saying: "If the last decade's trends continue unchecked, juvenile arrests for violent crime will double by the year 2010."

But the trends turned around in the last years of the twentieth century. Violent crime—particularly by juveniles— steadily decreased in the late 1990s, though it was still much higher than in the 1960s.

And still the fear of crime is there. Law-abiding people are afraid to walk the streets of their cities, particularly after dark. They are afraid to use automated teller machines or walk to their cars in shopping-mall parking lots. They are being told to bar their windows and lock the doors of their homes and cars when they are inside.

"I put an alarm on my car. I lock my doors when I ride around—I didn't use to," says McLennan. "I put a Club on my steering wheel, because I don't want anybody to take my car. I've got a kill switch on my car. I've got bars on my front door. I've got bars on my windows. I've got all kinds of deadbolt locks. I lock myself up like a prisoner, and I have an alarm on my house. The bad guys are running around free, and I'm locking myself up in jail. I think something is out of proportion here."

Few will argue against a law-abiding citizen taking these sorts of precautions, though most deplore the need for them. But when it comes to carrying a handgun for self defense, many people balk at the idea as somehow uncivilized.

"I think the problem here is that people are buying into the mythology that guns make us safer. The truth is that they don't, and there is no evidence to support that they do," said Robin Terry, communications director of Handgun Control, Inc., now known as the Brady Campaign to Prevent Handgun Violence.

Tell that to Greg Ferris, the San Antonio gun-store owner who was attacked in his store by three street-gang members in 1993. They did not charge into the store like coyotes after a jack rabbit just to rob. They were on a mission of murder to prove they were the toughest little gangbangers in the neighborhood. Only his custom handgun saved Ferris's life. His story is told in a later chapter.

Or tell it to any of the people featured in the "Armed Citizen" columns of the *American Rifleman*. The magazine of the National Rifle Association (NRA) scours the country's newspapers for incidents in which armed citizens win confrontations with criminals. Each month, the magazine relates six or eight such encounters.

It's not just that members of the anti-self-defense movement have chosen not to protect themselves, but in their elitist arrogance, they don't want you to either.

Listen to Robin Terry again: "We don't think that people should be walking the streets with a gun in arm's reach at all times, because we think that escalates the level of violence. Minor traffic altercations and minor arguments which could have turned into fist fights are now going to turn into gun fights."

In her statement, Terry betrayed an attitude typical of many in the gun-control movement—a lack of trust in the average law-abiding citizen.

"Working to keep handguns out of the wrong hands," bragged the letterhead of Handgun Control, Inc. Taking the word "Control" out of its title when it changed its name to the Brady Campaign was designed to make it appear more palatable to middle America. Now it claims to believe "a safer America can be achieved without banning all guns," according to its web site. It talks of supporting "sensible gun laws." But make no mistake, they mean taking the guns out of the hands of anyone who is not a law-enforcement officer.

Paxton Quigley was a founding member of the gun-control movement. Following Robert Kennedy's assassination, she helped found the first gun-control political-action committee—the National Committee for Handgun Control. After two of her friends were raped, her house burglarized twice, and her car stolen in front of her eyes, she changed her mind. Author of the book, *Armed & Female*, she now teaches women how to defend themselves with guns.

Members of the gun-control movement believe there are far too many guns of all kinds in American society and that these guns are responsible for much of the violence. This is probably true. Guns facilitate violence. A killer can do in a fraction of a second by exerting a few pounds of pressure on a trigger what it might take him ten minutes and a lot of exertion to do with a baseball bat.

But it is also true that guns prevent violence. Many years ago, when my wife was about seventeen, she was stuck in a traffic jam in a San Antonio park. A man in his mid-twenties opened her door on the passenger side and got into the car. Anita pulled a small .25 semi-automatic out of her purse with her left hand and laid it across her right forearm. As she kept it trained on him, she told him to get out. He did.

"To this day, I don't know if he intended to chat me up or if he had something more sinister in mind," she says.

It was illegal in those days for her to be carrying a loaded gun for protection in Texas—it still would be for a seventeen-year-old—so naturally she never reported the incident to police.

Marguerite Everheart of New Mexico has twice been accosted at highway rest stops. On one occasion, she was driving north on Interstate 25 to Montana to shoot in a rifle match. She had her son, who was about six years old, with her in the car. While she was traveling through Wyoming it started raining so heavily she felt it was unsafe to continue. She pulled off into a rest area and decided to catch some sleep. Everheart opened the driver's window about an inch so the windows would not fog up and went to sleep. She woke to find a man in his thirties trying to push down her window and force his way into her car.

"He wanted me to open up the door, but I wasn't going to do that," Everheart said. "When I'm on the road I always carry at least two handguns with me. And I had my handguns very close to me."

Everheart pulled her Beretta 9mm from under the blanket and pointed it at the man. He realized the error of his ways and left in a hurry. When the rain stopped she drove on.

"If I hadn't of had the gun with me, I don't know, I may have lost my car and everything that I had in the car," she said.

On the second occasion, Everheart was driving to another rifle match. She was on the highway between Santa Fe, New Mexico, and Las Vegas, Nevada, when she again pulled into a highway rest stop. Leaving her son asleep in the car, she went to the women's restroom. She had a Colt .380-caliber semiautomatic in her purse.

A man followed her into the restroom and tried to push his way into her stall as Everheart was trying to leave.

"Luckily I had my purse behind me in such a way that I could get to the gun, and I proceeded to explain to the man that it was loaded and that I knew how to use it," she said. "He left."

Everheart is not sure what the man had in mind, but without the gun, she almost certainly would have been raped, robbed, or even murdered.

Laura Poldson worked for the Texas State Rifle Association in a Dallas suburb. One morning she was driving to work when she stopped for gas at a filling station she often used. She is a concealed-handgun license holder and was wearing a gun. Poldson was filling the tank of what she refers to as her "Mom-mobile," a dirty white Oldsmobile Cutlass Supreme, when an older model sedan with two men in it pulled in behind her.

One of the men pumped gas, while the other leaned on the hood of his car and said: "Nice car you've got."

As her car was in no way special, warning bells went off in her head. Laura replied in a noncommittal tone: "It gets me where I want to go and back."

"Nice car; maybe I should get one like it," the man said. "Maybe I should take yours."

"The tone of his voice wasn't threatening, but it was not kidding either," Poldson said.

She decided she was through filling her tank whether it was full or not. She put up the pump nozzle with one hand and reached for her keys with the other. Meanwhile the man had straightened up and was no longer leaning on his car, though he had not moved towards her.

"What are you, ten-foot tall and bulletproof?" Poldson retorted.

"Have you got a gun?" the man asked in alarm.

"That's for me to know and you to find out," she replied.

The two men immediately got into their car and drove off. Poldson got back into her car, locked the doors, and sat there

shaking. After a few minutes, the manager came out of the convenience store and asked her if she was all right. She said she
felt scared to death. "I couldn't believe I just did that," she said.

Reflecting later on the incident, she said she probably
wouldn't have shot the men over her car. She just reacted because
she felt in danger. Poldson was wearing a .380-caliber semi-
automatic in a holster in the middle of her back at the time,
but never even had to draw it. None of these incidents was
reported to the police, so they never showed up in any statistics,
though these women may well have prevented serious crimes
because they were armed.

Professor John R. Lott Jr. of the University of Maryland
is author of *More Guns, Less Crime: Understanding
Crime and Gun Control Laws.* He contends that a woman
who defends herself with a firearm is 2.5 times more likely
to survive a violent confrontation with a criminal without
serious injury than if she were not to resist at all. If a
woman resists a criminal attack with anything other than
a firearm, she is four times more likely to be hurt than if she
uses a gun. Men who resist crime with guns also fare better than men who do not resist or resist without firearms,
but the difference is less dramatic. When a woman produces
a gun the dynamic of the confrontation changes more radi-
cally than if a man defends himself with a gun.

"When you are talking about a male criminal attacking a
female victim there is a larger strength differential than when
you're talking about a male criminal attacking a male victim
on average. The presence of a gun represents a much bigger
change in a woman's ability to defend herself than it does for
a man," Lott said.

While women benefit more from using a gun to defend themselves against criminal attack, comparatively few women go
through the process of getting a concealed-handgun license.

In Texas, only 18 percent of license holders are women, while in Florida, it is a mere 15 percent.

For many women, like Jennifer Palmer, it takes a life-threatening incident to make them realize they are responsible for their own safety, and a gun is the most efficient tool to accomplish this. For Carol Lane of Waco, Texas, it was when she awoke in the middle of the night to see a man in her bedroom going through her possessions.

Lane and her husband were asleep on a cold January night in their three-bedroom single-story house in a residential neighborhood of Waco. Like most mothers of young children, she was a light sleeper. Their eighteen-month-old son was sleeping in his own room across the hall from their bedroom. In the early hours, something woke Lane.

"I lifted my head up from the pillow just a tiny bit to see and kind of get my eyes adjusted to what little light there was," she said. "I could not believe it that there was a guy in the bedroom."

There was a night light on in her son's room and some light from the moon outside, so Lane could see the man was wearing a ski mask. He had his back to her and was rifling through her husband's personal effects— wallet, wedding ring, change— on the dresser.

"I just immediately laid my head back down on the

Carol Lane and her son David shortly after the burglary.

pillow and froze. I just couldn't think. My heart was pounding so hard I thought he might hear it. I just couldn't move; I couldn't think of one thing to do."

Then the man turned towards her. He walked over to her side of the bed, heading towards her dressing area and the bathroom.

"At that point, my husband rustled around in the bed, and the guy stopped and looked right at me. It was terrifying," Lane said.

After what seemed an eternity, the man turned around and left the bedroom. She woke her husband and told him there was a man in the house. At first, he didn't believe her but then he saw the beam of a flashlight flickering down the hall. He got up and picked up a large brass lamp, the only weapon he could find in the bedroom, Lane said. But by the time they were ready to check on their son, the man had gone.

They called police, but the man escaped, taking with him Lane's purse that had been on the kitchen table, her husband's wallet and wedding ring, some silver flatware, and a clock off the wall. He had taken a pillowcase from the spare bedroom to carry his loot.

In the days following the burglary, they received news that the burglar had used their credit cards to buy knives at a local mall and other things. The police later caught him, and he confessed to the Lane burglary and numerous others. He was on parole and had attacked one woman who awoke while he was in her house, but otherwise the burglaries were non violent, Lane said. They never got any of their property back.

"He was a young white guy with a drug problem, and he stole to support his drug habit," Lane said.

A few days after the incident, Lane called Deputy U.S. Marshal Parnell McNamara. At the time, she was teaching kindergarten at St. Paul's Episcopal School and McNamara's daughter was in her class. She discussed the burglary with him and asked his advice. As a result, they put in a security system and

McNamara suggested she buy a gun and learn how to shoot. Neither Lane nor her husband owned any guns or had any interest in them, she said. She had never fired a gun.

"We were talking about how to protect your home and things you could do and so on, and he said: 'I really think you ought to consider getting a gun and learning how to shoot.'

"I said: 'Parnell, that's not me. I don't know a thing about guns,'" Lane recalled.

McNamara told her that his wife and daughters all knew how to handle a gun and persuaded her to give it a try. He let her try several different types of handguns, and Lane discovered that she was a good shot—better than her husband.

"I was well motivated, and I was determined that I could do this if I needed to," she said. "From a kindergarten teacher to a pistol-packin' mama."

McNamara has a rifle and pistol range on his property and taught her to shoot. He said he started with safety procedures then had her shoot at a large bullseye target from five to seven yards. She then graduated to silhouette targets at longer ranges.

"She was a natural shot," McNamara said. "She was very serious about what she was doing. There was no question that she was determined to learn how to shoot well so this would never happen to her again. She told me: 'I never want to be that frightened again in my life.'"

Lane and her husband bought a .38-caliber Smith & Wesson revolver, which they kept locked in a box in their bedroom to keep it away from their son. Since that terrifying night, Lane has not been faced with any more traumatic incidents. But for several months she suffered from post traumatic stress, and she was afraid to be left alone in the house. She said the gun did provide moral support, and the burglary has made her more aware of her surroundings.

"I'm probably a little more aware than someone who didn't go through that," she said. "Maybe it was a cheap lesson."

Christi Kincannon was somewhat better prepared than Carol Lane when a man broke into her house in Waco. At least she had a gun.

She was living in an older house, built in the 1920s, and although it wasn't very wide, it stretched a long way back. Her bedroom was at the back. It was a Friday night, and she had gone to bed early, about 10 p.m., read for a time, then turned out the light. About 11 p.m., her doorbell rang.

Kincannon was divorced and had been seeing a man she didn't want to see again. She thought it might be he, so she got up without putting on any lights and crept to the dining room window. When she peeked out she didn't see any car in the driveway. She stood there puzzled for a few moments, then saw a figure under the streetlight on the corner walking along the sidewalk towards her driveway.

"I could tell that the individual was a tall black male, and I could tell that he was looking towards my house," Kincannon said.

She expected him to walk on past her house and down the street. He didn't. He turned into her driveway and walked directly towards her front door. She heard the man at the front door, but he did not ring the bell. She ran back to a butler's pantry in the middle of the house where there was a wall phone and dialed 9-1-1.

"What really disturbed me more than anything else was how quickly all this took place. From the moment that I first heard him at the door, actually fooling with the door, until the time he got into the house was no more than maybe ninety seconds," she said. She told the police dispatcher that someone was trying to break in at her front door. The dispatcher was trying to calm her down.

"I was scared to death, I really was. I had the dispatcher on the phone; I could hear the guy at the door, and I told the dispatcher that I was going to go get my gun," Kincannon said.

The dispatcher told her not to move but to stay on the phone with him. She told him she would come back to the phone when she had got her gun. At the time, she was regarding the dispatcher as her lifeline, but after hearing the tape of the call later she said he sounded patronizing and could have given her better advice.

"He really didn't do me any favors," she said.

He could have asked her if there was a back door so she could have escaped, but he didn't. It never occurred to her to go out the back door or turn on the lights so he would know someone was home, Kincannon said.

"But I went and got my gun and got ready for a fight."

As soon as she got back to the phone, armed with her .22-Magnum-caliber revolver, things happened quickly.

"I heard a little pop, and I heard the door open in the living room, and I knew he was in the house," she said. "Then it was very quiet."

There were two ways to the kitchen and the butler's pantry where Kincannon was on the phone, through the dining room or through a den. She knew he would be coming towards her by one route or the other.

"I decided I wasn't going to sit there and wait for him to find me, so I went to the dining room door."

She held the revolver in her right hand with the muzzle pointing up at the ceiling. She pushed the heavy dining-room door open and stepped through. She was silhouetted against the window, and she knew he had seen her. The man was standing in the middle of the living room.

"He took a step towards me. I just brought the gun down, straight down in front of me, and fired," she said.

The bullet hit the living room wall and the intruder fled out of the front door. Kincannon ran after him.

"You go from being scared beyond belief to being totally enraged," she said. "So I went after him and ran out on the front porch. He was running in front of my neighbor's house, and I took another shot at him. He dove, he actually went horizontally into her bushes on the side of the house."

She went back to the phone and told the dispatcher what had happened. He told her to put the gun down as the police were arriving. Shortly after, about twenty police officers crowded into her house. When they realized what had happened, they laughed and joked about the incident, Kincannon said.

She was concerned that she should not have fired the second shot at the man, but the officers told her not to worry about it. She was also afraid the man might return, but they told her: "Lady, he's not coming back; he's gone on to a new career by now."

The incident made her feel more confident that she could handle anything that came her way, though she wishes the man had been caught.

For some people, it takes a change in geographical location to convince them of the value of a gun for self defense. Eliza Sonneland is a radio talk-show host in San Antonio, Texas. However, she is not a native Texan. She grew up in New York, living in Manhattan and on Long Island. There, she had no exposure to guns.

"There were no guns. There were no conversations about guns," she said.

At one point, she lived in a particularly unsafe area of New York City called Hell's Kitchen. She carried Mace, but it never occurred to her to protect herself with a gun. As an adult, she absorbed information from the media about guns, but it was all negative.

"What am I getting from the news and information out there? Bad guys are shooting people—bad. Kids are accidentally getting shot—bad. Famous people are being assassinated—bad stuff. What's the message? We've got to get rid of guns. I mean, it's a given."

Then she moved to Texas where there are lots of guns. She arrived in San Antonio in June of 1983 to visit a college

Eliza Sonneland.

roommate and never went back. She soon got a job as a radio producer, became co-host of a morning talk show, and later got her own radio show.

The first time she actually held a handgun was when the public information officer with the San Antonio Police Department insisted she go to the police range and shoot.

"I'd never felt the weight of a gun in my life," she said.

She was impressed by the way Sergeant Paul Buske repeatedly checked the handgun to ensure it was unloaded even though he knew it was unloaded. He showed her how to dry fire the gun before she was allowed to actually shoot it on the range. When she hit the target, she felt an unexpected thrill.

Sonneland said she grew up with a very negative view of hunting and hunters. She was even a vegetarian for part of her life.

"I still believed that hunters were nothing but a bunch of sadistic killers. They got their jollies from killing things. I mean, who are these people? And why would anyone want to talk to them?"

At the time, she was living on three acres outside the city, and she kept chickens. She was upset because raccoons were killing the chickens, biting their heads off.

"They seem to kill them for the thrill, and all of a sudden I don't want to drive to work swerving around raccoons. I want to run over them. All of a sudden, I have this different look on nature—something I never imagined would happen."

One talk-show guest provided her with more food for thought. He said there are no quiet, gentle deaths in nature. They tend to be brutal and terrifying.

"I had never thought about that," Sonneland said.

She realized that short of deliberate torture, anything humans do to animals while hunting is likely to be quicker and less terrifying than the way nature disposes of the old or infirm. That was a big shift in viewpoint, she said.

However, a bigger shift was yet to come.

"I was having one of my I-know-more-than-anybody kind of conversations with listeners about guns and why we must do something, and a woman called me up. She was an elderly woman and she said, in a very matter-of-fact voice, without being emotional or scolding to me, that she had been raped, and now she carried a gun.

"That was it. Who was I to tell her she couldn't? Well, if I'm going to accept that nobody can tell her she couldn't, who was I to tell anyone they shouldn't?"

Her next attitude-changing experience happened when Ralph Voss, the owner of a local shooting range called "A Place To Shoot," persuaded Sonneland to take the Texas concealed-handgun-licensing course. After missing several classes and being prompted by Voss, she and a co-host finally turned up to take the course. She was surprised to find that the others in the class were normal people "with lives and jobs." She was impressed with what she was learning.

"I'm learning through this concealed-handgun course that the last thing I want to do is pull a weapon out and shoot somebody with it. I'm thinking: why isn't everybody taking this course whether they ever intend to own a weapon ever?"

The result of all these experiences and her willingness to open her mind and question everything she had believed was that her attitude about guns changed completely.

She took a three-day defensive-tactics course at Thunder Ranch shooting school and took up Cowboy Action Shooting, where she goes by the name of the "Sunshine Kid." When Clint Smith of Thunder Ranch was quoted on the CBS show "60 Minutes," as saying that there are some people who just need killing, she was not appalled and it made sense to her.

Now, when she interviews people about guns, she tries to remember that it took her years and many experiences to change her mind. Sonneland urges shooters to invite others to go shooting and let them feel the thrill of hitting the target as she did.

"It's the hands-on experience that will give someone an education that no amount of argument, verbal abuse, or anything else will do," she said.

Another woman who changed her mind about guns and took up the cause of concealed carry is Candy Ruff. Until 2007, Kansas had no provision for concealed carry by civilians. Ruff is a Kansas state representative for Leavenworth who had much to do with getting a shall-issue concealed-handgun law through the Kansas Legislature in 2006. She had been pushing for such a law since 1996. Until then, concealed carry was not an issue she took any interest in.

She was elected in 1992 as a Democrat. In 1996 the issue came before her committee, and she asked her husband, who was a lieutenant with the Leavenworth Police Department, about the issue. He told her that "the last thing cops are afraid of is law-abiding citizens."

The first woman to testify before Ruff's committee was a rape victim, who came from a wealthy community known as the Gold Coastline. Ruff describes her as "the lady-that-lunches type." The woman was returning to her car after lunch at an upscale restaurant in Johnson County.

"She was accosted and kidnapped. She was brutally raped and sodomized, beaten severely, and left to die. She came to tell us that, after she had gone through this horrific experience, she was trying to put her life back together, trying to figure out how to protect herself, because her perpetrator was not caught," Ruff said.

The rapist took the woman's credit cards, driver's license, and everything that was in her purse. He, therefore, knew where she lived and all about her.

"She was trying to decide how she was going to protect herself away from her home and was told by the police department there in Johnson County that she couldn't protect herself with a handgun away from home; that she would then be the criminal. She would be the person who would be arrested for carrying a concealed handgun, and they would have to arrest her. She was appalled by that, and I couldn't believe it either.... I was very moved by her testimony and became very interested in supporting the issue from there," Ruff said.

That weekend Ruff went home to Leavenworth and got a call from a woman in her community. She too had been raped.

"She had been accosted in a Wal-Mart parking lot, 2 o'clock in the afternoon with her two-year-old child. She too was somebody who had a small handgun that she was now carrying with her, and she asked me personally to get involved in this issue and make it so she would not have to be a criminal by defending herself," Ruff said.

"I became very interested in this issue, and it became mine. It is something I have worked very hard on."

After the Kansas Legislature passed a concealed-handgun law in 1997, the Republican governor vetoed it. She found most of the attention concerning concealed carry was focused on men and the NRA.

"I decided to pull together the women in the Legislature who supported this issue, and we made it a women's self protection issue."

She has talked to more than twenty women who have been sexually assaulted. Most of them have not reported the rapes to police, and their attackers have not been caught. They live in fear that their rapists will return and need to be able to protect themselves without becoming criminals, Ruff said.

"They have all told me the same thing: other than the death of a child, there is nothing worse than being assaulted, sexually assaulted. It changes your life forever," she said.

The women told her that, if they had been armed with a handgun at the time, it probably wouldn't have made any difference, because at the time none of them thought she was vulnerable.

"It didn't even cross their minds that they weren't safe, especially the lady that lunched in Johnson County. She thought she was in the safest place in Kansas," Ruff said.

The women told her that they are constantly aware of their surroundings and who is near them.

"They have taken handgun lessons; they have taken self-protection lessons; they know what to do. They think constantly and train constantly for all eventualities," Ruff said. "I feel that those women who have gone through that should not have to be breaking the law in order to protect themselves."

Gary Kleck, criminology professor at Florida State University, conducted a national survey of nearly five thousand people in 1993. Extrapolating on the data he accumulated, Kleck estimated that about 2.4 million Americans each year use firearms to defend themselves in confrontations with criminals. Interestingly, guns were fired in only about a quarter of the incidents. In three-quarters of the cases, the threat of a gun was enough. Probably, in the majority of those cases where a crime was prevented and no one was hurt, the incident was not reported to police.

Even in cases where a shot was fired, the shooter may not have informed police, because only a third of them claimed to have hit anybody.

"If you believed what they said, they might have actually wounded somebody as much as 8 percent of the time maximum, but my impression is that they are probably guessing in a number of cases," Kleck said.

He thought it more likely that only about 2 percent wounded or killed their assailants.

Before the Republicans took Congress like Sherman marched through Georgia, the Democrats rammed through federal legislation that mandated a five-day waiting period and a background check for a handgun purchaser, with the ridiculous expectation that it would keep guns out of the wrong hands. They also slapped a ban on some semi-automatic firearms of military appearance, as well as magazines holding more than ten rounds. But while the federal government was restricting firearms in the statistically suspect belief that it would reduce crime, a movement was sweeping the states like a California brush fire. State legislatures passed laws to allow residents to carry concealed handguns for self defense.

As of the fall of 2007, thirty-eight states have laws requiring officials to issue residents concealed-handgun carry licenses, provided they meet certain criteria. These states and their criteria are examined in the final chapter. In addition, one state, Vermont, has never required residents to have licenses to carry handguns, concealed or in the open.

This brush fire of legislation produced an absolute furor in the anti-self-defense community, which is doing everything it can to discredit the movement. While most of the states with "shall-issue" laws passed them in the 1990s, Florida's concealed-carry law went into effect October 1, 1987. As the first state in recent years to pass such a law, Florida has become the standard by which others are measured.

"In eight years, they had a total of fifty-four revocations for committing a crime with a gun, which means roughly seven a year out of about 150,000 who have a permit at any one time," says criminologist Kleck. "If that were the violence rate of the United States as a whole, we'd be more peaceful than Switzerland."

The Metro Dade Police Department, which enforces law in Miami, Florida, is the only city police organization that has kept tabs on license holders themselves. From January 1, 1988, until May 31, 1990, Metro Dade police recorded any incident in which a license holder came to their attention. By 1990, more than eighteen thousand licenses had been issued to Dade County residents.

But in the twenty-nine-month period, only fifty-seven incidents occurred, including twenty-two where the license holder was arrested. Eight of the arrests were for aggravated assault; the others varied from the serious—a license holder fired a couple of shots at a motorist who cut him off in traffic—to the less serious—the permit holder was arrested for drunk driving and his gun was found in the car. In other incidents, in which license holders were not arrested, they thwarted five robberies, interrupted four burglaries, and prevented one rape.

Despite claims by the Brady Campaign that "law enforcement across the country has consistently opposed" concealed-carry legislation, Florida police chiefs and sheriffs don't oppose it. In December 1994, Charlie Wells, then president of the Florida Sheriffs' Association, admitted he had been "apprehensive as hell" about the law before it went into effect. But after seven years his fears had not been realized.

"The bottom line is that it's an absolute no-factor. There's no reason to be concerned about it," Wells said.

About the same time, Karen Beary, executive director of the Florida Police Chiefs Association, polled fifteen of her members. None voiced any problems with the concealed-carry law, she said.

At the other end of the country, Washington state has had a "shall-issue" handgun permit law since 1961. "It's part of the way of life," said Eugene Cotton, executive director in 1994 of the Washington Association of Sheriffs and Chiefs of Police.

While the law is accepted with mixed feelings by some law-enforcement officers, "there are those of us that figure it's a constitutional right," Cotton said.

"The real problem is the crook who carries one [a gun] and has no permit," he added.

On the fifth anniversary of Governor, now President, George W. Bush's signing the Texas Concealed Handgun Act into law, several legislators and supporters of the law held a birthday celebration and news conference at the Capitol in Austin. In 1995, when Bush signed the bill, public opinion was polarized, with major newspaper editorial boards almost unanimously against law-abiding Texans being given the opportunity to carry concealed handguns to defend themselves.

Former State Senator Jerry Patterson, one of the authors of the law and now Texas Land Commissioner, spoke at the press conference in May 2000 in support of the law and praised its success. The comments in 1995 of the state's major newspapers forecasted carnage in the streets and shootouts at every four-way stop, Patterson said.

"In other words, the doomsday scenarios were predicted universally by most of the editorial boards in the state and by many citizens," he said.

Patterson kept a newspaper clipping file and found these comments were similar to those made in Florida newspapers in 1987 when that state passed its concealed-carry law.

"The exact same comments, almost verbatim, lifted from the Florida dailies to the Texas dailies," he said.

The predicted carnage had not materialized, and some opponents of the law changed their minds, Patterson said. He read from a letter dated December 16, 1999, sent to him by John Holmes, then district attorney of Harris County, which includes the city of Houston.

"As you know, I was very outspoken in my opposition to the passage of the Concealed Handgun Act. I did not feel that such legislation was in the public interest and presented a clear and present danger to law-abiding citizens by placing more handguns on our streets.

"Boy was I wrong. Our experience in Harris County, and indeed statewide, has proven my initial fears absolutely groundless," Holmes wrote.

Patterson also quoted a statement by Glenn White, president of the Dallas Police Association, in the *Dallas Morning News* in December 1997.

"I lobbied against the law in 1993 and 1995 because I thought it would lead to wholesale armed conflict. That hasn't happened. All the horror stories I thought would come to pass didn't happen. No bogeyman. I think it's worked out well, and that says good things about the citizens who have permits. I'm a convert."

However, many supporters of stricter gun controls believe that any attempt to reduce the number of guns in society is good and that an unarmed society is a safe society. They contend that self defense is not a valid reason for keeping or wearing a gun. The people who support this view tend to be people who know little or nothing about guns and are afraid of them. If nobody had guns, we'd all be safer, they reason.

This line of thinking was promulgated by Gregory Curtis, then editor of *Texas Monthly* magazine. In the May 1995 issue, he addressed the pros and cons of the recently-passed law that would give Texans the right to carry concealed handguns for self defense. He acknowledged that those who carried guns would be safer than those who didn't. But if everyone carried a gun, nobody would be safer, Curtis claimed. He seemed to think it is unfair to all the potential victims out there for some individuals to improve their safety by carrying a gun. This is akin to outlawing burglar alarm systems because not everyone can afford one.

Some people say carrying a handgun and learning how to use it for self defense is a logical extension of being responsible for your own safety. This school of thought is represented most vocally by the NRA, whose officers and members generally feel that the Second Amendment to the Constitution guarantees Americans the right to bear arms, not just while hunting or target shooting, but for self defense against criminals and against government tyranny. That is one factor that proponents of gun control, like the Brady Campaign to Prevent Handgun Violence and the Violence Policy Center, conveniently overlook. This country became an independent nation because a group of colonists used their arms against British tyranny.

The Second Amendment states: "A well-regulated Militia, being necessary to the security of a free State, the right of the people to keep and bear Arms, shall not be infringed."

Anyone who researches the context in which that sentence was written can hardly fail to realize that the framers of the Constitution intended that "the people" should have the right not just to own, but to carry, arms and that the first half of the amendment did not refer just to the National Guard. It was customary in the eighteenth century for people to wear swords and handguns without restriction. The Second Amendment specifically affirms that right to "the people." Yet the gun controllers and confiscators try to twist that sentence to say it refers only to some kind of part-time army. It is well to remember that the amendment says "the people," not "the people who have never been convicted of a felony" nor "the people who have passed a training course." Just "the people."

However, the reality is that ever since the amendment was signed judges and legislators have been whittling away at that right in the elitist belief that "the people" cannot be trusted with guns. And it doesn't happen just on the national level. Many states have similar clauses in their constitutions, only to find the right has been breached more than honored.

Both sides in the long-running gun-control debate support their positions with statistics and studies, and each side derides the other side's figures and conclusions with an almost Cold War fervor. The NRA says that the states with the most restrictive handgun controls, like New York, Illinois, and California, have the highest violent-crime rates. The Brady Campaign says states like Florida, which have allowed citizens to carry guns for self defense, have seen an increase in violent crimes.

Who's right? Both sides pick their statistics carefully, but the gun-control advocates seem to play fast and loose with the truth. In 1999, the Texas Department of Public Safety released figures on how many concealed-handgun license holders had been arrested in the license program's first three years and for what reasons. Based on these figures, the Violence Policy Center put together a report which it entitled: "License to Kill, and Kidnap, and Rape, and Drive Drunk." Under this headline, the VPC trumpeted that license holders had been arrested for "nearly two crimes" a day and "more than one serious violent crime per month." The figures also revealed that fifteen license holders had been charged with murder or attempted murder. The report did follow up several of the more serious cases to show two license holders had been convicted of murder.

The media accepted the VPC report at face value and reported it without any attempt to put it into context. This irritated Bill Sturdevant, a chemical engineer from Navasota, Texas, and a concealed-handgun license holder, when he read an article on the VPC report in his local paper. "I was really dismayed at the total lack of perspective in the article," he said.

He decided to do something about it. During the next few weeks, he put together his own seventy-five-page report entitled: "An Analysis of the Arrest Rate of Texas Concealed

Handgun License Holders as Compared to the Arrest Rate of the Entire Texas Population (1996–1998)." Later he updated his study to cover the first five years of the concealed-handgun license program from 1996 through 2000. His analysis put the arrests of license holders in perspective.

"The average Texan is much more likely to be arrested for violent crimes than the average concealed-handgun-license holder is," Sturdevant said.

Sturdevant concluded that the entire population of Texas over the age of twenty has an arrest rate for violent crime more than five times higher than do Texas concealed-handgun-license holders. A Texas resident does not qualify for a license until the age of twenty-one. Texas license holders are even less likely than adults generally to commit violent crimes frequently indulged in by habitual criminals, such as forcible rape and robbery. The rates are fifty-four times more likely and thirty-seven times respectively.

However the gap is much closer with violent crimes likely to be committed by non-professionals, though license holders are still more law abiding. Texans twenty-one years or older are 1.2 times more likely to be arrested for murder or non-negligent manslaughter than license holders. The rate for aggravated assault is 2.4 times. Of course, not everyone who is arrested is convicted. License holders such as Gordon Hale III of Dallas (Chapter 6) and Ralph Williams of Fort Worth (Chapter 11) have been exonerated by grand juries. Others like Pete Kanakidis (Chapter 11) were acquitted after a trial.

Sturdevant found the arrest rate for license holders to be much higher than the conviction rate. As of June 30, 2001, for those license holders arrested for crimes of violence, 26 percent had been reported to the Department of Public Safety as convicted while 44 percent had been acquitted.

Violent crime rates are too complex to be much affected by a single law. So far, no one has proven conclusively that citizens carrying handguns for self defense are a major deterrent to violent crime, but there are certainly some strong indicators.

John R. Lott Jr. and David B. Mustard, then working at the University of Chicago, found that violent crime decreased significantly after passage by states of concealed-carry legislation. Their study, "Crime, Deterrence, and Right-to-Carry Concealed Handguns," published in July 1996, analyzed crime statistics from 1977 to 1992 by county before and after right-to-carry laws took effect. It is probably the most extensive examination of the subject yet undertaken.

When state right-to-carry laws took effect, murders dropped by 8.5 percent; rapes by 5 percent; and aggravated assaults by 7 percent, Lott and Mustard found. They also found a substantial increase in the number of property crimes when states passed right-to-carry laws. Criminals appeared to change their behavior, switching to crimes where they were less likely to confront an armed citizen, Lott and Mustard said. Thus it seems that even citizens who choose not to carry guns benefit from right-to-carry laws.

License holders themselves are probably the most carefully screened group of people in the nation. This is particularly true in states that have passed right-to-carry laws in the last decade. The few states that have had "shall-issue" laws for many years tend to be comparatively relaxed about handing out permits. The cost of the permits or licenses is relatively cheap, and often no training course is required. But applicants still have to pass criminal record checks.

In states where laws have been passed more recently, applicants have to jump through a lot more hoops and be prepared to shell out more money. It cost me about $300 to get licensed in Texas, including $140 for the license and $150 for the training course. The result is that the percentage of licensees whose permits are revoked for abuse is tiny. Despite predictions to the contrary, the sky has not fallen, and the streets are not running with blood in states that have passed concealed-carry laws.

Former NRA President Marion Hammer helped pass the Florida law. "It gives law-abiding individuals the ability to choose whether or not to carry a firearm for protection. In effect, those people who refuse to be victims and want to be able to protect themselves can get licenses to carry and do not have to be concerned about being prosecuted for carrying a firearm," Hammer says.

Some states, like Maryland, Massachusetts, and New York—and like Florida before 1987—have a discretionary license system in which the politically connected and those showing need can get permits to carry handguns. The wealthy get to carry guns to protect their jewelry and the merchants to protect their cash.

"I find it most offensive that government would place a higher value on money or jewelry than the life of an individual, and that's exactly what they were saying," Hammer says.

David Kopel, research director of the Independence Institute in Golden, Colorado, has studied concealed-handgun licensing laws. He was asked what Texas could expect when its law took effect January 1, 1996.

"Based on what we have seen so far, we certainly are not going to get any increase in crime, and there's not strong enough evidence to show that there will be a decrease," he said.

Kopel found that in states which have "shall-issue" concealed-carry laws, only between 1 and 4 percent of the population bothers to get a permit. So the predictions of the doomsayers—that everyone will be carrying a gun and shooting each other at the least provocation—are just not true.

In the mid 1980s, long before the Killeen massacre, Ron Wilson was in Austin when he got a phone call that would have a lot to do with Texans' ability to carry handguns legally for self defense in the 1990s. At the time, Wilson was a Democratic representative in the Texas Legislature for a Houston constituency. His wife and children were temporarily living in an apartment while their new home was being built.

"I got a call, saying that my wife had been attacked," Wilson said. He got on the next plane and returned to their apartment in Houston.

"My wife had gone to take the trash out with my two-year-old son. When she returned to the apartment, someone jumped out of the bathroom—a guy, a black male—jumped on her."

The man tried unsuccessfully to rape her. When he asked her where her kids were, Mrs. Wilson fought like a lioness defending her cubs and drove him off. But not before he stabbed her in the head and chest. As he left, the man threatened to return.

It was that incident that started Wilson thinking about how to protect his wife from future attacks.

"That's where my interest came from," Wilson said of the bill that passed the 1995 session of the Legislature, giving law-abiding Texans the right to carry handguns for the first time in a century.

It couldn't be just his wife who was at risk, he thought. Other women are probably in similar situations.

"They ought to be able to protect themselves," Wilson said. "How can we, as policy makers, extend the right of self protection to individuals? I looked at a number of options: one is to put more money in the police force; another is hiring private security guards; another is requiring that individuals who own apartments provide on-site security. But those are all cost-prohibitive. And then I figured that the best way, after I looked at some other states, was just to give individuals a right to protect themselves, with deadly force if they had to. And that's where the idea came from. It took me about eight years to pass it."

Wilson says the first priority of a government in a democratic society is to protect its citizens. It provides military forces to defend against outside aggression and law-enforcement agencies to protect against domestic aggressors. Licensing citizens to carry handguns for individual protection is an additional step. "It's just a logical extension. There's nothing abnormal about it," Wilson says.

Besides, in Texas, citizens have long had the right to carry rifles everywhere except where alcohol is served and into government buildings. "Even before this bill passed, it was totally legal for me to walk down Main Street in Houston with a fully-loaded AK-47 and not break any laws at all," Wilson says.

People who were taking the training to become licensed gun carriers in Texas gave different reasons, but all felt they could not depend on the government to protect them adequately. U.S. courts have consistently held that law-enforcement agencies have no duty to protect an individual citizen. It is fine for U.S. Senators Charles Schumer or Edward Kennedy to rail against private ownership of firearms. They have never had to walk a mile in the moccasins of a woman being stalked by an abusive former husband who has threatened to kill her. In 1986, a bodyguard employed by Kennedy was arrested for carrying two submachineguns, a pistol, and 146 rounds of ammunition into a Senate office building. It's okay for Kennedy to be protected by firearms, but not for you. What hypocrisy!

In Texas, many people applied for concealed-carry licenses to legalize what they had been doing for years. Gary, 49, who owns a wholesale distribution business in San Antonio, has been carrying a gun since he was fourteen.

"The police can't protect you; they're there to write the reports," he said. "I don't believe in allowing my safety or my family's safety to be handled by someone who has absolutely no concern about it."

Gary wears his gun almost all the time—except when he goes into an airport, courthouse, or anywhere there is a metal detector. "When I get out of bed, it goes on," he said.

Gary has been stopped by police officers who found a pistol in his possession. They let him go after checking and finding he had no criminal record.

"We've done it before, when it wasn't legal to carry concealed, but we've always done it," he said.

M ost of the people taking training courses for a license are men. But many of the women are there because of previous incidents that have scared them.

Rochelle, 33, is office manager for a supermarket. She handles the money for the store and leaves work at 1 a.m. Ironically, neither of the incidents that prompted her to take the course occurred late at night.

The first happened about 2 p.m. in the parking lot of another grocery store. Rochelle had just come out of the store and was walking towards her car, when a man drove up next to her and ordered her into his car. When she refused, he drove beside her as she continued walking towards her car. As she reached her car, Rochelle pulled a can of Mace from her purse and sprayed it in the man's face. He wiped his eyes, then drove off, she said.

The second incident also happened in the afternoon. Rochelle returned home to find a pane of glass in the door broken. Undaunted, she entered the living room to find the television set had been moved and everything usually kept on top of it had been removed. Then she heard a noise upstairs.

"I realized then they were still in the house," Rochelle said.

She coolly used the telephone downstairs to call the police. When the dispatcher learned she was still in the house, he said, "Would you please go back outside and wait for the officers."

She had been out at the range, so she had a .380-caliber semi-automatic pistol in her car.

"I got the gun out of the car and went back into the house," Rochelle said. A couple of minutes later the police arrived and found her in the house. "I'm walking through the house with this gun and they go, 'Ma'am, do you live here?' I said, 'Yeah.' They go: 'Please put the weapon down.'"

While Rochelle was getting her gun, the youths had escaped. A couple of weeks later, however, she got a call from the police, who had recovered a handgun and some other property the thieves had stolen, she said.

Joe, 51, is a San Antonio radiologist who has a weekend farm near Comfort in the Texas Hill Country. He carries a revolver in the car when he is going to and from the farm and wants to be legal. Joe is also concerned about going into the hospital where he works late at night. Texas law makers prohibited the carrying of concealed weapons in hospitals, even with a license, if the hospital posts signs.

"I'm also a little concerned about the way society in general is going. If it hadn't happened now, in the next twenty years it will, because we're all at the mercy of criminals. If they want to do something, they're going to do it," Joe said.

Another man concerned about the way society is heading is Gordon, a retired dairy farmer, who still keeps some beef cattle on his farm. "I'm taking it [the course] for self protection. I live in the country, have all my life, and the country used to be a safe place," he said.

Recently a man was shot to death by an employee on a ranch near Gordon's home in Bandera County, he said.

Gordon, 63, grew up in an era when everyone had two parents at home. If he got into trouble at school, he got into worse trouble when he got home. "Nowadays, if a teacher touches a kid at school, he's got a law suit; the parents jump all over him. It's just turned backwards in my opinion," Gordon said.

While no one expects the carrying of handguns by law-abiding citizens to be a panacea, Land Commissioner Patterson, the NRA's Marion Hammer, and others believe armed citizens will make the country a little safer.

"I think the first time a carjacker follows what he thinks to be a victim home in a nice expensive car, pulls up behind him, and the victim drops a couple of carjackers bloody in the driveway, there will be fewer carjackings," Patterson said. "Overall I think it'll have a minimal effect, but it definitely will not have a negative effect."

So far he has been proved right.

Chapter Four

STAYING OUT OF TROUBLE:
NON-VIOLENT DISPUTE RESOLUTION

Robert Butler, U.S. Customs Special Agent and firearms instructor, was in Columbus, Georgia, when he visited the local outlet of Toys-R-Us with his father to pick up something for his children at home in Texas.

"I was walking in, and these three gangbangers drove by and almost hit me with their car," Butler recalls. "They said something, and I said something back: to watch where they're driving."

He had dealt with street-gang members before, both as a police officer and as a Customs agent, and knew how dangerous they can be.

The youths stopped, and Butler stopped. They stared at each other, then the youths drove off towards the parking lot. Butler and his father Grant entered the store.

"I thought they might drive down to the parking lot and wait for us to exit the store," Butler says.

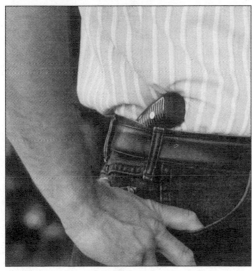

He carries a Ruger SP101 snub-nosed revolver without a holster, tucked into his belt behind his right hip. If he isn't wearing a jacket—and

How U.S. Customs Special Agent Robert Butler usually carries his five-shot Ruger SP101, hidden under his shirt or jacket.

119

he wasn't on this occasion—his shirt goes over it. He was concerned about what might be awaiting him and his father when they left.

"So while I was in the store, I moved my gun around inside my shirt to the front so I could just lift up my shirt for quick access to the weapon," Butler says.

"I was ready. When I walked down, I was looking both ways to see where they were. If they'd've driven up, that gun would have been in my hand."

As it turned out, the gangbangers were not in sight when Butler and his father left the store. But Butler was thinking ahead, planning for what might happen...and so should you, if you carry a gun and intend to protect yourself.

You have already reached adulthood, and some of you have even reached senior-citizen status, without getting killed or being convicted of a serious crime. You, therefore, possess certain life skills that have kept you safe up to now. The odds are that, whether you choose to carry a gun or not, you will die of what are generally referred to as natural causes—cancer, a heart attack, or just plain old age. Some readers may be destined to die in traffic accidents, others in fires, tornadoes, or earthquakes. A few may be murdered by felons wielding guns, knives, or clubs. The object of this book is to provide you with the knowledge and encourage you to acquire the skills to prevent you from becoming one of the latter—a victim of violent criminal attack.

Criminals generally are opportunists. They look for an easy target that has what they want—cash or valuables that can be converted into cash. The first step in taking charge of your own security is to become a less-attractive target. As Clint Smith, director of Thunder Ranch shooting school, says: "If you look like food, you will be eaten."

Few people look less like food than Robert Butler. He is more than six-feet tall, exudes self confidence, and is always alert. He has also survived one gunfight. The three little gangbangers were well advised not to mess with him. But had he been a five-foot tall, one-hundred-five-pound woman, they might have been waiting.

All self-defense instructors I have spoken to agree that a confident, alert demeanor will discourage most opportunistic criminals from choosing you as a target. If they do, you should have some warning and be able to take evasive action.

"You need to pay attention to your surroundings and to what's going on around you, primarily looking at people and evaluating what they're doing, how they're acting," says firearms instructor and former police officer Bill McLennan.

"We know that criminals size people up before they attack. They do this by watching a person's body language. They look for introverted people, people that aren't paying attention to what's going on. They'll prey on the weaker-looking people and the older people."

McLennan says we should be sizing people up and analyzing their movements. What seems out of place or unusual? A youngish man wearing a coat in an Arizona summer should set off the warning bells. It could be an undercover cop or it could be someone carrying a sawed-off shotgun under his coat with robbery on his mind.

I have watched journalists, who are supposed to be professional observers, walking from a newspaper building to where their cars are parked with their heads down, apparently staring at the sidewalk a few feet in front of them. Maybe they are trying to figure out a crossword puzzle clue or maybe they are afraid of stepping in something unpleasant.

You can wipe dog mess off your shoe; it's harder to erase the memory of a rape or purse snatching. Of course, if you are killed, after a few brief seconds of terror, the world will have to find someone else to revolve around. But it will devastate your loved ones.

John Long, the barber from Shreveport whose encounter with robbers is described in Chapter 2, is one of the civilians I have met who is most attuned to signs of trouble and is always alert. He recalls one occasion when he ignored the warning signs.

At the time, an insurance office occupied the store next to Long's in the strip center on 70th Street. One day in the late fall, Long was out talking to a customer in the car lot. He noticed two men, both wearing jackets, and both with their hands in their pockets as it was a cold day.

"They were walking in a manner that catches my attention, like leaning forward and looking around, glancing quickly," says Long. "There was something in me that said, 'Something's wrong here. Check it out.' But just as I thought that, a customer pulls up for a haircut, and I'm thinking to myself: 'Wait a minute, maybe I'm over-reacting. Maybe I'm letting my imagination get the better of me.' My instincts tell me to check this out. My logic tells me maybe this is somebody who has just run in to make a quick payment on an insurance policy."

Long goes into the shop and gives the customer a haircut. When the customer has left, a woman runs in and tells him she has been robbed. The woman was the only employee in the insurance office, and she was pregnant. The men had robbed her then locked her in the bathroom. She had just managed to escape and, although she was not injured, she was shaken up.

"These two men, armed with guns, took this poor little unarmed pregnant woman, locked her in the bathroom, took the money out of the cash box, and ran out the back door," Long says.

"When you've got an instinct or a feeling something's wrong, don't simply dismiss it, check it out. It could be something. That's what I've learned: to always trust your instincts on something like that.

"I felt guilty because I essentially had turned my back on my instincts that said, 'Do something,' and my brain told me that there's probably nothing there, and I was over-reacting. I felt guilty about that for a long time."

COLOR CODES

The late Colonel Jeff Cooper, one of the leaders in self defense and father of the "New Technique" of combat shooting, called it living "in yellow." One of his most valuable contributions was to adapt color codes for mental conditioning to overcome a normal person's reluctance to pull the trigger on another human being.

White is the condition of vulnerability. You are not paying attention to your surroundings. The ultimate Condition White is when you are asleep. You are not alert to anything that is going on around you. About the only place you can usually afford to be in Condition White, if you take your safety seriously, is when you are at home with the doors locked.

Yellow is the condition of being alert. Every time you step out of your door, every time you wear your gun, you should be in Condition Yellow. Your eyes are moving, scanning your surroundings, not just in front of you but also behind you. A stealth attack is usually made from the rear. When driving, keep your eyes on the rear-view mirrors for anyone following you. When you pull up to a stop light, be aware of the people and vehicles around you. Many attacks are made at stop lights. When you stop, leave enough room between your vehicle and the one ahead so you can pull around it and escape in an emergency.

When you get into your car, lock the doors as automatically as you put on your seat belt. Keep the windows rolled up so you cannot be reached. When Gordon Hale III, whose story you will read in chapter 6, was attacked, his pickup was surrounded by other vehicles stopped at a traffic light.

Afterwards, Hale's father said, "He said he'll never run with his windows down, and he'll never drive in the middle lane again."

Hale believes if he had been in the inside or outside lanes, he could have driven off on the shoulder or the median, and if he had had his windows rolled up, his attacker could not have reached him.

Some carjackers and criminals with other motives will deliberately bump your car from behind. When you stop and get out to inspect the damage and trade accident information, they will attack. If you don't feel comfortable about the situation, drive to the nearest police or fire station.

When approaching your car in a parking lot, glance under the car as you approach. Before you get in, look in the back to make sure no one is hiding there.

If you are walking, pay particular attention to bushes, doorways, and parked vehicles—anything that might provide cover for an attacker—and keep away from them.

Keep your back to a wall when you can. Take the seat against the wall in a restaurant or bar. Wild Bill Hickok ignored this rule, and it cost him his life in Deadwood, South Dakota, in 1876. He was playing poker when Jack McCall shot him in the back of the head. The cards Hickok was holding—two pairs, aces and eights—became known as the dead man's hand.

Be particularly alert when using automated teller machines. Many people have been robbed at gunpoint and forced to give up their personal identification numbers so their accounts can be looted. Sometimes they have been killed during these robberies.

Not being in Condition Yellow probably contributed to the death of San Antonio construction contractor Joe Ince on a January evening in 1994. Ince, 38, was lead trumpeter in the Trinity Baptist Church orchestra. He was returning home from music practice when he stopped to make a paycheck deposit at a bank teller machine. After putting the check into the machine, Ince was abducted at gun point by a seventeen-year-old youth and a thirteen-year-old girl. He was driven off in his own extended-cab pickup by Oscar Ortiz III, with the girl holding a .22 revolver to his head.

The pair forced Ince to give up his wallet, his ATM card, and his account access number. They drove around to several teller machines and made one withdrawal. At one point, Ortiz taunted Ince, asking him how it felt to have a gun to his head, according to the girl's testimony. The girl told a San Antonio jury that Ortiz grabbed the gun away from her, complaining she wasn't "doing it right." He then shot Ince once in the temple. After pushing the mortally wounded man out of the pickup, they drove to another teller machine and withdrew more of his money. In total they got about $600. Ortiz was sentenced to death by the jury in July 1995.

Most of the techniques used to avoid becoming a victim are available in pamphlets put out by police departments. The advice is generally good where it relates to alertness. However, beware of the advice that often accompanies these suggestions: not to resist. As far as we know, Joe Ince did not resist his abductors. One such leaflet gives the following advice: "If the attacker is only after your purse or other valuables, don't resist. You don't want to escalate a property crime into a violent confrontation."

If a man demands that you hand over your purse with an implied threat that you will get hurt if you don't, that is already a robbery, a crime of violence. And how can you be sure that all he wants is your purse?

While Condition Yellow is the state of general alertness, once you have identified a specific person or set of circumstances as a possible threat, you move into Condition Orange. You may deal with it best by avoidance. It can be as simple as turning around and walking back into the building you have just left. Your self-defense tactics are most successful when you don't know what might have happened if you hadn't taken avoiding action.

The two teenagers with their gimme caps on backwards who are hanging around your car in the mall parking lot should prod you into Condition Orange. Now you have a specific threat.

Your best course of action is to walk back into the mall and contact security. That may not fit in with your image of what an armed person should do, but it's good advice. As you will see in later chapters, shooting someone is often traumatic and expensive.

Even if they take a baseball bat to your windshield, you may do better to call the police rather than take them on. In some states, like Texas, it is legal to use deadly force in certain circumstances to prevent burglary or criminal mischief. In other states, it is legal to use deadly force only to protect yourself or another from serious physical harm. Know the laws regarding the use of deadly force in your state.

Even if it is legal to shoot someone smashing your car windows or running out of your front door with your television, it may not be wise. You may think I am advising you to wimp out. I am not. I am alerting you to the reality of today's America. If you have money or other assets like most middle-class citizens, you can be right and still lose everything. It is a lot cheaper to replace a windshield or a television than it is to pay a lawyer to defend your actions in court when the family of the kid you killed—or worse, crippled—sues you. This is something you should think about before it happens.

D on't think of a gun as your only salvation, even if you are carrying one. The mind, rather than the gun, is the weapon, according to David Ham, a fourth-degree black-belt *aikido* instructor. The mind can think of better ways of getting out of a tight situation than shooting your way out.

Several years ago, Ham, a businessman and chief executive officer, was driving his Infiniti Q45 in downtown San Antonio. He was returning home from teaching a self-defense class to a group of law-enforcement officers when he pulled up at a red traffic light. Looking to his left he saw, stopped beside him, a brown Ford Mustang, about twenty years old, with a blue stripe and lowered suspension. Ham immediately identified the three teenage youths in the car as likely gang members. Sure enough, the youth in the front passenger seat looked at Ham and flashed a gang sign with his hands.

"I naturally turned to the right to see who he was signing, and there wasn't anybody there," Ham says. "I'm trained to look out of my peripheral vision, so as I'm turning back to the left, I see this guy take a sawed-off shotgun and place it on the window sill. I could hear the thunk of the barrel on the window sill."

At the time, Ham had been practicing *aikido* for more than a dozen years. Unlike karate or *tae kwon do, aikido* is a defensive art. There are no attacks in *aikido* and there are no contests or competitions. *Aikido* philosophy is to use the minimum force necessary to remain undefeated. In fact the ultimate use of *aikido* is to avoid a fight entirely. This is not to say it is an anemic art: it can be lethal. It is particularly useful to police officers, as it enables them to take a violent suspect to jail without stopping off at the hospital first.

Despite *aikido's* defensive philosophy, Ham's first thought was aggressive when he saw the youth pointing the shotgun at him.

"I thought, as I was rotating my head, 'you stupid son of a bitch, I can kill you.' That was my first thought off the top of my head," Ham says.

He was unarmed and the young hoodlum had the drop on him from about three feet away. It was not that he was able to kill the youth but rather that, by pointing the shotgun, the teenager provided him with justification to kill him.

"You're stupid to make this opening because the effect of that is: I could legally kill you. That was the logic," Ham says.

The muzzle of the double-barreled shotgun was so close that Ham could see the marks of the hacksaw that had been used to chop down the barrel.

"It looked like a howitzer, man; I could have driven through the tunnel. I mean, it was just big. Interestingly enough, I was never frightened during the incident. I don't know why. Maybe that's because of my training."

Even before he had finished turning his head, Ham decided to use the subtler side of *aikido*. He faced the youth with a wide grin on his face. He lifted a hand above the rolled-down window and gave the kid a thumbs-up sign and uttered one word: "Cool."

"Yeah," the kid replied and lowered the shotgun. The lights changed, and the Mustang drove off.

Ham followed, staying back to write down the license plate number of the car, then turned off and drove to the police station. He recounted the incident to the sergeant in charge of the gang unit and learned later that the youths had been found and the shotgun seized.

Ham feels that even if he had been armed he would probably have been killed or seriously injured if he had tried to shoot it out.

As shown in Chapter 2, some of the most vulnerable people in our society are those, usually women, who are involved in domestic disputes. Messy divorces, spurned lovers, sexual jealousies, all produce strong emotions that often result in violence. Again and again, police are forced to tell people in these situations that they can do little until they are attacked. Stalking laws help, but essentially these potential victims find they are on their own. If you are being stalked or threatened by someone, it is important to report each incident to police to show a pattern of threatening behavior.

When San Antonio barber-shop owner Henry Gomez, 68, shot and killed a jealous lover in his home, he was not arrested. Gomez had recently broken off a relationship with one of his hairdressers. The woman started going out with Arthur Andrade Reyes, 54. But Reyes apparently felt his relationship with the woman was threatened as long as she kept working at Gomez's barber shop.

On July 10, 1996, Reyes came to Gomez's living quarters, behind the shop. He accused the barber of trying to make a fool out of him by letting the woman continue to work at the shop. Reyes told him that both he and the woman were going to die. Later the same day, Reyes returned, and Gomez told him the woman had agreed not to work at his shop any more. However, Reyes again threatened him. Wisely, Gomez told police of the threats, and officers took a report.

On July 13 Reyes returned. The barber saw a pickup pull up at the back of his house. He heard Reyes talking to one of his sons at the back door. At this stage, he was in Condition Orange, though he would probably not have known it by that name. He was faced with a specific threat. Gomez went into his bedroom and took a loaded .357 Magnum Taurus revolver from his dresser drawer, according to a police report. Reyes barged into the house. Gomez told him not to come any further, but Reyes took no notice. Gomez was now in Condition Red. He was ready to shoot if Reyes kept coming. Condition Red doesn't mean that you shoot, just that you have made the decision to shoot if necessary. If Reyes had stopped and backed off at that point, Gomez probably would not have pressed the trigger. But Reyes kept coming at the older man, keeping one hand in his pocket as though he had a weapon in it, Gomez later told investigators.

Reyes lunged at Gomez. Gomez fired one shot, hitting Reyes between the eyes.

It turned out that Reyes was unarmed, but Gomez fired when in fear for his life. It did not hurt that Gomez was an elderly man and that both his sons gave statements that supported his version of events. But the police report on file, alleging that Reyes had threatened Gomez previously, added valuable corroboration to the barber's story.

NON-VIOLENT DISPUTE RESOLUTION

When the Texas Legislature passed its concealed-handgun licensing law in the spring of 1995, it came with a lot of baggage. When the clock struck midnight on December 31 that year, Texas would allow—for the first time in living memory—ordinary citizens to carry handguns. It was a big change. Unlike many Western states, Texas had no open-carry law and no previous concealed-carry licensing system at all. For decades, a majority of Texas politicians had shown they did not trust ordinary citizens to carry guns for protection. As with Florida in 1987, there were many organizations and individuals, including the state's leading newspapers, predicting carnage in the streets.

Consequently, Texans wanting a concealed-carry license have to jump through more hoops and put up more money than the residents of most other states. One of the requirements is to take a training course of between ten and fifteen hours that includes classroom time and a fifty-round range course.

This course, which covers the laws governing concealed carry and self defense, may be costly and inconvenient, but it is a good requirement. Giving someone a license to carry a handgun without a training course is like giving out driver's licenses without a road test.

One of the subjects taught in the Texas course is non-violent dispute resolution. The course was designed by the Texas Department of Public Safety, which adapted for civilians some of what it teaches Highway Patrol officers about understanding confrontation and preventing it from escalating into violence. It was taught to me by Greg Ferris, who has educated hundreds of Texans in the concealed-handgun course. Much of what follows is his interpretation of the required Texas training course.

According to Dr. Eric Berne in his 1964 best-seller, *Games People Play*, we all have three "selves" or "ego states" within us. These are parent, adult, and child.

Berne observed that people easily change viewpoints, feelings, and behavior during interaction with others. They exhibit behavior that he linked to parent, adult, and child ego states.

Parent-like behavior is authoritarian. Under stress we become angry and protective. We tend to give orders and make judgments about what others are doing. Our parents told us, "Brush your teeth" or "Do your homework," while we were growing up. In the parent mode, we behave like our parents did. We say, "Quit that" or "You should know better."

Anyone who is spoken to like that tends to react in a defensive or child-like fashion with replies such as, "I will if I want to" or "Screw you." This escalates the conflict, which, if allowed to progress into a slanging match, may end in violence. In stressful situations, such as traffic accidents, parent-like and child-like behaviors tend to become dominant. A person in the parent or child ego state tends to be emotional and to speak in the first person, lacing his speech with "I," "me," or "my."

Berne's way of deescalating a conflict was to speak and behave in an adult way. The adult ego state is objective and logical. It is based on reasoning and life experience. The adult ego state is able to effectively analyze a situation: what caused it and how to resolve it. It can put its analysis into words in a non-prejudicial manner. A person in the adult ego state uses "we," "us," and "our."

"We have two sides to an argument; the adult ego state can express both sides," Ferris says.

The parent and child ego states prove useless in deescalating a conflict. We want to be in the adult ego state when we're in a dispute. We want to be objective and able to analyze what's going on.

"The adult always leaves room for the second person," Ferris says. "And that's the best way to resolve a conflict. It prevents defensive reaction, does not embarrass the other person, and allows them to save face and maintain their dignity."

Most adults will recognize signs of emotional disturbance in a conflict situation from their own life experience. For most people they will be reminders rather than anything new.

They are tip-offs or warnings you should be watching for in a confrontation. The signs include:

1. Eye Contact. It occurs in different ways. The person won't make eye contact. He is watching you through his peripheral vision or is casting you furtive little glances. More dangerous is the guy who bores a hole right through you with his eyes, like you're not there. This person could be waiting for you to finish talking so he can speak his piece. He knows exactly what he's going to say, and he's waiting for his opportunity to say it. He is not listening to what you are saying. Alternatively, he may be planning his moves. He may be waiting for an opportunity to attack. Again, he's not listening. Last and most dangerously, he may be devaluing you as a human being. If he's looking through you like you aren't there, he could be moving into Condition Red, where he is breaking down his natural inhibitions against killing you. He's looking at you like a target rather than a person.

2. Silence. Silence can be interpreted in much the same way as eye contact. He could be waiting for you to finish talking, he could be planning, or he could be dehumanizing you.

3. Crying. The danger here is that when you see him burst into tears, you will assume that you have won the argument, that he has submitted to you. You relax your vigilance and may even move closer to him. But you may be misreading him. He may have decided that his only option is violence. He knows that he may get killed or injured. He may actually have gone into mourning for himself, losing any inhibitions he may have had against taking your life. By comparison, you have let down your guard and will be taken by surprise when he makes his move.

4. Clenching Fists. This, along with tensing muscles and body tremors, indicates the body is pumping itself up with adrenaline, preparing for a fight.

5. Sweating. Look for it particularly where it doesn't occur as a result of heat—on the upper lip, on the forehead, and on the palms of his hands. If he's wiping his palms on his pants or shirt, he's getting ready for action.

6. *Erratic Breathing.* He may be taking long, deep breaths or he may be panting. Either way, he is pumping up, oxygenating his blood in preparation for violent action.

7. *Increased Blood Pressure.* His face or skin may flush, or you may be able to see the blood throbbing in his throat. While increased blood pressure will make you bleed more from a wound, it will also keep you fighting longer. If you lose blood pressure, you can go into a coma.

8. *Violent and Abusive Language.* As an argument gets closer and closer to violence, the decibel level goes up. It gets louder. The words used get shorter and more blunt. Factual argument turns into a personal, emotional quarrel.

9. *Tantrums.* Adults can and do throw tantrums, stamping their feet, kicking tires, or throwing things.

10. *Stuttering Speech.* People who normally speak coherently start to stutter and stammer. They may be so preoccupied with what is about to happen that they don't pay attention to the words they are saying.

This list is by no means complete. There are other signs, such as rapid blinking and nervous tics. People under stress tend to exhibit one or more of these signs. Watch for them and try to get distance between you and anyone showing these signs. Back up or move to get something such as a vehicle between the two of you.

The Texas Department of Public Safety course recommends analyzing the elements of your confrontation by asking the following questions and others that may occur to you. Remember the four categories by using the mnemonic PACE:

Problem. What is the problem? What is the conflict about? What brought the two sides into conflict? What are the risks and gains?

Audience. Who are the players involved in the conflict? What is their agenda? What do they have to gain and lose? How far are they willing to go? What are their cultural differences and similarities, their roles in the community? What signs of emotional disturbance are they showing?

Constraints. What are the obstacles to effective communication? They include: the time of day—we usually feel more comfortable during daylight; the weather—tempers are shorter in hot weather; location—we may be on their turf; ego states—those involved may be in the parent or child ego state; their beliefs and value systems—the gang member is going to have a more macho code of behavior than the straight-A high-school student; bystanders or family members can boost a person's courage and make him less able to lose face; language—in Florida, Texas, or southern California, people confronting you may speak only Spanish, while in San Francisco or New York they may understand only Cantonese.

Ethical Presence. The only person you can control in an argument or confrontation is yourself. Are you in control of yourself? Are you in the adult ego state? Are you speaking from the adult behavior perspective, not expressing parental or child-like emotions, personal feelings, opinions, or value judgments? Parent and child words and behavior only polarize and escalate the conflict.

Having used PACE to analyze the conflict, you need to deescalate the conflict. Use the mnemonic LEAPS to remember five techniques recommended to defuse a situation:

Listen. In a conflict, we become very self-centered. We want to talk and force our point of view on the other person. If we listen and nod occasionally rather than argue, much of the heat will go out of the situation. Listening is a very important communications skill and should not be confused with just hearing another person.

Empathize. Put yourself in the other person's shoes; see things from their point of view. Be sure to empathize aloud so the other person can hear you doing it. Agree with the person where you can with honesty. However, do not sympathize or become emotionally attached to their point of view. If you do, you will lower your guard.

Ask. Question the other person about specific facts. Remember the Five Ws: Who, What, When, Where, and Why. Try them out. But go further by asking questions like: "How does this make you feel?" "What would you do if...?" "How would this affect you?" Asking questions builds rapport and solicits input from the other person rather than pushing your perspective onto him.

Paraphrase. Put the other person's meaning into your words, and feed it back to him. This means you are understanding his point of view and giving him a chance to agree with something you have said. It is the only way to interrupt someone in mid-sentence without generating more hostility. The other person becomes a better listener because it is his perspective that is being played back to him. It creates empathy and generates an atmosphere of fair play: you have listened to him and made an effort to understand his perspective, therefore, he will be obligated to do the same for you.

Summarize. When we summarize, we move towards conclusion. Our tone and words should be shaped with decisiveness and authority. For example, you might end with one of these: "Based on what you've told me, why don't we do this?" "Let's do this." "Why don't we do this?" "If you do this, I'll do that." Note the use of "we" and be sure to make the resolution a winning proposition for both sides.

When you strap on your concealed handgun, you should be aware of two things:

First, the legal system will likely hold you to a higher standard of behavior than your untrained, unarmed neighbor. You need to be able to show that you did nothing to start or escalate an argument. President Theodore Roosevelt was the advocate of the philosophy, "Speak softly and carry a big stick." These are words for the civilian gun carrier to live by. You have your big stick—actually a small stick, but with a lot of punch—now learn to talk softly. Don't get into heated arguments; walk away. It is no longer okay for you to flip the middle finger or yell "a--hole" at someone who cuts you off in traffic.

I recently met a man who had done some plumbing work for my wife and me when we bought a house in San Antonio. He told me he had gone through the training course and had a Texas concealed-handgun license.

"Then I discovered that I had a case of chronic road rage," he said. If someone cut him off in traffic or did something else to anger him while driving, he was afraid he would lose his temper and shoot them. He said he had sold all his guns and did not plan to renew his license. I congratulated him on making a wise decision.

Second, be aware that, when you start carrying a gun, your personality may change. You may become more confident, but also more aggressive. You may go to places that you would not have gone before simply because you are armed. You may think you are invincible, but you're not. Remember, step softly and don't go into places where angels fear to tread.

However, having encouraged you to avoid a shootout if it is possible, there may come a time when you are faced with a life-or-death—your death—situation. What are you going to carry, and how are you going to react? The next chapters will help answer those questions.

Finally, in a chapter about keeping out of trouble, I make no apologies for repeating: trust your instincts.

Rory Vertigan was working as a security manager for a Phoenix real-estate company in 1999. On a March afternoon, he was about to leave his office when he picked up his

Beretta Bobcat and stuck it in his front pants' pocket. The Bobcat is a .25-caliber semi-automatic handgun good for exterminating rattlesnakes or as a backup gun. It is not a first choice for self-defense. Vertigan, then twenty-seven, stepped outside and was walking to where his car was parked, when he stopped, paused a moment, then retraced his steps.

Rory Vertigan.

Back in his office, he put the Bobcat back in the drawer and took out his Glock Model 31. The Glock is a full-size semi-automatic which can hold sixteen rounds in the powerful .357 SIG caliber. Carrying the Glock, Vertigan returned to his car. He said he had no idea why he exchanged the underpowered Beretta for the bigger handgun. Some sixth sense or instinct was guiding his action that day.

Within an hour, Vertigan was using the Glock to wound a Mexican drug trafficker, who had just shot and killed a Phoenix police officer. Although the bigger gun did not keep Vertigan out of trouble, he would have been in a heap more trouble if the little Beretta had been his only weapon.

Chapter Five

CHOOSING A HANDGUN:
SEMI-AUTOMATICS AND REVOLVERS

STOPPING POWER

The call was for "burglars in action."

When San Antonio police officer Bill McLennan and his partner arrived at the house, the homeowner told them he had just shot the burglar. He had come home from a hunting trip to find the burglar going out the door clutching his guitar. The homeowner had shot the thief with his hunting rifle, a weapon chambered for the .22 Savage Hi-Power, a high-velocity cartridge with ballistics close to the standard .223-caliber U.S. military round. The thief had dropped the guitar and run off.

"We knew the guy was hit, because there was blood on the guitar and there was a hole in it," McLennan said.

The homeowner told the officers the burglar was holding the guitar about waist level when he fired. The complainant gave them a description of the man, so while his partner took the report, McLennan started to prowl the area looking for a crook with a stomach ache.

He found nothing until he decided to check the bars in the area. More than half an hour after the shooting and half a mile from the house, McLennan was coming out of a bar when he saw a man walking towards him. The man seemed to fit the description of the burglar.

"But he seemed okay. As he approached me, it sounded like he was walking in water or his shoes were wet. It turned out, it was blood actually sloshing out of his shoes, and the guy was bleeding pretty good," McLennan said.

The burglar had taken a good hit from a high-velocity round, had walked half a mile, and was still standing half an hour later.

In most cases in which a homeowner shoots a burglar, the burglar flees, according to McLennan.

"Rarely do I recall finding one at the scene of the crime," he says.

If a high-velocity rifle won't put a man down with a single shot, a handgun certainly can't be relied on to do so.

McLennan, retired chief firearms instructor for the San Antonio Police Department, used to believe in the stopping power of a handgun bullet, but has changed his mind over the years.

"You have to destroy a lot of tissue; you have to make 'em bleed," he says. "They run out of oxygen, and they finally quit what they're doing."

Like many things in life, a handgun is a compromise. It is the least-effective firearm for self defense. Except at very close quarters—at arm's length—shotguns and rifles are much more effective in stopping a drug-hyped robber or rapist intent on making you pay for his lack of social skills. A handgun is the hardest firearm to shoot accurately, and, even when you hit what you are shooting at, your target doesn't vaporize in a red mist like on television.

I first learned this many years ago when I was working on a ranch in western Canada. I took a shot with a .45-caliber Smith & Wesson revolver at a coyote standing seventy-five yards away. At first I thought I had missed it, as I watched it run more than ten yards before keeling over. When I opened the coyote up, I found the bullet had ripped through its heart. It was a lucky shot, but that animal ran thirty or forty feet shot through the heart with a 260-grain, semi-wadcutter bullet. Imagine the coyote as a two-hundred-fifty-pound parolee armed with a butcher knife from your kitchen, and you're shooting at him across the living room.

Even if you hit him in the heart, he could still impale you on your own sausage slicer.

In choosing a handgun for self defense, remember that the gun has two functions. In some cases, presentation of the gun, coupled with a shouted order to "STOP, GO AWAY, BACK UP," will be enough to defuse the threat. It reminds the potential robber or rapist that he has urgent business in another county.

Keep the order short and loud. Don't say anything like: "Go ahead, make my day." It's too long, and it's not forceful enough. But more important, if you shoot and somebody overheard you taunting the person you just killed, a prosecutor or plaintiff's lawyer will make you look like some homicidal maniac. However, your expression should leave your potential attacker in no doubt that if he continues his intentions, you will shoot him. While any handgun will do, a large gun with a hole in the business end as big as a howitzer reinforces the seriousness of your intentions.

In cases where the threat is not enough, the gun is a delivery system for those little lead missiles, scarcely bigger than a cigarette filter, that rip and tear your attacker's anatomy. It is the bullet that stops the attack, not the gun. The size and weight of the bullet depend mostly on the caliber of the gun from which it is fired. So one of your first decisions in picking a gun is deciding on a caliber.

Caliber

Caliber is a confusing term. According to the dictionary, it is the measurement of the bore or internal barrel width of a gun in inches or millimeters. For example, a .45 barrel has a bore diameter of about 0.45 inches, and a 9mm has a bore diameter of about 9 millimeters. However, the measurement is not exact. A .44 Special or a .44 Magnum will have a bore diameter of 0.429 inches—closer to .43 than .44. The caliber which really upsets the system is the .38. A .38 Special has a bore diameter of 0.357 inches—about a .36 caliber. It shoots the same bullet as the .357 Magnum. In fact, a .38 Special round can be fired in a gun chambered for .357 Magnum. The reverse is not true, because the case of the Magnum is man- ufactured slightly longer to stop people from shooting the more powerful round in a gun not built to withstand the pressure.

We tend to talk of a revolver being of .38 Special caliber or of .44 Magnum caliber, or a semi-automatic as being a 9 mil- limeter Luger or a .45 ACP (Automatic Colt Pistol). Strictly speak- ing, it is the number only that refers to the caliber. The following words or letters usually refer to the cartridge case the bullet is fired from and thus the length and shape of the chamber. It may also give some hint about the cartridge's velocity: Magnum denotes a heavier powder charge and higher velocity than standard cartridges. When we talk of choosing a caliber, we are talking of the cartridge that we want the gun to shoot.

In self-defense shooting, the object is not to kill your assailant, though this may be a by-product. The intent is to stop him from continuing his attack on you. As a former police reporter in San Antonio, I know many people get killed by .25-caliber, fifty-grain bullets fired from cheap semi-automatics. But the victims don't usually die quickly, and they are often quite capable of shooting back, even when mortally wounded by such pip-squeak artillery. The reason people carry these "poodle shoot- ers" is because they are small, light, easily concealed, and cost less than $100.

At the other end of the handgun spectrum is Dirty Harry's .44 Magnum revolver with its six-inch barrel. It weighs almost as much as a six-pack and is about as easy to conceal. But a hit from a .44 Magnum bullet traveling at 1,350 feet per second is more likely than a projectile from any other handgun to end a gunfight in one shot.

The old rule of thumb was: the larger the caliber, the more effective the bullet is in stopping an attack. When asked why he packed a .45, the ol' time Texas Ranger replied: "Because they don't make a fifty."

This quote is somewhat dated now as they do make handguns in .50 caliber but most of them weigh about a much as a howitzer and consequently don't make very good carry guns.

Bill Davison, owner of Tac Pro Shooting Center in north Texas, says many American firearms instructors seem unduly fixated on the .45. He says you should carry whatever gun you can shoot accurately. Davison migrated from the United Kingdom several years ago after serving in the Royal Marine Special Boat Service. He spent time fighting IRA terrorists in Northern Ireland, where the standard-issue handgun was a 9mm Browning semi-automatic.

"If you can hit the cardiovascular triangle [upper chest area] every time with your nine mil as fast as you can pull the trigger, then carry a nine mil," Davison told students attending one of his three-day primary pistol classes.

When he first came to the United States everyone told Davison he shouldn't carry a 9mm because the cartridge was ineffective, he said.

"I can honestly tell you, gentlemen, that I have never had someone not die because I shot them with a nine mil. They all died immediately, and I'm really pleased with the cartridge," Davison said.

He believes that bullet placement is far more important than bullet size in a gunfight, and he had some of his students rethinking their assumption that bigger is better for a defensive handgun.

Gary Marcum, a Fort Worth police officer in the early 1980s, found Davison's statement compelling. He normally carried a single-stack .45 because, like many of us, he was convinced the caliber was the best.

"Bill's experience has a lot of power and in my mind eliminates a lot of argument," Marcum said. "Now I'm beginning to think I may carry a double-stack .40 simply because he's convinced me that it's a lot more important where you put the bullets than it is the diameter of them or the velocity."

Even a .45 cannot be relied upon to put a man down with one shot. An undercover drug operation a few miles south of San Antonio, in April 1991, erupted into a shoot-out that left as many dead as the gunfight at the OK Corral.

Domingo Moncada, 27, an undercover member of a narcotics task force, had brought a ton of marijuana to "sell" to drug trafficker Ben Gonzales, 24, for $1.3 million. The sale was to take place in a fenced area occupied by a battery of oil-field tanks beside a ranch road in rural South Texas. Moncada was accompanied by his brother, Juan Moncada, 33, who was acting as an informant, and sheriff's Chief Deputy Ken Meister, 45. The plan was to arrest Gonzales and his companion, Vincent Vargas, 23, when they handed over the money.

But Gonzales didn't bring any money. He was going to "rip-off" these men he believed were drug dealers—rob them of their dope. Before the meeting, he positioned Vargas's uncle, heroin addict Juan Flores Vargas, 60, in ambush behind a log in the brush. He was armed with a .22-caliber rifle.

When Domingo Moncada, Gonzales, and the others drove up, they parked and got out of their vehicles. Gonzales told them he was waiting for the man with the money. Without warning, Juan Vargas opened fire from ambush with his .22-rimfire rifle. He hit Chief Deputy Meister once in the chest and once in the back. Meister fell to the ground without firing a shot.

Meanwhile, Vincent Vargas and Gonzales pulled their guns and started shooting at Domingo Moncada—or that is how it appeared. Gonzales opened fire but Moncada thinks Vargas didn't get off a shot, though he was trying to.

"I think he had a single-action. He didn't know he had to cock the hammer back and then pull the trigger. I think he was just working on the trigger part," he said.

Moncada pulled his .45 semi-automatic from his waistband and ducked behind the Fiero he had driven there. He bobbed up and fired twice at Vargas, hitting him once, between the upper lip and the nose. Vargas went down.

Moncada fired at Gonzales who was now running towards a barbed-wire fence, shooting over his shoulder as he ran.

"He was running away, twisting, pointing a gun at me, when I shot him in the ass."

Moncada hit Gonzales as he was diving through the fence. The .45 bullet ranged up through his vital organs and lodged under the skin of his chest. He ran and crawled 160 paces through the brush before he collapsed. He died shortly after he was found by another officer. He was clad only in his socks and underwear as the rest of his clothes had been ripped off him by the barbed-wire.

Moncada and his brother both fired several shots at Juan Vargas, the sniper, one of the bullets wounding him superficially in the side. Meister died on the way to a hospital, while Gonzales and Vincent Vargas were dead at the scene.

In summary, Meister, who was also armed with a .45 semi-automatic, was put out of the fight by two shots from a .22 rimfire. Vincent Vargas was dropped by one shot from a .45, but Gonzales managed to travel 160 yards mortally wounded by another shot from the same gun. Had he been more inclined to fight than run, he might have done a lot of damage before he expired.

Moncada told me he loaded his .45 with three rounds of ball ammunition on top of hollow points. He downed Vargas with one of the ball rounds, but doesn't know if it was a ball or a hollow point that hit Gonzales. He said he loaded the ball ammunition in case he needed the penetration, for example, when shooting through a car door.

Despite the thousands of words that have been written about stopping power, the truth is that the effect a bullet has on a human body in a gunfight is a craps shoot. There are too many variables for accurate prediction. However, most gun experts agree that larger-caliber bullets that expand and stay in the body are more effective than smaller-caliber bullets that go right through the body and three apartment walls.

The shape of the bullet and velocity are important. Modern jacketed or semi-jacketed hollow-point bullets are much more effective than round- or flat-nosed bullets. A hollow-point bullet is designed to expand to more than double its original diameter when it hits flesh, creating a larger wound channel and slowing the bullet down faster. Thus it tends to expend all its energy in the body and not come out the other side.

For reliable expansion, a bullet needs to be going close to one thousand feet per second. A round-nosed bullet, however, tends to go through flesh like a darning needle through an old sock. If it doesn't hit bone, it'll go through the bad guy and two innocent bystanders behind him. And the crook may not even be aware he has been shot until someone asks him about the ketchup stain on his shirt.

Some of the best hollow-point rounds available are Black Hills, Cor-Bon, Federal Hydra-Shok, PMC Starfire, Remington Golden Saber, Speer Gold Dot, and Winchester SXT.

Bullet placement is a variable that can be controlled to some extent. A hit in the upper body or the head is better than a hit in the arm or leg—or a near miss. This is why we train and practice.

The variable over which you have no control is your opponent's will to fight. Most criminals are cowards who tend to run rather than fight—which is why producing a gun is often enough. But you can't count on it.

Many criminals going about their business are doped up to the point where they feel no fear and no pain. In such a state, they are resistant to the damage done by a bullet or even several bullets. Domingo Moncada thinks that Ben Gonzales managed to cover 160 yards when mortally wounded because he was hopped up on cocaine.

Other crooks are just plain tough. They'll fight and die rather than give up—like Michael Platt, the bank robber who killed two FBI agents and wounded five more with a Ruger Mini-14 semi-automatic rifle in Miami in April 1986.

So, what caliber gun should you carry? By now, you have probably reached the inevitable conclusion that there is no simple answer. Many experts feel that a gun of .38/9mm caliber is the minimum that should be considered for self defense. I agree with the principle but not the dogma, on the basis that any gun, even a .22 caliber, is better than no gun.

The weakest of the .38s in general use is the .380 Automatic, but some excellent pistols are made in that caliber. They will fit in a purse or fanny pack as well as a regular holster, offering maximum convenience for the civilian gun carrier, particularly in South Texas or Florida shirt-sleeve weather.

Anything more powerful than the .380 is worth serious consideration as a concealed-carry handgun. For semi-automatics, the 9mm round is the standard military and police round for most of the world. For many years, it was considered, like revolvers in .38 Special caliber, to be under-powered. However, with modern hollow-points, its performance has been improved.

The .40 Smith & Wesson has become very popular with law-enforcement agencies in the U.S. The more powerful 10mm is

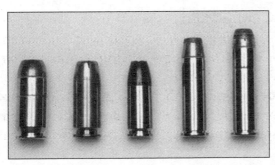

These cartridges with hollow-point bullets are commonly used in handguns for self defense. From the left: .45 ACP, .40 S&W, 9mm, .38 Special +P+, and .357 Magnum.

less popular and more of a handful to shoot, while the old .45 ACP is considered by many to be the ultimate in self-defense rounds. The new .357 SIG apparently performs well in gunfights, according to the Texas Department of Public Safety, which has adopted it.

There may be some occasions when a really small gun is needed due to hot weather or other conditions. Some good semi-automatics in .22 rimfire, .25, or .32 calibers are available, but normally they should be considered only for a backup or second gun.

A multitude of snub-nosed revolvers is available in .38 Special caliber and some in the more-powerful .357 Magnum. More effective yet are the .41 Magnum, .44 Special, and .45 Colt. While these make good home-defense guns, they tend to be large and heavy for concealed carry. The .44 Magnum is too hard to control for all but the experts, and even they would probably do better with a lighter load for defense against anything short of grizzly bears.

SINGLE ACTION OR DOUBLE ACTION?

Single action and double action refer both to how the gun works and the method used to shoot it. Sam Colt's percussion revolvers, invented in the first half of the nineteenth century, could be operated only one way. The shooter had to cock the hammer manually with the thumb before he could fire the shot by pressing the trigger. This is single action—cock the gun, squeeze the trigger. The Colt Peacemaker, the gun most seen in Western films, was a single action. But Sam Colt had competition from other revolver makers.

Robert Adams, a London gunmaker, manufactured a revolver which could be fired in two ways—one could thumb-cock the hammer and press the trigger or use a long pull on the trigger, which raised the hammer and dropped it to fire the shot. This gun was a double action—it could be fired in two different ways. While that is what double action originally meant, it has also come to mean shooting a gun by the long trigger pull, or trigger-cocking method, that raises the hammer and lets it fall.

THE REVOLVER

The single-action revolver is not ideal for self defense. It is slow to fire and slower to reload. However, the gun that helped win the West has its followers. It was probably the best self-defense handgun of the nineteenth century, and well into the twentieth century many western lawmen carried the Colt Single Action Army model. But single-action revolvers are outdated for self defense. Double-action revolvers are more efficient; they can be loaded and fired much more rapidly.

A revolving cylinder that usually contains five or six chambers identifies the revolver. To load the double-action revolver, move the cylinder latch with the thumb of the right hand (for a right-hander). Swing the cylinder to one side, using the first two fingers and thumb of the left hand, palm up. This is

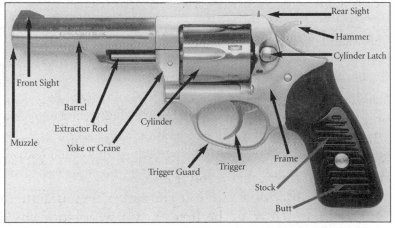

Main parts of a revolver.
Note: This is a Ruger SP101 in .22 caliber, six-shot.

also the way to see if the gun is loaded. Feed the cartridges into the chambers, then close the cylinder using both hands. Do not flip the cylinder into place using one hand, as is sometimes seen in the movies. It will damage the gun. We'll go into this in more detail when we discuss reloading.

Most modern revolvers are referred to as double action, but can be fired single or double action. In self-defense situations, the gun should almost always be shot double action. There will be no time to cock the hammer in most cases. To shoot a revolver double action, you just pull the trigger. The trigger will move about half an inch before the gun fires, and the pull will be much heavier than single action—eight to twelve pounds, instead of three or four. In addition to dropping the hammer, the long pull has to cock the hammer and turn the cylinder, so a new round or cartridge lines up with the barrel under the firing pin. Some pocket-size revolvers, like Smith & Wesson's Centennial, can be fired only double action because the hammer is enclosed so it won't catch on clothing during a draw from a pocket or concealment holster.

When the firing pin, propelled by the hammer, hits the primer in the base of the cartridge, the primer ignites. It sends a flame through the flash hole into the main body of the cartridge case, igniting the powder charge. Pressure builds up in fractions of a second. The only release for this pressure is to push the bullet out of the cartridge case, out of the chamber, and through the barrel. The rifling in the barrel starts the bullet spinning, stabilizing it on its course.

Despite the long and heavy trigger pull, the cylinder can be unloaded in a remarkably short time. For more than fifty years, Ed McGivern of Montana held the record as the fastest double-action revolver shooter. In January 1934, he fired five shots from a .38 Smith & Wesson revolver into a target at fifteen feet. He was clocked at two-fifths of a second and the holes made by the bullets could be covered with a playing card.

Recently, McGivern has had competition from Jerry Miculek. On July 24, 1999, Miculek set three world records with a revolver. He fired six shots from a Smith & Wesson revolver, chambered for .45 ACP, at a single figure target, reloaded, and fired six more shots in 2.99 seconds. Using a special Smith & Wesson .357 Magnum revolver with a cylinder that held eight rounds, he fired all eight shots into one target in one second. Using the same revolver, he then fired two shots on each of four targets in 1.06 seconds. While no one expects the average concealed-handgun-license holder to duplicate such shooting, it does give an indication of how fast an expert can operate a revolver.

In choosing a gun to carry, we have to compromise among convenience, power, and accuracy. Convenience means a small, light gun that is easy to conceal; power is a big, heavy, large-caliber gun with better stopping power; and accuracy is a function of barrel length and the user's ability. Major George

Jerry Miculek shooting the eight-shot Smith & Wesson Performance Center Model 627 that he used in 1999 to set two of his three speed records.

Aylesworth of the Metro Dade Police Department in Florida is convinced that after the novelty has worn off, many of Miami's concealed-carry-license holders leave their guns in their cars or at home. Carrying a gun is both uncomfortable and a big responsibility.

"It's a real pain in the butt," Aylesworth says. "It's heavy, it's bulky, and it jabs you in the side."

The smaller and lighter the gun, the more likely you are to carry it. A .25 in the hand is better than a .45 left at home because it was too big and heavy to wear comfortably. However, the smaller and lighter the gun, the harder it will be to control or to shoot fast and accurately in the medium-to-heavy caliber desirable for self defense.

A revolver for civilian self defense doesn't need a barrel longer than four inches. Longer barrels add weight, are less concealable, and are slightly more accurate. But most gunfights take place at a range of less than fifteen feet, and a civilian is unlikely to be involved in an exchange of shots at thirty or forty yards. Many police departments used to equip their officers with Colts or Smith & Wessons in .38 Special and .357 Magnum calibers. The patrol officers usually carried revolvers with four-inch barrels, while detectives used the two-inch models. There are many of these revolvers in good condition on the second-hand market and they make good carry guns.

If buying new, Smith & Wesson still produces an extensive line of revolvers suitable for self defense. Colt no longer produces its popular Detective Special and has drastically reduced its line of defensive handguns. Taurus is the only other manufacturer producing an abundant range of defensive revolvers for the civilian market. In the 1970s, Taurus and Smith & Wesson were owned by the same international conglomerate. Taurus acquired a reputation for producing cheap reproductions of Smith & Wesson revolvers. While Taurus revolvers tend to cost a little less than Smith & Wessons, the reputation is no longer deserved. Smith & Wesson is still the yardstick by which revolvers are measured, but no one need apologize for carrying a Taurus.

Smith & Wesson's Model 66 in stainless steel comes with a 2.5-inch or a 4-inch barrel in .357 Magnum caliber, which will also shoot .38 Special rounds. Stainless steel is more desirable than blued steel in a carry gun, particularly in a hot or humid climate. The 2.5-inch-barrel version is more versatile and can be carried more easily in a holster, fanny pack, or purse. The Model 65 Ladysmith with a three-inch barrel is also a good choice. These

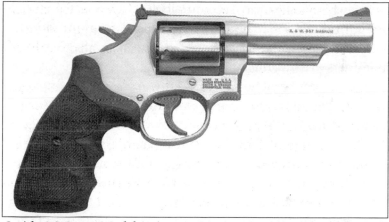

Smith & Wesson Model 66 in .357 Magnum/.38 Special caliber with four-inch barrel.

Smith & Wesson Model 65 LadySmith in .357 Magnum/.38 Special caliber with three-inch barrel.

guns are built on a medium frame and are not feather weights. They tip the scales at about two pounds.

In the smaller, J-frame Smith & Wessons, there are three options: the Model 60 or Chiefs Special, which has an external hammer; the Model 649 or Bodyguard, which has a shrouded hammer; and the Model 640 or Centennial, which has a completely enclosed hammer. The Chiefs Special also comes with a three-inch barrel, which ejects empties more positively than the two-inch-barreled version with its shorter ejector rod. However, it is less easy to fit into a pocket or small purse. These revolvers hold five rounds of .357 Magnum or .38 Special ammunition.

While any of these three models is excellent, the Centennial is my personal favorite. These guns are going to be fired at belly-gun range, double action, so the Centennial with its completely enclosed hammer makes more sense. There is nothing to snag on a pocket, jacket lining, or purse. It's as smooth as a cue ball.

The models mentioned above are stainless steel and weigh about twenty-three ounces. Each has an Airweight counterpart with a steel cylinder, but an aluminum frame and chambered for only the .38 Special cartridge. They weigh about fifteen ounces.

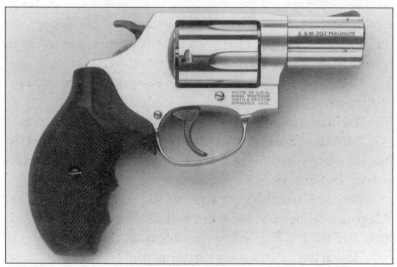

Smith & Wesson Model 60 Chiefs Special in .357 Magnum/ .38 Special caliber with two-inch barrel.

Smith & Wesson Model 640 Centennial in .357 Magnum/
.38 Special caliber with two-inch barrel.

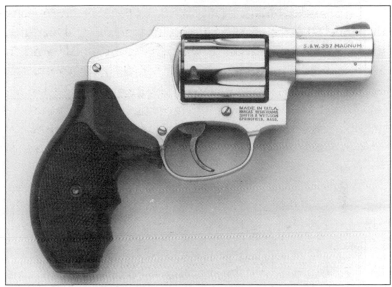

The Smith & Wesson Models 60 and 640 in stainless steel and .357 Magnum caliber compete with Ruger's SP-101. This little five-shot .357 is slightly heavier than the Smith & Wessons and comes in several barrel lengths. For convenience and concealment the two-inch barrel length is the best choice. It is the personal favorite of Robert Butler, U.S. Customs special agent, competition shooter, and firearms instructor.

"This little Ruger will fit in your pocket completely," Butler says.

It'll fit in a fanny pack, a purse, or the console of your car.

"You can have it in your hand in your coat pocket in a situation when you think you might need it. It's much more versatile," Butler says.

With the small S&Ws and the Ruger, buy them in .357 Magnum caliber, but use them with .38 Special +P ammunition and the recoil won't be a problem, Butler advises.

"Using the +P in a stress situation, you'll never feel the gun go off."

Ruger SP-101 in .38 Special caliber.

While Taurus produces competing five-shot revolvers in .38 Special and .357 Magnum calibers, the firm also makes a line of guns with seven-shot cylinders and two-inch barrels.

In a quest to make these small revolvers even lighter and to cater to the civilian concealed-carry market, Smith & Wesson and Taurus have introduced similar models using titanium for some of the components. The Centennial AirLite Ti Model 342 in .38 Special caliber, with aluminum frame and titanium cylinder, tips the scales at twelve ounces. Its Chiefs Special counterpart is the Model 337.

Taurus competes with its Total Titanium revolvers, which have frames and barrel shrouds made of titanium in addition to the cylinders. If these trends continue, eventually I expect we'll see guns that are lighter than the bullets they fire.

The latest line from Smith & Wesson uses small amounts of scandium mixed in with the aluminum from which the frames are made. This results in a stronger frame that can withstand the pressures of a .357 Magnum round in a J-frame revolver that weighs about twelve ounces. Scandium is a rare and expensive metal that has been used in Russian jet fighters, baseball bats, and mountain-bike frames.

Smith & Wesson Model 337 Chiefs Special AirLite Ti
in .38 Special caliber.

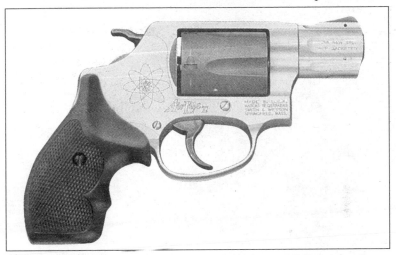

Smith & Wesson produces two of these scandium revolvers in .357 Magnum caliber. The Model 340 AirLite Sc is similar to the Centennial with an enclosed hammer, while the Model 360 AirLite Sc is more like the Chiefs Special with an exposed hammer. If the AirLite Tis are the Centennial and Chief Special on aerobics, these babies are J-frames on steroids.

Smith & Wesson does admit that recoil with these guns is a problem. I have not fired either model, but with full .357 Magnum loads I expect they have more muzzle blast than an elephant gun and are harder to control than a wildcat. But you probably won't notice it in a firefight.

Another offering from Taurus is the CIA (Carry It Anywhere) line. The model numbers are 850 and 650. The Model 850 comes in .38 Special caliber including a Total Titanium version weighing sixteen ounces, while the 650s are in .357 Magnum and are about twenty-four ounces. These are substantially heavier than the lightest offerings from Smith & Wesson, but weight is not the only consideration. Part of the compromise in choosing a revolver is the trade off between carrying weight and recoil. Personally, I have never found my S&W Model 640

Smith & Wesson Model 340 AirLite Sc in .357 Magnum caliber.

in stainless steel to be uncomfortable to carry all day in a belt holster.

Taurus produces a line of short-barreled revolvers in .38 Special and .357 Magnum calibers that hold seven rounds. These are certainly bulkier than the five-shooters, but the extra two rounds available without reloading could be crucial in a gunfight.

For those who want a small revolver in a caliber larger than the ubiquitous .357/.38 Special, Smith & Wesson, Taurus, and Charter Arms all produce comparatively light, short-barreled, five-shot revolvers in .44 Special caliber. Smith & Wesson produces three versions, including the Model 296 Centennial AirLite Ti with a concealed hammer and two-inch barrel weighing nineteen ounces. Taurus makes several configurations of its Model 445 including an UltraLite at twenty ounces with a ported barrel to reduce muzzle flip. Charter Arms manufactures the Bulldog, a five-shot .44 Special that weighs in at twenty-one ounces.

While there are other revolver makers, the manufacturers mentioned in this section are the best, and all have been in business for many years. If you are serious about your safety, always get the best. Your life depends on it.

All Ruger, Smith & Wesson, and Taurus revolvers can be carried and fired as they come out of the box. However, a good gunsmith can improve them. He can smooth the double-action trigger pull, lop off a hammer spur, and round the sharp corners. He can also polish the chambers to make extraction of empty cases easier and bevel the edges of the chamber mouths to make reloading easier. In addition, you can install different stocks that may make the revolver fit your hand more comfortably. Hogue and Pachmayr both make fine stocks to fit most popular revolvers and semi-autos. Nill-Grips, made in Germany by Karl Nill GmbH and popular in Europe, were available in the United States, but now can be ordered directly from the company. Instructions are on its U.S. web site: <http://www.nill-grips.com>.

Taurus Model 850 Total Titanium, CIA (Carry It Anywhere)
five-shot in .38 Special caliber.

Small revolvers with short barrels are often called "snub-bies." Usually they have a barrel about two-inches long and may carry five or six .38 Special or .357 Magnum rounds in the cylinder. They are very popular self-defense guns because they are small and light, but pack a significant punch.

I often carry a Smith & Wesson Model 640 in .357 Magnum caliber under an untucked shirt during the summer in South Texas.

Ed Lovette is also a fan of the short-barreled revolver. He has written a book entitled *The Snubby Revolver,* extolling its virtues. Lovette is a columnist for *Combat Handguns* magazine, a former firearms instructor with the New Mexico Law Enforcement Academy, and a former CIA officer.

"A lot of people are buying it for personal protection, but most of our training is geared towards the pistol or the semi-automatic," Lovette says. "If they choose to use the snubby as their personal defensive weapon, they need to get some training on it, and that's pretty tough to do today."

One trainer who specializes in snubbies is Michael de Bethencourt, the chief trainer for Northeastern Tactical Schools in North Billerica, Massachusetts. He teaches a popular course on short-barreled revolvers to law-enforcement officers and legally armed civilians. He holds courses around the country.

"We've all seen the fellow shooter who loads up his pistol and multiple magazines for range training, then closes out the day by packing away the pistol and magazines, and slipping a J-frame into his pocket. My view is the snub is both a comfortable gun and a convenient gun. If you're going to carry that five-shot only one day of the year, then you should dedicate at least one day a year to learning every fighting trick that snub has to offer," de Bethencourt says.

Lovette's personal recommendation is the Smith & Wesson Centennial, because its hammer is enclosed in the frame. It has no external hammer to catch on clothing when drawing it. Taurus makes a similar model called the CIA, while Ruger has an option on their SP 101 for a dehorned hammer.

"What that makes you do is you always shoot the weapon double action. So now you don't have to remember, should I cock it or not. You'll hear people say: 'Yeah, but if I've got a shot at twenty-five yards, and I can only shoot the head, I want to be able to cock the gun.' That's fine, but my preference is that the gun works one way and that you learn how to use it, because overwhelmingly everything we see suggests that, especially for the private citizen, it's going to be pretty close when it happens."

The SEMI-AUTOMATIC

Unlike the revolver, the semi-automatic pistol or auto-loader has no cylinder. It carries its rounds in a detachable magazine that fits into the butt. The butt is commonly referred to as the grip and the stocks as the grips. The frame contains the trigger and hammer. On top of the frame is the slide, which, as its name suggests, slides back and forth when the gun is fired. The slide also encompasses the barrel, which is a separate entity. The semi-automatic has a single chamber at the rear end of the barrel.

Semi-automatics are built in three styles—those that can be fired only single-action, those that can shoot only double-action, and those that can be shot both ways. For anyone but an expert, the more modern double-action semi-automatics are best for concealed carry.

A typical double-action semi-auto is carried with a round in the chamber and the hammer down. The first time the trigger is pulled, it feels similar to a revolver being fired double-action. The pull is long and heavy. The trigger action has to raise the hammer to full cock before it can snap forward onto the firing pin. The firing pin hits the primer, which ignites the powder charge, pushing the bullet out of the barrel. However,

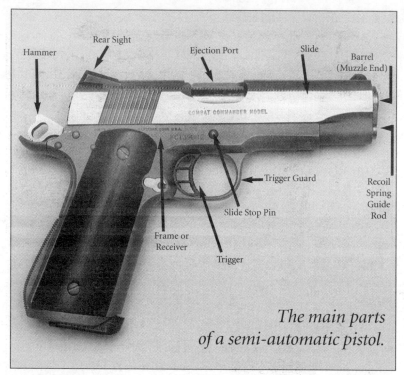

*The main parts
of a semi-automatic pistol.*

some of that recoil power caused by the burning powder is used to push the slide to the rear. The backward movement of the slide drags the empty cartridge case with it, flipping it out through the ejection port. The backward movement of the slide also cocks the hammer. As the slide shunts forward, driven by spring pressure, it strips another round from the top of the magazine and rams it into the chamber. The gun is now cocked and ready to fire. The second and subsequent shots are fired by a lighter, single-action pressure on the trigger.

This double-action mode for the first shot, single-action for subsequent shots, is not ideal and takes some getting used to. The trigger pull on most double-action semi-automatics is nowhere near as sweet and crisp as the double-action pull on a quality revolver.

When police departments across the country started replacing their revolvers with semi-automatics in the 1980s and

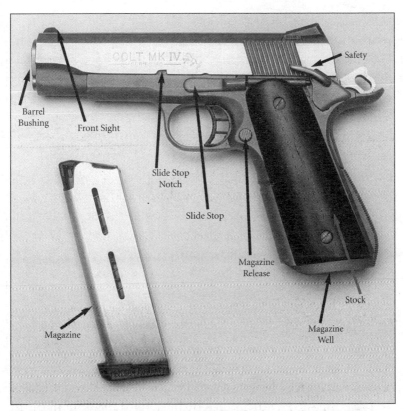

early 1990s, some gunmakers, notably Glock and Smith & Wesson, produced semi-autos that replicated the long double-action trigger pull of the revolver in the automatic. By this time, police departments were teaching their officers to use their double-action revolvers only in the double-action mode.

The double-action-only semi-automatics replicate the double-action pull of the revolver for every shot, not just the first. They do not cock the hammer when the slide slams to the rear. Each shot is fired with the same long-and-heavy trigger pressure. This is not a noticeable problem at three feet, when the shooter is crushing the trigger as fast as possible, expecting at any moment to feel the impact of a would-be carjacker's bullets. However, at twenty or thirty feet, it might be the difference between a disabling hit and a flesh wound.

Perhaps the best solution is the Glock. This space-age semi-automatic has a long half-inch trigger pull reminiscent of the double-action pull on a revolver, but it takes only 5.5 pounds of pressure to fire—barely more than the let-off for a single-action semi-auto. A good double-action pull on a revolver is seldom less than eight pounds. The Glock has no separate safety or decocking lever to complicate things either. Its only obvious safety is a small lever in the face of the trigger which is depressed as the finger squeezes.

Bill McLennan, former chief firearms instructor for the San Antonio Police Department and part-time instructor at Thunder Ranch shooting school, is a fan of the Glock.

"It's simple; it's tough; you can abuse it," McLennan says. "I think it's the best fighting pistol in the world. Next to that, I would probably go with a Smith & Wesson, Beretta, SIG—something of that nature."

Glock manufactures three different size handguns in the most popular self-defense calibers—9 mm, .40 S&W, .357 SIG, and .45 ACP. For example, in 9 mm the Model 17 is a full-size handgun, the Model 19 is a compact, while the Model 26 is a subcompact. All these models have polymer frames that are almost indestructible and come with the same constant double-action-style trigger pull of 5.5 pounds. The only problem with the subcompacts is that the butt is so short that for shooters with medium or large hands the pinkie tends to flap in the breeze.

McLennan still prefers the larger Glocks 19 and 23 and says they are easier to shoot—the longer butt makes them more comfortable—and are almost as easy to conceal. There is the added advantage of extra rounds—the Model 19 magazine holds fifteen rounds of 9mm while the Model 23 packs thirteen rounds of .40.

The Glock is the most popular sidearm of police departments in the United States and of many police agencies worldwide. In the age of terrorism even some British police officers are carrying Glocks.

Glock Model 17 (top) and Model 26, both in 9mm caliber.

Bill Davison and Dean Thompson of Tac Pro Shooting Center like the Glock because they believe it is the most reliable of the handguns available.

Ed Lovette became a believer in Glocks after he attended the scene of a plane crash in the mountains of Peru. A plane carrying a Drug Enforcement Administration agent smashed into the mountains, exploding in flames, and killing everyone on board. Lovette found the agent's Glock some yards from the scene. It was scorched and battered but it still worked.

Glocks are made with a polymer frame and a steel slide. This format has been widely followed in recent years by other handgun manufacturers. Many of the major manufacturers have produced handguns with polymer frames. Browning has its Pro-9 and Pro-40; CZ has its 100B, also in 9mm and 40 S&W; Heckler & Koch has polymer frames on its USP Series; Kahr produces the P and PM Series pistols; Smith & Wesson, its M&P Series; Springfield Armory has introduced the XD in several calibers; Taurus has the Millennium Series; while Walther has

Springfield Armory XD 45 (Extreme Duty in .45 ACP caliber).

the P99. Most of these are full-size auto pistols, though Taurus Millennium and Kahr handguns are compacts that are light and small enough for convenient carry.

Smith & Wesson produces a good selection of compact, concealable semi-automatics with double action on the first shot or double-action-only operation. They range from the 3913 LadySmith in 9mm caliber with its alloy frame, through the .40 caliber semi-autos such as the 4013, to the Model CS45 in .45 ACP. The company also manufactures the Sigma Series with polymer frames in 9mm and .40 calibers.

SIG Sauer turns out some excellent double-action first-shot and double-action-only semi-autos, from the P220 in .45 ACP to the P229 in 9mm. The compact P239 in 9mm, .357 SIG, and .40 S&W calibers is an excellent choice for concealed carry. It weighs between twenty-five and twenty-seven ounces, depending on caliber, and sports a 3.6-inch barrel. For a smaller and lighter semi-auto, SIG makes the P232 in .380

caliber with its Walther-influenced profile. Which brings us to the classic Walther PPK made famous by fictional British secret agent James Bond. Several models are available in calibers from .22, through .32, to .380. Walther also makes the P99, a polymer-frame semi-auto in 9mm and .40 S&W calibers. Ralph Williams used his Walther P99 to good effect when he was attacked in the Dallas/Fort Worth area. (See Chapter 11.) Walthers are distributed in the U.S. by Smith & Wesson.

IMI (Israel Military Industries) is famous for its massive Desert Eagle series of pistols that are about the size and weight of a small howitzer. Desert Eagles in .44 Magnum and .50 AE are not the sort of handguns that lend themselves to concealed carry. However, the company's Baby Desert Eagles, also known as Jerichos, in 9mm, .40 S&W, and .45 ACP are less well-known and imminently concealable. They are particularly comfortable, at least in my hand. IMI products are distributed in the United States by Magnum Research, Inc.

Smith & Wesson Model 3913 LadySmith in 9mm caliber.

SIG Sauer Model P239 in 9mm, .357 SIG, and .40 S&W.

SIG Sauer Model P232 in .380 caliber.

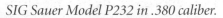

Baby Desert Eagle by IMI in 9mm and .40 S&W.

Beretta makes some fine medium-frame semi-autos in its Cheetah Series in .380 caliber, as well as some holster guns in 9mm. The company also makes a line of vest pocket autos in .22 and .25, if that is your taste.

Heckler & Koch makes the USP Compact line of conventional pistols. The company also makes a unique handgun in 9mm—the P7. This handgun, colloquially known as the "Squeeze Cocker," has a lever on the front of the butt. When the shooter takes a firm grip, the lever is depressed, which cocks the gun. This action is unique, but the P7 fits low in the hand and is very pleasant to shoot when you get used to it.

Another choice might be one of the small double-action-only semi-autos from Kahr. They come in 9mm and .40 S&W caliber. They weigh around twenty-two ounces and have a sweet double-action trigger pull.

There will be times when concealing even one of the current crop of .380s may prove inconvenient. Or occasionally a civilian gun carrier may want to pack a backup gun, maybe in a pocket or an ankle holster. Far better than going down caliber

Kahr MK 40, in .40 S&W caliber.

to a .25 or .22, consider the .32 ACP. For some years now, the small firm of L.W. Seecamp has been making a fine little .32. The Seecamp .32 is not much bigger than a cigarette packet. It was as popular as a millionaire's daughter and as scarce. The manufacturer doesn't appear to want to expand and didn't keep up with demand. As a result, gunstores seldom had any in stock and the occasional Seecamp that turned up at a gun show often sold for several hundred dollars more than its $400 list price. The Seecamp was originally made in .25 caliber. A few years ago, I saw a pair—a .32 and a .25 with the same serial numbers—at a gun show. The asking price for the pair was $2,300.

In response to this unsatisfied demand, North American Arms introduced a copy of the Seecamp called the Guardian. It looks like the Seecamp, feels like the Seecamp, but fortunately is much easier to get. It too is chambered for the .32 ACP, holds six rounds in the magazine, weighs about fourteen ounces, and is double-action only. This brought down the price paid for a Seecamp. The last one I saw at a gun show was priced at $400, while I paid less than $300 for a Guardian. North American

A North American Arms Guardian in .32 caliber.
The .380 is similar in shape, but larger.

Arms has introduced a slightly larger and heavier version of the Guardian in .380 caliber.

Perhaps to take up some of the slack in the demand for the Seecamp, Beretta introduced a larger-caliber version of the Bobcat .25, called the Tomcat, in .32 ACP. At five inches long and about a pound in weight, it fits handily in a jacket or pants pocket. With Winchester Silvertips, the double-action/single-action Tomcat packs an effective punch. Another useful .32 caliber semi-auto is the Kel-Tec P32. This double-action-only pistol is similar in size to the Tomcat. With its polymer frame, the P32 is the lightest of these poodle-shooters, weighing about half a pound. It is also the least expensive. Trading on its popularity, Kel-Tec introduced a .380-caliber version that is only fractionally larger and heavier.

Beretta Model 3032 Tomcat in .32 caliber.

Kel-Tec P32 in .32 caliber.

My favorite 9mm handgun is the CZ-75, which I bought to shoot in practical competition in Canada in the mid-1980s. I recall very few malfunctions. It is an engineering masterpiece and has been widely cloned. At that time, it was almost impossible to get in the U.S. because it was made in Czechoslovakia, then a communist country. The only modification I ever made was to lop off about half of the hammer spur, which had a habit of biting me in the web between my thumb and trigger finger. The CZ-75 has a smooth double-action first shot. However my IPSC (International Practical Shooting Confederation) instructor, Murray Gardner, urged me to carry it "cocked and locked" like a single-action semi-automatic. The thumb safety is in such a good location that I have always carried it that way.

Carrying a single-action semi-auto for self defense is like single-malt Scotch—an acquired taste. After a tune-up from a master pistolsmith, the Colt 1911 Government Model and its clones are thought by many experts to be the best fighting handguns but only for someone who is prepared to spend

CZ-75 in 9mm caliber. Originally made in Czechoslovakia (now the Czech Republic), but much copied.

as much time training as a TV anchorman spends with his hair. They are not for the casual shooter who keeps a gun in his glove box and dusts it off once a year to go to the range.

For decades, the Colt Government Model 1911 in .45 caliber—and in other countries the Browning Hi-Power 9mm—was carried by the military in flap holsters with a full magazine, but no round in the chamber. To fire the pistol, the shooter had to rack the slide (pull it to the rear and let it go) to chamber a round, then pull the trigger. This made for a slow first shot.

Texas Rangers unofficially adopted the Colt Government Model as their sidearm. They liked the capacity of the Colt—seven rounds in the magazine plus one in the chamber—and the caliber—.45 ACP. They also liked the ease and speed of reloading—slap another magazine in, rather than fumble with loose rounds. (This was in the days before speedloaders.) They carried the Government Model cocked and locked—that is with a round in the chamber, the hammer cocked, and the safety on. The shooter had only to slip the safety off during the draw for a very fast first shot—as quick as any double-action revolver or semi-auto. Texas Ranger Charlie Miller tied down the grip

Browning Hi-Power Mark III in 9mm caliber.

safety on his Government Model with a piece of rawhide to deactivate it. Asked if it wasn't dangerous to carry the gun that way, Miller reportedly replied: "It had better be."

Even without the grip safety tied down or pinned, cocked and locked is still considered by some to be a dangerous way to carry a handgun. Worried about liability, many law-enforcement agencies have prohibited their officers from carrying handguns that way. Jack Dean carried a Colt .45 cocked and locked for more than twenty years as a Texas Ranger. But when he retired in 1993 to become U.S. Marshal for the Western District of Texas, the Marshals Service would not permit him to carry a cocked-and-locked pistol.

Thanks to Jeff Cooper, the Colt Government Model 1911 and its clones became very popular among combat-style competition shooters. As a result, many gunsmiths became expert at altering and adding to the former U.S. military sidearm, making it a superb defensive weapon. Not that the competition guns are ideal for carrying. The trigger pull—usually about three pounds—is too light for a defense gun. In a life-threatening situation, it's too easy to fire an accidental shot with a trigger pull that light. A four-pound trigger pull is considered an absolute minimum on a defense gun.

One major problem with the Colt Government Model 1911 for concealed carry by civilians is that it is big and heavy. A better choice is the Colt Commander, which has a shorter barrel than the full-sized Government Model, or the Officers Model, which is smaller yet. Some of these models come with aluminum frames, which make them lighter. I frequently carry a Colt Defender, which is about as small, light, and handy as a .45-caliber semi-automatic is likely to get. It has several of the features that previously would be found only on an after-market Colt—an improved grip safety and a beaver tail. But, remember: the lighter the gun, the more you will feel the recoil.

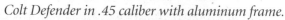

*Colt Mark IV Series 80 Combat Commander in .45 caliber,
customized by San Antonio pistolsmith Greg Ferris.*

Colt Defender in .45 caliber with aluminum frame.

Many clones of various qualities have been made of the old Colt Government Model and its smaller offspring. Some of the better quality ones make good carry guns, including those manufactured by Springfield, Kimber, and Para-Ordnance. There are several smaller gun makers—like Bill Wilson of Wilson Combat and Les Baer—who produce top-of-the-line, single-action semi-autos for those who want the best.

The Browning Hi-Power is a favorite with many professional gun carriers in countries other than the United States, where 9mm is the standard handgun and submachinegun round. I carried one as an officer in the British Army's Royal Military Police in the 1960s. The only way to carry a single-action semi-automatic for self defense is cocked and locked. With the Browning and the Colt Government Model, the thumb safety is located too far aft and requires an extension for easy operation.

Para-Ordnance has introduced a series of semi-autos that are styled like Colt single actions but are double action only. The Para Companion and the Para Carry are the most suitable for carrying concealed. The Para Carry is about the

Kimber Ultra Elite Special Edition .45 ACP.

Para Companion by Para-Ordnance. Looks like a single-action 1911, but it's double-action only.

size of a Colt Defender or Officers Model, while the Companion is somewhat larger. According to Todd Jarrett, handgun champion and professional shooter who represents Para-Ordnance, the trigger pull out of the box is about six pounds. I can attest that the examples at the 2002 SHOT Show in Las Vegas had about the lightest and smoothest double actions I have ever tried.

REVOLVER VERSUS SEMI-AUTOMATIC

Which makes a better self-defense gun, a revolver or a semi-automatic pistol? More words have been written about that question than are written about Republicans and Democrats in an election year. The experts still disagree.

Bill McLennan, president of Small Arms Consultants, has trained thousands of police officers in defensive shooting and tactics. He thinks the double-action revolver is the worst choice possible, particularly for people of small stature without a lot of hand strength, including most women.

"It's extremely hard to shoot in the double-action mode, and that's the only way that you should shoot it. Most of these people go for it because it's got a heavy trigger pull and they think they're not going to have accidents. That's not the way to prevent the accidents. For safety, the finger goes straight [alongside the trigger guard] until I get ready to shoot the gun," McLennan says.

More accidents do happen with semi-automatics than revolvers, but the reason is poor training. If you open the cylinder of a revolver, it is easy to see whether it is loaded or not. In fact, it's easy to see whether a revolver is loaded without opening the cylinder. The shooter can see the rims of the cartridge cases, and the shootee can spot the glistening hollow-point bullets staring unblinking at him from the muzzle end. This may indeed be an advantage if a gun is performing in the deterrent role.

U.S. Customs Agent Robert Butler and top gunsmith Greg Ferris think revolvers are better for the average civilian because of their simplicity of operation. Butler recommends a five-shot revolver such as Smith & Wesson's Chiefs Special or Ruger's SP101 loaded with a light 110- or 120-grain hollow-point bullet in a +P round. It'll fit in a purse, fanny pack, the console of your car, or in a pocket.

"A semi-automatic is too hard to operate in a stress situation," Butler says. "Is there a round in the chamber? Is it off safe? Is it a double-action? Do you have to cock it? Quite often I see students, when I run them through stress courses, who will hit the magazine release by accident and drop the magazine. When a semi-automatic doesn't fire, or if for some reason it doesn't cycle or it jams or something, you have to go through a procedure."

Butler makes a good point. Semi-automatics are more complicated than revolvers. Many people have been killed or wounded because someone took the magazine out of a semi-auto and thought it was unloaded, forgetting there was a round still in the chamber.

"A properly maintained revolver will almost always fire," Butler says. "Very seldom do you have a problem with it. Usually when a revolver doesn't fire it's because you have run out of bullets or you have a misfire."

Butler does acknowledge that you run out of bullets more quickly with a revolver, but he doesn't think that will make much difference.

"It's not like TV. I've been doing this for twenty years, and the most I've ever shot was six rounds out of a gun."

Revolvers usually carry fewer rounds loaded than do semi-autos of similar size and power. The Smith & Wesson Chiefs Special and the Ruger SP101 in .38 Special caliber or .357 Magnum both carry five rounds, compared with the eight rounds of .380 in the Walther PPK/S American and the same in the SIG Sauer P232. And once they are shot dry, revolvers are more difficult to reload. Even with speedloaders that carry five or six rounds ready to be inserted into the cylinder in one movement, they are slower to recharge. An expert can reload a revolver in three or four seconds, while a fresh magazine can be slapped into a semi-automatic in two or three seconds. That extra second is a long time in a gunfight. A trained shooter can get off several aimed shots in that time. Also, the stress of combat tends to coarsen motor skills, making those five or six rounds in a speedloader into extra thumbs as you try to coax them into the chambers.

Paxton Quigley, author and self-defense teacher, arms the women who attend her training seminars with revolvers. They are simpler and safer for beginners to operate and maintain. As she points out in her excellent book, *Armed & Female,* semi-automatics tend to jam if fired without a locked wrist. Racking the slide to load the gun or clear a jam may be difficult for a woman without a strong grip. Even on the range, it may result in frustration and broken nails. In a gunfight, broken nails may be the least of her worries.

Each year handgun manufacturers produce new models. With the explosion of state concealed-carry laws, they are catering to the civilian gun carrier. The models mentioned in this chapter are good, and their makers can be relied upon to produce quality guns. The best way to decide which gun to buy is to shoot as many different models as possible before making a decision. Choose a gun that fits your hand and feels comfortable.

AMMUNITION MAKERS:

Black Hills Ammunition, Inc., P.O. Box 3090, Rapid City,
SD 57709; 605-348-5150; <www.black-hills.com>
Cor-Bon/Glaser, 1311 Industry Road, Sturgis, SD 57785;
605-347-4544; <www.corbon.com>
Federal Premium Ammunition, 900 Ehlen Drive, Anoka,
MN 55303; 763-323-2300; <www.federalpremium.com>
PMC Ammunition, P.O. Box 940878, Houston, TX 77094;
<www.pmcammo.com>
Remington Arms Co., Inc., P.O. Box 700, 870 Remington
Drive, Madison, NC 27025; 800-243-9700;
<www.remington.com>
Speer Ammunition, 2299 Snake River Avenue, Lewiston, ID
83501; 208-746-2351; <www.speer-bullets.com>
Winchester Ammunition, Olin Corp., 427 North Shamrock,
East Alton, IL 62024; 618-258-2365;
<www.winchester.com>

GUNMAKERS:

Les Baer Custom Inc., 29601 34th Ave., Hillsdale, IL 61257;
309-658-2716; <www.lesbaer.com>

Beretta U.S.A. Corp., 17601 Beretta Drive, Accokeek, MD 20607; 301-283-2191; <www.berettausa.com>

Browning Arms Co., One Browning Place, Morgan, UT 84050; 801-876-2711; <www.browning.com>

Charter Arms, 273 Canal Street, Shelton, CT 06484; 203-922-1652; <www.charterfirearms.com>

Colt's Manufacturing Co., Inc., P.O. Box 1868, Hartford, CT 06144; 800-962-2658; <www.colt.com>

CZ-USA, 3327 North Seventh Street, Kansas City, KS 66115; 800-955-4486; <www.czusa.com>

Glock, Inc., 6000 Highlands Pkwy, Smyrna, GA 30082; 770-432-1202; <www.glock.com>

Heckler & Koch Ashburn, 19980 Highland Vista Drive, Suite 190, VA 20147; 703-450-1900; <www.heckler-koch.com>

Kahr Arms, One Blue Hill Plaza, P.O. Box 1518, Pearl River, NY 10965; 845-735-8535; <www.kahr.com>

Kel-Tec CNC Industries, Inc., P.O. Box 236009, Cocoa, FL 32926; 321-631-0068; <www.kel-tec.com>

Kimber Manufacturing. Inc., 2590 Highway 35, Kalispell, MT 59901; 406-758-2222; <www.kimberamerica.com>

Magnum Research, Inc., 7110 University Avenue NE, Minneapolis, MN 55432; 763-574-1868; <www.magnumresearch.com>

North American Arms, 2150 South/950 East, Provo, UT 84606; 801-374-9990; <www.NorthAmericanArms.com>

Para-Ordnance Manufacturing, Inc., 980 Tapscott Road, Toronto, Ont., M1X 1C3, Canada; 416-297-7855; <www.paraord.com>

L.W. Seecamp Co., Inc., 301 Brewster Road, Milford, CT 06460; 203-877-3429; email seecamp@optonline.net.

SIG Sauer, Inc., Corporate Park, Exeter, NH 03833; 603-772-2302; <www.sigsauer.com>

Smith & Wesson, 2100 Roosevelt Ave.,
    Springfield, MA 01104; 800-331-0852;
    <www.smith-wesson.com>
Springfield Armory, 420 West Main St., Geneseo, IL 61254;
    309-944-8994; <www.springfield-armory.com>
Sturm, Ruger & Co., Inc., 1 Lacey Place, Southport, CT
    06890; 203-259-7843;
    <www.ruger-firearms.com>
Taurus International, 16175 NW 49th Avenue, Miami, FL
    33014; 305-624-1115; <www.taurususa.com>
Wilson Combat, P.O. Box 578, Berryville, AR 72616;
    870-545-3618; <www.wilsoncombat.com>

HANDGUN STOCKS:

Hogue Grips, P.O. Box 1138, Paso Robles, CA 93447;
    800-438-4747; <www.getgrip.com>
Karl Nill GmbII, ln Schlattwiesen 3, D-72116 Mossingen,
    Germany; (+49)7473/9434-0; <www.nill-grips.com>
Pachmayr, Lyman-Pachmayr-Trius Products, 475 Smith
    Street, Middleton, CT 06457; 800-225-9626;
    <www.pachmayr.com>

BOOKS:

Lovette, Ed. *The Snubby Revolver: The ECQ, Backup,
    and Concealed Carry Standard.* Boulder, Colo.: Paladin
    Press, 2007.

Chapter Six

HOW TO CARRY:
HOLSTERS AND OTHER ACCESSORIES

Gordon Hale III was a forty-two-year-old master electrician, who spent much of his working day in the less savory industrial areas of Dallas and Fort Worth. He worked for a welding company and drove his pickup from job site to job site, repairing electric welding machines. He carried a lot of expensive electronic gear, including a radio to keep in touch with his company.

"He's the perfect kind of person to be carrying a concealed handgun," said his lawyer, Vincent Perini. "At least if you agree with the concealed-handgun law, he's a perfect example of the kind of person who needs it."

In October 1995 Hale took the concealed-handgun course at the Academy for Firearms Training in Grand Prairie, the Dallas suburb where he lives. The concealed-handgun license became effective in Texas on January 1, 1996. Hale received his license early in January and started carrying his gun, a .40-caliber Beretta Centurion Model 96D, in his pickup.

"It's like buying insurance: you hope you never use it," said his father, Gordon Hale Jr.

About 10 a.m. on February 21, Hale was driving his Dodge pickup westbound on Mockingbird Lane. He had made one call in the Mockingbird area and was returning to Kennedy Air and Gas where he worked. Despite its rustic name, Mockingbird Lane is a major urban thoroughfare with three traffic lanes in each direction. Hale was driving in the middle lane when his pickup and a van on his right brushed mirrors.

A neat, fastidious man, Hale took a lot of pride in his truck. The Dodge and the equipment it carried were his livelihood.

*It was a Beretta Centurion like this that Gordon Hale III,
carried on the seat of his pickup.*

The mirror was on the passenger side, and he couldn't see what
damage it had sustained. He sped up and tried to wave the driver of the van to the side of the roadway so they could check
for damage.

The driver ignored him. After several attempts to get the
van driver to pull over, Hale dropped back behind the van. He
wrote down the license number of the vehicle and the courtesy phone number. His sister worked at an office about half
a mile further on, so he decided to go to her office, check for
damage, and call the police from there.

Hale stopped in heavy traffic for a red light a few blocks before
he reached his sister's office. The van now pulled in behind him.
The van driver, a muscular Pacific Islander weighing about two
hundred fifty pounds, approached Hale's open window.

As Hale's father recounted it, the conversation went somewhat as follows:

"What did you want?" asked the driver of the van, 33-year-old Kenny Tavai.

"Well, you hit my vehicle, and I wanted to stop and look, see what was the trouble," replied Hale.

"I didn't hit you; you hit me," Tavai argued.

"No, you hit me."

"No, you hit me."

"Well, regardless, I'm going up to my sister's place of business, and I'm going to check my truck out and call the police," Hale said.

"Don't do that."

Tavai had moved from Seattle about two weeks before and apparently had a Texas identification card, but no Texas driver's license. He was a trainee driver for Marquis Messengers, Inc., and had been on the job for two days.

"I've got to do that," Hale said. "If there's damage, I've got to do it to collect the insurance."

"Don't do that," Tavai repeated.

"Yeah, I'm going to do that."

Tavai reached in through the open pickup window and grabbed Hale by the neck of his polo shirt and started smashing him with his fist. The first blow hit Hale on the side of the face and head. Hale was strapped in by his seat belt and boxed in by traffic in front of him, on each side of him, and by Tavai's van behind him. He couldn't go anywhere, so he tried to duck below the window as Tavai continued to pound his head with a large fist.

"Stop, stop," Hale yelled, but Tavai kept hitting him.

According to lawyer Perini, the only thing witnesses differed on was how many times Tavai hit Hale.

Hale had his semi-automatic in its usual place, on the seat of his pickup under his jacket. He reached back behind him and grabbed the gun.

Still begging Tavai to stop beating him, Hale brought the gun up towards his assailant's chest and fired once. The

Winchester SXT jacketed hollow-point bullet hit Tavai under the heart.

The man stopped hitting him immediately, walked back to his van, and leaned up against it. He slid down the side of the van until he was sitting on the ground. Tavai was rushed by ambulance to Parkland Memorial Hospital, where he died several hours later.

When the police arrived at the scene, they arrested Hale and charged him with murder. He suffered some eye damage from the pounding he took and needed glasses prescribed. He was later no-billed by a grand jury.

Former Texas State Representative Ray Allen taught the training course that Hale attended at the Academy for Firearms Training as a prerequisite to getting his license. Allen says he doesn't give advice about where or how people should carry their handguns. However, he does tell his students that, if they choose to carry their guns on the front seats of their vehicles, they have to be concealed.

"We certainly tell people that it's legal to carry a firearm on the seat of your car, if it's concealed with a newspaper or a jacket or something of that nature. But we didn't give Gordon, for example, any advice about carrying it in his car," Allen says.

Wearing a gun is a hassle, especially for a civilian. The gun is heavy—at least a pound and often more than two. Then you must conceal it and keep it concealed, not just in front of the mirror, but when you work or go to the store or collect the kids from school. When you first start wearing a concealed handgun, you feel about as self-conscious as a teenage girl wearing her first mini-skirt. Depending on where you are wearing your gun, you learn to bend your knees instead of your back when you pick things up, you avoid stretching to reach something on a high shelf with your gun hand, and you sit down and get up carefully.

Finally, there are all the places a civilian, by law, is not supposed to carry a gun. For example, in Texas the current law states that a concealed handgun cannot be carried into a school, college, university, bar, court, racetrack, sporting event, polling place, prison, or the secured area of an airport. In addition, many businesses, local government buildings, and public transit authorities display signs prohibiting the carrying of firearms. Employers may also prohibit you from carrying a gun while you are working. In some states the validity of many such prohibitions has yet to be tested in court; however, it seems that many business owners and public officials do not trust their customers, employees, and voters to defend themselves. They would apparently prefer them to die passively like Post Office supervisors rather than resist violent criminals.

These restrictions have helped make carrying a concealed weapon so inconvenient that, after the newness has worn off, many license holders will leave their guns at home or in their cars. As firearms instructor Bill McLennan puts it: "Most people will quit doing it, because you have to want to do this. If you're a gun carrier, you're not going to be concerned about how big the gun is. You know that it's a pain, and you'll put up with it."

If a concealed-handgun-license holder finds that wearing a gun is too much trouble, and decides to keep it in the car, favorite places are in the glove box, in the console between the front seats, and under the front seat. The glove box is particularly difficult for the driver to reach without making a production out of it.

Gordon Hale's father is convinced that if his son had kept his gun in the glove box of his pickup, he would not have been able to reach it when he needed it. Leaving it on the passenger seat under a jacket or newspaper worked well for Hale. It's invisible but instantly accessible. However, if the driver stops suddenly, the gun can slide off the seat onto the floor. This is what happened to one of the FBI agents during the shoot-out with bank robbers in Miami in 1986. He spent most of the gunfight scrabbling on the floor, trying to find his gun. McLennan says his father carried a gun in a holster attached to the front of his seat. He covered it with a towel when he got out of the car. You might want to rig up something similar.

However, wearing a gun is still the best way of ensuring that you'll have it when you need it. A man will most often wear his handgun in a holster, while a woman will usually carry hers in her purse.

Hip Holsters

Many people spend several hundred dollars buying a gun, then buy a generic holster for it at a gun show for $20. This, as McLennan says, is like buying a Cadillac and equipping it with the cheapest tires you can find. A good gun requires a good holster, a good belt (if it is a belt holster), and a good pouch to carry a spare magazine or extra rounds.

Alessi, Bianchi, DeSantis, Galco, Kramer, Don Hume, Mitch Rosen, Safariland, and Milt Sparks all build great holsters. There are other holster makers who are probably just as good, but you won't go wrong with these. Most of them, such as Bianchi and Galco holsters, can be bought off the rack in good gun stores, while others, like Sparks, make them to order. The best holsters are still made of leather, though in recent years established companies such as Safariland and others such as Blade-Tech and Fobus have been turning out holsters made of space age plastics. They are generally well molded to fit the guns they are designed for and cost a lot less than a good leather holster. Steer clear of woven nylon holsters.

The ultimate in concealment for a full-sized gun is an inside-the-waistband holster such as Milt Sparks's Summer Special, the Galco Royal Guard, or Bianchi's Pistol Pocket. All these holsters have leather loops that snap around the belt, rather than spring clips to hold them in place. My own favorite of this type is Milt Sparks's Executive Companion, which is almost rectangular in shape. This breaks up the outline of the gun and is comfortable.

Fobus Standard Holster, made of injection molded plastic.

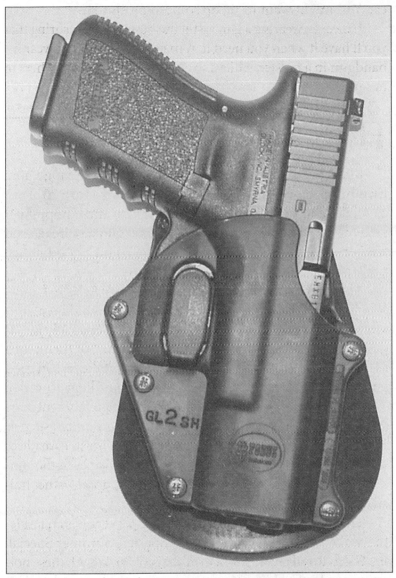

The best of the inside-the-waistband holsters have a strip of steel sewn around the top to keep them from collapsing like an empty grocery bag when the gun is drawn. If the holster keeps its shape, the gun can be reholstered easily with one

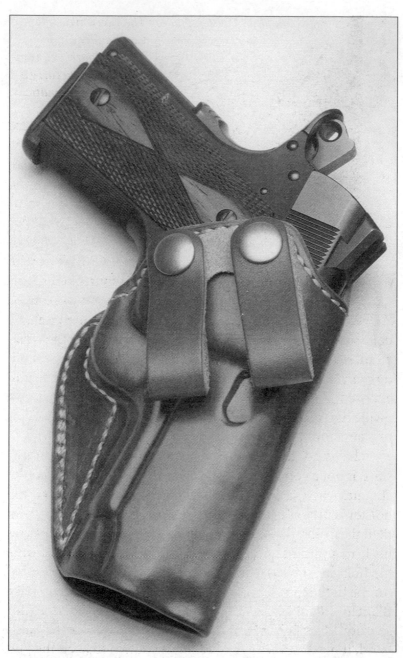

Milt Sparks's Heritage Model is an updated version of his classic inside-the-waistband Summer Special.

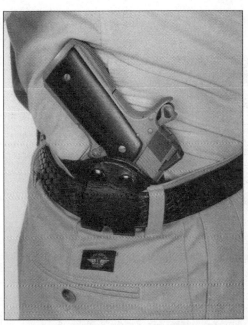

The Executive Companion by Milt Sparks is a comfortable way to carry a large semi-automatic.

hand. A medium-sized handgun can be well hidden in an inside-the-waistband holster under a short jacket, vest, or loose shirt. In summer weather, a T-shirt with an unbuttoned sports shirt over it will conceal an inside-the-pants rig quite successfully. The gun is less likely to be seen inside the waistband, say on a windy day or if the shooter is running, than if it is carried in a regular belt holster. The only part of the gun exposed is the butt. Remember that when wearing a gun inside the waistband, you'll need to buy your clothes a size or two larger in the waist or eat less.

That is not to say a hip holster, worn outside the pants or skirt, is not a good carry. It is excellent in temperate or cooler climates where jackets are heavier and bulkier. The regular hip holster is probably a fraction of a second faster to draw from than the inside-the-waistband type. The gun carrier is also less likely to grab a handful of shirt along with his weapon. Some hip holsters, such as Galco's Avenger, have tension screws that can be tightened to hold the gun more securely. Others, like Bianchi's Shadow, have a thumb-break retaining strap for security. As a general rule, if the holster is worn outside the waistband, it needs some type of retaining device to keep the gun from falling out when you bend over or run or during other physical exertion. Pressure between the belt and the body

Galco's Avenger. Note the tension screw and how the leather is molded to the gun.

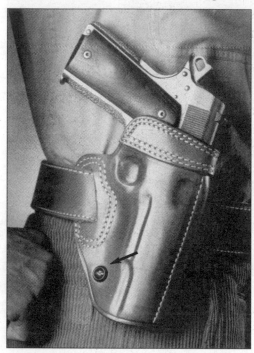

should keep the gun in an inside-the-waistband rig.

The outside-the-waistband hip holster has several configurations. The more traditional type of hip holster has a belt slot on the back of the scabbard, like the Bianchi Thumbsnap models. The pancake holster, like the Shadow, has belt slots fore and aft of the gun, which gives the leather a more circular, or pancake, outline. Other holsters, such as Galco's Speed Paddle, have a curved plastic plate, or paddle, that fits inside the pants, while the leather scabbard hugs the outside over the belt. Some holsters are held to the belt by a spring clip. This makes them easy to remove for putting gun and holster in the glove box when you have to enter a building, like a courthouse, where guns are prohibited. A cheap holster of this type can come off the belt with the gun during the draw, but this won't happen with those from reputable makers.

Then there are the bikinis of holsters, like Milt Sparks's and Galco's Yaqui Slide. They cover the trigger guard, the adjacent part of the slide, and little else. While some police officers are fond of these, they are not the best solution for the civilian. If you are going to carry your gun in a holster on the outside of your belt, choose a model that covers the barrel completely. If you inadvertently expose the bottom of your holster for a moment, an observer may be unsure that what he has seen actually contains a gun. It might contain a camera, a cell phone, or a pair of glasses. However, he will be in little doubt if he can see the black snout of your .45 auto protruding from beneath your shirt.

The secret of carrying a large gun in a belt holster is to use a heavy belt at least 1.25 inches wide. A thin trouser belt will cut into your midriff like a cheese wire and won't anchor the holster well.

Of course, there is also Special Agent Robert Butler's solution, which is mentioned at the beginning of Chapter 4: just tuck a small revolver like the Ruger SP-101 or a J-frame Smith & Wesson into your belt, butt forward, behind your hip. It is not a position for a fast draw, but it is comfortable, relatively secure, and convenient. Instead

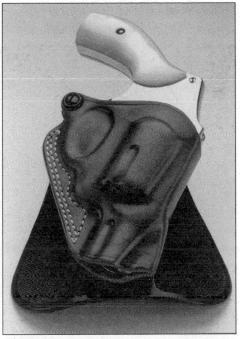

Galco's Speed Paddle. The plastic paddle fits inside the waistband.

Galco's Yaqui Slide.

of the hassle of putting on and taking off a holster, it takes only a moment to tuck the gun into your waistband.

OTHER HOLSTERS

While hip holsters seem to be the favorite way of carrying, there are many other ways of packing a handgun concealed.

Cross-draw belt holsters do not conceal well under a jacket, because they need to ride close to the navel for easy access. They are easier for an attacker to grab, as the butt of the gun is pointing towards him. A hip-draw requires a vertical motion of hand and gun; a cross draw is a horizontal movement and is more difficult to stop on target. However, a cross-draw is very fast to get into action. The weak hand pulls the coat to one side while the strong hand scoops out the gun and sweeps it onto the target.

Some of the same problems are evident with a holster riding on the belt in the appendix position. It may be faster than a hip holster, but does not conceal the gun as well unless it is worn under the shirt. But the main thing I have against the appendix position is that the gun is carried with the muzzle pointing at the family jewels. One of the men who competes at a local shooting club carries a .45 cocked and locked in an appendix holster. I can never look at where his muzzle is pointing without inwardly cringing.

A small-of-the-back holster, such as Galco's appropriately named S.O.B., is a better option for a belt holster that will conceal a small revolver or semi-automatic comfortably. With these holsters, don't bend over at the waist or the gun will "print" against the back of your shirt or jacket. If you have to pick something up, squat down, bending your knees rather than your back. This is the best way to pick up a heavy load anyway, as it is less likely to damage your back.

Galco's S.O.B. worn in the center of the back.

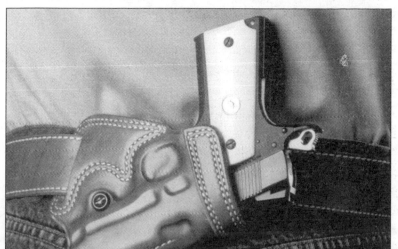

A belly band is an under-the-shirt belt with a built-in holster. It is usually a nylon and elastic belt about four-inches wide worn just above the waist. Some are equipped with a shoulder strap which helps carry the weight of the gun. In addition to a built-in holster, the Bianchi Ranger belly band has pockets for such essentials as money. The belly band can be worn so the gun can be reached through the shirt front in a cross draw. The draw is easier if one shirt button is left undone or if the shirt has snaps instead of buttons. The gun can be worn for a cross or side draw under a shirt that is not tucked in. One hand pulls up the shirt while the other goes for the gun.

Shoulder holsters are another option. I used not to like the type that hold the barrel of the gun horizontal and pointing aft. The Miami Classic by Galco, worn by actor Don Johnson in the "Miami Vice" television series, is one of these. Detectives in one small South Texas city have a penchant for this type of holster, and in the police station often wear their rigs without jackets. Walking behind one of these officers and looking

Galco's Miami Classic positions the barrel of the gun horizontally—disconcerting for the person walking behind you.

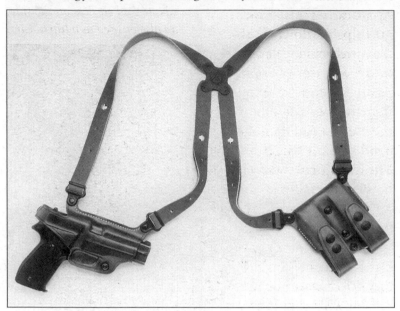

down the barrel of a .45 semi-automatic is downright disconcerting. It also breaks one of Jeff Cooper's safety rules: "Do not point your gun at anything you are not willing to destroy."

I decided to give the Miami Classic a try after noticing that it was the favorite holster of Bill Davison, owner of Tac Pro Shooting Center and a former professional bodyguard. The big advantage of the shoulder holster is that it makes the gun much more accessible when you are in a vehicle with your seatbelt on. Try getting to your gun when it's in a hip holster under a jacket and a seat belt. It's not easy. I found that from a standing start, a hip holster was much faster than a shoulder rig. However, under Bill Davison's instruction I found that I could fold my arms across my chest with my right hand on the gun under my jacket and my thumb on the thumb snap. That made for a speedy draw. If you do a lot of driving, a shoulder rig may be the best holster for you.

Other shoulder rigs, such as Bianchi's Special Agent, carry a small handgun upside down with the barrel pointing directly into the wearer's armpit. Again, I tend to recoil from these styles as I think they send a bad message about muzzle direction. The traditional shoulder holster, which carries the gun muzzle pointing down, is more acceptable.

Bianchi's Special Agent points the muzzle into your armpit. Note the belt slots on the side; it can also be used as a hip holster.

While many people like shoulder holsters, and they do conceal a gun reasonably well, many ranges and shooting schools ban them, along with crossdraw rigs, because of the possibility of endangering your neighbor on the firing line with your gun muzzle during the draw.

Ankle holsters are not too practical except for perhaps carrying a backup weapon. Most good holster manufacturers make them. Alessi makes a good one. However, a gun on your ankle is going to be inconvenient during any vigorous physical activity such as running or fighting. It is a poor choice for a main gun, but acceptable for a secondary weapon, though it does tend to become exposed when the wearer sits down. Be sure to practice getting it into action. This sort of rig cannot be worn with tight pants.

Moving up the leg from the ankle, we come to the thigh holster. Women can carry a small revolver or semi-automatic on the inside of the thigh. The holster is mounted on a wide garter that holds it to the thigh. A garter belt around the lady's waist with a suspender leading down to the holster provides additional support. No lace in sight on the Galco example, but drawing the weapon certainly requires some provocative skirt hiking.

For those people carrying a very small weapon, whether it be as main armament or backup, there is the pocket holster.

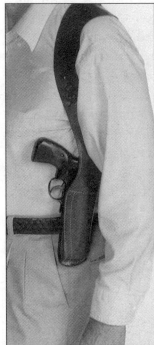

It beats just shoving the gun into a pocket. A holster holds the gun in a constant position in the pocket so the butt is easily accessible. It will make the outline of the gun less obvious and reduces pocket wear. If you anticipate trouble, you can have your gun in your hand before exposing it. A hand in your pocket is natural and nonthreatening. You can even shoot through the pocket if you are attacked at close range.

A traditional shoulder holster by Bianchi holds a large revolver with the muzzle pointing down. The bottom of the holster attaches to the belt.

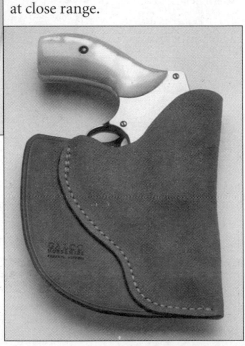

Galco's Front Pocket model.

Fanny Packs, Purses, and Other Carrys

When choosing a fanny pack, purse, or briefcase in which to carry a concealed handgun, get one designed to do the job with a built-in holster in a separate compartment.

Fanny packs are popular, particularly in the Sun Belt, as a casual alternative to a purse for a woman and to serve the same function for a man. They carry keys, coins, wallet, street map, sunscreen, almost anything you might carry in your pants or jacket. And they will carry a bigger gun than anything that fits in a pocket. Some fanny packs have a tag or loop which can be pulled diagonally downward with the left hand (for a right-handed shooter), unzipping two sides of the gun compartment and exposing the butt of the gun to the right hand. Fanny packs, such as Galco's Escort, also have compartments and pouches for anything else you wish to carry. I know one FBI agent who carries his service semi-automatic in a fanny pack, at least during the summer months.

My .32-caliber North American Arms Guardian came in a DeSantis nylon pouch that clipped to the belt. It was opened

Galco's Escort, a fanny pack with built-in holster.

with a zipper, while inside was an elastic holster for the gun and room for an extra magazine. It was about the size to contain a personal digital assistant or PDA such as a Palm Pilot.

Gun carriers can also conceal their weapons in women's purses and briefcases that have special compartments built into them. A purse with a shoulder strap and an opening in the side closed by Velcro allows a woman to slide her hand onto the gun without drawing it. The disadvantage of packing a concealed handgun in a separate container rather than wearing it is

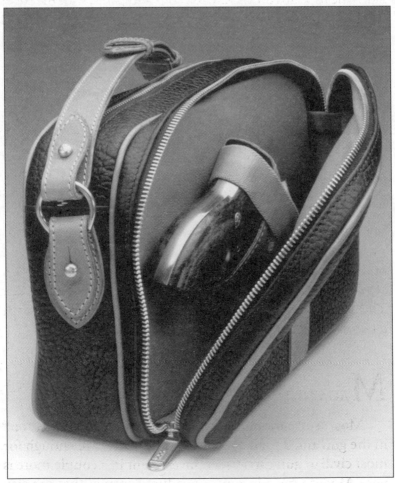

Galco's Le Nouveau Sac purse with built-in holster.

that purses and briefcases can be detached from their owners. They can be snatched, or they can just be left and forgotten in a store, car, or office. This is also true of daytimers and books with built-in compartments to conceal a handgun.

   With more and more people carrying concealed firearms, manufacturers are coming out with new and innovative ways of packing them. One such innovation is the Pager Pal. This is a pancake-shaped flap of leather with a holster sewn to one side and a dummy pager clipped to the top on the other side. The flap slips down between shirt and pants, with the pager hooking over the top of the belt. A real pager or a compact cell phone can be substituted for the dummy. For a right-handed shooter, it is best to position the holster between the left hip and the belt buckle for a cross draw. To draw the gun, grasp the pager with your left hand and pull upwards until the butt of the gun appears above the belt. You can then draw the gun with the right hand. The Pager Pal comes in three sizes—large, small, and mini. The mini fits the Seecamp or the .32-caliber North American Arms Guardian. The small Pager Pal will take some of the small semi-automatics such as the Colt Mustang .380 and the Beretta Tomcat .32. The manufacturer claims the larger holster will carry some of the double-column-magazine semi-automatics like the Glock 23 and the CZ-75. However, concealment and comfort would obviously be better with the single-stack semi-autos like the SIG Sauer P232 or the Colt Officers Model. The larger model will also carry a small-frame revolver with a two-inch barrel such as the Smith & Wesson 640.

MAGAZINES AND SPEEDLOADERS

   Most semi-automatics are sold with two magazines: one in the gun and a spare. While two magazines are enough for most civilian gun carriers, an investment in a couple more is wise. Modern metallurgy has produced springs that can stay

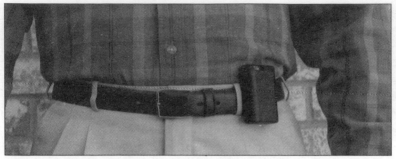

Pager Pal fits on the belt like a standard pager.

Pulling up on the pager exposes the gun butt.

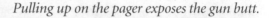

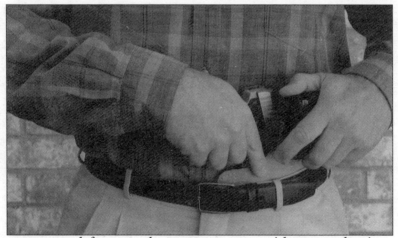

compressed for months or even years without weakening. However, I like to keep two magazines full and two empty, and change them around from time to time. Damaged magazines are often a cause of malfunctions in semi-automatics, so having spares on hand is a good policy. You will also need the extra magazines if your practice routine extends to any form of combat competition. More on that later.

In addition, you will want some means of carrying your spare magazines. Depending on the number of rounds your gun carries and your own personal preference, you will need a single- or double-magazine pouch. Most of these fit on the belt, either outside or inside the pants. Some shoulder holsters have double-mag pouches built into the harness on the opposite side from the holster to balance the weight of the gun.

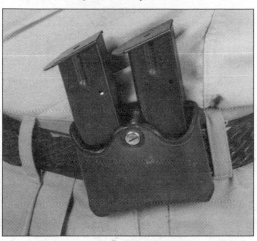

A magazine pouch like this can hold an extra thirty rounds of 9mm ammunition.

The fastest reload is from a single or double pouch mounted on the belt on the side where the left hand drops naturally to it. The magazines are positioned vertically, bullets pointed forward, and the pouch does not have a flap and a snap. A good mag pouch should have enough friction to keep the magazine from falling out, but should allow an easy draw with the left hand.

A single pouch with a flap and snap might be mistaken for a sheath for a folding knife, which could be an advantage. Flaps also protect the jacket lining from the sharp corners of some double-column magazines. Most of the good holster manufacturers also make magazine carriers to match their holsters.

The fastest way to reload a revolver is with a speedloader, like those made by HKS Products. However, unlike a spare magazine, which is flat and easy to conceal, a speedloader is bulky and awkward to pack. Speedloaders can be mounted on the belt in pouches or on the harness of a shoulder holster. The pouches will require flaps and snaps. Several holster makers provide much flatter pouches

An HKS speedloader containing five rounds of .38 Special ammunition, ready to insert into a revolver cylinder.

A Bianchi Speed Strip.

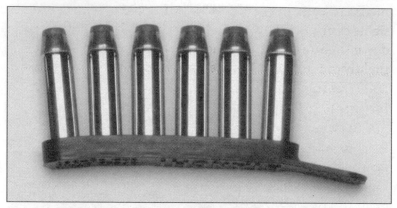

carrying five or six loose rounds that dump into the hand when opened. Galco has a belt-slide cartridge pouch holding six rounds in pairs, which makes for easier reloading, particularly in the dark. No fumbling with six rounds in your hand, trying to get them into the cylinder without dropping some. Another solution is the Bianchi Speed Strip which holds six rounds to a flexible plastic band. The rounds can be loaded two at a time and fit flatly into a pocket or pouch.

OTHER ACCESSORIES

Having shelled out for gun, leather, and ammunition, you need two more pieces of gear before you head for the range—eye and ear protection. If you need glasses to see the sights, and the lenses are made of plastic rather than glass, your prescription glasses will probably do fine. However, if you are in your forties or fifties, you may have noticed a deterioration in your eyesight. When I was in my early fifties, I found I could not get a crisp sight picture. My solution was to get a special pair of trifocals. Most trifocals have the bottom of the lenses for reading, the middle for intermediate distance, and the top for long distance. I had the optometrist change the prescription so the long distance parts of the lenses were in the middle and the intermediate distance segments were at the top. The intermediate segments were made so I could see my handgun sights clearly at arm's length. Now when I shoot, I tilt my head down slightly until I have the sights in focus and the target is slightly out of focus. This seems to be compatible with a normal Weaver or isosceles stance. (See Chapter 8.) These glasses take a little getting used to, but I wear them all the time. The optometrist told me he occasionally ordered similar prescriptions for pilots who have to see dials and gauges above and below the plane's windshield.

If you have 20:20 eyesight, you will need to get a pair of glasses to ensure you keep your eagle-like vision. Most ranges require shooters to wear eye protection, and even if they don't, you should. It is as wise as wearing a seat belt in a car. It won't guarantee to save your eyesight from a lead shaving or an exploding barrel, but it sure improves the odds. AO Safety Peltor and Silencio are among the companies that make non-prescription shooting glasses. Get the wrap-around kind that provide protection from the side. This is protection that ordinary prescription glasses do not provide. However, if you are in a line of shooters on the range, it is possible that a lead shaving or other flying debris may come at you from the side. This is particularly likely if your neighbor is shooting a revolver with a cylinder slightly out of alignment.

I started shooting handguns in the 1950s, when ear protection meant rolling up gun-cleaning patches and sticking them in your ears. It wasn't until the late-1960s, when I was taking a physical examination, that I realized I had lost some of my hearing. Nowadays we are much more conscious of the importance of protecting our hearing. Remember, once lost, it doesn't return.

Foam ear plugs, such as those used by workers around noisy machinery, provide the simplest and cheapest ear protection. These are much better than nothing, but not as good as a pair of ear muffs of the type made by AO Safety Peltor or Silencio for $20 and up. You can also buy hearing protectors, such as Pro-Ears made by RidgeLine, Inc., that electronically filter out the noise of gunfire but allow voices through for normal conversation, and even enhance low-level sound. These are a lot more expensive, often more than $200.

I have a pair made by Peltor that have worked flawlessly for several years. The only maintenance required is to change the AAA batteries from time to time. Companies such as Electronic Shooters Protection and Walker's Game Ear, Inc. make custom molded electronic hearing protectors that fit inside the ear. They allow speech and normal sounds to get through clearly but block the sounds of gun shots. However, they are expensive, with analog systems costing several hundred dollars and digital protectors up to $2,000.

HOLSTER MAKERS:

Alessi Holster, Inc., 2465 Niagara Falls Boulevard, Amherst, NY 14228; 716-691-5615; <www.alessileather.com> (at press time, this website was temporarily down due to back orders)

Bianchi International, Inc., 27969 Jefferson Avenue, Temecula, CA 92590; 909-676-5621; <www.bianchi-intl.com>

Blade-Tech Industries, 2506 104th Street Court South, Lakewood, WA 98499; 253-581-4347; <www.blade-tech.com>

DeSantis Holster and Leather Goods Co., 431 Bayview Avenue, Amityville, NY 11701; 800-424-1236; <www.desantisholster.com>

Fobus Holsters, 76 Vincent Circle, Ivyland, PA 18974; 267-803-1002; <www.fobusholster.com>

Galco International Ltd., Aztec Business Park, 2019 West
Quail Ave., Phoenix, AZ 85027; 623-434-7070;
<www.usgalco.com>
Don Hume Leathergoods, Inc., 500 26th Street Northwest,
Miami, OK 74354; 800-331-2686; <www.donhume.com>
Kramer Handgun Leather, P.O. Box 112154, Tacoma, WA
98411; 253-564-6652; <www.kramerleather.com>
Pager Pal, 200 West Pleasantview, Hurst, TX 76054;
800-561-1603; <www.pagerpal.com>
Mitch Rosen Extraordinary Gunleather, 300 Bedford Street,
Manchester, NH 03101; 603-647-2971;
<www.mitchrosen.com>
Safariland Ltd., Inc., 3120 East Mission Blvd., Ontario, CA
91761; 909-923-7300; <www.safariland.com>
Milt Sparks Holsters Inc., 605 East 44th St. #2, Boise, ID
83714; 208-377-5577; <www.miltsparks.com>

OTHER ACCESSORIES.

AO Safety Peltor, 5457 West 79th Street, Indianapolis, IN
46268; 800-327-3431; <www.aosafety.com>
Electronic Shooters Protection, 15290 Gadsden Court,
Brighton, CO 80603; 800-767-7791;
<www.espamerica.com>
HKS Products, 7841 Foundation Drive, Florence, KY 41042;
800-354-9814; <www.hksspeedloaders.com>
Ridgeline, Inc., 101 Ridgeline Drive, Westcliff, CO 81252;
719-783-4161; www.Pro-Ears.com
Silencio, 56 Coney Island Drive, Sparks, NV 89431;
800-648-1812; <www.silencio.com>
Walker's Game Ear, Inc., 531 Gilbert Street, Media, PA
19063; 610-565-8952; <www.walkersgameear.com>

Chapter Seven

AVOIDING ACCIDENTS: SAFETY AND HANDLING

It was late in the afternoon of January 19, 2004, in Miami, Florida. Travis Jenkins had just picked up his three-year-old son from Shummarah Murphy, the child's mother, and was driving him home, when he stopped to visit a family friend. It was a fatal decision.

Jenkins, twenty-six, was driving a rented Chrysler Pacifica sports-utility vehicle because his own car was being repaired. Travis Jr., who had turned three just sixteen days before, was not strapped into a child-safety seat.

According to a report in the *Miami Herald*, Jenkins had been mugged during the previous year in a drugstore parking lot. As a result he had acquired a Florida concealed-weapons license. His gun, a 9mm Taurus semi-automatic, was loaded with eight rounds in the magazine and one in the chamber, according to homicide Detective Kevin Ruggiero.

Jenkins stopped the vehicle on the street in front of the house where the friend lived. A woman in her late fifties, she had apparently had once dated Jenkins' uncle. When Jenkins got out of the vehicle, his gun, which was in a nylon holster without a safety strap, was lying on the hump between the front seats, according to Ruggiero.

Jenkins and the woman were talking on her porch in sight of the vehicle, but left the toddler for at least five minutes, the detective estimated.

"The lady realizes the car is running," said Ruggiero. "She told him to go turn the car off. He goes back to turn the car off. He goes back to the porch to talk, all the while leaving the gun on the floorboards."

Suddenly, they heard a shot. Jenkins raced back to the Chrysler to find his son had got the gun out of the holster and shot himself in the forehead. Jenkins drove the child straight to Jackson Memorial Hospital where doctors tried to save his life. The little boy was pronounced dead the following day.

Ruggiero said, after checking with the medical examiners, measuring the child's arms, and noting the stippling pattern from the gun left on the toddler's face, he realized how the accident had happened. "The trigger would have had to have been pulled with his thumb, so I guess he was trying to look down the barrel."

After the investigation, Jenkins was arrested and charged with culpable negligence, a felony. "It's the toughest arrest I've ever made," the detective said. "And seeing the autopsy of a baby isn't pleasant."

The accident that cut short the life of Travis Jenkins Jr. is a cautionary tale for anyone who carries a gun. It takes only a few moments for tragedy to strike. Whether his father spends time in prison or not, it is unlikely he will ever forgive himself for those moments of inattention.

To put these tragedies in perspective, there has been a steady decline during the 1990s in the accidental deaths of children under the age of fifteen caused by firearms, according to the National Center for Health Statistics. In 1999 eighty-eight children died as a result of such accidents with firearms, compared with 227 in 1990. And children were far more likely to die in accidents with other causes. In 1999 children under fifteen were twenty-nine times more likely to die in motor-vehicle accidents; ten times more likely to drown; eight times more likely to suffocate; and six times more likely to die in fires. That said, any child's untimely death is a tragedy, whether from a bullet or from playing with matches.

A gun is a tool, but like a car, it can do a lot of damage if not used correctly and treated with respect. It doesn't have a brain, and it can't shoot by itself. Therefore, in order for it to shoot, somebody has to pull the trigger, either by accident or on purpose. As firing a gun by accident can lead to serious injury or death, it is important to follow a few simple safety rules. As with most rules, there are exceptional circumstances where they may not apply, and I'll point out some of them. But the following rules are a good guide.

Safety Rules

1. TREAT ALL GUNS AS THOUGH THEY ARE LOADED.

Guns that people thought were unloaded are the biggest cause of firearms accidents. If you handle all guns as though they are loaded, you will avoid such tragedies. All defensive weapons should be kept loaded and handy all the time. An empty gun or a loaded gun kept locked in a gun safe is not going to be much good if you need it in a hurry. However, you must ensure that children and other adults do not have access to your guns. Their handling habits may not be as safe as yours.

2. ALWAYS KEEP THE MUZZLE POINTED IN A SAFE DIRECTION, UNLESS YOU ARE DEFENDING YOURSELF OR OTHERS.

A "safe direction" is defined as where, if the gun goes off, there will be no injury to man, woman, or beast, and there will be minimum property damage. That means keeping the gun pointed at the backstop when on the range and never at people or pets. Pointing the gun at the ground is usually fairly safe, but remember that walls, particularly apartment walls, are not necessarily bullet-proof. Always practice drawing your weapon and dry firing it in a safe direction. If you shoot enough, you will almost certainly fire a shot by accident at some time, but if you always keep the muzzle pointed in a safe direction, the result will do no more than scare the daylights out of you. In a shooting career that has spanned more than forty years and

many thousands of rounds, I have fired three shots accidentally. Two of the bullets went harmlessly down range. The third
one left a .45-caliber hole in a window before burying itself in
a stream bank outside. I had been practicing the draw and thought
the gun was unloaded. In each case, the gun was pointed in a
relatively safe direction, and in each case I was shocked and embarrassed. Develop safe habits. Don't let the muzzle cover anybody
when you are turning or passing a gun to someone. I have seen
people who should know better wave their guns around,
casually covering anyone in range when they "know" the gun
is "empty." As mentioned above, it's only "empty" guns that kill
people by accident. I make no apology for repeating it. Imagine
that your gun has a wooden dowel or a laser beam extending
from the barrel. This way you will always be conscious of
where the muzzle is pointing.

3. **KEEP YOUR FINGER OUTSIDE THE TRIGGER GUARD
    UNTIL YOU ARE ON TARGET AND HAVE DECIDED
    TO SHOOT.**
    When I was taught to shoot in International Practical
Shooting Confederation (IPSC) competition in Canada, we were
taught to load, reload, unload, and move from one firing
position to another with the trigger finger lying alongside
the trigger guard—not on the trigger; not inside the trigger guard.
I remember being ordered off the range during the first string
of a match for reloading with my finger on the trigger. I
learned, and now whenever I pick up a gun, my finger automatically slips into position alongside the trigger guard. It touches
the trigger only when I am pointing the gun at the target and
have decided to shoot. A couple of decades ago, most holsters
carried the gun with the trigger exposed. Today almost all of
them enclose the trigger so that a finger cannot reach the
trigger until the gun is drawn. Get into the habit of putting your
finger on the trigger only when the gun is coming onto the target and you intend to fire.

4. BE SURE OF WHAT YOUR BULLET WILL HIT BEFORE YOU SHOOT.

Trick shooter Ed McGivern fired thousands of rounds at aerial targets in rural Montana in the 1930s. I shot tin cans thrown into the air in the wilds of British Columbia in the late-1960s. However, there are fewer and fewer places where this can be done safely anymore. It is certainly unsafe to shoot into the air in a city, but bullets fired horizontally can also take unexpected paths if they hit a hard surface and ricochet. Remember skipping flat rocks across a pond as a kid? Bullets can also bounce off water in the same way. Imagine being attacked by a mugger in front of the polished granite wall of a bank. You fire three shots at your assailant. Two hit, but the third strikes the granite wall and ricochets, striking a woman standing half a block away at a bus stop. Now, you almost certainly face a civil suit. If your life was in danger, your decision to shoot was right. It's better to be alive and facing a civil suit than dead and facing the undertaker. But it is something to think about. Remember, most apartment walls and many house exterior walls are not bullet-proof. I have seen many houses with stucco walls that have been shot up by gang members armed with rifles, shotguns, and handguns. Many of the bullets went in through the front wall, pierced several interior sheetrock walls, and went out through the back wall. Invariably the reason I was there was because someone, often a sleeping child, had been wounded or killed, and I was reporting the story.

5. EVERY TIME YOU PICK UP A GUN, CHECK TO DETERMINE WHETHER IT IS LOADED.

With a revolver, open the cylinder to see it is unloaded. With a semi-automatic, first remove the magazine, then lock the slide back, and look into the chamber. I also recommend looking into the slot from which you removed the magazine, in case a round is somehow stuck there and could be kicked into the chamber when the slide goes forward. Gunsmith and firearms instructor Greg Ferris thinks making shooters chamber conscious is as important as making them muzzle conscious. He instructs them to check "what is in the chamber, what can be in the chamber, what has access to the chamber." If someone checks to see the gun is unloaded, then hands it to you, don't accept that it is unloaded. Go through the procedure of checking for yourself. When you are on the range and you are going forward to check the targets, lay the gun down on the bench, unloaded, with the cylinder open or with the magazine removed and the slide back. Lay a semi-automatic down with the ejection port uppermost so people can see at a glance that the gun is safe. After having checked for yourself that a gun is unloaded, still treat it as though it were loaded.

6. DON'T HAND A LOADED GUN TO ANYONE, AND DON'T ACCEPT ONE.

Handguns should be passed from one person to another unloaded and with the muzzle pointed in a safe direction. This is a good general rule, but I can think of some exceptions to it. A range officer or instructor may accept, very carefully, a loaded gun from a student on the range if it jams or malfunctions and the student can't clear it. The muzzle should be pointed down range with fingers outside the trigger guard during such transactions. In another situation, you might want to hand a second gun to an ally during a gunfight. Otherwise, always transfer guns unloaded.

7. DON'T DRINK OR USE DRUGS BEFORE OR DURING SHOOTING.

There are exceptions to this, but it is a good rule of thumb. Some people are permanently on drugs for medicinal purposes. There is no reason they can't enjoy shooting. Just don't shoot or handle firearms when you are impaired. People tend to do stupid things after a few drinks, so if you know you are going to a party or function where you are going to drink, leave your gun at home.

8. DON'T LEAVE A LOADED GUN UNATTENDED.
An exception, of course, is when the gun is left in a strategic position for self defense at home, at the office, or in the car. People, particularly children, are curious, and a gun is a curiosity for many. You cannot assume that others have been schooled in gun safety. If someone shoots himself, herself, or someone else with a gun you have left unattended, you might avoid being charged criminally, but you will certainly be paying legal fees and jury judgments limited only by your ability to pay.

9. ALWAYS USE EYE AND EAR PROTECTION WHEN SHOOTING.
The only exception to this is when you have to use your gun in self defense. Otherwise wear shooting glasses or prescription glasses with lenses made of plastic. As I mentioned earlier, I lost some of my hearing by shooting without adequate ear protection.

10. AVOID LEAD CONTAMINATION.
Ingestion of lead particles through the skin or by eating with unwashed hands after a session at the range can cause brain damage. (This may be why seasoned shooters are often regarded as weird by non-shooters.) Wash your hands and face after leaving the range and certainly before eating anything. Shower and wash your clothes as soon as conveniently possible. Also wash your hands and face after cleaning your gun. You will minimize your exposure to lead contamination by shooting bullets totally jacketed in copper. Most major bullet manufacturers now make bullets of this type. However, be sure to observe the precautions mentioned above, as other people may be shooting

less-safe bullets, and most primers contain heavy metals that can do you harm with prolonged exposure.

TRAFFIC STOP SAFETY

Most of us don't often meet a police officer face-to-face. Frequently when we do, it is because we have become the subject of a traffic stop. This is usually not a pleasant experience for the person being stopped. He or she is usually accused of committing some infraction of the traffic laws, and the experience is probably going to be costly in terms of a ticket. It is not a particularly pleasant experience for the police officer either. Many police officers are killed during traffic stops. So they are often edgy when they stop us. How should you, the driver, behave during a traffic stop if you are a concealed-handgun-license holder and have a gun?

Different law-enforcement organizations have different ways of handling a traffic stop, and you might do well to ask your local police what their procedure is and how you should respond. Most police officers will approach you in your car, though some will order you to get out of the car.

When you pull onto the shoulder of the highway or to the side of the street and stop, you should immediately lower your window then put your hands on the steering wheel in the 10 minutes to 2 o'clock position. This enables you to talk to the officer when he approaches you and reassures him because he can see your hands. Officers are trained to watch hands, because only by the movement of your hands are you likely to be a threat. Never at any time during the stop make any quick or furtive movements with your hands. If you are stopped after dark, turn on your dome light so the officer can see you more easily.

As soon as the officer speaks to you, tell him you have a concealed-handgun license and tell him where the gun is. If you have the license but are not carrying a gun, it is good policy to tell him so, because in most states when he checks your driver's license he will know that you have a concealed-handgun license. It is better that he hear it from you rather than find it out on his own. In Texas the law stipulates that if a police officer asks you for any type of identification, you are required to give him your concealed-handgun license without specifically being asked for it. In many other states you are required to show the license only if asked for it. However, it is good policy to volunteer your license wherever you are.

Once you have told the officer that you have a license and are armed, follow his instructions and cooperate with him as fully as possible. Police have the right to disarm you if they feel you are a threat. Some officers realize that if you have a license you are more likely than the average person to be law-abiding. Some officers, particularly the young and inexperienced, may view you as a threat. Whatever the attitude of the officer, be polite and pleasant.

CHILDREN AND GUNS

In November 1997 a Denver television station—KMGH TV—and the Lakewood Police Department conducted an experiment to see how children would behave when they found guns. Lakewood is a suburb of Denver only a few miles from Littleton and Columbine High School. The experiment resulted in a three-part series on Channel 7 news called "Kids and Guns."

Two empty and disabled handguns were hidden in a room among various toys. Groups of two or three children were put into the room and left to explore, while their parents watched what they did from another room by means of two hidden cameras.

Two mothers watched in horror when their sons picked up the guns, pointed them around, and repeatedly pulled the triggers. Both mothers said they hated guns and would not let their children have anything to do with them. They acknowledged afterwards that perhaps their children needed to be taught about guns.

Reporter Susan Parks said that several other children had picked up or touched the guns. One mother seemed certain her son and his cousins would play with the guns. But they were the only kids who did the right thing. They didn't touch them and went to tell an adult. These kids knew about guns because family members had been jailed for using them, said Parks.

Charlie Johnston, Lakewood's police chief at the time, is a strong advocate of formal gun-safety training for children. He said parents need to be aware that most children, at one time or another, will come across a gun.

"Shying away from it, avoiding it, or feeling that: 'I don't want guns in my house,' isn't going to work, because kids will find guns," Johnston said.

He urged parents to expose their children to guns and allow them to shoot under supervision as part of an education process. This will alleviate their natural curiosity. In the experiment, the kids who had been exposed to guns behaved more responsibly when they found the guns, he added.

Johnston said it is also important to show children the damage guns can do. This can be effectively demonstrated by shooting a plastic jug full of water, a watermelon, or a large, unopened can of tomato juice.

"We teach our kids very young that when a stove is hot, it burns you," Johnston said. "We say, 'Here, this is what "hot" means, and if you touch it it will hurt you.' We need to do the same kinds of things with kids as it applies to guns."

If you intend to keep a gun or guns ready for self defense, and you have children in your house, you have a problem. You have two conflicting priorities. You don't want your children or their friends to hurt themselves or anyone else with your guns.

But a gun kept for self defense must be kept easily accessible and ready to shoot at a moment's notice.

Some states, such as Texas and Connecticut, have passed laws making it a criminal offense to allow an unsupervised child access to a firearm. In Connecticut, the owner of a firearm is guilty of a Class D felony if a child gains access to his gun and causes injury or death with it to himself or another person. In Texas, the same offense is a Class A misdemeanor.

Just allowing a child (younger than seventeen) unsupervised access to a "readily dischargeable" firearm is a Class C misdemeanor in Texas. However, regardless of whether it is against the law, you don't want the sense of guilt that comes with a tragedy caused by your negligence. Even if the guilt doesn't get you, the civil lawsuit will likely bankrupt you.

What to do? One leaflet, called "Dealing with Gun Violence" and funded by the U.S. Department of Justice, makes the following recommendation: "If you choose to own firearms—handguns, rifles, or shotguns—make sure they are unloaded and securely stored. Invest in trigger locks, gun cabinets with a lock, or pistol lock boxes. Lock up ammunition separately."

This advice is given in a leaflet, sponsored with your tax money, that urges you to consider removing guns from your home altogether and urging your children "to organize against handgun violence," by which they probably mean gun ownership.

However, the advice is fairly standard: lock up your guns unloaded in one place and the ammunition somewhere else. Even Smith & Wesson in its instruction manual states: "Store your unloaded firearm and ammunition separately and in places inaccessible to children and unauthorized persons." Good advice when referring to a hunting handgun or a target pistol. Also good advice to absolve the manufacturer from lawsuits. But not very practical for keeping a gun to save your life.

How do you keep a self-defense gun instantly ready for action, but safe with children around? Police officers face this quandary every day. They have some advantages over most civilians. When they go to work, the gun goes with them. This is not always true with civilian gun carriers. Their employers may forbid them to take a gun to work. Most states with recently enacted concealed-carry laws allow employers to prohibit their employees from carrying a gun at work. This is true for all non-law-enforcement employees of the federal government. Many people don't want to leave expensive guns in their cars in unsecured parking lots, so they will leave the guns at home.

Another difference between law-enforcement officers and civilians is that in many jurisdictions the officers are required to carry their guns even when off duty. However, they may carry a smaller, lighter, and more convenient gun off duty rather than their service weapon. This means they may leave their service handgun at home when not at work and their off-duty gun at home when they are working. They still have the same problem. What to do with the gun when it's not readily at hand?

I asked several police officers how they cope. Most of them say they make it clear to their children that their guns are off limits and that they haven't had any problems.

"Being on the police department, I've seen so much tragedy," homicide Sergeant Ray Torres said. Torres comes from a police family. His father was a police officer, and so was his older brother. When I spoke to him, he had a girl aged seven and a four-year-old boy.

But it was an accident involving his brother's wife and his infant niece that has made him particularly conscious of gun safety. It happened in the early-1970s at a holiday home on Lake LBJ when his brother's family was visiting. Someone had carelessly left a revolver on the counter where a five-year-old boy got hold of it. The gun went off and the bullet hit Torres' sister-in-law's wedding ring—on her hand—while she was holding her baby daughter. The bullet shattered and pieces of it embedded themselves in her arm. Luckily, Torres' niece was unhurt.

Torres said his daughter had recently asked him to teach her to shoot, and his son, who was not as disciplined, had started showing an interest in his father's gun. Torres was thinking of buying a gun safe or a trigger lock.

Homicide Detective Jimmy Holguin kept his gun locked in his briefcase most of the time when he was at home. At night, he kept the case unlocked and close to the bed. "I want the gun accessible," he said.

Holguin had two boys, aged seven and nine. He let them hold the unloaded gun to satisfy their curiosity. On one occasion, a teacher at school told one of the boys that guns were bad. This confused the boy, who worried that his father must be bad if he carried a gun.

"I had to tell him: guns aren't bad; they are dangerous," Holguin said.

Sergeant Joery Smittick and his wife had three daughters, ages twelve, eight, and two. When he arrived home from work, Smittick took off his issue .40-caliber Glock semi-automatic.

"First thing I do, I unload it, take out the clip, take the round out of the chamber, and separate them," he said.

Smittick kept his gun and another handgun high up on the dresser in his bedroom. He kept the gun and the loaded magazine near each another. If he needed the gun in a hurry, all he had to do was grab it from the dresser, slap in the magazine, and rack the slide.

"It's still convenient enough that I could get to it and use it if I have to," Smittick said.

His daughters showed little interest in the gun, though Smittick was thinking of taking the oldest to the range sometime soon. "I told my daughters they don't touch that thing; I put the fear of God into them," he said.

That may work well for girls, but boys tend to develop a fascination for guns when they see them on television.

As former Lakewood Police Chief Charlie Johnston says, the best way to make a child safe around firearms is education. When they start reacting to firearms they see on television, it is probably time to teach them about guns and take them to the range. Former police officer and firearms instructor Greg Ferris says you have to satisfy their curiosity and show them what a firearm can do.

Ferris recalls as a youngster watching a television series about the FBI. He remembers totally unrealistic stunts such as seeing "Efraim Zimbalist Jr. go into the old FBI crouch, fire from the hip with a two-inch revolver .38 Special, hit a car doing sixty miles an hour; it flips over, explodes, and burns everybody inside to death."

"They do things on TV with firearms that firearms cannot do," Ferris says. "Children need to understand that what they see on TV is not the way it works in the real world."

Children must be taught a healthy respect for guns, but they must be given a realistic appraisal of what a firearm is capable of. Teach them how to operate the gun, then take them out to the range and let them shoot it. This might be a good time to show them something spectacular by firing at a plastic jug full of water or a watermelon.

You will get one of two reactions. The child will be afraid of the gun and not want to shoot anymore or, like Ferris' son, he'll call for more ammunition. Either way, you have satisfied the curiosity. If he or she enjoys it, you can have some good parent/child time together whenever you go to the range. If they hate it, don't make them shoot. Come back in several years and try again. Ferris took his son to the range the first time before he was four. As a parent, it is up to you to decide at what age to take a child shooting.

Sergeant Tim Rupp, who is a strong advocate of education in making children and guns compatible, makes this suggestion when taking a child to the range: load the gun with only one round. That way, once the gun is fired, it is no longer in a dangerous condition.

The National Rifle Association has taught firearm safety to millions of children through its Eddie Eagle Gun Safety Program. It teaches children who find a gun to "STOP! Don't

Touch; Leave the Area. Tell an Adult." The program is taught in schools and has wide support from law enforcement, with many officers involved in teaching it. The NRA estimates the program has been taught to more than twelve million kids. Certainly due in part to the Eddie Eagle program, accidental firearms deaths among children are half what they were in the mid-1970s.

The best way to keep your self-defense handgun out of the hands of children and others is to wear it. If you are not wearing it and it isn't under your direct control, it must be made secure. Putting the gun on a high shelf will keep it out of reach of a toddler, but not a teen. Hiding it is also not a good approach. Remember when you were a kid? Was there anywhere in your house that you hadn't explored? I remember, as a kid, finding a .32 semi-automatic and ammunition in a drawer in my father's dressing room.

One of the best ways to secure your guns is to invest in a gun safe. They are big and heavy—five- or six-feet tall, two- or three-feet wide, and eighteen-inches to two-feet deep. They will store rifles and shotguns vertically in racks and have shelves for handguns, ammunition, and anything else of value you may have from cameras to jewelry. They vary in price and sophistication from about $700 to several thousand. In addition to being child- and burglar-resistant, some safes are advertised as being fire-resistant. Get a safe that you can bolt to the floor, as burglars sometimes arrive equipped with a dolly and wheel out the unopened safe to a waiting vehicle. When robbers walked into a retired pawnbroker's house, they tied up his wife and wheeled the safe, containing twenty-six firearms, as well as nineteen Rolex watches and other valuables, out on a dolly they had brought with them. Heritage and Liberty specialize in making full-size gun safes. Other safes bear the names of well-known firearms' manufacturers, such as Browning and Winchester, and may or may not be made by the company concerned. Browning makes its own safes, while Winchester safes are made by Granite Security Products, Inc.

A gun safe is a good place to keep guns that are not likely to be used for self defense—your hunting rifles; your shotguns for doves, ducks, or sporting clays; and your hunting and competition handguns. Whether you keep them loaded in the safe or unloaded and whether you have another safe or hiding place for the ammunition is up to you. Personally, I am of the Elmer Keith school and believe that all guns should be kept loaded all the time. If everybody in the house knows this, there should be no accidents. A gun safe is also a good place to keep self-defense handguns that you leave at home when you go out.

If you can't afford a gun safe or if it is too bulky, several companies make handgun security chests that are much smaller and usually quicker to get into if you need the gun in a hurry. GunVault, Inc., makes two security chests for handguns, one with one shelf and another with two. The smaller one costs about $170 and measures 12 x 8 x 5 inches. The advantage of the GunVault is that it has a combination lock that can be operated by feel in total darkness. The top side has finger grooves with raised buttons in them. By placing your fingers in the grooves,

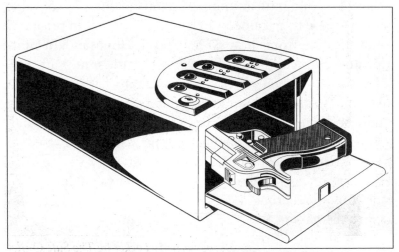

GunVault's MiniVault keeps a handgun secure at home or office.

you can operate the buttons in sequence and the door pops open. It is not as fast as a holster, as its advertising claims, but it's a lot faster than a regular gun safe and much more secure than leaving your gun in a closet.

Another option is a small safe that will fit into a house wall between two studs, such as those made by The Safe Outlet. Their Riflelocker is five-feet tall and will take several long guns as well

The Home Security Locker by The Safe Outlet holds two handguns and other valuables.

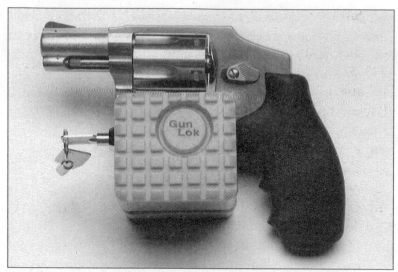

A trigger lock.

A bore lock.

as handguns. The Home Security Locker and Gunlocker are smaller and are designed to hold handguns.

There are various other ways to disable a handgun, but they are not particularly suited to your defensive handgun. A trigger lock, as its name suggests, is a clamp that goes over the trigger guard enclosing the trigger and locking into place. It requires a key to unlock it, but the price, about $10, is very reasonable. Another way of disabling a handgun is a bore lock. It is a rod that goes down the barrel of a revolver or semi-automatic and locks into place. Bore locks cost about $20.

GUN SAFES AND HANDGUN SECURITY CHESTS

Browning, One Browning Place, Morgan, UT 84050; 800-333-3288; <www.browning.com>
GunVault, Inc., 23910 North 19th Avenue, Suite 48, Phoenix, AZ 85027; 800-622-4903; <www.gunvault.com>
Granite Security Products, Inc., 4801 Esco Drive, Fort Worth, TX 76140; 817-561-9095; <www.granitesafe.com>
Hcritage Safe Company, P.O. Box 349, Grace, ID 83241; 800-515-7233; <www.heritagesafe.com>
Liberty Safe and Security Products, 1199 West Utah Avenue, Payson, UT 84651; 800-247-5625; <www.libertysafe.com>
The Safe Outlet, 28822 Front Street, #201, Temecula, CA 92590; 951-506-6899; <www.gunlocker.com>

FIREARMS SAFETY PROGRAM

Eddie Eagle Gun Safety Program, National Rifle Association, 11250 Waples Mill Road, Fairfax, VA 22030; 800-672-3888; <www.nra.org>

Chapter Eight

BASIC HANDGUN SHOOTING: WATCH THE FRONT SIGHT

Sergeant Robert Butler was irritated. The officer who had used the patrol car before him had not replaced the field contact cards he had used.

At the time, Butler was a patrol sergeant with the Terrell Hills Police Department. Prior to joining that department, he had been a Highway Patrol trooper with the Texas Department of Public Safety. Butler had just stopped a man he suspected was a burglar, and he wanted to fill out a field contact card.

Terrell Hills is an upscale suburb of San Antonio with its own small police department. It is mostly residential, containing some of the most expensive homes in the area—attractive targets for a burglar.

It was a November night about 9:30 and foggy. Butler had the man's identification and had patted him down lightly before rummaging through the patrol car looking for a contact card. He checked above the sun visor where they should have been; he checked in the glove box, but found nothing.

"It took my mind off him. I was mad at the officer who used the car with me 'cause he always used things, and he never put cards back and so forth, left things dirty," Butler recalled.

As he got back out of the patrol car, the suspect fired at him six or seven times with a .25 caliber Raven semi-automatic, then ran off up the street. Initially Butler didn't realize he had been hit. A car drove by about the time the suspect opened fire, and Butler thought someone had tossed some firecrackers from the car.

It wasn't until he tasted blood that he realized he was wounded. One bullet had gone in under his right arm, through his right lung, bounced off his breast bone, and through the other lung. Both lungs were bleeding and were starting to collapse.

"Then it dawned on me that I might die," Butler said.

He was building a house at the time, and the thought flashed through his mind that he might never see it completed. As quickly as the thought came, it went, and he was back on the street with a felon running from him.

"I thought, I'm going to kill him. I figured if I was going to die, he was going with me."

Butler called in on the radio, telling the dispatcher he had been shot. He walked around the car and saw the suspect running along the street, going uphill.

"I drew out my service revolver, and I shot at him four times and missed him."

Suddenly Butler felt the presence of the man who had taught him how to shoot, Texas Department of Public Safety range instructor Reeves Jungkind, there beside him.

"I remember him talking to me, standing to my left, telling me, sight alignment, trigger control, basic functions, basic things that you use for shooting a handgun. And so on the fifth round, I pulled the hammer back, in single action, and aimed for his shoulders, slowly squeezed it off, and I shot him.

"The bullet went in the back of the left knee, almost dead center and blew out his whole kneecap. They said all that was left was ends of the bone. And I shot another round into where he fell. I remember he yelled at me, 'Stop shooting, you've shot me.' And I remember thinking, tough."

Automatically, Butler reloaded his revolver before calling again for the ambulance.

"What you are trained to do is what will come out," he says.

When they measured off the distance, Butler had hit the fleeing man at a range of 422 feet. Butler recovered to become a U.S. Customs agent, a competitive shooter, and a firearms instructor in his own right.

Bill McLennan, former chief firearms instructor for the San Antonio Police Department, says seven officers over the years have told him that they heard his voice while they were involved in a gunfight. They heard him saying: "Step to cover and shoot," or "Slow down and shoot accurately."

Most firearms instructors agree that in a gunfight you will do what you have been trained to do. That is why it is so important to develop good shooting habits. Two of the most important aspects of shooting a handgun accurately are the things Butler heard Reeves Jungkind say to him on that November night. They are sight alignment and trigger control.

If you grew up on a diet of film and television Westerns, you will have a quite false impression of what a gunfight is all about. Remember the scenes where the good guy in the white hat downed the bad guy with one shot fired from the hip at fifty yards; or the hero shot the gun out of someone's hand? While action scenes became somewhat more realistic as time went on, we were still subjected to Clint Eastwood wasting several gunmen at twenty yards or more, fanning a single action Colt from the hip. All this is fantasy.

The old-time gunfighters of the West, such as Wild Bill Hickok and Wyatt Earp, raised their guns to eye level and used the sights, or at least squinted along the barrels, of their six-shooters.

In his biography of Hickok, Joseph G. Rosa quotes Luther North, whose brother Frank North used to shoot at targets with Wild Bill near Cheyenne, Wyoming. Luther later wrote that Hickok "was very deliberate and took careful aim closing his left eye. If he could shoot from the hip he never did it there."

As one old gunfighter put it, "Speed's fine, but accuracy is final."

That lesson is still being taught to police officers and civilians at shooting schools such as Gunsite and Thunder Ranch.

"Watch your sights; watch your sights," is the refrain hammered home to students by the staff throughout the Thunder Ranch Defensive Handgun I course.

One film that gets the shooting right is John Wayne's final movie, *The Shootist.* Wayne plays a gunfighter who is dying of cancer. Rather than die in agony of natural causes, he arranges to meet three antagonists in a saloon. All the shooting in the film is done with revolvers held at arm's length and at eye level.

The only difference between the old gunfighters' style of shooting and modern technique is that we have learned that getting both hands on the gun provides a more stable mount. However, there is still a place for unsighted fire with the gun held close to the body below eye level—but only at very close range.

Frank Hamer, the Texas Ranger captain who tracked down and killed Bonnie Parker and Clyde Barrow, was eminently qualified to speak on the subject.

According to his biographers, H. Gordon Frost and John H. Jenkins, Hamer was said to have killed fifty-three men in close to one hundred gunfights.

He believed that shooting from the hip was a lot of nonsense invented by Hollywood. Hamer once told a friend he shot from the hip only when his assailant was so close "I didn't have room to raise my gun and point it properly."

However, there are certain things common to shooting with or without sights. One of these is the grip.

THE GRIP

The way a person picks up a handgun gives a good clue to how familiar and proficient he or she is with it. When an expert picks up a gun, the barrel is automatically in line with the forearm and the forefinger is lying alongside the trigger guard.

To get the grip right, start with the hand empty. Open the hand so the thumb and forefinger form a V, with each about forty-five degrees off a center line extended from the forearm. Take the gun by the barrel in the left hand, for a right-handed shooter, and push the top of the stocks firmly into that V or web of the right hand so that the barrel is an extension of the forearm. Now wrap the three lower fingers around the stocks. The trigger finger should lie along the outside of the trigger guard. Every time you pick up the gun, fit it into your hand like this until that grip becomes automatic.

It is important to get a high grip on the gun to reduce the torque produced by the recoil. Firearms instructor Greg Ferris likens a handgun in recoil to an L-shaped teeter-totter. The lower your grip, the more the gun will rise in recoil. With a high grip, you are holding the gun closer to the axis of the barrel, and recoil will be absorbed by the arms and body.

On a revolver, the thumb should be pointing down toward the trigger. On a semi-automatic, there are two options, depending upon the gun and the shooter. Some people like the thumb down, pointing toward the trigger, particularly when shooting a double-action semi-automatic. With a single-action semi-automatic of the Colt Government type, most shooters like the thumb to ride on top of the safety. Your grip should be as high on the stocks as possible.

When raising the gun to eye level, the finger enters the trigger guard and rests on the trigger. If shooting single-action, the pad of the trigger finger should rest in the center of the trigger. If shooting double-action, the trigger can be pulled with the pad or the first joint, as this gives better leverage for the heavier pull.

This is the correct grip for the right hand of a right-handed shooter, whether firing with one hand or two. When using the two-handed grip, the fingers of the left hand wrap around the fingers of the right hand. The forefinger of the left hand should rest on top of the second finger of the right hand just under the trigger guard. Some semi-automatics, such as the Glock, have the forward end of the trigger guard shaped like a finger rest to take the first joint of the left forefinger. Ignore it. Keep your left forefinger under the trigger guard. The heel of the left hand should press into the stock in the gap between

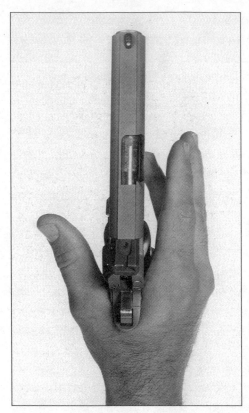

Semi-automatic grip (at left): Hold the gun by the barrel with the weak hand (not shown here) and push it back into the V of the shooting hand so the barrel is in line with the forearm.

Wrap the fingers of the strong hand around the butt, finger alongside the trigger guard and thumb resting on top of the safety, if using a single-action semi-automatic. Note: with double-action pistols, the thumb can be curled down toward the middle finger.

Wrap the weak hand around the strong hand.

When the sights are on the target, the right thumb presses off the safety and the trigger finger enters the trigger guard.

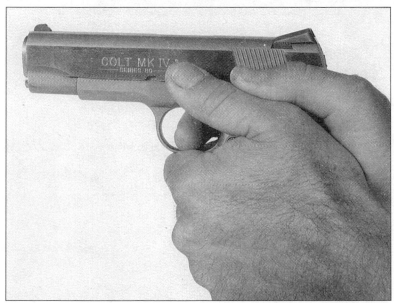

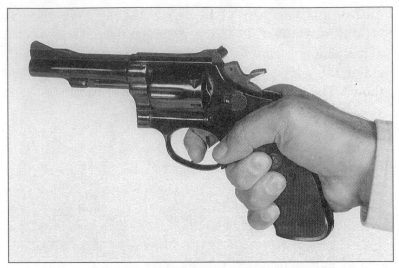

Revolver grip: Curl the thumb down toward the fingers of the strong hand for the strongest grip. Some shooters prefer to let the thumb rest on the cylinder latch.

Wrap the fingers of the weak hand around the strong hand under the trigger guard. Squeeze the trigger with the first joint of the finger.

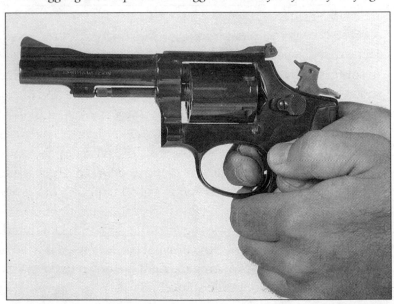

the heel and fingertips of the right hand. If the right thumb is pointing down at the trigger, the left thumb rests on top of it. If shooting a single-action semi-auto with the right thumb riding the safety, the left thumb rests underneath the right thumb. The grip should be like a politician's handshake—firm but not vise-like.

Where possible, always bring the gun up to eye level and use both hands. You will recover more quickly from recoil with both hands on the gun. I found that recovery time between shots on a .45 Colt Commander with full loads using two hands was about a quarter of a second. Using one hand, recovery was about a third of a second from shot to shot. However, it is important to practice shooting with one hand, using left and right hands, in case one hand is disabled or you are hanging onto something with the other hand.

The Stance

Two types of standing body position are currently favored for shooting a handgun with both hands: the Weaver stance and the isosceles stance.

The Weaver stance was invented by Los Angeles Deputy Sheriff Jack Weaver, one of the early contestants in practical shooting in southern California in the late-1950s. With a right-handed shooter, the left foot is a short step forward of the right and points toward the target or just to the right of it. The right foot points up to ninety degrees to the right of the target. The knees are slightly bent but the body is erect. The trunk of the body is turned about forty-five degrees to the right of the target. Some say the right arm should be locked straight, but photos of Weaver show both arms bent. The left arm is noticeably bent downward. The right hand pushes against the pull of the left hand. The gun is held slightly below normal eye level so the head is canted to the right side to bring the right eye down to the sights. The Weaver is almost a rifle stance.

Weaver stance:
Turn the legs and body
at an angle to the target;
tilt the head to the side;
bend the left arm
downward.

In the isosceles stance, the shooter faces the target squarely with the feet side-by-side at least shoulder-width apart. The legs can be locked straight or be very slightly bent, but otherwise the stance is erect. The arms are extended evenly, forming an isosceles triangle. It is necessary for the shooter to lean more into the gun with this stance to prevent being thrown off balance by the recoil.

Some research indicates that the isosceles stance is more natural and is more likely to be used in the stress of combat. Bruce Siddle, of PPCT Management Systems, states in his

Isosceles stance: Stand with the legs and body square to the target; extend the arms out straight, forming an isosceles triangle with the chest as its base.

book, *Sharpening the Warrior's Edge,* that even police officers trained in the Weaver stance revert to the isosceles stance under stress. Siddle and other authorities say facing a threat squarely is a natural human reaction. Jerry Lane, a firearms instructor who has worked for Smith & Wesson, Glock, and Heckler & Koch, has trained thousands of police officers in the Weaver stance, but has changed to teaching the isosceles stance as a result of the research done by Siddle and his colleagues.

Most people develop a shooting stance that is a mixture of the Weaver and the isosceles. I prefer a stance with the left foot

Author's modified-isosceles stance: Right foot back for stability, but body square to the threat, head erect, and arms almost straight.

forward, knees slightly bent but facing the target squarely, elbows bent slightly but left elbow bent more. Experiment and settle into the stance that suits you best. But remember, when the gangbanger screams at you that he's "gonna kill yore ass," your feet may not be planted in the perfect stance. You will have to draw and fire from where you are. So practice drawing your gun and shooting from different positions.

The legs should be bent enough to enable you to turn your body from the hips, not the shoulders. When you move the gun from one target to another, turn from the hips or by swiveling on the balls of your feet if the targets are widely separated.

Massad Ayoob, director of Lethal Force Institute, teaches what he calls a turret stance, which is an isosceles above the waist but with the legs in whatever position you find yourself when you have to shoot.

Bill McLennan teaches a modified Weaver he calls a boxer stance: feet about shoulder-width apart with one foot forward and one back. It gives you greater stability than the pure isosceles. Most gunfights take place at very close range, and you may be fending off the robber with your left hand while you

A one-handed shooting stance can vary from turning the body almost ninety degrees away from the target (as shown at left), to facing the target squarely. Note that the shooter is leaning aggressively into the weapon.

are trying to shoot him with the right. If you need to kick, you can kick from this position, McLennan says. He prefers certain aspects of the Weaver stance, in part because turning your body at an angle to the threat helps to keep your holstered gun away from your attacker when you are within grappling range.

Try the Weaver and isosceles stances. Have someone push you backward when your feet are in the isosceles stance. Then change to the Weaver—one foot back, one foot forward—and have them try to push you back. You'll soon see which foot position is more stable.

On the practice range, while waiting for the signal to shoot, hold the gun in both hands, elbows bent sharply so your forearms and the gun barrel are horizontal. Keep the muzzle pointing down range at the target. The safety is on with a single action, and the trigger finger is straight alongside the trigger guard. This is the ready position as taught by Bill Davison at the Tac Pro Shooting Center. It makes better sense than the traditional ready position, with arms extended and angled down, so the gun is pointing at the ground a few yards in front of you or at the bottom of the target. On the signal to fire, push the gun forward and upward until it is at eye level, press off the safety, place your finger on the trigger, acquire a good sight picture, and squeeze off the shot. The ready position is also good for checking out a real-life threat. You don't want to check out a threat in your house or anywhere else with your finger on the trigger. Anything that startles you is likely to result in an involuntary contraction of your trigger finger and an accidental shot.

When shooting with one hand, you can face the target squarely and raise the gun to eye level in the center of the body, as recommended by such experts as Captain W. E. Fairbairn, of Shanghai Police fame, and competition shooter J. Michael Plaxco. Or you can shoot with the shoulder of your gun arm extended toward the target and the body turned from forty-five to ninety degrees away from the target. Bill McLennan prefers to turn about forty-five degrees from the target, as he finds it easier to move, particularly backward. Practice shooting one-handed using both your dominant and your weaker hands.

SIGHT PICTURE

Achieving a proper sight picture with regular sights means getting the front sight centered in the notch of the rear sight, with the tops of both sights level and with the top of the front sight right where you want to hit on the target. If you do that and your trigger control is perfect, you will hit what you are shooting at every time. Sounds easy, doesn't it?

It is, but there are some complicating factors. First, you need to determine your master eye. Extend one of your arms. It doesn't matter which one. Lift your thumb up, and with both eyes open, line it up with some mark on the opposite wall. Close your left eye. Does your thumb appear to move in relation to the mark? If it stays anchored to the mark, your right eye is master. Try closing your right eye. If your right eye is master, your thumb should move to the right. If your left eye is master, your thumb will stay still.

If you are right-handed and your right eye is master, you are in good shape. If you are left-handed and your left eye is master, that's okay too. If you are right-handed, but your left eye is master or *vice versa*, you should still be able to handle a handgun without a problem, but you may have trouble shooting a rifle or shotgun. Always align the sights using your master eye.

It is better to shoot a handgun with both eyes open, particularly in a defensive situation, because two open eyes can see more than one, and you don't want to be outflanked on your blind side. If you have trouble shooting with both eyes wide open, try half closing your weak eye. After some practice, most people are able to shoot with both eyes open.

No one can hold a gun absolutely steady. Whether you are an Olympic contestant shooting a free pistol at fifty meters or an average Jill or Joe trying to fend off a street-wise scumbag, you are looking for an acceptable sight picture, not a perfect one. The only difference between a tyro shooter and a pro is that the pro's front sight wobbles over a smaller area on the target than the beginner's.

Many instructors in combat shooting teach their students to concentrate on the front sight. The human eye can focus on only one thing at a time. If you focus on the target, the sights will be fuzzy and your accuracy will suffer. If your focus is on the front sight, the rear sight will be a little fuzzy and the lettering on scumbag's T-shirt twenty feet away will be blurred.

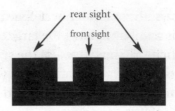

Correct sight alignment.

Any time you are shooting at something or someone more than a few feet away, you need to get that front sight on the target. Think front sight. Concentrate on the front sight. Focus on the front sight.

Greg Ferris teaches his students to keep the front sight in focus, but to concentrate on equalizing the bars of light on either side of the front sight within the frame of the rear sight. If you find this approach helpful, go for it.

When that juvenile gangbanger is pointing a sawed-off 12-gauge at your just-eaten dinner, it's really hard to get your eyes to focus on the front sight. Only constant repetition in practice will overcome your natural reaction to focus on that drain-pipe-sized barrel. Frequently people are mesmerized by their assailant's weapon and actually shoot at it rather than at the person wielding it. *Aikido* Sensei David Ham refers to that as "the mind captured by the weapon." Train yourself to focus on that front sight, though in a shoot-out you may not be able to tear your attention from your attacker.

Bill McLennan puts it this way: "If you don't look at your sights when you practice, you're not going to do it in the field. We say look at your sights. Realistically, you may be looking at the target, but you're aware of the sights. You've spent thousands and thousands of repetitions learning to use your sights, so that one time you didn't use your sights you still went to that learned position. You did everything exactly the same. Probably for all practical purposes you were using your sights, but it was a muscle-memory thing."

He says he used to shoot at close range by indexing the cylinder of his revolver against the target. He was persuaded by colleague Richard Stengel to use the sights. "Until I started using the sights, I never had rounds that were almost touching each other on the target, and Richard was always doing that," McLennan says.

"The problem with my cylinder indexing, like all point-shooting techniques, was that it fell apart when one or more of the indices—distance to target, target size, target angle, time allotted—were significantly changed. You may not be able to control target distance, size, or angle, but you can and must control the speed at which you shoot. There is only a split second between deadly accuracy and a miss; you must not shoot any faster than you can be sure of hitting your intended target."

SIGHTS

Sights on self-defense handguns will usually be improved with a little color to draw the eye to them, particularly in low light. Sights with three white dots, one on the front sight and one on each shoulder of the rear sight, are popular. White can also be used to outline the rear sight notch. Some people like red or fluorescent orange on the front sight. You can use model paint or you can get specially colored sights from makers like Millett. The trouble with red is that it doesn't show up any better than black in poor light. A relatively recent development is the fiber-optic sight. This is a red or green tube that gathers available light and concentrates it into a bright dot. TRUGLO, Inc., and HiViz Sight Systems make these sights. Smith & Wesson has installed a green or red fiber-optic sight on some of its models.

However, my favorite sights on a self-defense handgun are the XS Express Sights. Express sights were first used on English double rifles built for taking African dangerous game such as elephant, Cape buffalo, and lion. The rear sight is a wide, shallow V, while the front sight is a bead usually white and often made of ivory. John "Pondoro" Taylor, in his book *African Rifles & Cartridges*, expressed a preference for a large-bead front sight.

"The general run of animals shot in Africa justify a larger bead which can be picked up much more quickly if a quick shot is called for .... For the big rifle I like an extra large bead because it can be picked up instantaneously in heavy forest wherein the light is frequently bad," Taylor wrote.

The light is frequently bad and the range short in the typical gunfight. The game is also extremely dangerous—it is likely to be shooting back. Therefore, the large bead and open V of the XS Express Sights are very fast to align. XS Sight Systems, Inc., provides two sizes of white bead—standard and large. I recommend the large. While the white beads pick up whatever light there is, they can be ordered with a tritium insert. The rear sight is a shallow V with a vertical bar point-ing to the bottom of the V. This bar is white or tritium. The lat-est version is both: tritium outlined in white.

The sights are aligned so the bead perches on top of the ver-tical bar or in the bottom of the V of the rear sight. At close range the bead is placed over the area to be hit. Although these

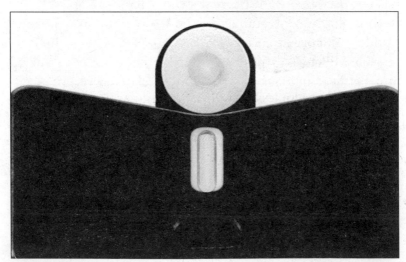

Sight alignment with XS Express Sights and on a handgun (at right).

sights might seem less accurate than regular handgun sights, I do not believe this is so. After XS Express Sights were fitted to my CZ 75, I had no trouble keeping most of my shots on a steel head-and-shoulders target at one-hundred yards. I have worn glasses all my life, and I found I could align these sights even without my glasses, something I could not do with standard sights.

If using regular sights for a self-defense gun, choose a ramp front sight that will not snag on clothing, whether you draw it from a pocket, a fanny pack, or an ankle holster. For the same reason, the rear sight should not be easily adjustable. In fact, most sights on self-defense guns can be adjusted by drifting them laterally in their dove-tail notches. Smith & Wesson semi-automatics come equipped with Novak's fixed sights, which have a low, clean profile that would be hard to snag on anything.

Some people swear by night sights—those tritium inserts that make your sights glow in the dark. Most gunfights take place in conditions of poor light, so they can be an advantage. Bill McLennan is a great believer in night sights.

"I think they're excellent. Probably one of the most innovative and best pieces of equipment that I've seen come along in my thirty years in law enforcement, as far as guns go," he says.

However, night sights are no substitute for learning to shoot using a flashlight. You always have to identify your target, and night sights aren't going to do that for you. SureFire makes an excellent line of small tactical flashlights with lithium

SureFire flashlight illuminates the sights and the target.

batteries that can be used with handguns. They can be attached to handguns, but this is usually not practical for pistols that have to be concealed.

Shooting instructor and gunfight survivor Greg Ferris dislikes night sights and recommends this experiment to show why. After dark in a lighted room, take a very unloaded gun with three-dot night sights and point the gun near the door where the light switch is located. Your partner in this experiment should be armed with a pen-sized flashlight. Without getting in line with the door or your muzzle, have him turn out the light. After getting accustomed to the sudden darkness, you will be able to line up the dot on the front sight between the two dots on the shoulders of the rear sight. Have your partner briefly flash the pen light at you to simulate an assailant's muzzle flash or your own. Suddenly, you will see at least six dots instead of three, making it almost impossible to get a good sight picture.

Some people swear by night sights with luminous inserts; others don't. However, anything that gives you an edge in poor light is worth considering, even if they only help you land the first shot on target. The first shot is the most important, as gunfights tend to be won by the person who makes the first hit.

Another sighting accessory that is becoming increasingly popular for use in poor light is the laser sight. These sights put a red dot on the target where the bullets will impact at normal gunfight ranges. They work best in bad light or indoors.

Crimson Trace makes laser sights that are molded into the left grip of a revolver or a semi-automatic. They are activated by a small button in the front of the grip just below the trigger-guard. When grasping the gun in a firm grip, the middle finger depresses the button, and the laser comes on. It can be turned off by a small switch at the bottom of the grip, but is normally left on. The laser is powered by two flat, round batteries about the size of quarters, located in the grips. The laser is offset between half and three-quarters of an inch to the right and slightly below the bore. It is usually zeroed at about fifty feet. This means that the gun will shoot slightly to the left of the red dot at ranges closer than fifty feet and to the right beyond fifty feet.

LaserMax makes a laser sight that fits under the barrel of many semi-automatics. The unit replaces the guide rod and spring assembly under the barrel of some pistols made by Beretta, Glock, SIG, Springfield Armory, Taurus, and many 1911 Government model clones. These units are turned on and off by an ambidextrous switch, which replaces the slidelock lever and is within reach of the trigger finger. LaserMax also makes a unit that attaches to the accessory rail under the barrel found on some tactical pistols. Both LaserMax and Crimson Trace make models to fit small J-frame, five-shot, Smith & Wesson revolvers. Crimson Trace lasers provide a constant beam, while LaserMax units emit a pulsing beam. Both types cost between $250 and $350, depending upon the model and the retailer.

The first time I tried a Crimson Trace sight on a borrowed Glock, I didn't like it. I shot it at a rack of steel plates from about thirty feet in bright sunlight and found myself trying to find the red dot instead of looking at the regular sights. This of course was exactly the type of light condition where laser sights are least useful. Later on I fitted Crimson Trace sights to my CZ-75 semi-automatic and my Smith & Wesson Model 640 revolver. They are still there. After trying them indoors and in poor outdoor light, I came to realize how useful they could be under typical gunfight conditions—at close range, in low light, and with movement of shooter and target.

Trainers like Bill Davison of Tac Pro Shooting Center stress that lasers are a good secondary sighting system.

"But they do not take over from the primary sighting system. You still have to work with your [regular] sights, get them working when you get into the fight. Then if for some reason, shooting around cover, or you're in an awkward position, or falling over, you need a secondary sighting system, that's when you need to go to the laser," Davison says.

Gila Hayes of the Firearms Academy of Seattle refers to them as an adjunct sighting system and emphasizes that most practice on the range should still be with the shooter focusing on the front sight. You should not become too dependent on laser sights, because any electrical system that uses batteries and wires can fail, particularly if not well maintained.

However, you should practice shooting at close range— between three and six feet—when you don't have the room to raise the gun to eye level. The laser provides a good check of where your bullets are going to impact.

Michael de Bethencourt of Northeastern Tactical Schools is a strong supporter of laser sights. "There is no downside— none. If you don't want it you can turn it off. The more I use it the more I like it."

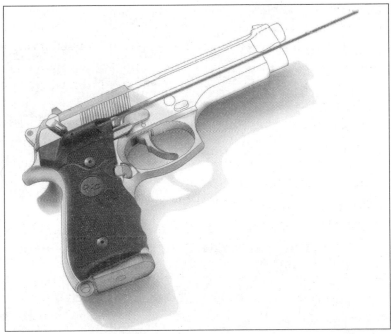

Laser sight on outline of a Beretta semi-automatic.

Several handguns equipped with laser sights suitable for concealed carry.

As mentioned earlier, he teaches courses on the use of snubby revolvers, many of which can be fitted with lasers. They are particularly appropriate for the short-barreled revolvers.

Davison agrees: "I think it makes the J-frame a very usable tool because a lot of the J-frames don't have good enough sights to see in low-light conditions."

It is hard to argue with success. Ed Lovette wrote a series of columns about laser sights for *Combat Handguns* in which he analyzed eight shooting incidents involving law-enforcement officers. Of the eighteen shots fired by the eight officers, all hit their targets. This is an incredible hit ratio. Usually only about 25 percent of rounds fired by law-enforcement officers in gunfights hit their targets.

Travis Noteboom of Crimson Trace says in the feedback the company has received about shootings involving laser sights, the hit ratio has been about 90 percent, and the officers tend to fire fewer rounds.

"You've got fewer shots going down range because you're getting hits; you're not spraying and praying. That improves the ratio," he said.

Lovette thinks laser sights give the shooter the best of both worlds.

"That's what works when you can't acquire your [regular] sights; when you're in an awkward position; when you're totally focused on the threat, as opposed to trying to get your eye back onto that front sight," he says.

Lovette has interviewed many people who have been involved in gunfights, including many police officers only trained in the use of the front sight.

Lovette says, "It's almost impossible to find somebody who remembers seeing a front sight if they were involved in a shooting. And a lot of that goes to the fact that you're looking at the threat. That's the natural thing to do—what's not natural is to try to break that eye contact from the threat and bring it back to the front sight."

That said, however, he agrees that you need to train to use the front sight and try to focus on it if you can under the circumstances.

"But if you can't, if the situation has happened up close and personal, the lighting may not be the best, the sympathetic nervous system has kicked in—all those things that happen—you're under the influence of survival stress, and the authorities are going to tell us that you're probably not going to be able to see the front sight because you lose your near focus, you'll find that you were really glad that you spent some time doing some really close-range stuff with the target focus, and that's where the laser grip really comes into its own," says Lovette.

The laser also has a deterrent effect. Law-enforcement officers have reported that often suspects have surrendered much more quickly than they would have otherwise after seeing that red dot on their chests.

But lasers are not a panacea. When the laser is on, the bad guy can see where you are. Things can become confusing when searching a darkened room with windows or mirrors. These glass surfaces can multiply the number of red dots you can see.

If a confrontation should happen to take place outside in bright sunlight, you are not going to be able to see that red dot easily even at ten feet, particularly if your attacker is wearing a multi-colored shirt or jacket with some red in it.

Bill Davison recommends zeroing the laser to about an inch below where the regular sights are pointing. This means that. if you are using your sights, you won't be able to see the laser dot with your dominant eye.

"If you can see it when you're looking at both your sights, what's going to happen is you're going to play 'which one should I look at?' And the only time you should be looking at the laser is when your sight picture is inoperable: like it's too dark; it's too shaded; you've just had a light flashed in your eyes; you're scared so much that you're looking at the target. These are times when a second sighting system allows you to carry on with the engagement."

One person who could have benefited from laser sights is Rory Vertigan of Phoenix. In March 1999, the off-duty security manager engaged a Mexican drug trafficker who had just shot and killed a Phoenix police officer.

Vertigan, then twenty-seven, was taking a shortcut through an industrial area on the west side of Phoenix in the late afternoon. He is a big man—six-feet five-inches tall and just over three hundred pounds—and he was squeezed into a very small Kia Sephia.

The driver's side window was rolled down to let the smoke escape from the cigarette he was smoking. His Glock 31 containing fourteen rounds of .357 SIG caliber was lying on the passenger seat. He had no spare magazines and no backup gun.

He was about three-hundred feet from an intersection when a white Lincoln Town Car came careering out of the side road, running the stop sign, and burning rubber as it swung in the same direction Vertigan was traveling. As he approached the intersection, he saw a marked police car follow in the same direction as the Lincoln with its bar lights flashing.

The Lincoln stopped in the middle of the street, and Vertigan saw one man run from it toward a nearby building. Another young man got out, but stayed near the driver's door of the white sedan. He had a .357 Magnum Smith & Wesson revolver in his hand.

As the squad car approached the Lincoln, the young man raised the revolver and opened fire at the police car as it approached him, then he tracked it, still firing as it passed him.

Vertigan reached for the Glock on the passenger seat of his car. He rolled to a stop about fifty feet behind the Lincoln Town Car. He watched horrified as the young man fired at the police car. His window was down, but he didn't hear the sound of the shots or the wail of the police siren. He did see the revolver bucking in the man's hands. He saw the officer slump down in the squad car. The police car slowed, veered off the street to the left, and smashed into a utility pole, snapping it in two.

The shooter, later identified as seventeen-year-old Felipe Petrona-Cabanas, turned towards Vertigan still holding the Smith & Wesson revolver in both hands. He thinks Petrona fired a shot at him.

"I'm not sure if he actually fired a round at me or not but I know the gun was pointed at me after he fired on the officer," Vertigan said.

He passed his Glock from his right hand to his left so he could shoot out of his window.

"I just saw the gun coming at me, and I thought I had to lay some rounds down, or he was just going to stand there and pluck me off."

Vertigan pointed his semi-automatic out of the window in Petrona's direction. He was unable to align the sights on his Glock, because his head was inside the car, his gun was outside, and his target was directly in front of his car. Vertigan's sights were not between his eyes and the target; they were off to the side. This is where laser sights would have been useful; he could have shot more accurately had he been able to see the red dot on the target.

"I just pointed the gun in his direction and started firing," Vertigan said.

After a further exchange of fire, Vertigan hit Petrona once in the shoulder then held him until the police arrived. For a full account of this incident, refer to my book, *Thank God I Had a Gun: True Accounts of Self-Defense.*

Trigger Control

The purpose of trigger control is to squeeze the trigger and fire the shot without disturbing the sight picture or moving the gun. The way to do this is to increase pressure on the trigger steadily until the gun goes off. The let-off should be a surprise to the shooter, even though the time period with practice can be compressed into a few hundredths of a second. With a double-action revolver or semi-automatic, this means a long squeeze against anything from five to twelve pounds of resistance over about a half inch of travel. With a single-action semi-auto, it means taking up the slack in the trigger, then pressing to a sharp break at around four pounds. The double-action trigger should be pulled by the first joint of the trigger finger. The end pad of the forefinger squeezes the trigger of a single-action. In all cases, the pressure on the trigger should be straight back and not to one side or the other.

With both types of action, the trigger should return forward under control of the finger. Do not allow the trigger to go all the way forward, but just enough for the sear, which holds back the hammer, to reengage. You will feel the click. The finger should not come off the trigger when going forward; keep a little pressure during the release.

It is important to grip the gun the same way, with the same amount of pressure, and to squeeze the trigger identically each time you fire a shot, because the gun starts to recoil before the bullet is out of the barrel. Therefore the recoil pattern must be the same from shot to shot.

Greg Ferris teaches his students to allow the gun to recoil until it runs out of energy, and if you are relaxed, it will quickly settle back to where it was when it fired.

"You don't fight recoil, you ride it," Ferris says.

In fact, experienced shooters need that recoil to develop a rhythm to their shooting cycle. The shooting cycle starts with the sight picture and the trigger press. The trigger breaks in the middle of the cycle.

"The end of the shooting cycle is when the gun has reached its apex in recoil," says Ferris. "Once it does that, now your cycle starts again. You release the trigger as you come down and start your trigger take-up as your sights come back onto the target."

You should keep your eye on that front sight even while it is rising in recoil. Of course, if one shot puts your attacker down, you will never develop a rhythm; but as long as he is a threat, you need to keep shooting.

Even if you fire only one shot, you need to bring your sights back into line with the target after you break the shot. This is called follow-through.

At some stage, most shooters will flinch or anticipate the recoil of the gun. It usually produces a low left shot on the target for a right-handed shooter. To test for this, have someone else load your gun or magazine with a dummy round among the live cartridges. When you get to the dummy, the click of the hammer will be accompanied by an embarrassing and noticeable dip of the front sight as you anticipate the recoil. Continued shooting with live and dummy rounds will usually cure the problem.

Bill McLennan thinks that trigger control is more important than sight picture in close-range defensive shooting. Despite deteriorating eyesight which affects his sight alignment, he still shoots better than most of us. "Consequently I think the trigger is what's most important," he says.

When you start practicing, don't hurry. Shoot deliberately, and strive for accuracy. Speed will come later. You might start with a figure target at twelve feet if you have never fired a handgun before. It is better to make hits at four yards than misses at twenty-five. On the other hand, it is possible to be too accurate. Bill Davison of Tac Pro Shooting Center says, if you are making a two-inch group on the target, you need to shoot faster. A four- or five-inch group is accurate enough for defensive shooting.

If possible get a professional instructor to teach you the basics. This is important because an instructor can teach you the proper technique and correct any bad habits before they become ingrained. There is nothing more frustrating than unlearning a bad habit.

THE DRAW

Most people who carry handguns on a regular basis wear them in holsters. The ability to draw your gun from a concealed holster and fire an accurate shot at close range in less than a second is a skill worth acquiring. It could save your life. But remember, the fastest draw is to have the gun in your hand.

We'll start with the draw from a hip holster on the right side, for a right-handed shooter, concealed by an unbuttoned jacket. The holster can be inside or outside the waistband. Most shooters go to the range to practice without a jacket and wear the gun exposed. Practice drawing the gun from the position it will be in on the street, that is, with the gun hidden under a jacket or under a shirt that is not tucked in.

Thunder Ranch teaches an effective five-step draw. When the individual steps are mastered they should be combined into a smooth, flowing whole. Do not try for speed; concentrate on relaxed smoothness. Speed will come later. When reholstering the gun, reverse the cycle as exactly as you can, as this will help with muscle-memory training. Experts say it takes three thousand repetitions of an action for it to become a reactive response. When you draw, do not look at the gun. Keep your eyes on the target, and shift your focus to the sights only when the gun appears on the line of sight between your eye and the target. Also, do not look at the gun or the leather when you reholster. You should keep your eyes open for any other threats. Felons often travel in pairs or packs.

Assume a relaxed stance with hands at your sides. Later you can practice with your hands up or on top of your head. These hip-draw instructions are for a right-handed shooter:

STEP 1: HAND TO GUN.

There are several ways to clear an open jacket or vest to draw a handgun from a concealed hip holster. The one I like is to bring the right hand up to chest level and run your thumb across your chest in a horizontal movement until the garment is far enough back for the hand to drop down onto the butt of the gun. Bill Davison prefers to grab the coat much lower down and swing it back in the direction of his left shoulder.

I watched Todd Jarrett, a professional shooter for Para Ordnance, perform both coat clearances. He said the first method was faster. Which ever method you use, while sweeping the coat to the side, bring the left hand, with fingers horizontal to a position just in front of your belt buckle. With your right hand, grasp the gun in a perfect shooting grip.

The thumb breaks the thumb snap if there is one, and the forefinger extends downward on the outside of the holster where it covers the trigger guard. With a single-action semi-automatic like the Government Model, the thumb should ride on the top of the safety, but don't take it off safe yet.

This should be the slowest and most deliberate step in the draw. How well you shoot when the gun reaches eye level depends largely on how good a grip you get on the gun when it is in the holster. Also, if you start your draw slowly, it will take your attacker just a little longer to realize what you are doing. If you make a quick snatch at the gun, your opponent's reaction will be quicker.

STEP 2: CLEAR HOLSTER AND ROTATE MUZZLE TOWARD TARGET.

Lift the gun upward until the muzzle clears the lip of the holster. Rotate the muzzle forward and upward until it is horizontal and pointing at the target. The forearm rests against the ribs

Steps in the hip draw:
1: Hand to gun.

2: Clear holster
and rotate muzzle to target.

or pectoral muscles. From this position the gun can be fired at an assailant who is at arm's length and crowding you.

This is called the retention position because it keeps the gun back from your assailant's grasp and is accurate enough to hit him. If you are fending off an attacker with your left hand, don't shoot him through your own arm. It has happened, according to Thunder Ranch's Clint Smith.

STEP 3: BRING HANDS TOGETHER.

The gun hand moves the gun to the front of the body at mid-chest height, where the left hand rises to cup the gun in a two-hand grip. The hands come together about six inches in front of the sternum, with the insides of the forearms resting against the ribs.

At this point the safety is still on, and the trigger finger is pointing straight alongside the trigger guard.

STEP 4: GUN TO TARGET.

Punch the gun forward with the gun hand against a slight restraining pull of the left hand. At this point, you have two options, depending upon whether you have definitely decided to fire a shot or not.

With a single-action semi-automatic, the thumb of the gun hand slides the safety off. If you have decided to shoot, your finger goes into the trigger guard while the gun is traveling forward. The trigger finger takes up the slack on the trigger as the gun reaches the end of its forward

3: Bring hands together.

movement. The gun stops when the gun arm is almost straight and the gun is between you and the target at eye level.

If you have not yet decided to shoot, your finger stays out of the trigger guard until that decision is made. With a double-action revolver or auto, if you are definitely going to shoot, the trigger stroke is started as the gun goes forward into battery. If you do not need to shoot immediately, your finger stays out of the trigger guard, and the draw ends here. If you need to shoot, continue with the next step.

STEP 5: SIGHT PICTURE AND TRIGGER SQUEEZE.

As the gun reaches the firing position, shift your focus from the target to your front sight. Do not try for a perfect sight picture. You should start your compressed trigger squeeze on an acceptable sight picture. Keep steadily increasing the pressure on the trigger until the gun fires with a surprise break.

4 and 5: Push the gun forward, raising it to eye level. Open fire if necessary.

Practice your draw extensively with an empty gun, striving for smoothness. Speed is the economy of motion and will come with practice. You want to be very certain of the mechanics of your draw before you start doing it with a loaded gun. This applies to any draw.

In hot weather a vest such as those worn by photographers will cover the butt of an inside-the-waistband holstered gun. The vest is cleared in the same way as a coat. You may choose to wear a T-shirt and an unbuttoned sports shirt to cover the gun. Again, clearing the clothing is done in the same way. However, if the shirt is buttoned but outside the pants, clear it by grasping the hem of the shirt with your left hand and lifting it above the gun.

Once the gun is out of the holster and in front of the sternum, the left hand comes down and across to take its grip. Be careful not to allow the left hand or arm to get in front of the gun muzzle.

Drawing from a shoulder holster or cross-draw belt rig starts with the left hand pulling open the jacket. The right hand moves to the gun and secures a solid shooting grip. The thumb breaks the thumb snap if there is one, or the hand pulls against the spring if there is not. Bring the muzzle down in a vertical arc, trying not to point the barrel at you or anyone else until

Shooter lifts his shirt with his left hand to reach the gun with his right.

the gun is in front of your chest, where the left hand can wrap around the fingers of the right hand. From there, the draw is similar to the hip draw—the gun is punched out into the firing position.

The draw from an ankle holster is different. If right-handed, the best way to wear an ankle holster is inside the left ankle. The best way to bring a gun into action from an ankle holster is to step back with the leg that doesn't hold the gun and kneel on that knee. Clear the pants cuff with your left hand. You need loose pants legs for the ankle holster, both to hide the outline of the gun and to get it into action. Draw the gun

and shoot from the kneeling position. Kneeling makes you a smaller target, and you don't have to bend down from the waist, losing your balance, or center, as the martial artists say, and perhaps losing sight of your adversary.

Ankle Draw: Shooter pulls up his pants cuff with the left hand and draws with the right.

With any of these draws, speed is fine, but accuracy is what counts. An illustration of what happens all too typically when that lesson is forgotten occurred on the west side of San Antonio a couple of days before Christmas 1994. Four sheriff's deputies, equipped with a warrant for drugs, had to break down the front door of the house they had come to search. As they rushed in, a man in the living room raised a .22 caliber rifle and fired one shot at them. The deputies fired fifty-three rounds from their .40-caliber Glocks at the man, hitting him ten times. Only two of the hits were considered life threatening. They hit the man with only one shot in five at a distance that could not have been more than fifteen feet.

According to FBI statistics, the average number of rounds fired in gunfights involving police officers in the 1980s was three. However, in the 1990s, the average quadrupled to about twelve rounds. Undoubtedly this coincides with the switch from revolvers to high-capacity semi-automatics.

As Thunder Ranch's Clint Smith puts it, "If you've got more, you'll shoot more."

FLASHLIGHTS

SureFire, 18300 Mt. Baldy Circle, Fountain Valley, CA 92708; 800-828-8809; <www.surefire.com>

SIGHTS

Crimson Trace Corporation, 8089 Southwest Cirrus Drive, Beaverton, OR 97008; 800-442-2406; <www.crimsontrace.com>

HiViz Shooting Systems, 1941 Heath Parkway, Suite 1, Fort Collins, CO 80524; 800-589-4315; <www.hivizsights.com>

LaserMax, 3495 Winston Place, Rochester, NY 14623; 800-527-3703; <www.lasermax.com>

Millett Sights, 16131-K Gothard Street, Huntington Beach, CA 92647; 714-842-5575; <www.millettsights.com>

Novak's, Inc., 1206½ 30th Street, Parkersburg, WV 26101; 304-485-9295; <www.novaksights.com>

TRUGLO, Inc., 1710 Presidential Drive, Richardson, TX 75081; 972-774-0300; <www.truglo.com>

XS Sight Systems, Inc., 2401 Ludelle Street, Fort Worth, TX 76105; 888-744-4880; <www.xssights.com>

Chapter Nine

ADVANCED SHOOTING:
BACK UP AND MOVE TO COVER

The first time Leo Arredondo got into a gunfight, he was on his lunch break. He and his friend Raul "Bear" Garza were at De La Rosa Home and Auto Supply on Nogalitos Street in San Antonio when a red pickup pulled up in front of the auto-repair-shop bays. It was shortly after 3 o'clock in the afternoon. They knew there was likely to be trouble when they saw the driver, seventeen-year-old Valentino Garcia Jr. and his uncle, Ricky Garcia, twenty-five, get out of the pickup.

Three of the five people in the garage that day had had problems with the Garcias. Eddie Mireles had been threatened. A couple of weeks before, Raul had been beaten with a pool cue by one member of the Garcia family, while another held a gun on him. Several months before that, Leo had gone to Raul's assistance when two of the Garcias attacked him. According to Leo, the Garcias had threatened to kill him. So he had bought a .380-caliber Davis semi-automatic.

"They had already been there harassing us, saying they were going to get us and stuff like that; they were going to kill everybody at the garage," Leo said.

The day of the shooting, April 30, 1992, Valentino and Ricky Garcia were looking for Mireles. They stood beside their pickup, waving handguns and taunting him to come out of the garage. When it became apparent that Mireles was not coming out, the Garcias got back into their truck as though to leave.

Then they apparently spotted Raul and got out again. Valentino started swearing at the stocky part-time mechanic. Raul said he didn't want any trouble and suggested they leave.

Ricky came around the front of the truck brandishing a .45 semi-automatic and yelled: "I've got something for you, too."

He started walking toward Raul, shooting as he came. Raul ducked behind his large Snap-on toolbox where he kept a .38 Smith & Wesson revolver. He grabbed the gun and emptied it at Ricky Garcia. Ricky went down, hit in the left shoulder and right side of the abdomen.

Meanwhile Valentino had come around the pickup to help his uncle. Leo was taking cover behind a vehicle parked in one of the garage bays. He says Valentino fired one shot at him with a snub-nosed .38 revolver. Leo says he fired twice with his .380 Davis, using one hand, but concentrating on the sights, at a range of about fifteen yards. He saw Valentino fall, hit in the chest.

Ricky picked himself up and helped his nephew into the passenger side of the pickup. He got into the driver's side and drove off. Less than two blocks away, Ricky apparently lost consciousness and the truck hit a utility pole in the front yard of a house.

By the time police arrived, Valentino was dead and Ricky was in bad shape. The wounded man was rushed by ambulance to a nearby hospital. He recovered, but refused to tell police what had happened, except to say that it was Raul who had shot him. An autopsy revealed that Leo's bullet entered Valentino's chest high on the right side and had gone through his right lung, causing massive internal bleeding. He also had cocaine in his system, according to the medical examiner's report.

Raul and Leo fled the scene but later turned themselves in to police and gave statements. A case for murder and attempted murder against Raul and Leo was rejected by the District Attorney's office.

Assistant DA Carl Lobitz, in rejecting the case, wrote: "Eyewitness statements indicate that complainants [Ricky and Valentino] sought out defendants at the garage, provoked a confrontation, and fired at defendants first. Therefore, defendants were justified in employing deadly force in self defense."

And that should have been the end of it. But blood feuds in Texas seldom die.

Four years later, on March 22, 1996, shortly before 10 p.m., Leo Arredondo was in the same garage on Nogalitos Street, helping a friend fix the brakes on a pickup. Again, a pickup, blue this time, pulled up in front of the loading bays, and two men got out. Again, they were both Garcias—San Henry Garcia, thirty-four, and his older brother, Valentine or Valentino Sr., forty, come to avenge his dead son. As they walked into the garage, Valentine pulled a short-barreled, pump-action shotgun from under his long, black overcoat.

According to witnesses, one of the Garcias demanded: "Where's that f---ing Leo."

Although he had never seen Valentine Sr., Leo knew they were Garcias and that they were there to kill him. He made a dash for the back of the shop where he had another Davis P-380 cached in a rack of tires. The Garcias opened fire with the shotgun and a .357 Magnum single-action Ruger revolver. Scooping up the Davis, Arredondo fired back.

When the smoke cleared, Valentine and Henry Garcia were lying on the garage floor, dead. Leo Arredondo had been hit in the legs by a shotgun blast and by a bullet that gouged his left thumb. He dragged himself toward the front doors before he collapsed.

This time, the shooting was very close and there was no time to take cover. Valentine was shot through the heart and Henry through the right eye with the bullet passing through the brain. That shot was fired from so close there was powder tattooing on Henry's face around the entrance wound.

According to the way the bodies, guns, and ejected cases were found, the shots were probably all fired from within ten feet or so. Police found five empty .380-caliber cases, indicating that Leo had fired all but one of the rounds in his Davis.

Four empty .357 Magnum cases were found in the Ruger single action. Evidence investigators found one more round in the cylinder that had apparently misfired. It was loaded with only five. No empty cases from the 12-gauge shotgun were found at the scene, but as the shooting happened after dark, they might have been missed. Certainly Leo was hit in the legs by at least one shotgun blast.

In his statement to police, Leo said he had recently taken a peace officer's course and had qualified on the range.

What can we learn from these two gunfights?

First, you don't have to have a modified, compensated, laser-sighted, double-stacked, $3,000 gun shooting low-yield nuclear rounds to win in a shootout. Both times, Leo Arredondo used a .380-caliber Davis semi-automatic that retails for about $100. Richard Stengel, the firearms expert at the Bexar County Crime Laboratory, who examined the gun, said it had a single-action trigger pull of 10¾ pounds. Stengel's opinion of the Davis is not high.

"The safety sometimes will come off when you pull the trigger," he said. "If the trigger pull is not really heavy, then if you drop the gun it'll sometimes go off."

In a gunfight, who is shooting and how is more important than the cost and quality of the gun. In both shootouts, all the guns used by the other shooters were far superior in quality to Arredondo's Davis semi-autos. In both incidents, Leo says he used the sights, except when the last assailant was almost on top of him.

Comparing the two incidents is instructive. In the first fight, the ranges were longer and the winners took cover. Raul would probably have been hit had he not taken cover behind the Snap-on toolbox. Police found a .45-caliber spent bullet inside the toolbox. Leo shot Valentino Jr. using a vehicle for cover.

In the 1996 gunfight, no one took cover and the range was much shorter, maybe a dozen feet or less, and everyone was hit by gunfire. When cover is available, use it, and increase the range between you and your assailants if you can. More about these tactics later in this chapter.

There was a common factor in both of these gunfights that we can't take to the bank. All four attackers went down when shot. That is probably the exception rather than the rule, whether you are using a .380 or a .45, and it is something you should never count on.

"If you don't take anything else out of this school with you, take the concept that when you shoot it's not going to work, and what will I do next?" says Clint Smith on the first day of a defensive handgun course at Thunder Ranch.

As previously discussed, just because you hit your assailant in a vital spot doesn't mean he's going to drop and quit the fight. He may still keep coming even after you've branded him with a brace of 230-grain slugs in the chest. Now what are you going to do?

Keep shooting until he goes down and is no longer able to do you damage. Cases have been documented where police officers have drawn their guns, fired twice, and reholstered their guns only to find that the bad guy is still coming on. The officers were trained in the double tap: draw and fire twice. They did under the stress of combat what they did in training. So when you practice, vary the number of shots you fire: sometimes one, sometimes six, and everything in between. Don't get hung up on the double tap.

W HERE TO AIM

"One of my pet hates is people saying: 'Shoot at the center of mass,'" says Bill Davison, owner of Tac Pro Shooting Center.

Many firearms instructors teach shooting for the "center of mass." Davison thinks this is bad advice. The center of mass is about where the stomach is located, and a person can survive multiple hits in the stomach for long enough to do a lot of damage.

"We need to be shooting at the cardiovascular triangle," he says. On a male, the cardiovascular triangle is found inside lines joining the nipples and the Adam's apple.

If you can see all of your assailant, aim for his upper torso: the heart and lungs area. It is the largest vital area, and sometimes one shot will put an attacker down. When you shoot at a target at usual gunfight ranges, you can see the holes in the paper. If you are concentrating on your front sight, you should not see the holes as they appear, but only afterward. However, when you shoot at another human being, who may be wearing a jacket, a sweater, or a patterned shirt, you may not be able to see whether you are hitting him. You may not see any blood. This is one reason it is important to use the sights, except at the closest in-your-face ranges. You should know whether you are making hits by the sight picture when you press the trigger.

If you are making hits in the chest area and your attacker is still coming on, it is time to shift your point of aim. Many police officers today wear body armor, but so, too, do some criminals. Bullet-resistant vests have been stolen from stores catering to law-enforcement officers. Criminals have been arrested wearing body armor. The odds are against it, but your well-placed bullets could be getting absorbed by a Kevlar vest. If so, there are two other vulnerable areas to aim for: the head from the bottom of the nose to the eyebrows and the pelvis.

The head at nose and eye level is the smallest target and the hardest to hit. The vital area is about three inches high and five inches wide. Why not aim for the whole head? A bullet through the cheek or jaw may spoil the punk's chances of an acting career, but, short of hitting the spinal column, there isn't much vital in the lower third of the face. Above the eyes, the skull curves away from the shooter and is at its thickest. Handgun bullets have glanced off this area or have penetrated the skin but zipped over or around the skull without penetrating.

Imagine a man bobbing and weaving to make himself a more difficult target and coming at you with an Arkansas toothpick. Hitting him in that vital area is going to take a lot of discipline and skill. If your attacker is smart and shooting at you from behind cover, his head may be all the target he presents.

The third vital area is the pelvis. This is probably the best target on someone who is charging you. A good hit in the pelvis should stop your attacker's forward motion. The legs don't work too well from a shattered pelvis.

When hits in the upper torso don't seem to be having much effect, shoot for the head and pelvis, and keep shooting until he goes down, advises Clint Smith.

Backing up

Most police officers who are killed by firearms are shot at a range of ten feet or less, according to FBI statistics. In the ten-year period from 1984 to 1993, 644 law-enforcement officers were shot and killed in the United States. Of those, 488 or 75 percent were shot by felons who were within ten feet of them. There are no comparable figures for civilians in gunfights, but it is reasonable to assume that the ten-foot zone of maximum danger applies to them as well.

"At this distance, he doesn't have to be good, he's only got to be lucky," says Clint Smith.

What can you do about it?

Maximize the distance to your attacker and minimize the target you present to him. This is what Thunder Ranch teaches very effectively in its Defensive Handgun courses.

Backing up during an armed confrontation is not an indication of cowardice. The graveyards are full of men who would not back up. It is both common sense and good tactics for three reasons:

- It makes you harder to hit. You are moving and with each backward step making yourself a smaller target.

Backing up: From your normal shooting position . . . (shown left) . . . take a long step back with your right foot (for right-handed shooters) . . . (shown center)

. . . and bring your left foot back until you are again in your normal stance (below right).

• It gives your superior skill a better chance to triumph over his willingness to shoot. Luckily for the rest of us, most criminals are not good marksmen. There are exceptions. If you are a licensed gun carrier, your skill should exceed that of most would-be robbers, rapists, or murderers.

• Any witnesses to the confrontation will tell investigating police officers that you were retreating and trying to avoid a gun-fight. This sounds good to grand juries and prosecutors.

There are two methods of backing up. The first, which is taught at Thunder Ranch, is particularly good on rough ground. You use a sort of crab-walk in which your legs are never crossed. This can be done to advantage up to about twenty yards. Beyond twenty yards, your chances of being hit by an assailant's bullet are greatly reduced.

Practice first with an empty gun on flat ground. The instructions are given for a right-handed shooter and should be reversed for a southpaw. Assume the Weaver or modified-Weaver stance. Your left foot should be half a pace ahead of your right, knees slightly bent, trunk of your body erect, gun in both hands, sights on the target. Lift your right leg and stretch it backward as far as you can. Put it down, toe first, then heel. Move your weight—or center, as the martial artists say—backward, until most of your weight is on your right foot. Bring your left foot back half a pace until you are in your original stance. Grope backward again with your right toe, and repeat the procedure. With practice, you can walk backward remarkably rapidly, keeping the sights nailed to the target and shooting all the while if necessary. Strive for smoothness, so your upper body is not bobbing up and down, but moves only to the rear. This makes it easier to keep the sights on the target. Get in the habit of shouting orders, such as "STOP" or "DROP THE GUN," in a loud, authoritative voice as you back up.

The second method of moving backwards or forwards is by using a gliding motion with your knees bent and your body erect. Bill Davison and experienced law-enforcement firearms instructor Jerry Lane prefer this technique. It is more like a short, ordinary walking step, but with the body moving only horizontally. In a normal walk, the head tends to bob up and down with each step. Try to eliminate this vertical movement. It is easier to keep the sights on the target with this method, and it is faster than the crab-walk. It is particularly useful on a flat, unobstructed surface such as a parking lot, where there is nothing to trip over.

If the cover is to one side or the other, again you have two options. You can get there by using a variation of the crab walk. To move to your right, take a step in that direction with your right foot. Move your left foot in the same direction, until you are back in your normal shooting stance. Take another step with the right foot and repeat the process. All the time, your gun should be in both hands, covering your attacker or shooting at him. With your knees bent and torso upright, you should be able to move quite rapidly, sideways to cover. To move to the left, reverse the process, leading off with a sideways step to the left with the left foot.

Bill Davison of Tac Pro Shooting Center shooting two-handed while moving from left to right towards cover.

Davison shooting one-handed as he moves from right to left towards cover.

You can also head for cover to one side or other of your assailant by using the same gliding walk used to advance or retreat. During this technique, your body will be facing towards the cover and you will be watching your attacker over your left or right shoulder. If you are right-handed and your attacker is to your left, you will be able to use both hands on your gun. If the threat is to your right, you will have to shoot one-handed.

Using Cover

There are two types of cover: cover from view, or concealment, and cover from fire. Anything that conceals you but won't stop a bullet is concealment. Examples are bushes, some exterior house walls, sheetrock walls between the studs, most modern interior doors, settees or sofas, car doors, and bodywork.

"You are not safe behind a car door," advises Robert Butler, firearms instructor with U.S. Customs. "Most of them are just a thin piece of metal. Unless the bullet hits the window frame or some other obstruction, the bullet will go through them."

As I mentioned in the chapter on safety, I have seen many houses that have been hit during drive-by shootings. Rifle bullets, handgun bullets, and shotgun slugs went through the front walls of these houses, through all the interior walls, and often out through the back walls. In many cases, occupants were wounded or killed by bullets that had gone through at least one wall and often several.

Firing a hollow-point bullet through sheetrock increases its penetration because the sheetrock will fill the hollow point and make it act like a round-nosed bullet. In other words, it will penetrate rather than expand. This is something to remember, if you have to shoot someone in an apartment that has neighbors just the other side of a sheetrock wall.

Cover from fire is anything bullets will not go through, such as thick tree trunks, concrete pillars, brick walls, or vehicle engine blocks. In seeking cover from fire, you must take into account what is being fired at you. Cover that will stop a pistol bullet may not protect you from an AK-47 or a rifled shotgun slug. But if there is cover available, take it.

Some people are reluctant to shoot through concealment cover to hit the man hiding behind it. Bill McLennan probably owes his life to a closed window. While circling a house looking for a felon, he passed a window. Later, when the man was captured, he told McLennan he was lucky to be alive because he would have shot him if the window had been open.

If you are caught in the open but there is cover nearby, you have several options for getting there. You can use the crab-walk taught at Thunder Ranch or the gliding walk favored by Bill Davison and Jerry Lane. With either of these methods, you can keep up accurate fire at your opponents. Or you can just run like hell. The faster you are moving, the harder you are to hit.

When you reach cover, get as much of your body behind it as possible. Your hands and part of your head are all your assailant should be able to see. You can reduce the target area available to him by 90 percent under ideal circumstances. You can rest an arm or hand against hard cover, but don't let the gun touch it. However, it is better to stay back from the cover so nothing protrudes forward of it. Don't stick your arms out beyond a wall or doorway. The bad guy may be closer than you think and may take your gun away from you.

You don't even have to be that close to cover to use it. For example, if you can keep a tree trunk between you and your attacker, you don't have to be pressed up against it. It is better to have the tree closer to you than to him, but it isn't essential.

Once you have reached cover, don't hide blindly behind it. Try to maintain at least visual contact with your assailant until he is no longer a threat. If you lose sight of him, he may be circling around behind you to attack you from the rear.

Always use cover to reload if you can.

OTHER SHOOTING POSITIONS

Most of your shooting will be done from a standing position, but you should also practice shooting from other positions. Kneeling is useful for shooting around and over cover, such as a vehicle. It also reduces your size as a target if used out in the open. Most gunfights take place at short range, so it is faster and more versatile to extend both arms toward the target. It also gives you the ability to swing the gun onto a new target without moving your legs.

The traditional kneeling position has the weak arm supported by the knee. If your elbow is actually on your knee, it will wobble. Make sure your elbow is just below and forward of your knee. That will give you a steadier position.

Lying prone is a very strong shooting position. You can rest your arms and hands on the ground to give you a steady position for a long-range shot. Perhaps your adversary is armed with a rifle. Lying down also minimizes your exposure as a target. It is not for nothing that soldiers are trained to drop to the ground when they come under enemy fire. Take advantage of low cover such as a tree stump or a curb while shooting from prone.

Kneeling position for fast shooting.

Bill McLennan shooting from the lying or prone position.

Students at Thunder Ranch practice shooting while lying on their backs (supine) and struggling to their feet.

You should also practice shooting at a standing adversary while lying on your back and while getting to your feet. You may have tripped while backing up, or you may have been knocked down by a fist or a bullet. You could be grappling with an attacker on the ground while his friend is trying to shoot you. Practice shooting while on your back and while struggling to your feet, but be sure your shots don't hit your legs or go over the backstop.

RELOADING

Reloading is like taking a pee. As my uncle used to say: "A wise man when he can and a fool when he must." There are two types of reload: the reload when the gun is empty and the tactical reload. They apply to both semi-automatics and revolvers, although the procedures are different.

Competition shooters plan the way they will shoot a stage in a practical match so they never run the gun dry. They reload, dropping live rounds and partly loaded magazines on the ground as they race to the next shooting box. This is fine for competition shooters, who know ahead of time where all the targets are and who have no shortage of magazines or speedloaders.

However, in a gunfight, you will probably not count your rounds, and you will likely shoot your gun until the hammer clicks on an empty chamber or the slide locks back. You will probably have only one spare magazine or speedloader—or two at most—and you won't know how many more rounds you will need. The bad guy might be down, but he may have friends you haven't spotted yet. You can't afford to drop live rounds.

There is a perception that shooting a gun until it is empty is bad luck or bad form. Not so.

"An empty gun is not bad luck," says Clint Smith. "It simply means you've been in a really good fight. What you need to do is get the gun loaded or you'll be having some bad luck."

EMPTY RELOAD— SEMI-AUTOMATIC

If you are armed with a semi-automatic, you should have one or two magazines in open-topped pouches on your left hip, if you are right-handed. Almost half the magazine should be exposed above the magazine pouch and belt.

Steps in the empty reload procedure for a semi-automatic: 1. Slide locks back.

Again, we will assume the shooter is right-handed. When the slide locks open, remove your finger from the trigger and lay it along the outside of the trigger guard. Bend your right arm, moving the gun back towards you. Some instructors recommend keeping it at eye level. This allows you to keep your eyes on the gun and the threat in front of you at the same

2. Weak hand grasps a full magazine.

time. Others advise bringing the gun down so it is in front of your chest. This shortens the distance the magazine has to travel and gives you better control.

At the same time, drop your left hand to the magazine on your belt. Grasp it between thumb and curled middle finger, with your forefinger pointing downward along the front edge of the magazine. If you are wearing a shoulder holster, the magazines are likely to be hanging upside down under your right armpit. Grasp the magazine in the same way as if it were on your belt. Press the magazine release catch with your right thumb, dropping the magazine to the ground. You may have to shift your grip on the gun to reach the catch.

Draw the magazine with your left hand, letting the tip of your forefinger rest on the exposed bullet. As you move it toward the gun, turn your wrist over so the magazine is the right way up to enter the magazine well. Guide the magazine into the well with your forefinger, then use the heel of your hand to ram it home.

3. *Strong hand depresses the magazine release, and the magazine drops.*

Put your left hand back on the gun. Drop the slide by racking it, rather than by depressing the slide stop with your left hand. If your slide is not locked back, but the gun was still empty, rack the slide.

There are two ways to grasp the slide when racking it. You can hold it between your thumb and curled forefinger, with the thumb on

4. *Weak hand guides the new magazine into the magazine well.*

the right of the slide. This is the slingshot method.

A better technique is to grasp the slide overhand, with your curled fingers on the right side of the slide and the thumb on the left side pointing toward the rear. Instead of pulling the slide back sharply and letting it go, hold the slide with your left hand and push the gun sharply away from you. After the slide has shunted forward, keep pushing the gun forward into the firing position, pick up your sight picture, and press the trigger, if necessary.

When there is a lull in the action, you can retrieve your empty magazine. The overhand technique for racking the slide is easier to use when you are under extreme stress and your fine motor skills deteriorate.

Bill Davison teaches his students to kneel while reloading in the open where there is no cover. He says this makes you a smaller target and enables you to pick up your ejected magazine more easily.

5. *Seat magazine with heel of the weak hand.*

6. *Rack the slide using the overhand technique. Resume firing position.*

TACTICAL RELOAD— SEMI-AUTOMATIC

Use a tactical reload to top up your gun during a break in the action. You may have disposed of one adversary but suspect he had company, or you may be behind cover.

Keeping the gun trained on the threat, move your finger off the trigger. Grab the new magazine with your left hand in the same way as for an empty reload. As you bring the new magazine up toward the gun, curl the forefinger down on the left side of the magazine so it is held between the fore and middle fingers. As your left hand reaches the bottom of the gun, depress the magazine release.

Drop the old magazine into your left palm, gripping it between your thumb and forefinger. Insert the new magazine into the gun, and ram it home with the heel of your hand. Put

Tactical reload—semi-automatic:
1. Draw a full magazine from its pouch and curl your forefinger down,
so the magazine is held between your fore and middle fingers as you bring the magazine
up to the gun.

2. Depress the magazine release with your strong thumb, and drop the partly-loaded magazine into the palm of your weak hand, grasping it between thumb and forefinger.

3. Insert the full magazine and seat it with the palm of the weak hand.

the old magazine into a
pocket on your left side,
where you can reach it if you
need more fire power. Put
the left hand back on the gun,
and resume firing if necessary.

Empty Reload—
REVOLVER

The way you carry your
spare ammunition has a lot

Empty reload using a speedloader:
1. Operate the cylinder latch with
the thumb of the strong hand.

to do with the way
you reload a
revolver. The
fastest way is to
use a speedloader
which holds all
five or six rounds
ready to be dropped into
the cylinder at once.
The problem with
speedloaders is that
they are bulky. This is
fine for a uniformed
patrolman who can
wear them in the open
on his Sam Brown belt.
It is not so good for
the plainclothes officer
or civilian gun carrier.
A speedloader is
almost as difficult to
conceal as the gun
itself. Therefore, many

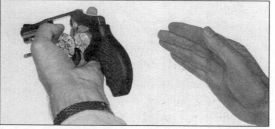

2. Open the cylinder with the weak hand.

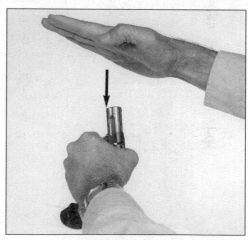

3. Turn the gun muzzle upward. Hit the
ejector rod sharply with the heel of the
strong hand to eject empty cases.

4. Point the muzzle down. Grasp a full speedloader from pouch or pocket, and insert the rounds into the chambers.

5. Flick the speedloader out of the way, and close the cylinder.

6. Resume the firing position.

civilians will either carry no spare rounds—not recommended—or will carry them loose in a pocket or in a flat pouch on the belt.

WITH SPEEDLOADER: As with the semi-auto, some people like to keep the gun at, or just below, eye level while reloading, enabling them to see any potential threat. Others bring the gun back until it is in front of the chest. Take your finger off the trigger and out of the trigger guard. Move your left hand forward under the gun.

Use your fore and middle fingers to grasp the cylinder on the right side and use your thumb on the left. Operate the cylinder latch with your right thumb: push it forward with a Smith & Wesson, pull it back with a Colt. Open the cylinder with the fingers and thumb of the left hand.

Take your right hand off the gun. Turn your left wrist a quarter turn to the right so the barrel is pointing vertically upward. Smack the ejector rod sharply downward with the heel of your right hand, knocking the empty cases out of the cylinder.

In some short-barreled revolvers, like Smith & Wesson's Chiefs Special and Centennial, the ejector rod is very short, and it may not punch the empties clear of the cylinder. You may have to pluck some of them out with your right hand.

When the cylinder is empty, turn your left hand back a quarter turn to the left and bend your wrist downward so the muzzle is pointing at the ground.

Grab your speedloader with your right hand with your fingers extending over the cartridges. Guide the bullets into the cylinder. Turn the knob on the back of the speedloader, releasing the rounds to drop into the cylinder. Flick the speedloader forward out of the way, then grasp the butt with your right hand. Close the cylinder with your left hand. Resume your two-handed grip, and get the gun back into action.

There is another method of ejecting the spent cases, using the right hand. When you bring the gun back toward you, leave your finger inside the trigger guard. After opening the cylinder with both hands, take your left hand off the gun. Allow the gun to roll back in your right hand, using the trigger finger inside the trigger guard as a pivot. The barrel should now be vertical. Use the right thumb to press down on the ejector rod, punching out the empties.

Transfer the gun to the left hand, holding the cylinder open with thumb and two fingers as described earlier. The reload is completed as in the first method. I prefer the second method because it is the same technique I use for a partial or tactical reload. However, using your thumb to eject the cases is not quite as positive as giving the ejector rod a sharp tap with the heel of the left hand.

WITHOUT SPEEDLOADER: For most civilians, this is the more likely scenario. Spare rounds are likely to be kept loose in a left-side pocket or in a flat pouch on the left side of your belt. Galco makes a flat pouch that holds six rounds in pairs,

Reloading a revolver without a speedloader:

1. After opening the cylinder, let the weapon rotate on the trigger finger until the muzzle is pointing up. Eject empties with the thumb of the strong hand.

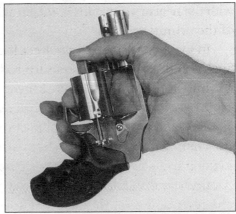

2. Point the muzzle downward and put the tip of the strong hand thumb into one of the empty chambers. Slide a fresh round down that thumb into the adjacent chamber.

which is ideal for this type of reload. True, it is slower than using a speedloader, but the rounds are held flat to the belt. Don't use a slide that keeps individual rounds in belt loops. Rounds kept this way for any length of time will grow green mold on the outside of the cases and are slow to get out of the loops. Use the second technique described earlier to eject the empties, keeping the gun in the strong hand.

Once the cylinder is empty, bring the gun down to waist level. Flip the gun forward at least one-hundred-fifty degrees, using the trigger finger through the trigger guard as a pivot. You are now gripping the gun in your right hand by its butt, with the muzzle pointed down at about a sixty-degree angle.

Take your finger out of the trigger guard and lay it alongside the frame.

While you are ejecting the spent cases with your right hand, your left reaches for your spare rounds. Depending on how you carry them, take one, two, or more to the cylinder. Holding the gun by its butt in your shooting hand, push your thumb forward into the mouth of one of the chambers. You use your thumb to index the cylinder as you feed in the rounds using your thumb as a guide. Holding one or two rounds at a time, slide them down your right thumb into the chambers. With a Smith & Wesson or any revolver with a cylinder that turns anticlockwise when fired, use your thumb in the empty chambers to move the cylinder clockwise as you feed in the rounds. With a Colt, which turns its cylinder clockwise when firing, use your thumb on top of the rounds you have just loaded to move the cylinder anticlockwise.

Using the thumb to index the cylinder enables you to reload your revolver in total darkness or in daylight without looking down at it. The other advantage is that you can stop the reloading process at any point after loading the first round or two, close the cylinder, and the gun will fire. When you close the cylinder, make sure the empty chamber your right thumb was holding is in the 12 o'clock position.

Most instructors teach students to reload single rounds with the right hand, holding the gun in the left hand as for loading with a speedloader. They say that under the stress of combat, your right hand will be able to manipulate the rounds into the chambers more easily than your left. Try both methods and pick the one you like best.

TACTICAL RELOAD—REVOLVER

There will be times when you have fired three or four shots from your revolver, and you have time to reload, even though your gun is still partly loaded. There are two methods of reloading a revolver that has been fired but still contains some live rounds.

METHOD 1. Rather than fumble, trying to pull out the empty cases with your nails, dump empties and loaded rounds and start again. But don't dump them on the ground. Use the second method described earlier to empty the cylinder. Use your right thumb on the ejector rod, and cup your left hand under the cylinder to catch live rounds and empty cases. Put them into a pocket from which you can grab the live rounds later if you need them. Now reload as you would an empty revolver.

METHOD 2. Point the muzzle vertically downwards and open the cylinder. Push up on the ejector rod with the left hand just enough to enable you to grasp the empty cases and pull them from their chambers one by one. Replace them and close the cylinder. Resume firing if necessary.

IMMEDIATE ACTIONS OR IAs

Everyone who shoots a semi-automatic will, at some time or another, experience a malfunction or jam. You may be able to drop all your shots into the eyeball of a figure target in the blink of an eye at fifty yards, but until you can keep your gun running under adverse conditions, you are not an accomplished pistol fighter.

Many handgun enthusiasts, the author included, have a long-running love affair with the Colt Government Model 1911 and its clones. In .45 ACP caliber, it is undoubtedly one of the finest fighting sidearms ever invented. However, it is temperamental, particularly after it has been accurized. In a class of twenty shooters at Thunder Ranch, about half were equipped with the 1911 type of semi-automatic, and all the malfunctions came from their end of the firing line. The following immediate actions, or IAs, as taught by Bill McLennan, will clear most malfunctions in a semi-automatic.

First Immediate Action:

1. Twist the weapon to the right so the ejection port is downward. Tap the bottom of the magazine with the heel of the weak hand to make sure it is seated properly.

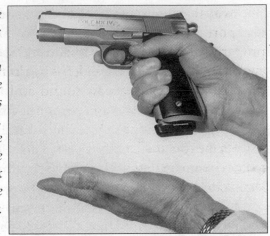

2. Rack the slide and resume the firing position.

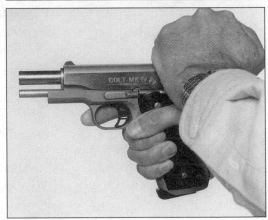

FIRST IA—TWIST, TAP, RACK, READY: If you press the trigger and your gun fails to fire, either the gun is empty—in which case the slide will be locked back on most semi-autos—or you have a malfunction. If your gun is empty, perform the empty reload described above. But perhaps your magazine is not seated, and the slide failed to pick up a round on its way forward; an empty case failed to eject and is stuck vertically, like a stovepipe, in the ejection port; or you had a dud round that failed to go off. Whatever, Twist, Tap, Rack, and Ready is your first immediate action.

Twist the gun to the side about sixty degrees so the ejection port is down. Tap the magazine to make sure it's seated properly. Grasp the slide overhand and sharply push the gun away from you, racking the slide. As you let the slide go, it shunts forward, picking up a new round and feeding it into the chamber. You are now ready to resume firing if necessary.

Some instructors teach a different technique to deal with a stovepipe case stuck in the ejection port. They teach students to knock the case out of the port with a wiping motion of the left hand. However, if the slide did not travel far enough to the rear to eject the empty case, it may not have traveled back far enough to pick up a new round. If this happens, you wipe away the stovepipe, and the slide slips forward onto an empty chamber. You will push the gun forward into the firing position and press the trigger—CLICK. Now you need to rack the slide. It is better to use Twist, Tap, Rack, and Ready to clear a stovepipe. The twist is specifically to let the stovepipe case fall clear of the gun. True, you may eject a live round, but you will be back in the action.

You can practice this at the range as follows: insert a loaded magazine in the gun; rack the slide to feed a round into the chamber; press the magazine-release button, and withdraw the magazine about an eighth of an inch. Take up a firing position and press the trigger. The gun will fire, but the slide will not pick up another round on its way forward. When you press the trigger again, the hammer will click on an empty chamber. Now twist the gun to the right, tap the magazine to seat it, rack the slide, push the gun forward into the firing position, and press the trigger.

SECOND IA: Sometimes the First IA won't work. For example, it won't clear a double feed. A double feed is when there is a live round or empty case still in the chamber, but the slide has picked up another round, which it is pushing up against the back of the one in the chamber, locking up the gun. When attempting to clear the gun with the First IA, you should be aware

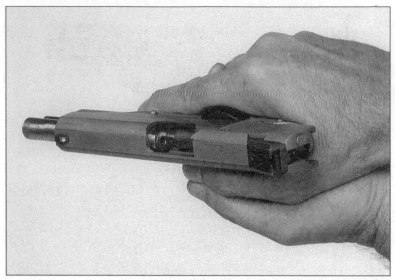

A malfunction where the slide sticks three-quarters of the way back like this is probably caused by a double feed.

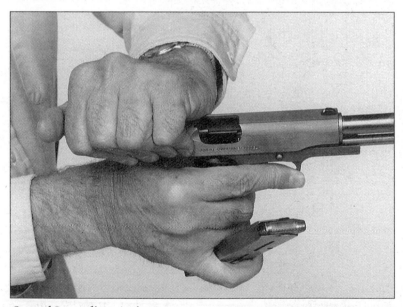

Second Immediate Action:
1. Lock the slide back, take out the magazine, hold it between the ring and little fingers of the strong hand, and rack the slide three or four times.

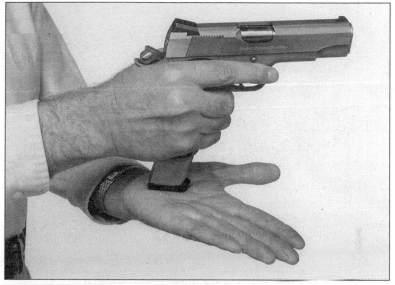

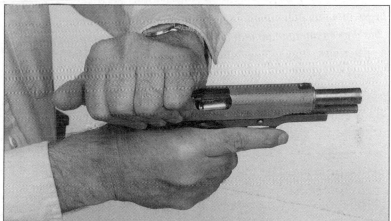

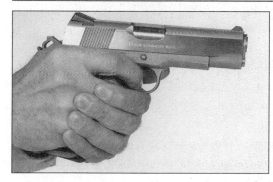

2. (at top) Replace the magazine.

3. (center) Rack the slide.

4. (at left) Resume the firing position.

when you attempt to rack the slide that it is almost in the locked-back position and travels forward perhaps only a quarter of an inch.

Now you use the Second IA: Twist the gun to the right, adjusting the grip of your right hand so your right thumb can reach the slide stop. Grasp the slide and pull it to the rear. Lock it back with the slide stop. Withdraw the magazine. Put it in your pocket if you have another loaded magazine available. A damaged magazine can be the cause of the malfunction, so it is better to replace it with a fresh magazine if you have one. If not, tuck the magazine between the ring and little fingers of your right hand. Rack the slide three times to make sure you have removed the round or empty case in the chamber or anything else that caused the gun to lock up. Insert a new magazine or the one you have been holding in your gun hand. Rack the slide to load a round, and you are ready to fire.

You can practice the Second IA as follows: Lock the slide to the rear with the gun empty. Point the muzzle at the ground, barrel vertical. Drop a dummy round into the chamber. Keeping the muzzle pointing downward, insert a fresh magazine with a dummy round on top. Ease the slide gently forward, so a dummy round at the top of the magazine pushes up against the back of the dummy round in the chamber.

Bring the gun up into the firing position and press the trigger. Nothing happens. Bring the gun back toward you at belt level. Twist the gun to the right side, ejection port downward. Lock the slide back. Remove the magazine and put it in your pocket or tuck it between your ring and little fingers. Rack the slide several times. Reload and fire at the target. If you are practicing with a partner, you can take turns setting up malfunctions for each other. It is important to use two dummy rounds in setting up this situation. If a live round is used in the chamber, it is possible for the nose of the second round to hit the primer of the chambered round hard enough to set it off. If the top round in the magazine is live, hitting the chambered

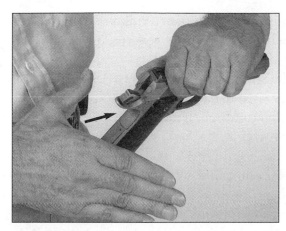

Third Immediate Action: Hold the weapon by the slide in the weak hand, and strike the butt high up under the hammer with the palm of the strong hand.

round can knock the bullet back into the case compressing the powder charge. This can lead to enough pressure when it is fired to blow up the gun.

THIRD IA: If the slide is seized and will not move, grasp it in an overhand grip with the thumb pointing to the rear. Release your grip on the weapon with the right hand, and with your right palm strike the butt of the gun several times, trying to push it forward. You'll usually be able to free a seized slide this way. Rack the slide, and get the gun running again. The slide can seize due to defective ammunition, like extruded primers, deformed cases, etc. If the Third IA doesn't cure a seized slide, you can rest the ejection port or rear sight against some object like the edge of a table, and try the palm strike from there.

H IP SHOOTING

Having emphasized in the last chapter the importance of using the sights at any range beyond arm's length, there are other schools of thought about self-defense shooting that you should be aware of.

Some experts can do amazing things shooting from waist level without using the sights. This is commonly referred to as hip shooting, though the gun is usually held forward of the hip. Former Border Patrolman Bill Jordan could shoot aspirin tablets off the fender of a car without hitting the car. Ed McGivern was also a pretty fair hand at hip shooting, hitting a one-inch bull's-eye most of the time at fifteen feet.

Bill McLennan practiced hip or point shooting in his earlier days and got quite good at it. He used a .22 caliber K-frame Smith & Wesson, similar in size and feel to his .357 Magnum service revolver.

"I could afford .22 ammunition, and at fifteen feet or so I could get match boxes drawing and shooting from the hip. But I was on the range and shot three hundred and four hundred rounds a day for months on end, and I got real good at it. I no longer have that skill because I haven't stayed at it. Within months it had diminished, and within a few years it was gone. I can hone it back probably quicker than a person can learn it, but it doesn't stay with you."

So unless you can afford the time and money to shoot more rounds than McDonald's has hamburgers, stick with the advice of Wyatt Earp and Frank Hamer: get that gun up to eye level whenever you shoot at something beyond arm's reach.

Point Shooting

In the 1920s and '30s, the Chinese city of Shanghai was a violent place. Gunfights between the British-led police force and local criminals exceeded six hundred over a 12½-year period with the police winning most of them. The credit goes to Captains W. E. "Dan" Fairbairn and E. A. "Bill" Sykes, who developed a close-range shooting system that gave the police more edge than a two-handed sword. During World War II, Fairbairn and Sykes taught their skills to British commandos and secret agents. Their system was introduced into the United States by Colonel Rex Applegate, who taught it to agents of the Office of Strategic Services, forerunner of the CIA.

Unlike the "New Technique" as taught by Jeff Cooper, Clint Smith, Chuck Taylor, and others, the shooter using the Fairbairn-Sykes-Applegate technique, also known as the "point shooting" method, ignores the sights and shoots mostly one handed. The shooter adopts a crouch, shoulders square with the target, gun in one hand. He, or she, keeps the gun on the center line of the body and raises it with a straight arm to eye level. The shooter squeezes off a shot or several, focusing on the target, without using the sights. In their book, *Shooting To Live*, Fairbairn and Sykes recommend teaching this method at ranges of six feet and twelve feet. At greater ranges, Applegate recommends a two-handed point-shooting technique, while still ignoring the sights. Further still, the point shooters use two hands and align the sights.

Some teachers and advocates of the New Technique and the point-shooting method tend to become polarized and think their technique is the only correct one. In fact, the two methods are closer to each other than some of their advocates acknowledge. Both techniques use one-handed, unsighted fire at close range, and both use two-handed, sighted shooting at longer ranges. The main difference between the two techniques is the determination of when to change from one type of fire to the other. As students, we can learn from both.

Teachers of the New Technique advocate shooting with both hands on the gun and using the sights under most circumstances. Point shooters tend to use one hand and ignore the sights. However, New Technique shooters also practice firing with one hand, in case the other is holding onto something or is disabled, and point shooters use both hands and the sights at longer ranges. Two hands make a steadier gun platform than one, so it makes sense to get both hands on the gun when there is time and both hands are free.

For close-in work, teachers of the New Technique recommend shooting from a "retention draw" position. In this technique the gun is held as in Step 2 of the draw described in the

Retention-draw firing position.

previous chapter. Shots are fired with the gun well below eye level, one-handed, with the forearm against the side. The other hand can be used to push away an attacker. This position is remarkably similar to the "quarter- or close-hip position" as illustrated in the book by Fairbairn and Sykes. They recommend practicing this position at a range of three feet.

Other teachers with excellent qualifications vary in the amount of emphasis they place on using the sights at ranges from arm's length to seven yards.

The late Jim Cirillo, a former member of the New York City Police stakeout squad and a seasoned gunfighter, taught his students to find the sights "subliminally," as he called it. He said his students shot better with the sights taped over, using the silhouette of the gun to aim.

Massad Ayoob, one of the best defensive handgun trainers in the nation, has made a scientific study of contemporary gunfights. In his book, *StressFire*, he recommends looking over the top of the gun, but getting the front sight onto the target. He suggests that trained police officers miss with three out of four shots fired in gunfights because they allow their focus to be drawn to the target instead of remaining on the sights. However, when it is too dark to see the sights, Ayoob recommends an isosceles point.

Brian Enos, one of the top practical competition shooters, talks of looking through the sights at the target, rather than focusing on them, for fast shooting at close range.

As mentioned earlier, law-enforcement firearms instructor Jerry Lane says that for most of the last decade police officers have principally been taught the Weaver stance. The shooter stands at an angle to the target, with the support arm bent sharply at the elbow, almost as though holding a rifle, and with the head canted to one side to line up the sights.

"It is totally opposite of what we will do during periods of extreme stress," Lane says. "What we will do is, we'll step forward, square to the target, and both arms will go out in front of us. We'll bend slightly at the knees, lean forward, and look at the target."

This applies at ranges up to twenty feet, where most gunfights take place, Lane says. Beyond twenty feet, the trained person feels less threatened, will slow down, and will use the sights.

Even officers who have been trained only in the Weaver stance will adopt a different position under life-threatening conditions at close range.

"They get in a shooting, they square to the target, use the isosceles shooting position, and it's like 78 percent of the time," Lane says.

Bruce Siddle of PPCT Management Systems teaches the law-enforcement and special-warfare communities how to condition people for combat stress. He says that under extreme stress the eyes dilate and you cannot physically focus on the front sight.

In his book, *Sharpening the Warrior's Edge*, Siddle states that the body's reaction to extreme stress results in changes to the visual system. Your ability to focus your eyes on anything close, such as sights or instruments, deteriorates, and you have difficulty in visual tracking. You also lose peripheral vision.

"You lose near vision, so you can't see your front sight," Siddle says.

Your focus will be on the threat. If you have had "Watch the front sight" drilled into you in training, but suddenly you are faced with a real-life threat, and you can't see the front sight clearly, you will be disconcerted. You may even panic.

However, Cirillo, in his book, *Guns, Bullets, and Gunfights,* stated that during his first shootout as a member of the New York City Police stakeout squad he was able to see his sights as clearly as if he were on a target range. Different people will react differently at different times.

Robert Butler, U.S. Customs firearms instructor, says that at really close range you can just point and shoot. "You need to go to the range; teach yourself how to hold that weapon and proper trigger control. Your arms are pointed straight out, you've got a proper grip, and that weapon will be pointed pretty well at the center of the target."

These differences in technique by different experts should not confuse the student. It's just a matter of choosing the right technique for the shooter and conditions. At ranges of four to eight feet, it is not difficult to hit the torso area of a figure target without using the sights. With practice you can extend this easily to twelve or fifteen feet. You should practice this because most gunfights happen in poor light when you can't see the sights anyway. Practice shooting in twilight and semi-darkness.

At arm's-length range, up to about four feet, practice shooting one handed with the forearm pressed against your ribs, where it is difficult for an attacker to grab your gun. This is Fairbairn's "quarter- or close-hip" position, while at Thunder Ranch it is referred to as the retention-draw position.

If you are attacked at arm's length, you will draw and fire your first couple of shots as soon as the gun comes out of the holster, from the retention position. As you back up, you move into a two-handed point without aligning the sights, and eventually you concentrate on the front sight for fast-aimed fire. The distance at which you change from one position to the next depends upon your preference and skill level and upon the circumstances—that is, can you see the sights or is it too dark? Personally, I change from the retention position to the two-handed point at about four feet and from the point to aimed fire using the sights, or at least the front sight, at about twelve feet.

However, if you are backing up while shooting and your attacker is bobbing and weaving, you will need to align the sights to keep making hits even at close range. Try out these pointing techniques and see which ones are best for you, but most of your practice shooting should be done by aligning the sights and focusing on the front sight. Taking a flash sight picture not only improves your accuracy but teaches your body a muscle memory that is part of the two-handed, eye-level pointing technique. If in doubt, focus on the front sight.

Chapter Ten

WINNING A GUNFIGHT: MIND-SET AND TACTICS

Gunsmith Greg Ferris had just started working on a customer's .45 semi-automatic in the workshop part of his San Antonio store when he heard the front-door buzzer sounding. Out of habit or paranoia—he had been held up before—he poked his head around the doorway into the counter area.

What he saw was not a customer. Three stocky Hispanic teenagers in street-gang garb were charging across the display area, heading straight for him. The youth in the lead was grasping a small, chrome-plated semi-automatic, which was pointed at him.

Ferris ducked back behind cover, his hand reaching for the custom .38 Super semi-automatic that was ready for action in a wall mount attached to the side of his work bench.

"Get your ass back out here, motherf----r," one of the attackers yelled.

"I did lean back around the corner, weapon now in my right hand unsupported, bringing it up to eye level with the muzzle trained to the front display area, while I remained hugging as tight to the corner as I could, so as to keep the solid wall between us," Ferris said.

As he looked over his sights, he saw another robber crashing through the swing door at the end of the counter. He was wielding a 12-gauge, pump shotgun, and it was pointed at Ferris's face. "At this point," Ferris said, "everything went into super slow motion."

He didn't realize until afterward that the robber with the shotgun fired the first shot. People who heard the sequence of shots said they heard a big bang first. The load of bird shot

307

whipped past Ferris's right shoulder, missing him by less than a foot, and smashed into the gun safe behind him, blasting a six-inch circle on the black-painted steel.

Ferris began firing at the youth with the shotgun.

"I don't recall seeing the sights, but I can remember visually noting my weapon was recoiling with each shot."

While shooting, Ferris yelled for his assistant, Mike Falcon, to get the Remington shotgun that was kept loaded with buckshot and slugs for such emergencies.

The youth with the pump shotgun dived to the right, onto the floor by the display counter. Ferris yelled at him to drop the shotgun, not realizing he had hit the robber in the chest.

"He was lying on his right side, looking straight at me, and attempting to work the action of the shotgun," Ferris said.

Aware the robber was trying to reload and fire at him again, the gunsmith fired another shot at him. This action convinced the robber to quit the fight. He then rolled onto his back and released his hold on the shotgun.

As Ferris looked up, he saw the other two robbers crowded around the front door. The one with the chrome-plated semi-automatic was turning in a crouch toward Ferris with his arm extended. Afraid the robber was going to shoot him, the gunsmith again opened fire.

"I fired until color and motion were no longer present in the doorway," Ferris said.

The two thugs he was shooting at ran out of the store and were picked up by a fourth, who was the driver of the getaway car. Ferris returned his attention to the downed robber behind the counter. He heard a noise near the front door and turned his gun toward it. It was his assistant Mike Falcon coming through a door from another room holding a shotgun.

"We both swung our weapons almost to bear on each other and then, as if we hit our muzzles on an invisible barrier, stopped together upon recognition of each other and swung the muzzles away," Ferris said.

He told Falcon the other two had escaped onto the street. His assistant ran out in time to fire two quick shots at the fleeing car.

Meanwhile, Ferris's wife, Melinda, came into the display area armed with a .38 Special Derringer she had taken from a briefcase in the office.

The robber on the floor started whining: "Don't kill me, don't kill me; think of my family."

Ferris told him to shut up.

When police and paramedics arrived, the robber on the floor was rushed by ambulance to a nearby hospital with a single bullet wound to the chest. He died about two hours later. He was identified as a seventeen-year-old gang member.

An eighteen-year-old, suspected of being the robber with the chromed semi-automatic, was dropped off at another hospital with three gunshot wounds. He survived and was charged in the attack.

While I have called these gang members robbers out of convenience, it is doubtful that mere robbery was all they had in mind. Police intelligence later determined they were on a mission to increase the reputation of their gang and, had Ferris not been armed and ready to shoot, he, his assistant, and his wife may well have been murdered.

What can we learn from this incident?

First, Ferris was prepared. He had been robbed four years previously. He and his customers had been forced to lie on the floor while two robbers looted his store. It was only through their inattentiveness that Ferris managed to get to a shotgun and opened fire, wounding and paralyzing one robber and capturing the other. He was determined never to be caught off guard again, so he took precautions. He placed several guns at strategic places in the store, so he would never be far from one of them. Hence the shotgun was readily available to his assistant, and the .38 Super that saved his life was within arm's reach while he was at his work bench.

While both of Ferris's gunfights have happened in his gun store, yours may occur somewhere else—in your home, in your car, or on the street. Carjacking, a term unheard of a decade ago, is now a household word. In fact, the getaway car used in Ferris's shootout with the gang members had been taken from a woman at gunpoint shortly before they attacked the gun store.

Carjacking—or vehicle-jacking—was on James Turner's mind early on the morning of February 17, 1997. It would cost him a lot of blood.

Jim Eichelberg ran a trapline of vending machines in northwest Houston. He serviced these machines early in the morning before the traffic got too heavy. He often had a few thousand dollars on him from the vending machines, so he had a Texas concealed-handgun license and usually carried a gun.

The gun was a snub-nosed Smith & Wesson Model 37 five-shot revolver which weighed 13.5 ounces. In it he carried MagSafe rounds in .38 caliber. These rounds kick less than regular ammunition in the light gun, and the bullets are designed to fragment on contact, so they won't go through three apartment walls and hit a little old lady two rooms away. Eichelberg had been shooting most of his life. He practiced with his father-in-law at least once a week, he said.

That morning he left his home about 5 a.m. when it was still dark and started his route. About 5:45 a.m., the forty-nine-year-old Eichelberg was driving his 1985 Ford van east on Milwee towards the Northwest Freeway. Just before he reached the stop sign at the freeway service road, he passed a man walking in the direction he was driving.

Eichelberg pulled up at the stop sign and waited for the traffic to clear on the service road. As he waited, he looked in his rearview mirror, but he couldn't see the man he had just passed. Wondering why the man had disappeared, Eichelberg looked at the rearview mirror on the passenger side. He saw the man running along the passenger side of the van. The man was holding a revolver in his right hand.

"You could see that gun. It was almost like there was a spotlight on it because the street light down the street was reflecting off that gun," Eichelberg said. "I got a real good look at that gun."

Eichelberg had no doubt the man was going to try to rob him or hijack his van. His gun was on the floor of the vehicle under his jacket and a mass of paperwork. He groped desperately for the gun. By the time he found it, the man was yelling at him through the passenger door window.

"He had his face against the window. His nose was almost touching it, and he had the gun next to his head," Eichelberg said.

The man was later identified as James Turner, 32, a skinny black parolee who was dressed all in black. Turner was shouting at Eichelberg and pointing the revolver at him through the window. However, with the noise of the traffic on the service road and the windows being closed, Eichelberg couldn't hear what he was saying.

"I didn't figure he was there to sell me newspapers."

Eichelberg brought his gun up and fired one shot at Turner.

The window shattered, and Turner's face disappeared. Eichelberg thought he had hit him, but he wasn't sure. He was deaf and half-blinded by the explosion of his gun inside the van. He was aware he was not in a good position if the man came back, so he jumped out of the van. He started running towards the back of the van, still holding his revolver. Eichelberg was hoping to put some distance between himself and his would-be attacker.

Turner apparently had the same idea. He started running back the way he had come. The two men met at the back of the van.

"Bam! He fired at me. I wasn't hearing too good, but I heard a three-fifty-seven being shot at me," Eichelberg said.

He stopped and fired at the moment when Turner was stationary.

"It was just like the concealed-carry class. There's the silhouette target for half a second."

He estimated the range at eight or ten feet. He said he couldn't see the sights because it was still dark. Turner started to run away. He jumped across a ditch on the shoulder of the road then stopped, turned, and fired again at Eichelberg from about twenty feet.

"There's that silhouette target again for half a second. Bang! I fired one off, right then, right quick," he recalled. "I didn't know if I had got him or not."

They exchanged more shots as Turner ran towards the corner of a fence in an overgrown lot.

"He got right to where the fence made a corner and that's the last time he shot at me," Eichelberg said. "This last time he took aim at me, but he was just too far away. And I let fly one right there."

He and his father-in-law later measured the range at fifty-one feet. Turner disappeared into the darkness. After a few moments, Eichelberg returned to his van and drove to a nearby service station where he used a pay phone to call police. He told them someone had tried to hijack his van, that he had exchanged shots with the man, and that he was a concealed-handgun-license holder.

After a few minutes, two police cars arrived, but they didn't seem too interested in picking up Eichelberg. The officers asked him where he had last seen the would-be hijacker, then drove off and began to search the area. Eichelberg waited patiently at the gas station until another police car pulled up and the officer told him to get in.

"I jumped in the front seat and he said: 'You got him,'" Eichelberg recalled.

The officer drove him to a convenience store about a block from where Eichelberg had last seen him. Turner had apparently collapsed from loss of blood in front of the store.

The police officers immediately recognized Turner as someone they had arrested more than once in the past. Turner whined that somebody had shot him but denied that he had shot anyone or that he had had a gun. Police asked Eichelberg whether he was sure Turner had a gun.

"I know he had a gun. I know a muzzle flash when I see one, and it was pointed at me, by God. There's a gun," Eichelberg told them.

Jim Eichelberg standing at the corner of the fence where James Turner fired his last shot.

The police searched Turner's trail back and found the gun wrapped in Turner's jacket some distance from where he collapsed. They showed Eichelberg the gun, a Smith & Wesson .357-caliber revolver with a four-inch barrel. It had five empty cases in the cylinder and one live round.

Both men had fired five shots. Turner had missed with every shot; Eichelberg had scored with all his.

"I made six wounds with five shots," he said.

The first shot hit Turner in the chest and would probably have killed him if Eichelberg had been shooting regular hollow points or ball ammunition.

"The police told me that I put one right over his heart, and they said there was a pattern of about two inches, so it was glass and shrapnel. The bullet had exploded when it hit that window."

With his next four shots, Eichelberg had hit Turner twice in the buttocks and once in the thigh, and one bullet went through his hand into his groin.

Later when Eichelberg was giving detectives a statement at the homicide office, the doctor at Ben Taub Hospital who treated Turner phoned up. "He asked me what I had shot this guy with. He was full of holes," Eichelberg said.

Apparently the bullets had exploded on contact leaving shrapnel wounds. Despite having been hit by five bullets, Turner was stitched up and sent to jail the following day.

Eichelberg was not the only person who called police from Milwee and Northwest Freeway. They received a 9-1-1-call from Jim Barber, a man who had been filling his car at a nearby gas station. It became apparent that before he had accosted Eichelberg, Turner had tried to carjack Barber's vehicle. He had stuck his gun in Barber's chest and demanded his wallet and keys. However, Turner had been unable to find the right key to start the car and had fled on foot. The keys were later found in Turner's pocket at the hospital. Some crack cocaine was also found on him, and police believe he was high when he attempted to rob Barber and Eichelberg.

Afterwards, a detective from the burglary division called Eichelberg on the phone. "He was mad. He said: 'Why the hell didn't you carry something bigger?' I explained to the guy, it's not my responsibility to do anything but defend myself."

As a result of this incident, Turner was sentenced to fifty years in prison as a habitual criminal. Jim Eichelberg started carrying a Charter Arms Bulldog five-shot .44 Special with hollow points.

MIND-SET

The first lesson about gunfight survival is the Boy Scout motto: "Be prepared." And that means a lot more than just having a gun within reach and knowing how to use it. To win a gunfight, you need to be more than able to shoot your attacker: you must be willing. When I took the course to become a Texas concealed-handgun instructor, the section on the use of deadly force was taught to us by Commander Albert Rodriguez of the Texas Department of Public Safety Training Academy. The first thing he asked us was: "Are you mentally prepared to take a life?"

If you do not believe you can kill another human being, you have no business carrying a gun. It is true that, in most of the encounters between crooks and honest citizens, production of the gun is enough to deter a criminal attack—but only if the criminal believes you will shoot. You would have to be a very good poker player to bluff a street-wise crook into believing you will shoot, if you have serious doubts about it. Unless you are mentally and morally able to drop the hammer on another human being, carrying a gun is not for you. Most law-abiding citizens have a natural reluctance to pulling the trigger, and this is a good trait.

As mentioned in an earlier chapter, Jeff Cooper originated the color-code system to progressively overcome that reluctance in time for law-abiding citizens to effectively protect themselves. Old-time Western gunfighters used to say that the winner of a gunfight was usually the man who first realized he was in a shooting situation. Realizing as quickly as possible that you are in a shooting situation is critical, and Cooper's color code helps you do this.

Imagine for a moment that you have just finished work in a downtown office building, and it's dark. You ride down in the elevator still thinking about the budget for your department that you have been working on. You are still going over the details of that budget in your mind as you mumble, "Good night," to the security guard at his desk by the doors.

As you step out onto the street, you are wondering if you allocated enough money for paperclips. You turn automatically to your left and start walking toward your car in the parking lot three blocks away, as you have done every work day for the last three years. Your head is bent, and your eyes stare unseeingly at the sidewalk a few feet in front of you. You fail to notice the youth across the street, acting as a spotter. As you reach the corner of the building, you are estimating the toilet paper requirements of your department.

This is Condition White. You are oblivious to your surroundings. As Clint Smith would put it: you are food, about to be eaten.

As you turn the corner, you almost bump into two youths with their caps on backward. You are surprised; they are not. One of them has a black handgun pointed at your midriff.

"Gimme your wallet, motherf----r!" rasps the one with the gun.

What do you do? You are caught completely off guard. Moving from that state to survival mode takes longer than you have. You may be robbed, and you may be shot and killed.

Let us change the scenario. As you leave the building, you are alert. You scan the street up and down, looking for potential threats. You know it's late, and this is not the best part of downtown after dark. You are in Condition Yellow. You notice the spotter standing on the corner on the other side of the street, drawing on a cigarette. There seems to be no reason for him to be there at this time of night. But he might be waiting for a friend. You think he's seen you, but when you look at him, he's looking elsewhere. You feel that he's a threat, and as you walk toward the corner you're trying to figure out what he's going to do. You cast glances all around you to make sure he has no pals with him. You have identified a possible threat. You are in Condition Orange.

As you reach the corner, you take it wide in case there is someone waiting. Out of the corner of your eye, you see the spotter making a movement that could be a signal. You think about turning around and walking back to the building, but it's too late. You are on them. But you are not surprised. You know this is a shooting situation when you see the youth with the gun. You are in Condition Red.

"Gimme your wallet, motherf----r."

"Okay, okay. Don't shoot."

You reach back, but it's your gun you reach for, not your wallet. You are about six feet from the youth with the gun. He is the most obvious threat. There is no hesitation. As your gun reaches eye level, you fire. Several times. You couldn't miss, he's so close. You are backing up, still shooting, as you have been taught. You are going to use the corner of the building as cover. Suddenly, your right leg gives way, and you are on the ground, on your back. You must have been hit. Your attacker is still shooting at you. He's leaning toward you. You must keep fighting. Your sights are on his chest. You fire again, and again. He goes down. His buddy is running down the street. Your slide is locked back. You reload, still lying on the ground. You are trying to see the spotter. You see him running away. The guy who shot you is lying on the ground, not moving. You've been hit, but you have survived.

The color code ratchets up your readiness and willingness to shoot. Another approach that may help you to pull the trigger on another human being is to dehumanize him. Think of your assailant as a target, rather than a person possibly with a wife, a mother, children. When we go to war with another nation, we try to dehumanize our enemy. We talked of "Gooks" and "Japs" in an attempt to make killing them easier. It may help you to pull the trigger if you look on your attackers as "trash" or "peckerwoods" or "scumbags."

The politically-correct crowd may have a field day over such advice, but who cares, if it helps keep you alive? Jeff Cooper recommends turning fear into anger or righteous indignation. How dare this man take my belongings at gunpoint? What gives this man the right to point a gun at me?

Shoot for the man, not for his weapon. Pick a spot on the "target" that you want to hit. It may be a belt buckle or a shirt button. This also helps you avoid allowing your mind to be captured by his weapon. People who analyze police gunfights have noticed that a disproportionate number of rounds fired hit the weapon being fired by the other combatant. This is not the result of a misguided attempt to shoot the gun out of his hand, *a la* Hopalong Cassidy. It is the result of the officer's attention being so concentrated on his opponent's weapon that he hits it.

The scenario above illustrates some other principles of winning a gunfight. The robber has a gun. This makes him all-powerful in his own mind. He is not expecting you to fight. You reinforce this belief when you appear to accede to his demands, saying: "Okay, okay. Don't shoot."

There is nothing fair about a gunfight. Take every advantage you can. Lie and cheat. If you can misdirect him while you draw and shoot, so much the better. If he is holding a gun on you, give him no warning—draw and shoot. It may appear that he just wants to rob you, but you can't take the chance. Maybe he wants to take you on a tour of automated teller machines as he loots your bank accounts. And maybe he'll kill you for fun along the way, as happened to San Antonio contractor Joe Ince. Never, ever let a crook take your gun. Despite the whining of the gun-control activists and the propaganda of some government agencies, people who fight crime at gunpoint are less likely to be killed or injured or to lose their property than those who offer no resistance.

Most of the time, action beats reaction. As a concealed-handgun-license holder, whether you are in your own home or on the street, you will be reacting to the attacker's action. You will be playing catch up in most deadly-force situations. The criminal will be the one who initiates the action creating the dangerous situation; and you will be reacting to his threat. He is likely to decide first that he is going to use deadly force. The person who initiates the action has a huge advantage.

If your first indication that something is wrong is when he starts shooting at you, you will need to move, draw your gun, and return fire. In April 2005 at the NRA convention in Houston, I watched Todd Jarrett, a professional shooter for Para Ordnance, draw his gun from concealment. The timer started with a beep. When he heard the beep, Jarrett cleared his tactical vest and drew his gun. He raised it to eye level and pressed the trigger to stop the timer. It took him about one second from beep to shot. Jarrett is an expert who fires many tens of thousands of rounds a year. I experimented doing the same drill at the range, and it took me an average of 1.48 seconds from beep to shot—almost half a second longer than Jarrett. I also tested how long I took between shots when firing my CZ 75 in 9mm as fast as I could, keeping the shots in the kill zone on a figure target at ten feet. I averaged 0.26 of a second. This means that if I draw and shoot at the sound of the bad guy's first shot, he is likely to get off at least five more shots before I fire one in return. This is why I have to move, preferably to some cover, to make myself a more difficult target. You might try these experiments for yourself.

However, if someone is holding you at gunpoint, perhaps during a robbery, and he has not decided to shoot you, it is possible to draw and shoot before he can respond—beat the drop, in Western parlance. From the figures we have just looked at, it seems impossible, right?

Habib Howard of Toledo, Ohio, was able to beat the drop when a robber tried to hold up his family's convenience store. Howard was wearing a Taurus semi-automatic in an inside-the-waistband holster and covered by his shirt.

Late one night in May 2004, Jose Custodia-Mota entered the store and picked up a twelve-pack of canned beer. When he approached the counter, he pulled a handgun on Howard and demanded money from the register. Habib gave him the money but kept his left side to the robber while his right hand was on the butt of his gun.

Custodia-Mota walked towards the door then raised his gun as though to fire at Howard, who drew his own gun and fired at the robber hitting him twice. Custodia-Mota did not get off a shot. Howard was able to beat the drop because he kept his gun side turned away from the robber and had his hand on the gun. This story is recounted in detail in my book, *Thank God I Had a Gun: True Accounts of Self-Defense.*

Habib Howard in his family's Toledo, Ohio, convenience store.

Photo courtesy *NRA News.*

Another way to beat the drop is to create a distraction, so the bad guy is thinking of something other than shooting you. Bill Davison of Tac Pro Shooting Center refers to it as making a window.

"We have to cause a distraction, a break in the train of thought of the bad guy, just get him to look in a different direction," Davison says. "That's what we call making a window."

It can be as simple as looking beyond the threat and saying: "No, it's okay, I can deal with it." You are speaking to someone who isn't there, but the bad guy doesn't know that for sure.

"It's very, very hard in a stress situation for someone to think: you're making that up; there is no one behind me. So when you say: 'It's okay, I'm dealing with it,' they want to look to see who you're talking to and when they look, bam, bam. You've got a window: he can't even see what you're doing, and you can go for the weapon," Davison says.

Throwing something also works as a good distraction. It might be your cap or hat, your wallet, a bank bag if you are taking receipts to the bank, or change from your pocket—anything that's handy. In the same way that it is difficult for the bad guy not to look when you talk to an imaginary person behind him, it will be close to impossible for his eyes not to follow a thrown object.

Davison tells of an occasion when he was competing in a tactical force-on-force competition, using a training system of plastic bullets fired from a modified handgun. More about force-on-force in Chapter 12. Competitors were searched before they were allowed to compete. They were allowed to have nothing on them but the handgun loaded with plastic rounds and a helmet for protection—no wallet, no knife, no keys, no change. Davison was given a piece of paper with the location of the next course of fire.

The scenario started with the competitor walking down a track with a woman who played his sister. Davison was told to stop and tie a boot lace, allowing the woman to walk ahead. While he was still kneeling down, the woman started screaming: "Bill, help me, help me."

When Davison reached his "sister," she was being held by two men. One had her by the throat and was holding a gun to her head; the other was standing beside them. Bill recalled the conversation this way.

Davison: "Look sis, leave him alone. You're always pestering people."

Bad guy: "Huh?"

Davison: "I'm sorry about that, mate. She's always picking on people; she's always doing stupid stuff. She's a bit crazy in the head, you know."

"Of course that wasn't their game plan, because they wanted me to try and rescue her, and I'm helping them beat her up verbally," Davison said.

Bad guy: "Well, you'd better do as we say."

Davison: "Yeah, no problem at all; just throw her down on the ground. I'll pick her up; it's no problem."

Bad guy: "You'd better stand still, dude."

Davison: "Well, what do you want?"

Bad guy: "Give me your money."

Davison: "Okay."

He started searching in his pockets and found the piece of paper with instructions on it.

"So I just lean slightly to one side, slip the piece of paper between my fingers, and threw it off to the left-hand side. As soon as I released it, I drew my weapon, dropped to one knee, and shot them both in the face. And guess what they were doing? Looking at the piece of paper."

This was an excellent example of creating a window by distracting the bad guys with whatever was available.

"You can make a window in many ways, but the more distraction there is the more chance you have of being totally successful," Davison added.

Another thing to bear in mind about reactions is that when you are shooting in defense of your life you will be laying down rounds as fast as you can. Even when you perceive that the threat is no longer there, it will take you as much as half a second to react and stop shooting. If for example, the attacker has turned to run away, you could pump a couple more shots into his back before you can stop shooting. This may be reasonable, but it doesn't look good to a jury. You will need an expert witness like Massad Ayoob to convince jury members of such reasonableness.

Winning a gunfight requires an attitude. Different experts have referred to it in different ways. Former U.S. Border Patrolman Bill Jordan named his book about gunfighting *No Second Place Winner.* Jordan's book title underlines the reality that, unlike in a shooting competition, "there is no second place winner in a gunfight." You cannot afford to be in second place in a gunfight. You have to win, or you will probably die.

It is the attitude displayed by Texas Ranger Captain Bill McDonald when he said, "No man in the wrong can stand up against a fellow that's right and keeps on a-coming." Once the fight starts, you must keep on a-coming, figuratively at least. Good tactics dictate that you may be backing up or moving sideways to cover, but figuratively you're still "a-coming," and you're still shooting.

Personal defense expert Jeff Cooper urges aggressiveness and ruthlessness in responding to a deadly attack. I would add determination.

Repeat to yourself: "I WILL FIGHT AND KEEP FIGHTING UNTIL THE THREAT GOES AWAY." It takes three thousand repetitions before a physical action becomes so ingrained that it becomes a reaction: an act performed without thought. Make a poster of those words, and hang it on the wall where you conduct your dry-firing practice.

Brainwash yourself: "I WILL FIGHT AND KEEP FIGHTING UNTIL THE THREAT GOES AWAY." It is what the winner of every gunfight, from Wild Bill Hickok to Leo Arredondo, has done.

You cannot let pain or fear stop you from continuing to fight. In a close-range gunfight, you may well be hit. Leo Arredondo, the auto mechanic on the south side of San Antonio, is a good example of a man who kept fighting after he was wounded. He was hit by a shotgun blast in the legs and went down, but he kept on fighting until both his attackers lay dead. You must keep on fighting whether you are still standing or lying on the ground.

This attitude toward self defense was articulated for a nation by Prime Minister Winston Churchill in the dark days of 1940, when Britain faced the threat of invasion from Germany. He told the British people, "We shall defend our island, whatever the cost may be; we shall fight on the beaches, we shall fight on the landing grounds, we shall fight in the fields and in the streets, we shall fight in the hills; we shall never surrender."

While the British people had months and years to defend their island, you will probably have only seconds to defend your life. However, the principle is the same.

As well as impregnating this attitude in your psyche, you can include it in your training. In martial arts we are taught never to stop a throw or move without completing it. Even if you have made a mistake, do not hesitate, but continue it through to the end. In the same way, when you are training for self defense, never allow a malfunction or an empty gun to stop you from hitting the target or completing the stage of fire.

Another lesson repeated frequently in the literature of Western gunfighters is that the man who wins in a gunfight is the one who takes the time to shoot accurately.

In his book, *They Called Him Wild Bill*, Joseph Rosa quotes Hickok's advice to a Colonel North in the 1860s: "Whenever you get into a row be sure and not shoot too quick. Take time. I've known many a feller slip up for shootin' in a hurry."

Luther North claimed his brother Frank regularly used to beat Hickok at target shooting. Wild Bill once told him, "Frank, you can beat the hell out of me shootin' at pieces of paper, but I can beat you when it comes to hittin' men."

In his biography of Wyatt Earp, Stuart Lake quotes the lawman as dispensing similar advice and recounting several incidents to illustrate his point. Earp apparently witnessed a gunfight in Deadwood, South Dakota, in which a man with the flamboyant name of Turkey Creek Jack Johnson took on two partners. The partners and Johnson closed on each other, conveniently right outside the cemetery, at a range of fifty yards. According to Earp, the two partners opened up with two guns each as Johnson walked toward them, gun in hand but not firing a shot. At about thirty yards, Johnson fired two carefully-aimed shots and killed both men. Earp said the partners fired sixteen shots between them at Johnson, causing him two or three minor flesh wounds.

Most civilians are not going to be trading shots with adversaries at thirty yards. They are more likely to be shooting at twenty feet, the range cited by Earp in a gunfight between Cockeyed Frank Loving and Levi Richardson in Dodge City's Long Branch Saloon. Richardson was a noted pistol shot, who had won several gunfights, until he took up gun fanning, according to Earp. Loving was about twenty years old and was a fair shot, who until then had never fired a gun at another human being. When they quarreled in the Long Branch, Richardson left to get his gun from his hotel room. When he returned, he shouted to Loving that he was going to kill him. Loving picked up his gun and stood up. Richardson started shooting, fanning his single action at a distance of twenty feet, according to Earp.

"While Levi was pumping lead at him, young Loving raised his gun as cool as you please and fired three shots," Lake quotes Earp as saying. All Loving's shots hit Richardson, killing him. One of Richardson's shots grazed Loving's hand.

It is natural, when your life is in imminent danger, to try to get your gun into action as quickly as possible and to shoot as fast as you can, sights be damned. This urge must be suppressed. Trained police officers have missed their attackers at ranges of six feet because they panicked.

"Wyatt Earp talked a lot about how you have to stand there and look death in the face, control your fear, and don't worry about this person shooting at you," says Bill McLennan. "I would say you ought to be moving and using cover, but you've still got to use those sights and control the fear."

Bill Jordan recommended convincing yourself the other guy is going to screw up and all you have to do is stay cool and make that first shot a hit. He quotes Texas Ranger Captain John Hughes: "If you get in a gunfight, don't let yourself feel rushed. Take your time, fast."

ADRENALINE AND SURVIVAL

The early morning of August 1, 1991, was a warm summer night with a partly cloudy sky, like many that had preceded it. But for San Antonio Police Officer Shayne Katzfey, it would be like no other. It was the night he shot and killed a man.

"The average person who's never been involved in a shooting cannot fathom the mental stress and the physical stress that you undergo right during the event and immediately afterward," Katzfey says. "It's nothing like anything I have gone through before, and I pray to God it never happens to me again."

Katzfey, then 25, was on routine patrol on the northwest side of the city. He had been a police officer for nearly three years. Shortly after 4:30 a.m., he and another officer were dispatched to an apartment complex for a report of two suspicious men, possibly trying to break into a vehicle. The resident who had phoned police told the officers he could see a man hiding in one of the enclosed yards behind the ground-floor apartments. The officers edged their way along the outside of the six-foot-high wooden fence that enclosed the yards, looking for the men. Katzfey was in front, holding his flashlight in one hand and his .357 Magnum service revolver in the other. All of a sudden, a man burst out of a gate in the fence right in front of Katzfey, his hands in front of him, apparently grabbing for the officer's gun. Reacting to his training, Katzfey fired, hitting the man once in the chest.

When you believe your life is at risk, your body takes measures automatically to ensure your survival. These changes affect different people in different ways and can be very disconcerting if you are not expecting them. Not everyone will experience all the symptoms, and different people will feel them to different degrees. Katzfey was quite unprepared for what happened in his body and for the aftermath.

Under stress the body dumps massive amounts of adrenaline into your system and with it a hormone called ACTH (adrenocorticotropic hormone), which sends messages to the brain, putting it into survival mode. The immediate effect prepares you to fight or flee.

Jean Souza, a counselor who worked with police officers and their families in San Antonio, has studied the effects of adrenaline and ACTH on law-enforcement officers, fire fighters, and paramedics. She taught at the San Antonio Police Academy and has consulted nationwide.

Souza says ACTH focuses attention to the lower brain, where the automatic survival functions are controlled. It restricts messages from the cortex, where reasoning and decision-making take place.

"In a survival situation, an officer or fire fighter has to be able to leap tall buildings in a single bound, without the cortex supplying him with too many details about how many floors are in the building or that he never was very good at the long jump," Souza says.

While she was talking about police officers and fire fighters, this also applies to anyone in a survival situation like a

gunfight. In this condition, the brain sends blood to the big muscles of the arms and legs. This is the condition that gives the
ninety-pound woman the strength to lift a car off her child or
husband. The fight or flight response has not changed since cave-
man days, when people fought with their bare hands or with
clubs and rocks. Extra strength was needed, and often is still
needed, to fight, run, and leap. So the lower brain directs
blood to the arms and legs. Katzfey says he experienced this rush
of blood to the big muscles.

"You can run like the dickens, and you're strong like you've
never been before," he says.

Unfortunately, this redirection of the blood and oxygen starves
the extremities. In particular, fingers get cold, numb, and
clumsy. Our bodies have not yet adapted to the possibility that
fighting may involve a delicate trigger squeeze. We can lose the
fine motor skills necessary for trigger pressing, reloading, or
clearing a malfunction.

The body also tries to eliminate anything superfluous to
survival. This is why some people mess themselves in a crisis,
while others vomit. After the shooting, Katzfey went behind
a dumpster and threw up.

"It was very embarrassing, because you don't do that at major
crime scenes," he says. "It's not because you can't handle the
thought or stresses you are under; it's because your body is reacting in a survival mode to make you be able to continue to fight,
should it be necessary."

Katzfey also experienced tunnel vision in which the eyes
focus on the assailant or even just the gun. This is why the gun
or the hand holding it are often hit by bullets during a gunfight.

"I could tell you everything just outside the shoulders
and from about the waist up on the person who attacked
me," Katzfey says, more than five years after the shooting. "I still
have a picture in my mind of just what that looked like."

Souza says tunnel vision is "a physical lock-on to the
threat." It is the body's way of focusing all your attention on

dealing with the immediate threat to the exclusion of anything else. It is a problem because you are focused on the target when, at anything further than halitosis range, you should be looking at the sights. You are also oblivious to any other threat, and criminals often travel in packs. Katzfey says the other officer a few paces behind him was his protection against tunnel vision.

"Had I been alone, I would've had no protection, and thank God there was no secondary threat that presented itself right that moment, because, frankly, I would have been defenseless against it," he says.

Since the shooting, Katzfey has trained himself to overcome tunnel vision. You can break the lock-on effect by moving your head or looking deliberately away from the threat. You won't do this unless you incorporate it into your training. Every time you fire at a target, look from side to side after you shoot until it becomes a habit.

Katzfey also experienced auditory exclusion, what he calls "tunnel hearing." Immediately after the shooting, he tried to use his radio to call for an ambulance. When you press the transmission switch on the radio, it emits a distinctive tone, and then you talk. Katzfey couldn't hear the tone while he was frantically calling for paramedics. In fact the radio was working perfectly, but he was aghast when he later heard a tape recording of his transmission played on a local television station. "Tunnel hearing" filters out anything that is not vital to survival, Katzfey says.

"There were witnesses at the shooting that said they heard people talking afterward, and I don't remember any talking afterward except me trying to get my radio to work," he says.

Loud noises such as gun shots do not seem as loud. Normally a .45 or .357 Magnum fired indoors without ear protection would make the shooter wince at the noise. Not so when you are in survival mode. The noise is filtered, and often a shooter will be unaware of how many shots she or he has fired.

In his second gunfight, Greg Ferris thought he had fired more shots at the shotgun-toting gangbanger than he did. Others have found themselves pressing the trigger again and again on an empty gun because they are not aware they have emptied it. Some instructors will tell you to always count your shots as you fire them. This may be practical in a competition, but not in a gunfight. The first indication you will likely have that you need to reload in a gunfight is when you are pulling the trigger on an empty cylinder or when you find the slide locked back on a semi-automatic.

Massad Ayoob, a nationally-known expert in personal defense, warns of the disconcerting effect of tachypsychia. This is a medical term for what Ferris experienced in his second fight—the slow motion effect experienced by many people during crisis situations. Katzfey's shooting incident was over in the blink of an eye, and he says he didn't experience this phenomenon. It is caused by the brain using its full power to gather and process data under the compelling effect of a life or death situation. If you haven't yet experienced this effect in an emergency, it can be disconcerting. It is the same slow motion experienced in dreams where you feel as though you are moving in molasses. Although you are in fact moving very rapidly, you can be panicked by this distortion of time, because you seem to be moving in slow motion.

Bruce Siddle of PPCT Management Systems believes these body changes are linked to heart rate. His research shows that fine and complex motor skills deteriorate between 115 and 145 heart beats per minute. However, law-enforcement firearms instructor Jerry Lane says there is more to these body changes than just an increase in heart rate.

"Probably most of all the adrenaline and the threat have to be there for the heart rate and the blood pressure and everything else to start really going up," Lane says.

He has raised his heart rate to 165 beats a minute on a treadmill, but there was no threat, and he experienced none of the other symptoms of extreme stress.

"This was a test I did," Lane says. "I went over and picked up a pen and just started writing. I was writing just fine, because none of these other things were present."

Bill Davison says when he was in the Royal Marine Special Boat Service he was part of an experiment to test the effects of stress on the ability to manipulate weapons. As a helicopter sniper he had to go through a process called dunking once a month. A helicopter body was suspended over a swimming pool that was kept at the same temperature as the North Sea. The marines were strapped into the helicopter.

"They spin it round this way, and they spin it round that way, then they turn the lights off while it's spinning, and it crashes into the pool upside down," Davison said. "Then you all have to get out safely."

This was the most stressful exercise they had to perform in training and would kick their heart rates up to about one-hundred-fifty beats a minute, he said. When they reached the side of the pool, they had to load rounds into a magazine and put it on the weapon. "We found everybody could get the magazine onto the weapon, but hardly anybody could get any rounds into the magazine," he said.

Davison recounts the death in Dallas of a police officer who was killed while reloading his pistol. "He was a good tactician, he was a member of a SWAT team, and he had been in a couple of fire fights, a couple of gun situations, and he'd always done really well," Davison says.

The officer was kneeling behind a police car. He had an empty magazine on the floor and a fresh magazine in the gun. The police officers with him saw him ineffectively trying to operate the slide stop lever with his thumbs. This is a fine motor skill, and the officer couldn't do it, Davison said.

"The bad guy ran up to the car and shot him in the top of the head at about a car's distance and killed him."

You need to be aware of all these possible changes that can affect your ability to coolly deliver aimed shots during a fire fight. They can also affect your memory of what happened. If you tell an investigator you fired only one shot, when in fact you fired several, your credibility will be destroyed with anyone who does not make allowance for these body changes. This is why it is best not to give police any statement of what you think happened until you have talked to your lawyer.

While these changes are affecting your body, making it more difficult to land your shots on the target, remember that the same thing is almost certainly happening to your adversary.

TACTICS

According to military doctrine, to attack a defended position you need to outnumber the defenders by at least two to one and preferably three or four to one. The annals of war are riddled with incidents where a small number of defenders kept a much larger army of attackers at bay for long periods.

In U.S. history the most celebrated such fight is the battle for the Alamo in the spring of 1836. At the former Catholic mission, about one hundred eighty frontiersmen with their long rifles kept several thousand crack Mexican troops at bay. For almost two weeks, this ragtag group of individualists, led by William Barret Travis and accompanied by the legendary Jim Bowie and David Crockett, defied the might of Mexico's army and changed history. Before the last shot was fired on March 6 and the last of the defenders shot, hacked, and bayoneted to death, hundreds of Mexican soldiers had breathed their last. The most reliable sources put the butcher's bill for the Mexican army under General Santa Anna at between six hundred and sixteen hundred killed.

Twenty-seven years later and seven hundred miles further south, about sixty soldiers of the French Foreign Legion were caught in the open by a well-armed Mexican cavalry force of eight hundred under a Colonel Milan. The legionnaires under Captain Jean Danjou fought their way to an abandoned farmhouse in the hamlet of Camerone. By the time they reached the farmhouse, the legionnaires were down to forty-six and the Mexicans were joined by reinforcements of twelve hundred infantrymen. For nine hours, a dwindling force of legionnaires beat back attacks by two thousand Mexican soldiers. When the defenders were down to five, the last standing officer, a Second Lieutenant Maudet, ordered bayonets fixed and led a final charge into the Mexican infantry.

Colonel Milan, impressed by the valor of the defenders, stopped the fight and allowed the surviving three to keep their rifles. Mexican casualties were estimated at about three hundred. The Battle of Camerone, fought on April 30, 1863, is celebrated each year by the French Foreign Legion as its proudest memory.

Not all such battles have ended with the massacre of the defenders, however. In 1879, King Cetewayo's Zulus were giving the British Army a bad time in South Africa. On January 22, a force of twenty thousand Zulus annihilated about seventeen hundred British soldiers camped at Isandhlwana. On the same day a few miles away at Rorke's Drift, 137 of their colleagues were attacked at a farm and mission station that was serving as a hospital and supply base. The defenders included thirty-six sick and wounded from the hospital and eighty-four soldiers of the 24th Regiment of Foot. They were led by Lieutenant John Chard of the Royal Engineers and Lieutenant Gonville Bromhead of the 24th, two undistinguished officers in their early thirties.

Given a few hours warning of the nearby massacre at Isandhlwana, the troops built fortifications of mealie bags and biscuit boxes to join the hospital and the storehouse.

About forty-five hundred Zulus attacked in the late afternoon. Attack followed attack with dead Zulus piling up around the makeshift fort until about 4 o'clock the following morning, when the attackers had had enough. About eighty of the defenders were still standing, while fifteen were dead, two dying, and the rest wounded.

They had fired twenty thousand rounds of ammunition. Eleven Victoria Crosses were awarded to the defenders, more than for any other single action. The Victoria Cross is the British equivalent of the U.S. Congressional Medal of Honor.

In each of these three actions, defenders, skilled in the use of their weapons, used cover to maximum advantage against assailants who had to push their attacks over open ground. Self defense against individuals is just war on a small scale. The same principles apply. The use of cover applies, therefore, to individuals just as it does to armies. Take cover, whether it's in your bedroom or behind a tree, and let him or them bring the attack to you.

If you hear someone breaking into your house, the smartest course of action is to barricade yourself in your bedroom and call 9-1-1. A cellular phone is particularly useful for this as its wires cannot be cut by intruders. However, there are situations when you will go in harm's way.

You are in the Luby's Cafeteria in Killeen with your family. You have eaten your lunch and are having a cup of coffee while you question your kids about how they are doing in school. You had a couple of fill-ups of ice tea earlier, and your bladder reminds you that you need to go. You are in the restroom when there is a tremendous crash. There are screams and the sound of gunfire: a steady rhythm—bang, bang, bang. Wisdom dictates that you stay in the bathroom and not put yourself in harm's way, but your loved ones are there. Nothing is going to stop you from going in.

Consider another scenario. You are asleep at home in your bed with your partner. You are awakened by the sound

Using cover, an instructor approaches an open door in Thunder Ranch's "Terminator," a range designed for practicing building-clearing tactics.

of breaking glass. You can hear other strange noises. You get out of bed and grab your gun from the chair with your discarded clothes on it. You pull on your jeans. Suddenly you hear a scream and a high-pitched voice filled with terror shouting: "Daddy, daddy," or "Mommy, mommy." You should stay put and dial 9-1-1 on the cellular phone, but those are your kids down the hall.

In both situations, you are going to go. It may not be the best decision for your own survival, but you will never forgive yourself if you don't go. The question asked by Thunder

Ranch director Clint Smith, is: "Are you gonna' go smart or are you gonna' go dumb?"

There are various procedures you can follow that may give you the edge to win a gunfight. They are called tactics. We have discussed some tactics already, such as maximizing the range by backing up to allow your superior weapons skill to prevail and minimizing your exposure to your assailant by use of cover. Tactics vary from maneuvering to keep the sun in your opponent's eyes to procedures to follow when coming to the aid of a family member or close friend.

It was more the latter that Clint Smith was referring to when he said: "The more that you know about tactics, the less you'll want to use them."

Here are some suggestions if you really feel you have to clear a house or other building. Now you must become the hunter. Move slowly and as silently as you can. Be aware that every step you take gives you a new field of view and field of fire. Those fields, while opening in front of you, are also closing behind you. Watch behind you for someone following you, and look up for someone hiding above you.

Keep your gun between you and the threat. Keep as far as you can from where the threat could be. This means that, if you are moving down a hallway and there is a doorway to your left, hug the right-hand wall of the hallway. This prevents your sticking your gun ahead of your field of view where someone on the other side of a corner can grab it. Don't peek around corners or from cover.

If you poke your head out for a quick glance and then move back behind cover, you have given your position away, and your opponent will just wait with his gun trained on the spot where you disappeared. When you look out from cover and you see someone who shouldn't be there, keep him covered and challenge him. Engage if he makes a clearly threatening move. Always look around cover, if possible, not over it. Reload behind cover, and try not to run your gun dry before you reload.

Doorways and hallways are particularly dangerous because they restrict your movement. When you approach a closed door, look for the hinge pins. If you can see them, the door opens toward you. Don't stand in front of the door when you open it. Remember most doors and interior walls are not bullet-proof. You can use this to your advantage, but so can those threatening you.

When searching for the threat, watch for shadows and movement. A quick movement will attract the eye faster than anything else. As you move, look for potential areas of cover you can use if attacked. Look for things out of place. A chair knocked over or a television set near the door are indications that someone has been there and may be waiting in ambush for you.

Look for reflections in windows, mirrors, glass panels in doors, or pictures. Adele Morris, the wife of a retired pawnbroker in San Antonio, was tied up with duct tape by a pair of robbers who told her not to look around. She was amazed to see reflected in the glass doors of her fireplace the dial of her safe, passing behind her as the robbers wheeled it out on a dolly.

Avoid being silhouetted against a window, a light-colored wall, or the sky, and beware of being backlit by standing in the doorway of a lighted room, if your assailant may be in the darkened hallway. Watch for toes or shoes under cars or drapes.

If you are trying to locate a potential attacker in the darkness, try throwing something to draw his fire: pocket change, your hat. When you shoot, move away from your muzzle flash before you receive an incoming burst of fire. Use a flashlight sparingly unless you are up against only one opponent, in which case you can blind him with it. In a dangerous situation, the fastest draw is to have the gun in your hand.

Above all, be safe. Remember your safety rules, particularly the ones about knowing what your bullet will hit and keeping your finger off the trigger until you are ready to shoot. You may mean only to keep him covered, but under the stress of a potentially life-threatening confrontation, your finger may ride that trigger too heavily. There are no excuses for shooting someone by mistake. Keep your finger off the trigger while you have someone covered. Shoot only at a genuine threat. Don't make a mistake and shoot a foreign student who doesn't speak good English or a drunk who wandered into your house by mistake. Even if you are cleared by a jury, you'll feel like hell, and your hard-earned money will be making some lawyer's payments on his Lexus or Jaguar.

As mentioned earlier in this chapter, individual self defense is just war on a small scale, and surprise is one of the principles of war. Perhaps the best tactic of all is: do the unexpected. When a man in his early twenties tried to rob a convenience store in Universal City on a late summer evening, the clerks thwarted him by not taking him seriously.

The man walked into the Diamond Shamrock gas station and convenience store on Pat Booker Road in the San Antonio suburb shortly before 10 p.m. He went to the back of the store and put a brown paper bag over his head. The would-be robber approached the counter where clerk Randy Larson, 45, was serving customers. He did not show a weapon, but kept his right hand behind his back inside his pants as though he had a gun.

"I don't want to scare anybody, but I need all the money in the cash drawer," the man said. "This is for real."

"Are you the unknown comic, or a robber?" asked Larson, referring to "the unknown comic" from the television program, "The Gong Show," in which one of the actors always wore a paper bag over his head.

The robber repeated his demand in a serious tone, so Larson turned to the other clerk, Claude Campos, 28, who was beside the coffee machine, and told him to call the police as they were being robbed. Larson turned back to the robber and told him he couldn't open the cash register. Meanwhile a ten-year-old boy came up to the counter to buy a piece of gum. He handed over the money, and Larson opened the cash register to accept it.

"You all are playing with me," said the frustrated robber and walked out. He was last seen walking rapidly across the road toward an apartment complex with the bag still on his head.

In this case, Larson realized that the robber was quite inexperienced and surprised him by not obeying his orders. In more serious cases, you will almost certainly surprise an assailant by launching an instant counter attack. You are rolling the dice by making such a response: you may be killed. But the last thing a robber or rapist expects when he points a gun at you is for you to pull a gun and fight back. This is where surprise works for you.

As Jeff Cooper, the grand old man of defensive pistolcraft, puts it: "May he never choose you—but if he does, surprise him."

Chapter Eleven

DEADLY FORCE:
WHEN TO USE IT AND WHAT HAPPENS WHEN YOU DO

It was one of those all too rare perfect days in Texas—not too hot, not too cold. It was late in April, and the bluebonnets along the highways were in full bloom. Ralph Williams was driving north on Texas Highway 121, a freeway that skirts the northwest edge of the Dallas/Fort Worth International Airport. He was driving a greenish-blue Porsche 928S4 with the windows down and the sunroof open, while listening to the stereo.

Williams had picked up the car that morning from LA Motorcars in Richardson, a suburb of Dallas, and had driven it to Fort Worth, where he had it thoroughly examined at a service station because he was thinking of buying it.

"It came back with a pretty clean bill of health," he said.

Williams, 35, had wanted a Porsche since he graduated from high school, and now he was about to realize his dream. After showing the car to his wife, he decided to buy it and had $1,500 in cash in his pocket for the down payment. He was driving the twelve-year-old Porsche back to the dealership in Richardson to make the purchase.

Life was good. He had no inkling of how dramatically his life was about to change.

Williams was driving about sixty-five miles an hour when he was passed by a green Porsche 944 traveling at a high rate of speed. "I remember seeing the Porsche because I was excited to see another Porsche owner on the road," Williams said in a statement he would write later. "I tried to flash my lights at him to say 'Hi,' but he was trying to get around another vehicle and was making hand motions like, 'Get out of my way.'"

Williams watched as the other Porsche driver took the next exit from the freeway and disappeared. "I just thought that he seemed to be in a big hurry," Williams wrote in his statement.

A few minutes later, Williams noticed a blue Honda Accord pulling alongside him. A young man was driving, and a woman was sitting in the front passenger seat. According to Williams, as the Accord pulled level, the driver started "honking and yelling" at him. Williams couldn't hear what the man was saying but had the impression that he wanted him to pull over.

"He seemed real upset to say the least," Williams said. "I wouldn't pull over because I didn't know who he was. After he persisted for probably a minute, he started swerving his car out of his lane into my lane, trying to cut me off or trying to force me to the shoulder of the road."

Williams slowed down hoping the Accord would continue on, but the other driver swerved into his lane and braked hard. Williams had all he could do to stop the Porsche without running into the Accord and without being hit by the cars behind him. Both cars stopped with only a few feet between them. Immediately, the driver of the Accord got out and ran back to the Porsche.

"He was yelling something about cutting him off or something, but he wanted me out of the car," Williams said.

Although Williams's door was not locked, the man could not open it. Williams said the door handles on that particular model of Porsche are fragile, and this one had been bent. It needed a special technique to open it.

"Unless you knew how to do it, you couldn't get it open, and luckily he couldn't get the door open," Williams said.

He tried to roll up the window by pressing all the buttons on the door. Williams didn't realize until the following day that the buttons controlling the windows were on the center console.

"He (the other driver) was enraged because I wouldn't come out of the car, and he couldn't get into the car, so he started punching me through the window of the car," he said.

Williams could not drive forward without hitting the Accord. He could not back up because there was traffic behind him. He was secured in place by his seatbelt, and he couldn't close the window.

He said he was "scared to death" because he didn't know why this man he had never seen before was attacking him. Was he the intended victim of a carjacking? Did the man somehow know about the cash he was carrying and plan to rob him? He had no idea why this was happening.

"I tried to protect my face with my hand, but one of his first punches hit me hard enough to blur my vision. I tasted blood in my mouth. At this point, I was scared to death. I was really afraid that I was starting to lose consciousness and might end up seriously hurt or even dead," Williams said in his statement.

Williams said he knew he had to do something before he blacked out. He had a Texas concealed-handgun license and was wearing his Walther P99 semiautomatic in a pancake holster on his right hip under his shirt. When he got into the Porsche, Williams moved the holster forward on his belt to where

The inside of a Porsche 928S4. The buttons to operate the windows are on the center console.

it was at his side rather than behind his hip. This was more comfortable and somewhat easier to reach. However, Williams was also sitting on the tail of his shirt which was over the gun. "It made it very difficult to draw the gun," he said.

He had to lean to his left so his right hand could reach under his shirt to draw the gun. Leaning to his left put his head closer to his attacker, who was still hitting him in the face, Williams said. "It was a struggle, but I got the gun out," he said,

He brought the gun up and, without using the sights, fired one shot. The 9mm Federal Premium Personal Defense bullet hit his attacker in the abdomen just under the ribcage on his right side. "I remember shooting him. I remember how loud it was inside the car. I remember looking down at the Walther after I shot him."

Williams said he thought his gun had jammed. He carried it with a round in the chamber and the hammer decocked. His first shot required a long, heavy double-action pull on the trigger. After he fired the shot, the trigger was further back ready for the short single-action pull for subsequent shots. He had not had the gun long, and this confused him momentarily.

"My first thought was: my gun has jammed, and I looked down at it. Then I realized the gun was fine, and it clicked in my head that that's normal," he said.

When Williams looked up from the gun, his attacker was there beside him. What he didn't realize was that, according to witnesses, the man had fallen down immediately after he was shot but had got to his feet.

"He was standing there, and he had put his hand down to the gunshot wound, and I saw a little drip of blood," Williams said. "At that point he stopped his assault, I mean stopped cold, took a step back and kinda threw up his hands and said he was sorry, screamed he was sorry at the top of his lungs, or at least it seemed like it to me."

The man turned and moved between the two cars to where his wife was getting out of the Accord. He spoke to her,

*Ralph Williams
of Fort Worth.*

*Williams wearing the
Walther P99 he used
to shoot his attacker.*

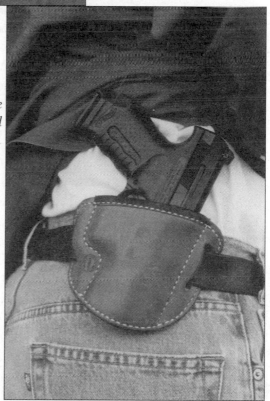

then he collapsed on the shoulder of the freeway, Williams said.

He had his cell phone with him and knew his attacker needed medical attention, and he probably did too. His could taste blood in his mouth, he was groggy, and his vision was still blurred. Williams called 9-1-1.

He said he knew he had to be careful about what he said, because 9-1-1 calls are taped, and the tapes can be entered into evidence. He told the 9-1-1 operator there had been a shooting on Highway 121. Williams realized the police would be at the scene in a few moments.

"I thought it would be best that I wasn't sitting there with a smoking gun in my hand," he said.

Williams could see on the floor on the passenger side of the car the empty casing from the round he had fired. Still on the phone to the 9-1-1 operator, he put the gun under the passenger side floor mat. The operator asked him if he was the person who did the shooting. He admitted that he was.

Moments later, several police officers arrived. According to the Grapevine Police Department report, the first officer on the scene was traffic officer Craig Johnson on a motorcycle. He saw the Porsche with Williams inside it stopped in the right-hand traffic lane and the blue Honda Accord a few feet in front of it with its backend in the traffic lane and its front wheels on the shoulder. The report stated that Johnson was told by witness Randall Rude that "the guy in the Porsche shot this guy."

Williams saw at least three police officers around the Porsche all with their guns drawn and pointed at him.

"I knew that I was going to be arrested, so I raised my hands up through the sun roof of the car because it was open," he said. "So they knew I wasn't a threat to them."

Johnson was on the passenger side of the Porsche and spoke to Williams through the open window. According to the report, he noticed the empty pancake holster on Williams's right side and asked him where the gun was.

"I told him it was underneath the floor mat on the passenger side of the car. I didn't point, I just kinda pointed with my head so I wouldn't make any sudden motions at all, because I do remember them saying something about 'we will shoot you.' I do remember hearing that very clearly," Williams said.

Johnson found the gun but did not move it, leaving it to be photographed in place by the crime-scene technician. The officer grabbed Williams's right hand while another officer took hold of his left. They put his hands together and handcuffed them, then told him to get out of the car.

"The seat belt was on, so they handcuffed me into my seat belt. They had to unhandcuff me, take off my seatbelt, and then rehandcuff me again," Williams said. "By this point, the officer who came through the passenger side of the car is physically on top of me. I mean he's got his knee on my leg; he's pretty much crushing down on me to maintain control of me."

The officer told him to swing his legs out of the car, but Williams couldn't move because he was being pinned down by the officer.

"I explained to him that he was laying on top of me, and I couldn't move. He said something about [me] being a smartass. I said: 'I'm not trying to be; really I just can't move.' I think once he realized I wasn't trying to be a smartass that he let off of me just a little bit, and I was able to swing my legs out the door."

Williams stood up. The officers unhandcuffed him then spun him around and pushed his upper body onto the car while they searched him. They asked him if he had any weapons and he told them he had two pocket-knives in his pocket. They took the knives and handcuffed him behind his back.

The police report stated that an officer read Williams a Miranda warning. He was then put in the back of a patrol car and was driven to the Grapevine Police Department.

Williams said that while he was in the patrol car he complained to the officer that the handcuffs were really tight. He said the officer told him he was sorry, but they wanted to get him to the police station before the media arrived on the scene.

"I admit that it hadn't even dawned on me that the press was going to be there," he said. "At that point I shut up because I thought, you're right, I don't want to be here when the press arrives either; let's keep on going."

Williams thinks it was when they arrived at the police department that he was asked if he was a law-enforcement officer. He believes this was prompted by the holster he was wearing. He told the officer that, no, he was not a police officer but a concealed-handgun-license holder.

Williams was taken into a holding area and booked. They took his shoe laces, belt, and everything that was in his pockets, including his wallet with his driver's license and concealed-handgun license. He was fingerprinted and photographed, then put in a cell.

Later he was taken to the detective office. According to the police report, he was interviewed on videotape by Detective Bob Murphy, who read him the Miranda warning again. Williams said the detective was "real nice." He told Williams he had investigated a lot of shootings, but he didn't know anything about this one. Williams had a concealed-handgun license so he was obviously not a generic criminal, the kind he deals with everyday, the detective said.

"I'm sure he's a nice guy, and he is because I've talked to him since, but I also saw it as this giant door that he's trying to open for me to just spill my guts," Williams said. "And at that point I still didn't know what I was spilling my guts about, so I didn't want to say anything,"

Williams originally phoned me as the author of *The Concealed Handgun Manual.* He said that some months before that fateful day, he had bought a copy of the book and had found it particularly helpful in knowing what to expect during and after the shooting.

"I read the book cover to cover enough times to know I wasn't going to say anything until I had talked to an attorney. I was really nervous, but I was calm. I wasn't upset; I just was worried because I had just spent already the better part of an hour sitting in a cell, contemplating that I might be sitting in one for the rest of my life. And I don't know why.

"So I explained to him that I first of all was a CHL holder, and that I had never been in problems with the law. I didn't even have a ticket on my record. And that I had never seen that guy before, and I didn't know why the whole incident happened, that he attacked me. I felt comfortable saying that much, but I wasn't going to go into any detail about why he attacked me, how he attacked me or anything, because I didn't want to give him any doors open to ask any more questions. I told him that I understood the job that he had to do, and I respected that, but I wasn't going to say anything more until I talked to an attorney."

Williams was returned to his cell. Meanwhile, the man he had shot, Uriah Ray Suhr, 18, was rushed by ambulance to Parkland Memorial Hospital in Dallas, where he went directly into surgery, the police report stated. Later, investigators were told Suhr had suffered injuries to his liver, pancreas, kidney, and vena cava, a major blood vessel. One of the doctors that operated on Suhr told police he was not sure that the wounded man would survive.

Back at the jail, Williams was allowed to make a phone call to his wife Karen with a jail guard standing close enough to hear what he was saying. He told her he was in jail and needed a lawyer. At first she thought he was joking, but he told her someone had attacked him and he had shot the man in self defense. His wife called her brother, Jeff Petrie, who also was a concealed-hand-gun-license holder. He contacted J. Don Carter, a Fort Worth criminal-defense lawyer, to represent Williams.

Later in the evening, Williams's wife came to the Grapevine jail, and he was allowed to talk to her briefly. Police told him he could not be arraigned because it was after 3 p.m., and no magistrate would be available until the following morning. He would have to spend the night in jail.

Williams said all his clothes except for his underwear were taken for evidence and he was given a paper jumpsuit to wear. He borrowed a paperback thriller from a jail guard and read it before he was released. It took him about twelve hours and helped keep his mind off what was happening, where he was, and, above all, why he had been attacked.

"I didn't want to think about what had happened because I couldn't understand it. I mean I knew what happened, but

I didn't know why it happened. You try to figure out what you did. I thought: did I cut this guy off in traffic? Is that why this happened, or was it something else? Was he trying to get the car; was he trying to get the money? I couldn't understand it."

Williams said it would have been much more scary if he had not been prepared for what to expect by reading *The Concealed Handgun Manual*.

"It was still pretty surreal," he said.

The following morning, Williams was arraigned before Judge David Florence on a charge of attempted murder. Carter, his lawyer, did not attend the hearing. Williams was expecting bond to be set at about $100,000, so was pleasantly surprised when Florence set it at $10,000. He felt the judge was aware that he was defending himself.

"I felt a lot better, right then," he said.

Before they released him, police asked if they could photograph Williams' face where he had been hit, he said.

"That surprised me because I had never mentioned anything about being hit. To me that was a positive, because they knew that I had been hit, and I hadn't said that. So they took pictures of my face."

His face was swollen but not bruised, he said. For some weeks, Williams had been taking medication for a pulled groin muscle, and he attributed the lack of bruising to the medicine.

He was finally released from custody about 1 p.m., still without any idea of why Suhr had attacked him. His wife picked him up from the jail, and for the first time in twenty-four hours he saw a newspaper. The shooting at Columbine High School in Colorado was all over the front page. The shooting Williams had been involved in happened on April 20, 1999, the same day Eric Harris and Dylan Klebold gunned down a teacher and a dozen fellow students before killing themselves.

While Williams was in jail the police had been busy interviewing witnesses and collecting evidence. According to the police report, several witnesses told police they had seen Suhr run from his car to the Porsche and that he appeared to be punching Williams through the open window before the shot was fired.

Police briefly interviewed Brandy Suhr, wife of the wounded man, while she was awaiting a ride to the hospital. They conducted a more detailed interview two days later.

Brandy Suhr said she and her husband were driving to a spot along the highway where they planned take photos of their five-month-old daughter Angelica among the bluebonnets, the report stated.

Suhr, his wife, and daughter were all in their Honda Accord when they left their home in Euless, a suburb south of Grapevine. They were driving west, towards Fort Worth, on Texas Highway 183. As they approached the entrance ramp leading to Highway 121, they spotted a green Porsche traveling in the same direction. Brandy Suhr told police her husband commented about how nice the Porsche looked and that one day he would be driving a vehicle as nice. Williams believes that they actually saw his greenish-blue Porsche on Highway 183.

As they drove north on Highway 121, they noticed traffic stacking up because one of the lanes was closed. Brandy Suhr told police her husband decided to get off the freeway because he "can't stand to be in traffic."

They pulled up at a red traffic light. When the light turned green, Uriah Suhr did not drive on immediately because he was turning down the bass on the car stereo, his wife said. The same Porsche she thought they had seen earlier was directly behind them, and the driver sounded his horn. The driver of the Porsche "flipped off" Suhr, who replied in kind, Brandy Suhr told police.

As the road becomes the entrance ramp to Highway 121, it narrows from two lanes to one. The Porsche tried to pass the Accord as the road narrowed. Brandy Suhr said the passenger side of the Porsche struck the Accord near the front of the driver's door and sped away.

Her husband took off after the Porsche which was heading north on Highway 121. She estimated Uriah Suhr was driving about ninety miles an hour, but the Porsche was doing one hundred twenty. She said she tried to call police on her husband's cell phone but could not get through. She asked Suhr to slow down, which he did. They were about to take the William D. Tate exit when she saw what she thought was the Porsche that had hit them and pointed it out to her husband.

He tried to get the Porsche to pull over, and when it did he walked back to the Porsche where she heard him "yelling things like: 'we have a baby in the car, what were you thinking?'"

The police report stated she saw her husband making hand motions like he was trying to slap something away just before she heard the shot.

When asked by police if she was sure the car Williams was driving was the one that hit their car, she said: "almost," according to the police report.

Witness Steven Michael Cutter told police he was behind the Accord when the Porsche cut in front of it and hit it. After looking at photos taken by police at the scene of the shooting, he said he thought Williams's Porsche was not the vehicle that clipped the Accord, the police report stated.

Police were not able to interview Uriah Suhr until June 7, seven weeks after the shooting, because he was in a coma. He

Porsche 928S4 like the one Ralph Williams was driving.

Porsche 944 like the one that side-swiped Uriah Suhr's car.

denied hitting Williams and said he just wanted to get insurance information from him when he approached the Porsche.

When police examined both cars, it appeared the Accord had been in a recent accident, but there were no corresponding marks on the Porsche Williams was driving. They took paint samples from Williams's Porsche and from where the Accord had been hit on the driver's side. Laboratory analysis indicated that the paint samples did not match, the report stated.

After reading news stories of the incident, Williams realized that the Suhrs had been hit by another Porsche. What triggered the realization was that the stories were saying he was driving a green Porsche. The car he was driving was blue but he had been passed by a green Porsche 944 moments before the Accord tried to pull him over. It was a case of mistaken identity.

Williams wanted to get the case over with, but his criminal-defense lawyer, J. Don Carter, said it would be a mistake to rush the District Attorney's office.

"He said we didn't want to do anything to stir up the police department or the district attorney. We didn't want to do anything to draw attention to the case," Williams said.

Consequently, it would be almost a year, March 9, 2000, before Williams was no-billed by a Tarrant County Grand Jury. Williams himself did not testify. It cost Williams $26,500 in total to defend himself. Carter charged him $16,500 for his criminal defense and bond. Williams said Carter worked entirely "behind the scenes" negotiating with the district attorney's office.

Williams also paid $10,000 to Rugger Burke, a civil attorney, when Brandy Suhr sued him on her husband's behalf. Ironically, Williams was not sued for shooting Suhr but for negligence in the traffic accident he was not involved in. The case was dismissed after he counter-sued and was awarded $10,000, which he said he is unlikely to collect. Medical bills for Suhr exceeded $600,000.

Williams effectively lost his job at Best Buy, a department store chain where he had worked for nine years. Best Buy would not let him return to work until the criminal charges were resolved. The company suspended him, but paid him only while he had unused sick time or vacation. After three months he had run through his benefits from Best Buy and was without a source of income. Williams was disappointed by the reaction of the people he had worked with at Best Buy.

"I was really surprised when all this happened. There was a barrier there. No one wants to talk to you; no one wants to know about it; everyone assumes the worst."

He resigned from the company and started his own business.

In retrospect, would Williams have done anything differently? Although he practices regularly with his handguns, he feels he should have known the Walther P99 better before carrying it. He also feels the incident would never have come to a shooting if he had known how to close the window on the Porsche. And the Porsche? He spent the down payment on legal fees and didn't buy it, but he still wants one.

This is the sort of thing that can happen to a concealed-handgun-license holder even when he is in the right. Here is another example.

Joe Archer (not his real name) was lying on the couch in his suburban home one night about 11:30 watching television when he heard what he thought were two gun shots.

"The dog was barking like crazy, so I knew somebody was out there," Archer said.

His first thought was that his pickup or boat was being broken into, as they were both parked in the driveway. He ran outside, dressed only in his shorts.

Looking down the slope to his left, he saw a young man on his neighbor's front lawn with what appeared to be a bag in his hand and a young woman at the intersection perhaps twenty-five yards away. "What are you doing?" Archer called out.

"It's none of your f---ing business. Go back inside," the youth yelled back.

"Do you live in this neighborhood?" Archer asked.

The youth said he was having a fight with his girlfriend and again swore at Archer.

"Well, don't you come on my goddamn property," Archer barked.

He turned and started walking back toward his front door. "That's when he started coming up the hill onto my property," Archer recalled.

The youth appeared very agitated, Archer told police later. "The man was too boisterous and too aggressive to be normal. I felt that he was under the influence of drugs or alcohol," Archer said in his statement.

At this time, Archer was fifty-seven years old. He had spent thirty years in the U.S. Army, including two tours in Vietnam, retiring as a command sergeant major. After retiring from the military, he had become a school district police officer in a nearby jurisdiction.

Archer went back into his house to get his gun and possibly arrest the youth for trespassing.

"I expected to get my gun, and he'd be out in the front yard and say, 'Come on out,' or something like that. I'm going to surprise him and say, 'Look, I'm a police officer, you're under arrest, you get down on the ground.' That's all I was going to do," Archer said. "Call the [city] police, and that would be the end of it."

The bedroom door in Archer's house is about six feet from the front door. Archer ducked into the bedroom where his wife was sleeping and retrieved his service revolver from under the bed.

When Archer came out of the bedroom, cocking the .357 Magnum as he turned toward the front door, the youth filled the doorway, an arm's length away.

Instinctively, Archer fired. The youth tumbled backward out of the door, shot through the brain. His blood spattered the wallpaper in the hallway.

Archer is still not sure what happened. It happened too fast. Was it the trained reaction of a former jungle fighter? Perhaps. In his statement, Archer said, "When he began to come through my door I felt threatened, and I was defending myself. It was not my intention to shoot: it just happened."

Archer likens his reaction to that of a baseball pitcher when a ball is coming straight for his head.

"Whether you do that by instinct or whether it's a planned process and you kinda turn your head to catch the ball, I don't know. All I know is I came out and cocked that pistol and had a vision in my mind of him being in the front yard and, as it was, he was right there in front of my face, coming in my house, and I shot."

Initially, it appeared that Archer would be exonerated, even though the man had not been armed. The "shots" Archer had heard earlier were the noises made by the youth hitting a wall with his bag in his rage at his girlfriend. Archer and his wife were questioned and gave statements, but he was not arrested.

However, when the District Attorney's office got the case, Archer found he was in a heap of trouble. The assistant DA said she could prove the man was outside the house when Archer shot him. Retired Texas Ranger Al Cuellar, who is familiar with the case, disputes this. He says the blood spatters on the wall paper near the door show the youth was shot while inside the front door.

The assistant DA also said the gun was touching the youth's face when he was shot.

"His [Archer's] biggest problem was that it was a contact wound," she said.

Archer is adamant the gun was three or four feet from the youth's face when he fired.

Archer got a lawyer, who took the case for expenses but no fee. To Archer, it appeared obvious the lawyer didn't want to take the case to trial. He pressured Archer to plead guilty to involuntary manslaughter. Archer tried to get another lawyer, but the man wanted $15,000 to go to trial. Archer said he never found out whether he was indicted or no-billed by the grand jury. Court records show he waived indictment and pleaded no contest. Archer said he was told if he didn't strike a plea bargain, he would be charged with murder. Under this threat, Archer pleaded guilty to involuntary manslaughter and received ten years probation.

"It's a sad story," says Cuellar. "He paid lawyers, his insurance went up, he lost his ability to own a gun in the future, he lost his job, and he was right—but he's alive."

Three years after the shooting, and after having threatened to kill Archer, the dead man's brother was released from a mental institution in another state.

Archer's case shows that for the law-abiding citizen who takes up arms, events have a way of getting out of hand. Archer had no intention of shooting the man. He just wanted to get control of the situation. But he was surprised into shooting when the scenario he was expecting changed abruptly. Once the legal system grinds into gear, the average person has no control of the outcome.

Archer realized these things almost immediately. When his wife asked him what had happened, he replied, "I think I just ruined my life."

"You start shooting, even if you're right, it's very difficult—and this guy's right," says Cuellar.

Investigators, prosecutors, and even your own defense lawyer all have their own agendas. The prosecutor is going to be pressured by the relatives of the person you shot to charge you with murder. They may go to the news media with their side of the story, which will increase the pressure on the DA's office. The DA is susceptible to such pressures, particularly before an election. Archer feels his case suffered from bad timing. The police officers accused of beating Rodney King were acquitted about the same time as Archer's shooting, and Los Angeles was aflame with riots. A local television news report even linked Archer's shooting with the Los Angeles riots, Archer says.

There are also pressures on defense lawyers that work against a defendant. Any lawyer who takes a case *pro bono,* for no fee, is going to want to dispose of it as quickly as possible, so he can continue earning a living from clients who pay. The lawyer also has to work within the system. He has to deal with your prosecutor and judge when your case is but a distant memory. Of course, these factors may make no difference, but you can never be sure. In the legal system, as in other areas of life, you tend to get what you pay for. Anybody who trusts the legal system to dispense justice is as foolish as the person who believes the police will protect him or her from crime.

For an investigator who just arrives on the scene of a shooting, you are the suspect, particularly if the other guy isn't alive to be questioned. This is true, as in Archer's case, even if the shooter is another police officer. The investigator's job is to get as much information as possible from the suspect—you— before you have had time to think of the consequences of being totally honest.

The investigator will take advantage of your urge to get it off your chest—to justify what you did. He may sympathize with you, saying anyone would have done what you did. But he will write the statement, and all the time he will be trying to fit you into one of several little boxes with labels like MURDER, MANSLAUGHTER, or JUSTIFIABLE HOMICIDE.

He knows each of the elements the prosecutor would need to prove to put you into each one of these boxes, and you don't. He will subtly try to discourage you from calling your lawyer, because he knows a lawyer will shut you up.

Archer said he didn't have his reading glasses when asked to read and sign the statement, so they gave him a magnifying glass. It wasn't the same as being able to read it properly. He also complained that the detective did not put everything he said into the statement, and he had to request that something he had said be added.

Many years ago, when I was a teenager in England, I was involved in a motorcycle accident. I was riding to work in heavy fog when another motorcycle appeared suddenly out of the mist. We collided at an intersection. Neither of us was hurt badly, although the other guy's motorbike was a wreck. When the policeman was filling in the accident report, he said: "The cause of the accident was the fog, right?"

I had been brought up to believe that an accident was always somebody's fault, and I had obviously been going too fast for the conditions. The policeman posed the question three times before I got the message. He was trying to assist me by putting the blame on the conditions. He knew what the right answers were to keep me out of trouble, and I didn't.

One of the legal requirements for the use of deadly force is that you be in fear of losing your life or of being seriously injured. This was not spelled out in Archer's statement, and Cuellar says that was one of the things that went against him when the case reached the District Attorney's office. You cannot rely on a helpful detective prompting you with: "You were in fear of your life, weren't you?" or some such leading question.

Archer said, before he testified in front of the grand jury, his lawyer prompted him to say that he was "scared to death." He ignored the advice. He explained it this way: "What is the first thing you have to do to go into a combat zone? You've got to overcome your fear. And that's taught on billboards, on posters, on every infantry training base that there is in the military. You overcome your fear. And you do that by building confidence in your ability to use these weapons, to be better at your skill than them."

For thirty years he had been a combat soldier, and "overcome your fear" had been part of his creed. He wasn't about to admit that he was afraid to anyone.

Bill McLennan, former chief firearms instructor for the San Antonio Police Department, advises politely declining to make any statement before getting a lawyer on the scene.

"I'd tell the police when they show up that I really don't want to make any statement until I've had an opportunity to talk to my lawyer," McLennan says.

Most police officers who know how the system works will give you the same advice. Talk to your lawyer before you give the police a statement.

McLennan recommends talking over your self-defense tactics with your lawyer before you get involved in any shootings. Memorize his home and office phone numbers so you can call him from jail if necessary. Call your lawyer when you call the police—immediately after a shooting.

"Tell the police there's been a shooting and nothing more," McLennan says. "Tell your lawyer exactly what happened and follow his advice to the letter."

Clint Smith of Thunder Ranch adds another suggestion. After explaining to investigators that you were in fear of your life, tell them you want them to arrest the person you just shot, even if he appears to be dead. Officers should record what you say at the time and should later testify to your statements in court if the case ever gets that far. The implication is that only an honest citizen would insist on the arrest of the other person. This is likely to make a positive impression about you to the judge and jury.

When Gordon Hale shot Kenny Tavai in self defense on Mockingbird Lane in Dallas, police arrested him. He gave them a detailed statement explaining what had happened, then they booked him for murder. He went to jail and had his mugshot and fingerprints taken, just like a common criminal. He appeared in front of a magistrate, who set his bond at $25,000. He had to pay a bondsman $2,500, or 10 percent, to post his bond so he could get out of jail. That $2,500 is the bondsman's fee and is non-returnable.

The legal bill came to more than $9,000. Most of that went to Hale's lawyer, Vincent Perini, but about $2,000 went for expert testimony from a pathologist. In total, it cost Hale almost $12,000 to prove his innocence. A month after the shooting, a grand jury no-billed Gordon Hale.

"That's what you get for being right," Hale's father says. "M'boy, my wife, everybody in the family hates that something happened like this, that the man's dead. We regret it, we sympathize with his family, but I'm glad my son's alive."

Joe Archer was able to find a lawyer to handle his case without charging him a fee, probably because he was a police officer, but he feels he was not well represented. Gordon Hale's defense cost $12,000, and his lawyer, Vincent Perini, did an excellent job. The reality is that if you shoot someone in self defense and you are justified, you may well be arrested, and your case will go before a grand jury. You will need a lawyer, and you may need some expert witnesses. Even if you are exonerated by a grand jury, you may be sued by your assailant or his family. Then you will need a civil lawyer and more money.

The jurisdiction where the shooting happens may have a lot to do with how you are treated. Geographically, the South and West are much more accepting of guns and shooting than are the Midwest and Northeast. You are also much more likely to find a sympathetic jury for a self-defense shooting in a rural community than you are in a big city.

Racism can also work against you. Bernhard Goetz became something of a hero to many New Yorkers when he shot four black youths on a subway train in December 1984. He said they were trying to rob him. He was acquitted of attempted murder by a mostly white jury in a subsequent trial, though he was convicted of illegally possessing a gun. In April 1996 a civil jury of four blacks and two Hispanics awarded Darrell Cabey, who was paralyzed by one of Goetz's bullets, $43 million in damages. Cabey's lawyer fought successfully to have the trial moved to the Bronx, where minorities would comprise a jury.

Politics may also play a part in your treatment. If you shoot the mayor's criminally-inclined son, you will almost certainly be arrested, no matter how justified you were.

The attitude of the police chief or district attorney toward the concealed-carry law may also affect your treatment. Former Dallas Police Chief Ben Click lobbied against allowing citizens to carry concealed handguns before the bill was passed. When it became obvious the bill was going to pass, Click ceased speaking out against it, said Click's spokesperson, Sergeant Jim Chandler.

"At that time he was no longer in any type of opposition to the bill, although his position remained: more guns on the street is not the answer to crime. That has been his position all along and continues to be his position," Chandler said.

Gordon Hale's father believes his son was arrested because of Click's opposition to the law.

"I think Ben Click was against it, and he had probably instructed his officers, 'if you catch someone, let's make an example,'" Hale's father says.

Chandler denies this. "That is totally incorrect. There was no instruction like that given. The case was handled the way it was because the detectives strongly felt . . . like the use of deadly force in that case was more than was legally justified. And it didn't matter that that man could legally carry that gun," Chandler says.

Deadly Force ☛ 363

It seems extremely unlikely that the police chief of a major city would give such instructions to his officers. However, knowing how a police chief feels about the law may have some influence on the officers' actions when deciding whether to arrest a self-defense shooter or to let him remain free pending a grand-jury verdict.

His lawyer believes Hale had two strikes against him from the start: the shooting occurred as a result of a minor traffic dispute; and the man he shot was unarmed—that is, he had no weapon.

The people who were against the concealed-carry law had argued that every minor traffic accident would lead to a shooting, and here was an opportunity to crow that they had been right all along. "It pushed all the buttons," says lawyer Perini.

Typical was the reaction of the *Dallas Morning News*, which attacked Hale's actions and misstated the law regarding the use of deadly force.

"The big problem we had early on in the case was that the spin the police and the *Dallas Morning News* put on this was that it was just somebody attacking with his bare fists and how dare he wield his gun under those circumstances. That's what outraged me," Perini says.

The *Dallas Morning News* said deadly force can be used only when a person "feels he is in imminent danger of being killed."

This is not true. In Texas and most other states, you can use deadly force to protect yourself from serious bodily injury. You don't have to sit there and be beaten up, because fists can inflict serious bodily injury.

"Movies and television trivialize the danger from fists," Perini says. "You can be very seriously injured by fists, and the movies make it look like you can be just pounded and pounded and pounded and then dust yourself off and go about your business. Most people who receive really good licks to the face have something to show for it. You lose teeth, you get a broken jaw, you crush your cheek bones, and you injure your eyes."

As a result of the beating Kenny Tavai inflicted on him, Gordon Hale has suffered some blurred vision and needs to wear glasses to do his work—something he never did before.

"In a Texas criminal case, that would qualify as serious bodily injury. Now the law doesn't require that you suffer serious bodily injury before you're entitled to shoot: you're entitled to shoot to prevent it. What he was really doing was he shot to prevent further bodily injury," Perini says.

While the Dallas police and the local media assumed that Hale used excessive force, probably because his attacker was not armed, a grand jury decided what Hale did was reasonable under the circumstances. Hale resorted to his gun once Tavai grabbed his shirt and started pounding his head and face. He was trapped in his pickup, which was stuck in traffic. Hale had two options: allow himself to be beaten senseless or even killed by the younger, stronger man, or use his gun. Could he have used the gun to threaten Tavai into backing off? Unlikely, and he ran the risk of Tavai taking the gun away from him and shooting him with it. Could Hale have avoided the attack by being less confrontational during his argument with Tavai? It is possible, but a man can hardly be faulted for insisting on calling the police.

There is some good news for people like Ralph Williams, Joe Archer, and Gordon Hale, who are forced to shoot in self-defense. For too long the deck of cards that is our legal system has been stacked against the law-abiding citizen who uses deadly force to defend himself, herself, or others from criminal attack.

On April 26, 2005, Florida Governor Jeb Bush signed into law a bill known as the Castle Doctrine or Stand Your Ground Law. This was the result of intensive lobbying by former NRA President Marion Hammer, who is the executive director of Unified Sportsmen of Florida. The new law passed the Florida Legislature with overwhelming majorities in the House and Senate.

The law takes away the duty to retreat if attacked in any place that you have a legal right to be—home, business, vehicle, or walking down the street.

"Previously in just about every situation you had a duty to retreat," Hammer said, explaining further that the problem was not so much with the law itself as with the courts' interpretation of the law, as reflected in the instructions given to jurors.

Prior to passage of the new law, anyone who was attacked in Florida outside the home, had a duty to retreat before using force or deadly force in self-defense. The new law allows you to stand your ground and fight back if attacked, provided you are in a place you have a legal right to be. You don't have to flee, risking a bullet or knife in the back. However, to justify using deadly force, that is shooting your attacker, you must believe you are in imminent danger of death or serious injury.

The new law also makes the presumption that, if someone breaks into your home, he is there to do you harm, and it gives you the right to use force or deadly force in response. That someone is illegally in your home is enough justification for using deadly force. The law also extends that presumption to you while in your vehicle.

The law also protects people who used force or deadly force from being sued civilly. Previously, the conviction of your attacker was your defense in a civil law suit, but the suit would still cost you for legal fees, and sometimes juries sided with the attacker, handing down judgments that could bankrupt someone for defending himself. Now the law prevents your attacker or his family from filing suit.

"If you legally shot somebody under the Castle Doctrine they can't turn around and sue you for injury or wrongful death or what have you," Hammer said.

There is a lot of confusion among ordinary citizens about what the law is and what their rights are in terms of using deadly force in self-defense. Even legislators who make the laws don't know what the law is.

"Everybody thinks that if somebody breaks into your home you have a right to defend yourself and your family. But if duty to retreat has been imposed, you could end up being the one who goes to jail. This legislation is designed to cure that and give people back the rights that most people believe they still have until they come face to face with handcuffs," Hammer said.

Before the law had even taken effect on October 1, 2005, the Brady Campaign to Prevent Handgun Violence started warning tourists in advertisements and with fliers at airports to be especially careful, or they were likely to be shot by trigger-happy Florida residents. As part of its disinformation campaign, the Brady bunch referred to the legislation as the Shoot First Law.

In the succeeding two years, a rash of states followed Florida's lead with Castle Doctrine laws of their own. Each state had its own approach, and you should check the specifics of the law in your state or any state you plan to visit. By mid 2007 sixteen states had passed versions of the Castle Doctrine law. In addition to Florida, they are Alabama, Alaska, Arizona, Georgia, Idaho, Indiana, Kansas, Kentucky, Louisiana, Michigan, Mississippi, Oklahoma, South Carolina, South Dakota, and Texas.

Hammer pledged to keep working until all fifty states have passed Castle Doctrine laws.

"It's taking back America. It's recognizing individual responsibility, and it's giving back rights that have been whittled away by bleeding-heart courts," she said.

Get a copy of all the laws affecting the use of deadly force in your state, and become thoroughly familiar with them. In many of the states that have recently passed concealed-carry legislation, you are required to learn about those laws as part of a mandatory training program. State laws vary on this. In some states you have a right to protect your property by using deadly force under some circumstances. Most instructors caution against this even if it's legal. Ask yourself: is it worth killing somebody over a television set? My advice to most people is to use deadly force only to protect yourself, a loved one, or a very close friend from the imminent threat of serious bodily injury or death.

Try to avoid getting involved in third-party disputes. If you see a shabbily-dressed man with long hair running from a bank with a gun in his hand, he might be a bank robber, but he might also be an undercover cop chasing a bank robber. Get a good description of him, note his direction of flight, and call police. Avoid domestic disputes. If you come across a man beating a woman, you are in a tricky situation. If you interfere, both of them may turn on you. He may accuse you of threatening him, particularly if you pull a gun on him. And when it comes to court, she'll almost certainly back him up. He's the only husband she has, and who'll feed the children if he goes to jail and can't work? On the other hand, if you ignore it and he kills or maims her, you'll feel bad.

Bill Davison of Tac Pro Shooting Center is a highly trained former Royal Marine in the British military. He feels he has a duty to protect the innocent and those unable to protect themselves. "I will not stand by and allow someone to recklessly murder or injure women and children in front of me. It's just not going to happen," he says.

Davison says many firearms instructors advise their students to disengage from a fight as soon as possible. Everyone has to make his or her own decision about when to use deadly force and when to become involved in a potentially violent situation. In making that decision, your skill and experience level need to be considered. Most people are not trained to Davison's level in the application of deadly force.

"When someone walks into the cafeteria and starts shooting everybody, I am not going to run out the back saying: 'well, it's not my problem,' because I can't do that," Davison says.

If you are forced to shoot in self defense, don't make any threats or statements that you wouldn't want a jury to hear later. There may be witnesses you can't see, but who can hear you. And, as the officers involved in the beating of Rodney King found out, there are a lot of video cameras out there.

"I'm gonna blow yore ass away, scumbag," or "Go ahead, make my day, punk," are not the sort of statements that make it look as though you were doing everything you could to avoid taking another person's life. Leave the heavy dialogue to Clint Eastwood or Bruce Willis. "Stop!" "Drop that gun, now!" or "Don't do it!" are much more acceptable to a grand jury.

After the shooting stops and he's lying on the ground leaking blood out of the holes you put in him, don't go up to him. He may still be dangerous. Stay behind cover or out of range and call first for an ambulance. Tell the dispatcher there has been a shooting and someone is hurt and give the location. Don't tell them you've shot anyone, just that someone has been shot. Then call the police and tell them the same thing. Remember that telephone calls to police and emergency medical services are recorded. If the guy you have shot runs off, let him go. It's not your job to chase him down and capture him. Your job is to survive.

When the police arrive, unless you are holding your attacker at gunpoint, put the gun away. If they drive up to the scene of a shooting, they don't know who the good guys are. Tell them you are a licensed gun carrier, and show them the permit. If it was a clearly justified shooting, tell them you were attacked and you shot in self defense, advises retired detective McLennan.

"I would be polite. I wouldn't be hard ass about it, but I would tell the police that I really don't want to make any statement until I've had an opportunity to talk to my lawyer," McLennan says.

This is advice Pete Kanakidis could have used.

Kanakidis was a quietly successful and law-abiding businessman, who owned River Oaks Automotive Center in an upscale

Houston neighborhood. He and his fiancée often worked late at his auto-repair shop and felt they would both benefit from being able to carry handguns legally. They took the training in the fall of 1995 and in due course received their licenses.

Late in the afternoon of May 30, 1996, Kanakidis heard Hispanic music blaring from the radio of a Suburban, even before it turned into his auto-repair shop. When three men got out of the vehicle and advanced towards him yelling and cursing, he knew he was in trouble.

Two of the men who got out of the Suburban were brothers who used to work for Kanakidis at his business. The third man was their friend, Alejandro Cruz Arroyo, 26. The brothers were angry because Kanakidis had earlier threatened to call the police in a dispute over some tools and money.

Kanakidis, then 27, left the customer he was talking to and walked over to the three men hoping to calm them down. But the brothers were in no mood to be placated. They kept cursing and threatening him. One of the brothers was poking him in the chest, while the other had his hands balled into fists. Kanakidis was aware that Arroyo had slipped behind him, apparently to cut off his retreat.

"I was trying to defuse the situation, but it was getting worse," Kanakidis said.

While he was arguing with the men, he saw his younger brother near the office. He yelled at him to call the police and stay in the office. As Kanakidis tried to walk away from the two brothers they launched into him with their fists, he said. He was knocked to the ground and beaten by the two brothers. He said he was not sure if Arroyo took part in the initial attack. "I don't know if it was just two of them or three of them, but I knew I was in big trouble."

Kanakidis managed to get away from his attackers, but they chased him and caught him. One of them broke his nose with an uppercut to the face. They bent him over a tire rack and beat him while one tried to choke him. Again, he broke loose and ran to his truck where he kept a .45 Colt semi-automatic. He grabbed the gun and pointed it up in the air so his assailants could see it. He didn't point it at them, he said. They backed off and walked across the street, though they did not seem particularly intimidated by the gun. Hoping the confrontation was over, Kanakidis put the gun back in his truck, then ran to the office.

"I'm constantly running back and forth, I'm hyperventilating, I can't breath out of my nose, I'm bleeding, and I'm telling them: 'Call the police. Call the police.'"

He ran outside to see the three men coming back across the street. He ran to his truck, pulled out his gun, waved it in the air again, and yelled at the men to leave. Again, the men retreated across the street, and Kanakidis put the gun back. He ran back to the office to find out why it was taking the police so long to arrive. When he emerged, he saw Arroyo back on his property, walking between the tire rack and a small white car. When Arroyo spotted Kanakidis, he changed direction and got into the Suburban.

The repair-shop owner hastened over to his pickup to get his gun, but changed his mind, thinking perhaps Arroyo was going to drive off peacefully. Kanakidis walked out to the street hoping to see the police arriving. He saw no patrol cars or flashing lights, so he walked back into the shop's parking lot. Arroyo was eyeing him in the rear-view mirror of the Suburban and appeared to be fumbling between the seats.

"I'm thinking to myself, this guy's going for a gun. That's when I really, really got scared," Kanakidis said.

He ran back to his truck and grabbed his Colt. Kanakidis felt he had to get Arroyo to leave before he or one of his customers got shot. He came up behind the Suburban, yelling all the time that he had called the police and for Arroyo to leave. He made eye contact with Arroyo in the rear-view mirror. He heard Arroyo gun the engine then he heard the thunk as the driver slammed the vehicle into reverse.

"I didn't take it that he was trying to leave. I took it that he was trying to run me over," Kanakidis recalled.

He ran back a few steps, then stopped. When he turned around he found the driver's door of the Suburban right beside him. He continued to yell at Arroyo to leave, but the driver started to open the door as if to get out. Kanakidis slammed the door. Arroyo tried to grab him or punch him through the window. Arroyo made a sudden movement downwards with his right arm.

"I couldn't see his right hand from where I was standing. I felt that he was pulling a gun out," Kanakidis said. "I felt that my life was in danger." Kanakidis instinctively raised his gun and fired.

The round-nosed jacketed bullet hit Arroyo in the mouth. It was a fatal wound.

Pete Kanakidis, owner of River Oaks Automotive Center in Houston.

*River Oaks Automotive Center. The altercation took place
in the yard to the right of the building.*

Arroyo had no gun, but police did find a sawed-off baseball bat under the front seat.

Shortly afterwards, the paramedics arrived and cleaned up
Kanakidis's face. Then the first police officer showed up. The
auto-shop owner was understandably upset and blamed the
police for not arriving in time to prevent the shooting. He said
the officer ambled casually over to him with his hands in his
pockets and asked what was going on.

Kanakidis jumped to his feet and angrily retorted: "What
do you mean, what's going on? Look around. None of this would
have happened if you guys would've showed up earlier."

It was a mistake.

The officer became angry and shouted questions aggressively at Kanakidis.

"I was scared. He was yelling at me," the repair-shop
owner said. "I didn't feel it was beneficial to me to say anything
at the time because of the way he was acting. I didn't feel he was
on my side."

Kanakidis declined to answer any further questions. He was
taken to a local hospital and treated for injuries he suffered during the beating. When he was released from the hospital,
police charged him with murder.

Kanakidis hired Mike Hinton, a prominent defense lawyer and former prosecutor, to defend him. Hinton says his client was charged with murder because the antagonistic attitude of the first police officer spilled over to the other investigators.

"It never should have happened this way. He never should have been charged," Hinton says.

Kanakidis had tried repeatedly to stop the confrontation from escalating, just as he had been taught in the training course for his concealed-handgun license, his lawyer says.

Several months later, he was indicted by a grand jury. Hinton would not let Kanakidis testify before the grand jury, he says, because the prosecutor would not let him see the offense report outlining the allegations against his client.

More than a year later, in August 1997, the case went to trial. Hinton said he and the District Attorney agreed that Kanakidis's concealed-handgun license was irrelevant to the case, as the shooting took place on his own property.

Assistant District Attorney Sally Ring, who prosecuted the case, said there was no evidence that Arroyo had been one of Kanakidis's assailants. "There was no evidence that the deceased ever laid a hand on Mr. Kanakidis," she said.

Ring said it appeared that when Arroyo backed up in the Suburban he was trying to get away rather than back over the auto-shop owner.

"I think he [Kanakidis] should have been convicted of murder, and I wouldn't have prosecuted the case if I didn't feel that way," she said. "If I thought it was genuinely self defense, it would not have been prosecuted."

A jury of seven men and five women deliberated about four hours before finding Kanakidis not guilty.

"Thank God the jury system worked and he was acquitted," Hinton says.

But the ordeal cost Kanakidis dearly—financially and emotionally. Before the incident, he had been planning to get married. He had to postpone the wedding until after the trial. His legal bills exceeded $75,000, and he had to pass ownership of his business over to his future father-in-law. And then there was the act of taking a life.

"It's something I think about a lot. It's not a good feeling to know that you've killed a man. It's something I have to live with for the rest of my life."

After the shooting, Kanakidis was so distraught he didn't even want to own a gun and decided not to renew his concealed-handgun license, but he has since changed his mind.

"That gun actually saved me. I think I am going to keep my license," he said.

The case of Pete Kanakidis illustrates how expensive it can be, even if you are justified in pulling the trigger. If the shooting is not a really clear-cut case of self defense, you can face more legal fees in a civil case.

The police will certainly take your gun as evidence, and they may handcuff you and take you to jail, as they did with Gordon Hale and Kanakidis. The auto-shop owner spent nearly twenty-four hours in a jail cell with thirty other prisoners, he said.

When firearms instructor Greg Ferris is teaching a class for concealed-carry licensing in Texas, he keeps a plaque at the front of the classroom which reads: "I WAS IN FEAR OF LOSING MY LIFE OR BEING SERIOUSLY INJURED."

In that single sentence is the justification for using deadly force. And the threat doesn't have to be real. It is your perception of the situation that counts. If someone is threatening you with an empty gun or with a realistic replica of a gun and you shoot them, you are justified, if you believed at the time you fired that your life was in danger.

Defending yourself in court following a self-defense shooting can be expensive. It cost Ralph Williams $16,500 to defend himself against criminal charges, and that doesn't include the $10,000 he spent defending a civil suit. Gordon Hale shelled out $12,000, and Pete Kanakidis more than $75,000. The Castle Doctrine should cut down on the number of ordinary citizens who end up in court for defending themselves, but is there anything else we can do to keep the legal system out of our pocket books? In some states, it is possible to take precautions.

Garry Brookman lives in Euless, a suburb just southwest of the Dallas/Fort Worth International Airport. He is a large man with diabetes and other medical problems that can be life threatening. He has a Doberman called Rusty that he and his wife adopted from an animal shelter. The dog is certified as a canine assistance animal and has been trained to lick Brookman's face if he collapses. If there is no response, he barks. If they are at home and there is still no response, the dog goes into the bedroom and pushes a button which sends a prerecorded message by telephone to the 9-1-1 operator.

Brookman has a Texas concealed-handgun license and is certified by the Texas Department of Public Safety as a concealed-handgun instructor.

On Saturday afternoon, June 25, 2005, Brookman, then 56, took Rusty to Meadowmere Park on Lake Grapevine so he could get some exercise. He said the temperature that day was over a hundred degrees.

"I was watching Rusty wading in the lake when suddenly I heard gunfire," Brookman said.

Several people on the opposite shore of the cove, about fifty yards away, were shouting: "Stop shooting. Put that gun away. There are kids in the water."

After a few seconds Brookman heard two shots and saw the bullet strikes in the lake close to Rusty. The dog ran out of the water, and Brookman took him back to his pickup. At that stage, he did not see who was doing the shooting.

"At 3:02 p.m. I contacted Grapevine Police Department through 9-1-1 and reported that someone was firing a handgun at Meadowmere Park," Brookman said.

The 9-1-1 operator said the police would attend. Brookman wrote down the license-plate numbers of five vehicles parked close to his truck. He started to drive south on the park road when he noticed a black two-door Cadillac and a green Honda CLX parked some distance from the other vehicles. Four teenage youths were standing beside them.

Brookman said the oldest youth was by the open driver's door of the Cadillac. He was holding a .22 caliber Ruger semi-automatic handgun in his right hand. He turned and was putting the gun on the floorboard behind the driver's seat when Brookman stopped his truck across the road from them.

"I was writing down their license-plate numbers when they noticed what I was doing. They began screaming profanities at me, asking: 'Why are you writing down our license plates?'"

He lowered his window and told them he had called 9-1-1.

"The teen with the gun screamed more profanities, then yelled: 'Get out of here man, or I'm going to shoot you!'

"I did not respond. The teenager started reaching down into the backseat of the Cadillac. Fearing that he was going for the gun, I drew my stainless Ruger P-90 semi-automatic .45 ACP caliber handgun from the center console of my truck. I got out of my truck and ordered the youth to step away from the vehicle," Brookman said.

Confronted with the gun, the youth urinated and defecated on himself but complied with Brookman's order, backing away from the car and sitting down on a park railing. Brookman said he lowered his gun, as he no longer felt threatened. He noticed two large grocery bags containing fireworks on the ground beside the Cadillac.

He again called the Grapevine Police Department at 3:08 p.m. and told the operator he was holding the youths at gunpoint and they should send officers immediately. The operator told him to put the gun away, so he put it in his truck. While waiting for the police to arrive, the youths told Brookman they often used to shoot in the park and had been shooting at passing airliners.

At 3:55, nearly an hour after his first call, two patrol cars arrived. According to Brookman, Officer Aaron Cox took possession of his gun and put it in his patrol car, while the other officer talked to the youths. Cox did not ask him any questions, Brookman said, but went over to where the other officer was questioning the youths. The officers seized the bags of fireworks, and Cox wrote the oldest youth a ticket for possession of fireworks in a prohibited place. The officer noted on the ticket that he did not search the vehicle, which was where the youth's semi-automatic handgun was.

"They never asked me anything—not one word. They talked to the kids first and came and told me I was under arrest. Had they said anything or asked me: 'What's going on?' or 'Why did you pull your weapon?' I would have said, 'There's a gun in the back of that car there.' I would have said that," Brookman said. "Had they searched the vehicle, or searched him, they would have found the gun."

The officers told him he was under arrest for deadly conduct. They handcuffed him and put him in Cox's patrol car. His truck was impounded and his dog taken to Grapevine animal control. His handgun, magazines, ammunition, holster, magazine pouch, and Texas concealed-handgun license were held as evidence. At the Grapevine police jail, he filled in a form listing all his medical problems and the medications he was taking, including insulin for diabetes.

"It was totally ignored," Brookman said.

Fortunately for Brookman, some months before he had signed up with the CHL Protection Plan. CHL stands for Concealed Handgun License, the name for the Texas concealed-carry document. The plan sells to license holders a legal-services contract that covers legal expenses after a self-defense incident with a handgun, up to and including the grand jury proceedings. It does not cover the cost of bail or civil law suits.

"We are not an insurance company, *per se*," says company president Rick Mackey.

The company started selling legal protection to Texas residents who have concealed-handgun licenses in 2005. As of mid-2007, it had about 2,500 customers and was selling contracts in Missouri, Oklahoma, Louisiana, and Arkansas, as well. It is hoping to have approval by 2008 to operate in Florida, Tennessee, Colorado, Kansas, and Georgia.

Allowed one phone call, Brookman dialed the toll-free number on his CHL Protection Plan card and explained to the answering-service operator that he had been arrested and was in the Grapevine police jail. The operator called Richard Fry, a lawyer in Austin, on contract to the plan. Brookman was put in a cell with another man overnight. He said he learned later that Fry called the jail to speak to him at least four times between 4 p.m. Saturday and 7 a.m. Sunday. Fry was told he was unavailable, so the lawyer called Brookman's wife. She brought his insulin to the jail that Saturday night, but it was put in the evidence bag with his wallet and other belongings he had had on him when he was arrested. He received no medical attention, food, or water.

By the next morning Brookman was called to appear before a magistrate. He was having pains in his left arm and said he could not get up. He said he was dragged out of the cell by a police officer and his cellmate and left face down on the floor where he passed out. Someone shook him into a state of semi-consciousness and told him he had to sign a form.

"It could have been a confession to murder for all I knew," Brookman said.

The magistrate set his bond at a thousand dollars and asked someone if he was all right. Grapevine Fire Department paramedics were called to examine him. They realized he was having a heart attack and put him on a gurney.

The last thing Brookman remembers as he was wheeled out of the jail area was the magistrate saying, "Get him out of here before he dies on us."

An ambulance took him to Baylor Hospital in Grapevine. A police officer guarded him, while he was handcuffed to the gurney in the emergency room. After he was treated for the heart attack and told his bond had been paid, the police officer removed the handcuffs and left. Apparently Brookman had only a mild heart attack, so his wife was able to drive him home. He is convinced his heart attack was caused by the incompetence of the staff at the Grapevine jail, who withheld medical attention and medication from him. His health insurance paid $2,900 for his brief hospital stay.

The youth who was issued a ticket for possession of fireworks appeared in Grapevine municipal court on July 12, 2005, and pleaded guilty. He was fined $123 and put on probation for ninety days. He was not charged with illegal possession of a firearm, because the police officers never searched his car and thus never discovered the gun.

The following Tuesday, Brookman went to the Grapevine Police Department and filed a criminal complaint against the four youths for violation of the Texas Guide Dog Protection Act. Attempting to kill or injure a service animal is a Class C felony. Brookman also filed reports of domestic terrorism with the FBI, Texas Department of Public Safety, and the federal Park Service. A park ranger met Brookman at the crime scene on Wednesday and gathered spent .22 caliber casings and expended firework remnants. He told Brookman that in the previous twelve months there had been more than two hundred reports of firearms-related vandalism in the Grapevine Lake area.

About ten days after his arrest, Brookman appeared in Tarrant County Criminal Court. Fry, the protection-plan lawyer, drove up from Austin to represent him. He subsequently relinquished the case to Walt Cleveland, a local lawyer from the

Fort Worth area. Cleveland had been a police officer and a felony prosecutor before becoming a criminal-defense lawyer.

Brookman was charged with deadly conduct, a Class A Misdemeanor, punishable by up to a year in the county jail and a fine not to exceed $5,000, Cleveland said. The offense is when someone performs an act that is clearly dangerous to human life, although no injury results.

"To make a long story short, it's pointing a gun at somebody," the lawyer added.

For his second court appearance, Cleveland met Brookman at the courthouse. The lawyer conferred with the prosecutor, who offered a deal. Brookman would get five years probation if he pleaded guilty to deadly conduct, took anger management classes, gave up his gun and any other guns he possessed for destruction, and gave up all firearms for five years. A lawyer is required to tell his client what the prosecutor offers, so the client can decide whether to accept it or not.

"I told Walt, 'No.'"

There was a suggestion that the police were planning to destroy Brookman's gun, so Cleveland subpoenaed it for ballistics tests. He filed a series of other motions. Cleveland threatened to take the case to a jury trial, at which the youths would be subpoenaed to testify. They could not be forced to testify against themselves, but they could be forced to give evidence against each other. The case never got as far as taking depositions, but the threat was there.

"I knew I was right, and in a misdemeanor court in a large county like Tarrant County, I was dealing with an attorney that had very little experience," Cleveland said. "And I also threatened to make it a very public trial."

Cleveland said the investigation was poor, and the police officers were lazy in not doing a more thorough investigation.

"They had a person with a gun. They thought that they had solved the problem by taking the gun and the person who had it. They just diffused the situation rather than investigate it and see what actually happened," he said.

The prosecutor decided he wanted to renegotiate. He offered to dismiss the charges if they could destroy the gun. Brookman turned down that offer too. Then the prosecutor offered to let the judge decide if he got his gun and ammunition back.

"I said, "Fine. I'll go with that,'" Brookman said.

On Friday, March 10, 2006, Judge Brent Carr, an ex-Marine and former federal prosecutor, dismissed the charge of deadly conduct against Garry Brookman. He also signed an order for Brookman to get back his handgun, spare magazines, ammunition, and holster.

"I got in my car and drove directly from the downtown Fort Worth courthouse out to the city of Grapevine and went to the little information window and asked for my property back," Brookman said.

A senior police officer verified the order, then told Brookman he would have to make an appointment for the following week. Brookman pointed out that Grapevine police had had his handgun for nine months, and he wanted it immediately. When the officer stalled, he threatened to have his lawyer call the judge and tell him that Grapevine police were ignoring his order. Brookman got his gun back that day.

He still needed to get his concealed-handgun license back. Grapevine police said they didn't have it. He called the Texas Department of Public Safety, which issues the licenses, and faxed the judge's order. He was initially told the department didn't have the license. Apparently they later found the license and, after many phone calls, it was returned to him on April 6, 2006.

I emailed this account to the Grapevine Police Department for their comments. Several days later, I received an email from Sergeant Kim Smith, which stated that the department's lawyers had advised to allow the account to stand without comment.

"Several of his [Brookman's] points ... are inaccurate and based on his own personal interpretation of the incident," Smith wrote. She declined to elaborate on which points were inaccurate.

Brookman saved several thousands of dollars in legal fees by belonging to the CHL Protection Plan. He was pleased with the representation he received from both Protection Plan lawyers, particularly Cleveland.

"He went way beyond what the contractual obligations were, which were just to defend me until it gets to a grand jury. He helped me get my gun back; he went to court four or five times and got the thing dismissed; got the judge to order them to give me my gun back," Brookman said.

Coverage for an individual through the CHL Protection Plan is $129 a year or $229 for a couple. Each client receives a wallet-size card with a toll-free phone number on it that will be answered twenty-four hours a day. The client will be referred to one of the plan's contract lawyers, who will handle the case. As of September 2007, the only claim for legal representation had been Brookman's.

For more information about the CHL Protection Plan, visit website <www.chlpp.com> or contact Rick Mackey, president of the plan, at 866-851-9744.

NRA members, whether they have concealed-carry licenses or not, can buy insurance against the costs resulting from a self-defense incident. The NRA Endorsed Insurance Program offers an insurance policy for self-defense coverage among its property and liability plans available to NRA members only. There are two levels of coverage: for a premium of $165 a year, a member gets a policy with a $100,000 limit; for $254 annual premium, the coverage limit is $250,000. The limit for a criminal charge is $50,000 for both policies, and it is paid only as a reimbursement for expenses, after the case is concluded and the member is absolved of any crime in connection with a self-defense incident. The rest of the amount covers the defense of a civil suit for damages due to bodily injury or property damage.

The plans are administered on behalf of the NRA by Lockton Risk Services. More information may be found at <www.nraendorsedinsurance.com> click on Self-Defense.

One thing that is going to happen if you shoot someone in self-defense is that the police are going to take the gun you used. They may test fire it to make sure it works or to match the bullets it fires with one or several the medical examiner dug out of the dead perpetrator who attacked you. Even if you are innocent of any crime, it may be a long time before you get your gun back. This may leave you defenseless for weeks or months at a time when you could be in danger from an attacker on bail or from friends and family of your assailant.

Susan Gaylord Buxton had to get help from the NRA and the Texas State Rifle Association to get her gun back after she shot a fugitive in the leg in her Arlington, Texas, home. On November 9, 2005, Buxton, then a grandmother sixty-six-years old, shot Christopher Michael Lessner in the thigh after he had broken into her house in the middle of the night. Lessner had stolen a pickup in a nearby suburb and was running from police. He was arrested shortly after limping from Buxton's house.

A female detective from Arlington Police Department took the little J-frame Smith & Wesson revolver Buxton had used, saying the police needed it for only a couple of days. After hearing nothing for several days, Buxton started calling the detective who took her revolver. She left messages, but her calls were not returned.

"Well, that's making me mad. They could at least call me back because I left messages, and they won't even give me the courtesy of calling me back," Buxton said. "And they had my personal property. Whether it is a gun, or a skillet, or a baseball bat, it's mine. And it didn't commit any crimes."

She got Jill "J.R." Labbe, a columnist for the *Fort Worth Star-Telegram*, involved. Labbe wrote a column that ran on December 11 headlined "What One Woman Wants for Christmas: a Returned Gun."

Apparently the District Attorney's office had instructed the police department to hold the gun until the legal process against Lessner was completed. Labbe was told that Lessner's defense lawyer was blocking the gun's return to Buxton.

It is hard to see what part the gun could play as evidence in the charges against Lessner. As Buxton put it: he was not charged with getting shot.

Albert Ross, an Arlington lawyer who is legal counsel to the Texas State Rifle Association, promised to help. Still nothing happened.

"I'm at the fuming stage now. They had my gun without cause. I'm one of these people who pays their bills on time. I don't owe anybody any money. And I was really starting to have some kind of a complex here, and feeling that I have done something wrong," Buxton said. "And I don't like being made to feel like a criminal."

It seemed as though she was not the only one outraged by what was happening. Labbe forwarded emails to her from all over the country from people writing in support of the gun-totin' granny.

Buxton appealed for help to the NRA. She received a four-page letter from Stefan B. Tahmassebi, deputy legal counsel for the NRA, citing four legal precedents that might be helpful in getting her gun back.

The letter said state has a right to seize illegal firearms and weapons that were used to commit a crime. The police and prosecutor still have a right to use the gun as evidence in a criminal prosecution if the gun is necessary evidence of a crime. However, if these circumstances are not present, the state has no right to seize or to refuse to return the gun.

Ross said there was no reason for the defense lawyer or the prosecutor to hold the gun as evidence. If Lessner had touched the gun and had his fingerprints on it, it would have been different. Ross made it known that he was about to file a motion with the court to have the gun returned. One of the cases that Tahmassebi cited left the government open to having to pay court costs if a citizen had to go to court to get property returned.

Susan Buxton.

"Nobody wanted to take responsibility for making a decision on it—to give it back to her," Ross said.

Eventually, the prosecutor drafted a court order for the gun to be released to Buxton and, on December 22, a judge signed it. But no one told Ross or Buxton the court order had been signed. Christmas delayed things until January 11, when Ross and Buxton went to Arlington Police Department to pick up the gun. Initially the police couldn't find the paperwork, then they had to check on the computer to make sure the gun hadn't been reported stolen. Finally, they had to conduct a criminal background check on Buxton. Her concealed-handgun license apparently was not good enough.

What should have taken a few minutes took most of the morning. It had taken two months and two days from the time it was seized for Buxton to get her gun back. Once the District Attorney's office decided Susan was not going to be charged with anything, her gun should have been returned immediately.

"It was a screw up by the numbers deal, what I call a Chinese fire drill," Ross said.

There was no real basis for the police to take the gun away from her, he said.

While she was deprived of her own revolver, she borrowed a similar gun from her sister Judy Gaylord. The Smith & Wesson Chief's Special was not a light-weight revolver like hers, but it was handier to carry around than her 9mm semi-automatic.

When Judy Kuntz shot and killed a man who had broken into her Indialantic, Florida, home on May 29, 2005, there was no question that she fired in legitimate self-defense. The sixty-four-year-old widow was interviewed by Brevard County homicide investigators, and the .38 Special caliber revolver she had used was seized. The investigation cleared her of any wrong doing. The man she shot, Jason Louis Preston, thirty-three, was dead, so there would be no trial. However, her revolver was not returned to her until nearly eleven months later. She did have a shotgun that was not seized, so Kuntz was not defenseless. However, anyone who carries a handgun for self-defense should consider keeping two similar guns in case one is seized after a shooting incident.

The full stories of the self-defense shootings by Susan Gaylord Buxton and Judith Kuntz are recounted in my book *Thank God I Had a Gun; True Accounts of Self-Defense.*

PSYCHOLOGICAL AFTER-EFFECTS AND RESIDUAL ADRENALINE

Rory Vertigan, the security manager for a real-estate company in Phoenix, Arizona, suffered major psychological trauma after shooting and wounding Felipe Petrona-Cabanas, a young Mexican drug trafficker who had just killed a Phoenix police officer. (See Chapter 8.)

When he arrived home late that evening at the apartment he shared with his mother, it seemed that everybody he knew was there. His mother had made phone calls to their friends, who came over to give her moral support. Rory had a few drinks and went to bed sometime after midnight.

He could not sleep. His mind kept replaying the incident. He felt guilty that he had not done more to save Officer Marc Atkinson's life. But he had another more urgent fear. He remembered seeing a bullet hole in the back window of Atkinson's squad car.

"I layed in bed so sick to my stomach because I was thinking to myself, my God, what if that was one of my rounds. What if it was my round that hit him? I thought, oh my God I'm going to go to jail."

The Phoenix police association paid for and arranged for Rory to get professional counseling by a psychiatrist to help him cope with the stress of the incident. He told the psychiatrist he had experienced an anxiety attack the night of the shooting.

"I told her I was sweating, I was sick, I was freaking out, because all this stuff was playing over and over again in my mind: Oh my God, what if that was my bullet?"

Even after he had been assured that none of his bullets had hit Atkinson, Rory still suffered from what the psychiatrist called night terrors.

"I'll wake up soaking wet. I'll sit straight up in bed, and there will be a perfect imprint of me in bed from sweat. And I'll wake up with images of that night in my head. It doesn't happen like it used to, but I would say for a good year, I probably had a nightmare or night terrors two or three times a week."

In addition to dreaming of that night, he had nightmares of being shot to death. The psychiatrist said he was suffering from Post Traumatic Stress Disorder. He laughed at her and said that was something that only people in the military got after intense combat. Not so. She told him anyone involved in even one shooting can suffer from it.

Later, he went to another psychiatrist at his own expense. That doctor wanted to put him on medication, but he refused. He said he would never take medication for that. Six years after the shooting, the nightmares occur only about half-a-dozen times a year, he said.

The shooting also likely cost him a relationship. He split up with his girlfriend of more than eight years, because she couldn't handle what he was going through.

"That was one of the biggest strains on my relationship. That's part of why we separated. She said she just couldn't handle the way my emotional mindset was after the shooting."

What troubled Rory the most after the shooting was the feeling that he didn't do enough to save Marc Atkinson's life. Even though investigators, officers, and friends all said he did all he could have, his mind still won't allow him to believe it.

"I've played it over in my mind a million times. I was probably the worst Monday-morning quarterback there was."

He speculated that he could have warned Atkinson by blowing his horn or that he could have rammed the Lincoln.

"Even today, it still bothers me. But I know I did everything I could do, but my mind would not let me think that," he said.

After the shooting, Rory said he found details of the incident coming back to him over a period of days and even weeks. It was sometimes confusing, because he wasn't sure whether he was remembering something he witnessed or something he had heard subsequently. This initial memory loss happens frequently to people who have experienced high-stress situations.

This is why it is a good idea to wait a few days before giving investigators a statement.

Dr. Mike McMains, a retired police psychologist, says Vertigan's experience is a classic case of what can happen after a shooting incident, even if you do not kill anybody.

"Anybody who feels the threat, whether they actually take any action or not, or feels the threat for people that they have an emotional attachment to, can experience this kind of thing," McMains said. "It seems to me that Rory was identifying with the police officer in the situation. That's where the impact I think came from."

Vertigan didn't know Atkinson personally, but as someone in the security business, identified with law enforcement, McMains said.

McMains retired from the San Antonio Police Department after twenty-two years as a police psychologist. Before that, he was a psychologist in the U.S. Army for five years. Between his Army and police experience, he has dealt with about a thousand people who have been involved in shooting incidents, he said.

It's not over when the shooting stops, and concealed-handgun-license holders need to be prepared for the aftermath.

"God forbid that people get involved in shootings, but if you do, it's important to know what goes on after the fact, so you can be ready for it," McMains said.

Psychologists used to think of post-traumatic stress as a disorder in which a person is overwhelmed by anxiety in a fearful situation that he, or she, could not control.

"That's not the way to think about it."

The way to think about traumatic stress is that it is a survival skill, he said.

A shooting unfolds in stages. The initial stage, called the Impact Stage, lasts from when you perceive the threat, through the actual shooting, to whenever the questions from investigators, family, and friends stop. This will take two or three days.

Once you recognize a situation where you are in danger, you react in the way you need to in order to survive, McMains said.

"You tend to go on autopilot. When that adrenaline hits you, your cerebral cortex begins to shut down; you go into survival mode; your actions are geared to survival, and they are pretty automatic."

That is when you do what you've been trained to do. You may also experience tunnel vision when your whole focus in on one threat to the exclusion of others. You may tune out the noise of shots being fired, and you may feel that everything is unfolding in slow motion.

After the shooting, it is important to talk to people about what has happened, but it is important to talk to people who will have your best interests at heart and will be supportive, McMains said.

You may be offered coffee, tea, or a caffeine-laced soda by investigators or friends. People who have just been in life-threatening situations have a lot of adrenaline in their systems. The last thing they need is more stimulants. A glass of water is a much better choice.

The second stage is the Recoil Stage, which is when things have settled down and you are trying to adjust to what has happened.

Physiologically, you got a tremendous surge of adrenaline, cortisone, and the other chemicals that provide us with the energy to survive. There have been changes in the nervous system.

"The recoil is that time period that it takes your nervous system to reset itself—a six-to-eight week period."

During this stage, people often become withdrawn. They don't want to be around folks. They are more irritable, because their nervous system is clearly jacked up.

"There is a tremendous amount of second guessing—what if?"

After a shooting incident in which a police officer was killed, McMains had to deal with another officer who should have been on duty that night. The man felt guilty at not being there and handling the call. During the Recoil Stage, the person is trying to figure out if he or she could have done anything differently that would have resulted in a better outcome, as in Rory Vertigan's case. The person is also trying to get emotional control of the situation.

"Somehow the more we go over it and talk about it, the closer we come to coming to terms with it. I think that is part of the process," McMains said.

During this period of time, you are very susceptible to other people's ideas and evaluations. So the people around you make a difference in the way you react to a situation.

Life-threatening situations produce a feeling of the world out of control, so maintaining some ritual and routine helps bring it back under control. Beware of overindulging in alcohol.

Some people react to a traumatic occurrence by putting themselves at risk. McMains mentioned a Vietnam veteran who came back to the United States, sold the family station wagon and bought a Corvette. In six months, he picked up twelve traffic tickets for speeds in excess of 120 miles an hour.

"Some folks push the envelope after a life-threatening event—just daring death almost."

Moderate exercise helps burn off excess adrenaline, but don't overdo it and recognize that you will not be operating at 100 percent for a while.

The last stage in the psychological process of coming to terms with a shooting incident is the Adaptation Stage, McMains said.

"The world is not the same anymore. You've been in a situation where you could have died, and all of a sudden the world isn't as safe as you thought it was. But the other side of that is: neither is it as dangerous as you feel it is now. So you have to come to terms with the fact that in some situations, yes, the world is a dangerous place; in other situations, it's not a dangerous place."

It is also important to understand that the survival response is not sickness. It is a positive thing. You are alive because your survival responses kept you that way, McMains said. People become more cautious, and that's not a bad thing, he said. They become more attuned to risk and danger. They pay more attention to what's going on in the street, and police officers are much more careful about checking their equipment.

Some people have flashbacks and dreams. The FBI did a study some years ago interviewing fifteen thousand officers who had been involved in shooting incidents. About 66 percent had experienced flashbacks or dreams about the incident.

One officer McMains treated experienced anxiety attacks when he moved into a new house. He would experience these attacks when he left for work, particularly at the corner with the street sign. The name of the street was the same as the name of the man he had shot and killed.

When Police Officer Shayne Katzfey fired the shot that killed the man who was diving for his gun, he was shooting in self defense. The dead man had powder burns on the inside of his forearms, which corroborated Katzfey's statement that the man's hands were reaching for the officer's revolver when he fired.

However, the officer who wrote the first report classified the incident, not as a self-defense shooting, but as an accidental shooting. The man who was killed was not a thief or burglar, but a resident in his own backyard when he came out of the gate and went for Katzfey's gun. The initial report on the shooting is a public document and was given to the news media. At a subsequent news conference, police officials said Katzfey was in shock, and they were relying mostly on what his partner told them about the incident. But the other officer was behind Katzfey and couldn't see the man lunge for the gun. The police officials told the media the shooting appeared accidental and referred to the dead man as "totally innocent."

The impression that the shooting was an accident was never publicly corrected. Consequently the media reported and reinforced the impression that Katzfey had screwed up.

"Everybody in the city is reading and hearing and watching and seeing that I made a mistake," he says. For months afterward, Katzfey was racked with self-doubt. He didn't find vindication until three years later, when a federal jury exonerated him by rejecting a claim for damages by the dead man's relatives.

Massad Ayoob of Lethal Force Institute has made part of his living for many years studying and reporting on gunfights. He includes education about post-shooting trauma as part of many of his self-defense courses. He says post-shooting trauma is caused at least in part by the way society views and deals with people who have killed others. Some people appear to believe it's wrong to survive by killing another person. Mostly, these are people who have never had their lives threatened by an armed criminal. There is a lot of truth to the old saying that the difference between a liberal and a conservative is one mugging.

Clint Smith of Thunder Ranch says one thing he can never predict for students is what form the threat will take. Most police officers and probably civilians who carry guns fantasize at some time or other about winning a gunfight. Invariably the person indulging in the fantasy imagines the antagonist is an armed adult with a criminal record who probably shoots first.

When the man you have just killed was unarmed, the clearly-justified fantasy goes out the window, and self-doubt creeps in. To some extent, how clearly justified your shooting appeared to be to you and, just as importantly, to others will affect how you react to it.

"If you are surrounded by positive information, positive feedback from your shooting; if it's cut and dried, you didn't have a choice, there was no two ways about it, and everybody on God's green earth understands that, then you are not as likely to have as many of those lingering effects," Katzfey says.

Immediately after Katzfey's shooting, his thoughts swung wildly between being thankful that the man didn't get his gun to oh-my-God-I've-just-killed-another-human-being.

"It's like standing in the surf, and the waves of emotion are just washing over you, and you don't know how to feel, and you can't control them," he says.

This emotional surf ride owes much to the adrenaline that was triggered by the need to survive. Katzfey was overdosing on adrenaline and its accompanying hormone ACTH that was still surging through his system. When you are taken to the police station to make a statement about what happened, you will probably be offered coffee or perhaps a cola. The last thing your body needs at such a time is caffeine on top of ACTH, warns Katzfey. What you need is lots of water, followed by hard exercise such as running, bicycling, or beating the stress out of your system on a punching bag in the gym, he says.

A*ikido* instructor David Ham was astonished at his behavior as he coped with the after effects of adrenaline. He says he was calm and felt no fear during the incident when he gave a thumbs up sign to the teenage gangbanger who had the drop on him with a sawed-off shotgun.

After the youths drove off, Ham made a detour to the police station to report the incident. Consequently, he arrived home later than anticipated. His wife, Lisa, chided him for being late and told him one of his *aikido* students had phoned to ask where "the heck" he was.

"I blew up, and I blew up like I've never blown up before in my life," Ham says. "I said something to the tune of: 'Well, blank him, and I really don't want to hear this right now.'

"She was stunned to say the least, by the intensity of the response, much less the language that was involved, so she tried to figure what the problem was.

"She said: 'Gosh, you seem to be...'

"I said, 'Just don't talk to me right now. I don't want to talk to you. I don't want to hear about it. I'm telling you right now, this is not the time. Don't you blankety-blank talk to me.'

"Her mouth dropped open, and I kept coming. I walked down the stairs into the living room, got in her face, and said: 'I'm telling you right now, don't blankety-blank talk to blankety-blank me.'"

He turned around and walked out of the room. Ham went to the bathroom and noticed his hands were shaking. He ran around the block and got himself under control. He returned to the house, apologized, and told Lisa what had happened.

"She immediately understood. She said, 'I thought you were having a mental breakdown,'" Ham recalls.

He says his outburst was totally out of character. Unknown to him at the time, he was dealing with the after-effects of the adrenaline rush caused by his brush with death.

Counseling psychologist Jean Souza says it can take months or even years for adrenaline and ACTH to dissipate out of your system. Meanwhile, you will experience symptoms such as irritability, restlessness, and uneasiness. You may have trouble getting to sleep and experience body jerking, teeth grinding, and nightmares when you do. You may have bouts of self-doubt, depression, crying, and headaches. These symptoms can lead to over dependence on alcohol or prescription drugs or to digestive problems, and can even result in marriage breakup and job changes.

Bill Stroud, the owner of the Tool House in Shreveport, suffered emotional stress after shooting the man who tried to rob him. (See Chapter 2.)

"I had what they call post-traumatic stress for a while, and it was just overwhelming," he said.

Stroud said the combination of the stress over the shooting and the city ripping up the street in front of the store hurt his business badly.

"My stress was so bad, I often cried. Especially at Christmas time, it tore me up," he said. "I couldn't forget this nineteen-year-old's mom who wouldn't have her son at Christmas. It broke my heart. I'm a youth minister and work with youths of that age. Even though the guy didn't deserve a second chance, and I still believe in capital punishment, it still hurt and really affected me emotionally."

Stroud said that the only thing that kept him sane was his belief in God.

Katzfey coped with the after-effect of his shooting incident by learning all he could about post-shooting trauma. He and Souza helped form San Antonio's Police Officer Support Team, a group of officers who have been involved in shooting incidents and who help other officers through the aftermath. Unfortunately, there are no such groups for civilians.

It wasn't until he went on a training course in Palm Springs about six months after the shooting that he realized other people suffered from the same problems. A doctor explained in layman's terms what Katzfey had been going through.

"I've never talked to this man, I don't know who he is, but the guy's inside my head. Because everything he's talking about I know about, because I've been going through it. I couldn't imagine that somebody could have that detailed an amount of knowledge about just how I had been feeling," Katzfey says.

Fortunately there are things you can do to help counteract the ACTH in your system. Souza recommends percussive exercise for at least twenty minutes a day. This includes running, fast walking, using a punching bag, weight lifting, playing racquet ball, and practicing martial arts. Moving the major muscles produces endorphins which counteract the effects of ACTH.

She also suggests taking psyllium, a water-soluble natural fiber that absorbs and carries cholesterol and ACTH out of the system. Psyllium can be bought over the counter in health food stores and pharmacies in brand names such as Metamucil, Fiberall, Konsyl-D, and Serutan.

"It is not a laxative designed for the elderly, and it is not even remotely related to Geritol," Souza says.

She recommends a maintenance dose of three to six grams of psyllium a day, depending upon the stressfulness of your job. Up to nine grams a day is appropriate after a shooting or similar high-stress incident. Coupled with psyllium, you need to drink between two and four quarts of water a day, Souza says. Alcohol, coffee, and sodas are no substitute for water, as they dehydrate the system and so require more water to counteract.

While the last thing you want to do is shoot someone, if you have to, knowing what to expect afterward will help you weather it. As Clint Smith says, "If you pull a pistol out and shoot, your trouble just begins, it doesn't end."

INSURANCE:

CHL Protection Plan, 12801 Midway Road, Suite 212, Dallas, TX 75244; 866-851-9744;
NRA Endorsed Insurance Program, P.O. Box 22108, Santa Barbara, CA 93121-2108; 877-672-3006;

Chapter Twelve

PRACTICE: YOUR LIFE DEPENDS ON IT

Ted Bonnet stood with his hands on the cash register. Suddenly he whipped out a battered .45 Government Model 1911 semi-automatic and ripped off two shots at each of the two on the other side of the counter.

Without a pause, he sprinted for the doorway of the store, reloading as he ran. He fired two quick shots at the one hiding behind a car parked beside the gas pumps about thirty yards away and a couple more shots at two heads showing above the pumps.

Bonnet carefully squeezed off two more shots, hitting another figure behind the car, which was almost obscured by the hostage he was holding . . . .

No, this was not a gas-station holdup, though it was set up to simulate one. It was "Walt's Garage," a stage of fire in the fifteenth annual U.S. Practical Shooting Association's (USPSA) National Pistol Championships.

Bonnet, a pilot from San Antonio, won the Limited Gun category.

USPSA is the national body of the International Practical Shooting Confederation, generally known by its initials, IPSC, and pronounced "ipsick." This type of competition, whether at a local or national level, provides excellent practice at shooting fast and accurately under pressure. Several of the top self-defense instructors, such as the late Jeff Cooper, Ray Chapman, and Massad Ayoob, have been IPSC shooters.

When Cooper and others created IPSC in 1976, the intention was to provide competition that would enhance self-defense skills. In the subsequent couple of decades, IPSC has become an international sport with professional competitors who have developed a minor arms race around winning. In the early days, competitors used fairly standard .45-caliber Colt Government Model 1911s with a few minor modifications. Now, the top competitors shoot optical-sighted, compensated race guns with double-column magazines. They cost several thousand dollars and are about as concealable as backhoes. In reaction to the expense and impracticality of these guns, a Limited Class has been established in which competitors use standard pistols with only a few modifications allowed.

While IPSC competition is good practice in many ways, its stages are nothing like the sort of gun battle a civilian gun carrier is likely to encounter. For safety reasons, IPSC shooters run sideways or forward from one shooting box to the next. They don't shoot while backing up. They tend to reload while sprinting from one firing position to the next, dropping partially filled magazines along the way. They are running against the clock. Most of the shooting is done at ranges between ten and fifty yards. Real-life gunfights most often occur between three and twenty feet. Competition shooters may run through thirty rounds at more than a dozen targets, a highly unlikely occurrence in a real shootout. Even in Limited Class, high-capacity semi-automatics are most frequently used, and the gun is not concealed but worn in full view. IPSC shooters do not use cover as much as they should, and inevitably the shooting is done during bright daylight, not in the dark or half-light of reality. Before an IPSC stage of fire, you get a walk-through, in which you examine the course of fire and plan your attack—your route, where you will reload, and how many shots you will need to fire at each shooting box. There are no walk-throughs in a real gunfight, although you should try to plan how you will handle a situation before the shooting starts.

Having said all that, however, IPSC shooting is fun, and it teaches accuracy and confidence. Most IPSC stages are scored by dividing the score on the targets by the time it took you to complete the stage. This cranks up the pressure and encourages you to shoot as fast as you can make hits.

IPSC stages have become more complicated over the years as competitors and their equipment have become better and more sophisticated. However, one of the old standards by which to measure your performance is the El Presidente. You start with your back to three IPSC figure targets, spaced about a target's width apart, with your hands up, that is, with your wrists above your shoulders. At the start signal, you turn, draw your gun, and fire two shots at each target, reload, and fire two more shots at each target. An expert such as Ted Bonnet or Rob Leatham can complete the drill in less than five seconds with center-chest hits. The exercise is usually done at ten yards, but can be done at any distance—twelve, seven, or five yards. If your gun is concealed and you do a tactical reload, it will take longer, and if you use a revolver, it will take a lot longer. Always strive for center hits, no matter what the range or whether the target is torso, head, or pelvis. Keep a record of your scores and compete against yourself.

Another popular exercise is the "Bill Drill." Face a single target, draw and fire six shots, or five if your are using a five-shot revolver, trying to keep your hits in the A zone of an IPSC target. This exercise can be shot at any range from five feet to fifty yards, but you should concentrate on the closer ranges. It teaches you to handle recoil and bring your sights back onto the target after each shot. Again, record your scores and times, so you can compare your ability from month to month.

NRA Action Pistol shooting is another competitive "practical" shooting style. Unlike IPSC stages, Action Pistol strings have specific time limits. Whereas no two IPSC stages will be the same, Action Pistol uses a limited number of stages that are always the same. Stages include moving targets, banks of steel plates, and shooting from behind barricades.

While both IPSC and NRA's Action Pistol provide training in shooting accurately under stress, the best of the practical shooting sports for honing real-life skills is a relative newcomer. The International Defensive Pistol Association (IDPA) was created by Bill Wilson, Ken Hackathorn, and several others with extensive experience in practical shooting. They believed IPSC had deviated too far from its initial concept of providing defensive-shooting practice under the stress of competition.

IDPA rules were written to make sure the guns and gear used were of the types that would normally be carried by concealed-handgun-license holders. Competitors are divided into four divisions according to the type of gun used. They cover practical handguns from out-of-the-box revolvers and semi-automatics to slightly improved semi-autos. Compensators and optical sights are not allowed. Magazines are limited to ten rounds, and holsters have to be practical. Shooting and reloading must be done behind cover where possible, and partly empty magazines may not be discarded. Any practical-shooting competition, or gunfight for that matter, is a compromise between speed and accuracy. IDPA competition places more emphasis on accuracy. IPSC is more oriented toward speed.

One complaint I have with IPSC and IDPA is the targets they use. The targets are rough approximations of the human body with head, but the best scoring area on both types of target is the center of mass or about where the stomach is on a person. The most vulnerable area in the body is the cardiovascular triangle, which is in the top third of the torso, not the middle. Shooting exclusively at IPSC or IDPA targets will teach you to aim at the wrong area on the body.

Another way of improving reflexes and defensive handgun skills is with video training. I have tried two versions put out by Advanced Interactive Systems. One system uses real handguns that have been modified slightly to fire plastic bullets from compressed air cartridges and can be erected in any indoor training setting. The other requires an indoor range that allows students or customers to use their own guns with full loads.

The plastic-bullet system projects scenarios onto a screen about eight by ten feet, and the shooter must react to what is happening. AIS has various programs for law-enforcement and civilian training on discs. Each program has about ten different scenarios, and each scenario has three or four options within it. The civilian version I tried was specifically oriented to the concealed-handgun-license holder. The scenarios had titles like Carjacking, Home Burglary at Night, and Robbery at Gas Station. In one option of Carjacking, the bad guy is armed with a gun, in another, a knife. The shooter first has to decide if and when to shoot and then make sure he hits the bad guy and no one else. The scenarios are realistic, and it is surprising how quickly a bad situation can develop. This type of training is both fun and educational.

An AIS spokesman said in 2007 that the plastic-bullet system has been replaced by a laser operation, but the live-fire system is still being sold. Most of these video systems are located on ranges used to train law-enforcement officers as well as civilians.

Some shooting schools run force-on-force courses, which are especially useful and in some cases humiliating for the shooter. Force-on-force pits students against one another or against an instructor, using replica or modified handguns that fire plastic bullets or pellets in the closest thing to a gunfight that can be replicated in training. Participants wear helmets with face protection to keep pellets from damaging eyes. Scenarios can be set up to replicate everything from an attempted carjacking to house clearing. This training brings home to students just how vulnerable they are and how likely they are to get hit in a real gunfight. Properly supervised, it is excellent training.

I had the opportunity of watching U.S. Customs agents at a quarterly weapon-training session. The handgun training was split into two parts. First, there was a shoot-and-move course, designed by Special Agent Robert Butler, where agents ran from one piece of cover to another, engaging figure targets or steel

Concealed-handgun-license applicant shooting the required course in Texas. It is advisable to shoot your state's qualification course at least once a year and record your scores.

plates at each stop. Butler, who was the range officer, ran along with each shooter giving advice and yelling at him to go faster. The shouting was designed to fluster the shooter and to add to the stress. Butler urged the agents to shoot and reload while behind cover. This was good. In IPSC or NRA Action Pistol, lip service is paid to using cover, but this was more like real life.

The second part of the course consisted of firing strings of shots, most from a standing position, in specific time periods at various distances up to twenty-five yards. While the first shoot-and-move stage was more interesting and realistic, the second, almost sedentary, course was the one that counted. Several agents fired tight groups by taking the full time limit for each string, rather than by firing as fast as they could make good hits. This is not as realistic for self-defense practice as it could be. However, any practice is better than none.

"I really can't stress enough on training," Butler says. "Shooting at different types of targets—not always the same standard target—blue or grey or black or whatever target you pick. But I would encourage them to seek cover. That is not on the [U.S. Customs] training program. If you're in a situation, move to cover first. If you're in a situation where you can't, then shoot it out and hope he misses and you don't."

Whether you choose to take part in any of the so-called practical or combat shooting disciplines or not, you should definitely practice self-defense shooting with the gun you normally carry, be it a Glock Model 22 or a Smith & Wesson Centennial, in the way you normally carry it. Don't do your self-defense practice with a fifteen-shot Para-Ordnance .45 from an unconcealed hip holster, if you normally carry a Walther PPK/S in a shoulder holster. You need to practice the things you don't do when you're competition shooting and what you're not good at, like shooting one-handed.

Fire at ranges from three to twenty feet. Shoot while backing up and while moving sideways to cover. Shoot while lying on your back, as though you had tripped when backing up or had been shot and had fallen. Shoot while scrambling to get up and back up further. Practice tactical and empty reloads, as well as immediate actions to clear malfunctions. Draw from concealed, and practice shooting in your regular clothes, be they a business suit or jeans and a lumberjack shirt. You may find your jacket is too tight around the armpits as you thrust your arms forward into a shooting stance. Practice shooting with one hand, left and right. If you can arrange moving and bobbing targets, so much the better.

Imagine every possible situation you may be in, and try to adapt your practice to it. For example, if you can get a vehicle onto your range, practice what you would do if someone tried to hijack the vehicle. Also shoot using the car as cover, preferably its engine block. Your practice should be limited only by your imagination, safe practice, and the rules of the range you are using.

Butler recommends a civilian gun carrier should practice at least once a month for the first year and a minimum of once a quarter after that. "I would stay with one gun, because in a stress situation you'll know how to use it," he says.

Shooting a lot of different guns and wearing them in different places may confuse you in a tight situation. "Beware the man with one gun" is an old and true saying.

Keep a record of your practice sessions—how many rounds you fired, at what range, and how well you performed. If your state has a mandatory course of fire required to obtain a concealed-carry license, it might be a good idea to shoot that course four times a year and record your scores. If you get into a shooting scrape, you may be questioned about your ability with a gun, and you will have an advantage if you can document your training. You also ought to keep a list of all the books you have read, like this one and others in the bibliography, so you can testify: "I was taught to keep shooting until my attacker was no longer a threat, your honor. I learned that in this book, and that magazine article, and this course at that shooting school."

In addition to targets and target stands, shooting glasses, and ear protection, a timer is a useful piece of gear for practice. A timer gives you a starting signal in the form of a "beep," then records the sound of each subsequent shot fired. It enables you to record how long it took after the beep for you to fire the first shot and the time between shots, as well as the timing for the whole string. Timers vary in sophistication and price from about $100 to more than $200. I have found a PACT Club Timer, one of the least expensive, to work reliably over several years. Competition Electronics, Inc., also makes a line of timers.

Dry FIRING

Dry firing is shooting with an empty gun to develop correct shooting habits and skill. It is usually done at home between sessions at the range. You should have a particular place to perform dry firing, preferably against a bulletproof wall. Fix up some kind of aiming marks. They could be small figure targets cut from cardboard or photographs taken from magazines. Don't use pictures of political figures, such as Teddy Kennedy or Diane Feinstein, whatever you think of them, because it sends the wrong message to anyone who might see them. For example, if you are forced to shoot a burglar or robber in self defense in your home, you will be playing host to a lot of police officers. Some of them may not like the idea of civilians carrying guns to protect themselves and may be looking for anything to cast you in a bad light. The last thing you want is for any of them to testify to your grand jury that: "Yes sir, he had pictures of Senator Feinstein on a wall along with other targets." Remember that your private space may one day be seen by investigators who may have a lot to do with how you are treated by the legal system. For the same reason, avoid incendiary bumper stickers on your car or elsewhere—the kind that say "Protected by Smith & Wesson" or "No One Ever Raped a .44 Magnum."

When you start your dry-firing session, unload your gun and leave all ammunition in another room. Practice snapping the empty gun at the targets as though they were real and the gun loaded. Dry firing is better if you are using a double-action revolver or semi-automatic because you can "fire" more than one shot at a time. Dry fire is not just snapping the gun to learn trigger control and sight alignment. It's practicing drawing and reholstering without looking at the gun; it's practicing tactical reloads and empty reloads. It's all of it.

When you have finished your dry-firing session, leave the place where you practice, and reload your gun. Then put the gun away or holster it and leave it alone. Of the three rounds

I have fired by accident in my life, one was when I had been practicing the draw and dry firing with a .45-caliber Smith &
Wesson revolver. I finished dry firing and reloaded the gun. Then
without thinking I did one more draw and . . . Bang! The 260-
grain Keith bullet made a neat hole in the window pane and
embedded itself in a creek bank outside. That happened in the
late 1960s, but I remember it as clearly today as if it had happened last week. Casual dry firing at the television, or whatever else presents itself as you wander around the house, is an
invitation to disaster. How are you going to explain to your husband or wife that hole in the photo of your mother-in-law?

TRAINING SCHOOLS AND COURSES

The best way to get a good grounding in using a handgun
for self defense is to take a course from an expert. Some of these
courses are taught at static training schools like Tac Pro
Shooting Center in Texas and Gunsite in Arizona. Others are
taught by instructors, like John Farnum of Defense Training
International and Chuck Taylor of the American Small Arms
Academy, who will travel anywhere in the country to put on
a course for a minimum number of students. A selection of some
of the best-known schools and courses follows. It is by no means
complete. There are many other excellent schools and instructors located around the country. Before putting up money for
any school or course, it is well to check it out with previous customers and other experts. The best known schools are not inexpensive. Some will charge more than $1,000 for a five-day course,
not including ammunition. Most schools require evidence that
a student has no criminal record. In addition to defensive-handgun instruction, most of the schools also teach other weapons
such as shotgun and rifle, and some give instruction in
unarmed defense.

AMERICAN SMALL ARMS ACADEMY

P.O. Box 12111, Prescott, AZ 86304; 928-778-5623;
<www.chucktaylorasaa.com> Chuck Taylor, director.

Taylor is well known to those interested in firearms as the author of over five thousand articles on weapons, tactics, and wound ballistics, as well as four books, including *The Complete Book of Combat Handgunning.* He was operations manager for Jeff Cooper at Gunsite during the school's early days and was the initial director of instruction at Front Sight Firearms Training Institute in California. The world's first 4-Weapon Combat Master, he has trained special-operations units and law-enforcement officers in the U.S. and abroad, with both the Swiss Army and Air Force, along with forces of other European countries, formally adopting his techniques. Although limited by writing commitments and intuitional obligations, Taylor still conducts civilian courses at select ranges and shooting schools around the country.

BLACKWATER TRAINING CENTER

P.O. Box 1029, Moyock, NC 27958;
252-435-2488; <www.blackwaterusa.com>
Gary Jackson, president.

Blackwater has a 5,200-acre training facility on the coast of North Carolina, about fifty miles south of Norfolk, Virginia. Although Blackwater's prime mission is to provide training for the federal government and law-enforcement agencies, it does provide training for civilians. Courses for civilians include a three-day pistol course, a five-day Pistol I, and a five-day Pistol II. In addition to safety and the fundamentals of handgun shooting, courses include the draw, malfunctions, speed shooting, shooting on the move, use of cover, low-light shooting, and building searches.

CHAPMAN ACADEMY OF PRACTICAL SHOOTING
4350 Academy Road, Hallsville, MO 65255;
573-696-5544 or 800-847-0588;
<http://chapmanacademy.com>
Ray Chapman, president; John Leveron, instructor.

Chapman has been involved in practical pistol training and competition since the 1950s, when he, Jeff Cooper, and three others used to compete at Big Bear, California. Chapman won the first World Practical Pistol championship in 1975, as well as more than two hundred fifty other practical-shooting competitions. He established the Chapman Academy in 1979, based on his experience as a Marine and a police officer. While Chapman is still president of the school, he is no longer involved in its day-to-day running. The school is located on fifty acres and contains fourteen ranges.

Besides carbine and shotgun courses, Chapman offers four dedicated pistol courses (Intro, Advanced 1, Advanced 2, Advanced Low Light), as well as a tactical scenarios course. Even the long-gun courses involve practical pistol work. The courses are geared towards concealed-carry and practical defensive-pistol work. All public courses are in a three-day weekend format, usually Friday through Sunday.

DEFENSE TRAINING INTERNATIONAL, INC.
P.O. Box 917, LaPorte, CO 80535; 970-482-2520
<www.defense-training.com> John Farnam, president.

Farnam has a military and law-enforcement background. He has been holding classes around the country, from Florida to California, New Hampshire to Washington, for more than twenty years. In June 1996 he received the Tactical Advocate of the Year award from the National Tactical Association.

DTI offers two-day weekend courses on defensive use of a handgun. Curriculum includes threat evaluation, lethal-threat management, low-light shooting, holding suspects at gunpoint, and performing under stress.

FIREARMS ACADEMY OF SEATTLE, INC.

P.O. Box 400, Onalaska, WA 98570; 360-978-6100; <www.firearmsacademy.com> Marty Hayes, director; Gila Hayes, staff instructor.

The Firearms Academy of Seattle is owned and operated by the husband-and-wife team of Marty and Gila Hayes. Both have solid backgrounds in firearms training. In addition to running his own show, Marty Hayes is a staff instructor for Lethal Force Institute and an adjunct instructor for Defense Training International. He is also a police officer and firearms instructor for his department. Gila Hayes is one of the few nationally known women instructors in self defense. She has learned from some of the best instructors in the country, including Massad Ayoob, Clint Smith, Chuck Taylor, the late Jim Cirillo, and Louis Awerbuck. She is field editor for *Women & Guns* and writes for other gun magazines.

The school occupies sixty acres and includes a variety of tactical ranges. Two-day training courses go from basic handgun skills to advanced techniques.

GUNSITE ACADEMY, INC.

2900 W. Gunsite Rd., Paulden, AZ 86334; 928-636-4565; <www.gunsite.com> Owen Buz Mills, owner.

Gunsite is the original home of the American Pistol Institute, which was founded by Jeff Cooper in 1977. Cooper sold the operation in 1992 to Richard Jee, who operated it until 1999, when it was bought by Mills. The school is located on more than fifteen-hundred acres of rolling juniper hills north of Prescott. It contains regular pistol ranges, shoot houses, and tactical ranges, including ravines and wooded areas. Gunsite offers defensive-handgun courses for students of different levels of expertise. Most last five days, cost more than $1,300, and require more than twelve hundred rounds of ammunition. Two- and three-day courses are available. Gunsite offers some courses for women, taught by women.

LETHAL FORCE INSTITUTE

P.O. Box 122, Concord, NH 03302; 603-224-6814;
<www.ayoob.com> Massad Ayoob, director.

Ayoob is a world-renowned firearms and self-defense journalist, author, and trainer. A most popular series of articles has been his "Ayoob Files" in *American Handgunner* magazine. In each edition, he relates and analyzes a shooting incident for the lessons it teaches. In addition to writing and teaching, Ayoob has appeared in numerous trials as an expert witness on self defense. He founded LFI in 1981.

LFI offers many courses in armed and unarmed self defense to civilians as well as law-enforcement officers. LFI-I: Judicious Use of Deadly Force is a forty-hour course that teaches students home- and street-defense tactics, psychological preparation for violent encounters, and justifying your actions in court, as well as combat shooting. LFI courses are taught at the home range in New Hampshire and at other ranges around the country and even abroad.

NORTHEASTERN TACTICAL SCHOOLS

8 Kingsbury Lane, Billerica, MA 01862; 978-667-5591;
<www.SnubTraining.com>
Michael de Bethencourt, chief trainer.

De Bethencourt is the chief trainer for Northeastern Tactical Schools, specializing in courses on snub revolver, weapon disarming and retention, and folding-knife skills, for both law-enforcement officers and legally armed civilians.

Two popular NTS courses include Essentials of the Defensive Snub Revolver and Mastering the Defensive Revolver. The curriculum includes snub advantages and limitations; top gunsmithing options for snubs; uncommon snub-loading tactics; laser-grips, flashlights, and snub skills; snubs tactics for multiple targets; snub malfunction; and one-hand-only reloading skills.

De Bethencourt teaches these courses at ranges and shooting schools around the country. Currently, he is working on the first volume of a three-volume set of skills, tactics, and tips for the snub-revolver shooter.

OPTIONS FOR PERSONAL SECURITY
P.O. Box 489, Sebring, FL 33871; 877-636-4677; <www.optionsforpersonalsecurity.com>
Andy Stanford, director.

Stanford has been involved in private-sector practical shooting since the 1970s. He has trained under many of the best firearms instructors. From the late 1980s through the mid 1990s, he worked as a weapons and tactics analyst for the U.S. Department of Defense in the Weapons Planning Group, a classified think tank. Stanford is the author of more than sixty articles on firearms and weapon training. He is the author of two books: *Surgical Speed Shooting* and *Fight at Night*.

OPS offers a series of intensive one- and two-day handgun courses at Sebring and at other ranges, mostly in the southeast. These courses include Point Blank Pistolcraft, Surgical Speed Shooting, Tactical Dynamics, and Fight at Night.

PEREGRINE CORPORATION
P.O. Box 170, Bowers, PA 19511; 610-682-7147; email: <www.peregrinecorporation.com>
Emanuel Kapelsohn, director.

Kapelsohn is certified as a firearms instructor by the FBI, NRA, and Heckler & Koch. He was a staff instructor for Jeff Cooper at Gunsite. He is a vice president of the International Association of Law Enforcement Firearms Instructors and a charter member of the American Society of Law Enforcement Trainers. He has trained and certified firearms instructors and armorers for major police departments nationwide. He is a prolific writer in the firearms field, a practicing trial lawyer, and an expert witness in court cases involving firearms and the use of force.

Kapelsohn teaches the use of handguns and other weapons for self defense to qualified civilians as well as law-enforcement personnel. Courses range from basic to advanced, are taught on location, and are geared to the specific needs of his clients.

RANGEMASTER

2611 South Mendenhall Road, Memphis, TN 38115; 901-370-5600; <www.rangemaster.com>
Tom Givens, chief instructor.

Givens came to RangeMaster in 1996, after twenty-five years in law enforcement and specialized security work. He has trained security officers and law-enforcement officers at all levels in the use of firearms. He is author of five books, including *Fighting Smart.*

RangeMaster has a twenty-five-yard indoor range with all the bells and whistles and a well-appointed classroom with audio-visual equipment. The range offers a series of handgun classes,

Bill Davison supervises a Primary Pistol class at Tac Pro Shooting Center.

Instructor checking a line of shooters at Thunder Ranch.

mainly of eight hours spread over two days. They vary from Level I Personal Protection Certification, which qualifies the student for a Tennessee handgun license, to Level V–Professional Pistol.

RangeMaster instructors also teach at other locations around the country. The range often books other nationally reputed experts as guest instructors.

SMITH & WESSON ACADEMY

299 Page Boulevard, Springfield, MA 01104; 413-846-6461; <www.smith-wesson.com>

Robert Barrett, training coordinator for civilian courses.

The academy was founded in 1969 to train law-enforcement officers. It was opened to civilians in 1994 with a wide range of programs covering basic firearms safety through advanced training. A $2.7-million expansion project was completed in 1997. The academy offers several two- and three-day defensive-handgun courses. They cover everything from safe gun handling to surviving an armed confrontation and include such topics as low-light shooting, movement, multiple opponents, and shooting with one hand. Smith & Wesson offers some courses for women only.

TAC PRO SHOOTING CENTER

35100 North State Highway 108, Mingus, TX 76463; 254-968-3112; <www.tacproshootingcenter.com> Bill Davison, director.

Bill Davison migrated from the United Kingdom in 1998. He is eminently qualified to teach weapon craft to civilians, law enforcement officers, and the military. He is a veteran of the Royal Marine Special Boat Service, the British equivalent of the U.S. Navy SEALs, and has taught and used firearms for more than twenty years, including action in Northern Ireland. In the early 1990s, he taught advanced firearms techniques and VIP protection to the civilian police in Britain. While still in the Royal Marines, he visited the U.S. to teach anti-terrorist tactics to the Dallas/Fort Worth Airport Police SWAT team.

Set in the gently undulating ranchland of north Texas, the Davisons's shooting school occupies five-hundred-fifty acres and contains eight ranges. They vary in size from twenty-yard pistol and submachinegun bays to one of the few privately owned thousand-yard rifle ranges in the state. Davison teaches Basic, Intermediate, and Advanced Defensive Pistol courses, each lasting three days. Topics include short-range confrontations, moving and shooting, stoppages, stress operation, and combat mindset. He also teaches a two-day Fight-at-Night course.

THUNDER RANCH, INC.

6747 Highway 140 East, Lakeview, OR 97630; 541-947-4104; <www.thunderranchinc.com> Clint Smith, director.

After more than a decade in the Texas Hill Country, this well-known shooting school closed its Texas facility at the end of 2004 and opened up in Oregon in 2005.

Smith is a Marine Corps veteran with two infantry tours in Vietnam and a former police officer involved in firearms training and SWAT operations. He served as Jeff Cooper's operations officer at the American Pistol Institute. He founded International Training Consultants, Inc., a mobile firearms-training program, which led to the development of Thunder Ranch in the Texas Hill Country.

Thunder Ranch offers three Tactical Handgun courses, plus a ladies-only course. Other handgun courses include Concealed Carry, Home and Vehicle Defense, High Intensity Tactics, and a revolver course. Standard courses are for three days and are limited to a dozen students. Only frangible ammunition which can be purchased through the school is permitted. Ranges provide for static targets, wobblers, lateral, and charging movers. The ranch also includes a pro shop and shoot house named Terminator 3.

YAVAPAI FIREARMS ACADEMY, LTD.

P.O. Box 27290, Prescott Valley, AZ 86312; 928-772-8262; <www.yfainc.com> Louis Awerbuck, director.

Awerbuck worked for Jeff Cooper as chief rangemaster at Gunsite until 1987. He has more than twenty-five years' experience in small-arms instruction to the military, police, and civilians. He is the author of three books, *Tactical Reality: An Uncommon Look at Common-Sense Firearms Training and Tactics*, *The Defensive Shotgun*, and *Hit or Myth*, and has contributed articles to *SWAT* and *Soldier of Fortune* magazines. He also served in the South African Defense Force.

Yavapai does not have a home range, but Awerbuck will travel to anywhere in the country to teach classes of twelve to eighteen students. He offers three-day Tactical Handgun courses which encompass gunhandling, marksmanship, and tactics. Yavapai offers other courses such as Home Defense Tactics.

In addition to the nationally known shooting schools and courses, good local instructors can provide lessons to individuals and small groups. Your local police department or shooting club may be able to put you in touch with such instructors.

Many good instructional videos and DVDs have been made in the last few years that will help the self-defense student improve. Bill Wilson of Wilson Combat and Clint Smith of Thunder Ranch have both produced video series. Others who have ventured into this medium include Massad Ayoob, the late Jeff Cooper, and the late Colonel Rex Applegate.

Much good information about firearms and self-defense tactics can be gleaned from magazines such as *American Handgunner, Combat Handguns,* and *Handguns,* as well as periodicals of more general interest, such as *American Rifleman, Gun Tests, Gun Week, Guns, Guns & Ammo, Gun World, Shooting Times,* and *Women & Guns.* A new periodical has recently been added to the list that deals with concealed carry. Unsurprisingly it is called *Concealed Carry Magazine* and is a publication of the United States Concealed Carry Association. It is relatively expensive but well worth it. You can check it out at <www.usconcealedcarry.com>

Handloading

If you practice as much as you should, you will need to reload—not just the gun, but the ammunition. With the price of store-bought practice ammo at between twenty and thirty cents a round, you need to do something to keep the cost of your range sessions down or your household budget will take on overtones of the federal deficit. Handloading can cut the cost of your practice ammo down to between three and ten cents a round, depending on caliber and whether you buy your bullets or make them. A two-hundred-round practice session with handloads should cost less than $20. This compares favorably to $40 or more for the same session with store-bought ammunition.

While Hornady, Lee, Lyman, RCBS, and other companies make good progressive reloaders, practical-handgun competitors overwhelmingly favor the presses made by Dillon Precision. For example, in the 1995 U.S. Practical Shooting Association's Open National championship, all the top-ten competitors used Dillon Reloaders. This is not the exception, it's the rule and has been for a number of years. For the beginning handloader, Dillon's Square Deal B is the least expensive press at about $320. According to the Dillon catalogue, the most popular and versatile of their presses is the RL 550B, which sells for about $380. I have made many thousands of rounds of ammunition of various calibers with my 550, and it has never given me any trouble. They are robust and reliable. For those who want to shoot a little more and invest a little more, the XL 650, at less than $500, is your own ammo factory in the basement.

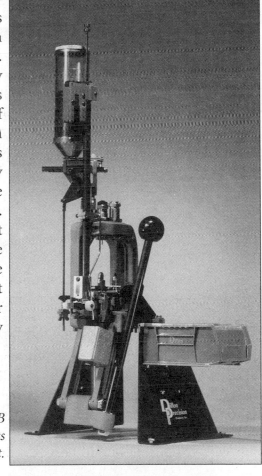

Dillon 550B handloading press on a Strong Mount.

You will also need a powder scale to set and check the powder charges thrown by the reloading press. Any of the manufacturers of good handloading equipment make balance scales and electronic scales. I have used a Redding balance scale for several decades and found it quite adequate.

Cases get dirty from burning powder each time you fire them, so a case cleaner and polisher is almost essential. Most case cleaners work on a vibration principle, but a few rotate. Both types use a cleaning medium made of ground corn cobs or crushed walnut shells to which some polishing liquid can be added. Dillon makes a case/media separator, but I have used a colander and a plastic bucket for years.

There are many other handloading tools and gadgets, but these are the basics. Casting, sizing, and lubricating your own bullets will save you more money in the long run, but lead and jacketed bullets can be bought for a reasonable price, and buying them means you spend more time shooting than reloading. When you get into handloading, you will need at least one good reference manual. Manufacturers of handloading tools, such as Lyman and Hornady, publish excellent handloading manuals, while powder manufacturers like Accurate and Hodgdon provide guides to the uses of their products.

A round of ammunition is composed of the case or casing, powder charge, primer, and bullet. The most expensive component is the case but, unlike the other parts, the case can be used repeatedly. Always use store-bought ammunition in your gun when you are carrying it for self defense. Shooting handloads in self defense just gives the lawyer for the shootee an opportunity to make you out as some gun-crazed weirdo who was just waiting to try out your cop-killing ammunition on his poor unsuspecting client. Besides, modern manufactured ammunition is as good as it gets for self defense. Some reputable brands are mentioned in Chapter 5. You should cycle your street ammunition through your gun and replace it perhaps once a year, although it should work effectively for many years.

You have several choices in acquiring cases for reloading your practice ammo. You can buy the ammunition complete, shoot it, and then reload the empties; you can buy unprimed or primed cases in bulk; or you can scrounge empties at your local range. Don't buy the aluminum-cased ammunition, because it cannot be reloaded. Powder and primers have to be bought either from your local store, at gun shows, or by mail order. You can cast your own bullets or you can buy them ready-made. Lead bullets are cheaper, but tend to lead up your barrel; jacketed bullets are more expensive, don't lead your barrel, and if completely jacketed are safer. There are no minute particles of lead exhaled from your gun into the air for you to inhale.

CARE AND CLEANING

With modern smokeless powders and non-corrosive primers, you don't have to clean your pistol or revolver after every trip to the range. However, you may want to do it just to keep your clothes clean. If you are in the habit of tucking a five-shot revolver into your waistband, like U.S. Customs Special Agent Robert Butler does, you don't want a lot of burnt powder and oil stains on your shirt or blouse.

Butler recommends a dry-cleaning method, particularly for a revolver. You need a bronze brush on the end of a cleaning rod. First, unload the gun. Push the brush through and pull it back through each chamber of the revolver's cylinder. Then clean the barrel in the same way, but make sure the end of the brush does not hit the firing pin hole. You can then use a mop or swab to wipe the powder and lead residue loosened by the bronze brush. Using another bronze brush, shaped like a toothbrush, clean all the places where there is a build-up of residue—the face of the cylinder, around the rear end of the barrel, under the star of the extractor. Wipe the loosened residue off with a rag or possibly an old toothbrush. and your gun is clean. You can put a drop of oil in the action and around the yoke or crane every once in a while, and your revolver should keep firing as long as you have ammunition for it.

An excellent tool for cleaning barrels and the chambers of revolvers is the Boresnake manufactured by Hoppe's, a division of Bushnell Outdoor Products. It is a fat, snake-like rope with one or two bronze brushes embedded in the front end. The brushes loosen the hard deposits and the rope wipes the bore clean. Boresnakes come in all sizes from .22 caliber to 12-gauge and they are washable.

Break-Free CLP is the best lubricating oil I have found. Never use WD 40 or any penetrating oil, because it will migrate into your ammunition and affect the powder or priming compound, causing misfires. WD 40 will air harden and freeze your action as effectively as squirting Super Glue into it.

The procedure for wet cleaning is much the same, but you use a solvent like Hoppe's No. 9 on your bronze brushes, then wipe out the bore and chambers with cloth patches. Wipe off the other parts with a rag, as in dry cleaning. Some people clean their guns by dropping the fouled parts into a container of a powerful industrial solvent such as Du Pont's Prep-Sol. Keep the sights, if they have inserts or are colored, and the stocks out of this stuff.

You can follow a similar procedure in cleaning a semi-automatic. Most semi-autos should be disassembled for cleaning. Unload the gun first. Remove the slide and barrel from the frame. Wet- or dry-clean the parts, then put them back together. Clean around the lips of your magazines. When you have finished cleaning, be sure to lubricate the slide rails, around the outside end of the barrel, the locking lugs, and where the hammer and sear engage. Rack the slide a few times, and wipe off the excess oil. Don't over-oil your gun, or you, as well as the gun, will be wearing the oil.

TIMERS

Competition Electronics, Inc., 3469 Precision Drive,
  Rockford, IL 61109; 815-874-8001;
  <www.competitionelectronics.com>
PACT, Inc., P.O. Box 535025, Grand Prairie, TX 75053;
  800-722-8462; <www.pact.com>

PRACTICAL-SHOOTING ORGANIZATIONS

Action Pistol, National Rifle Association, 11250 Waples Mill
  Road, Fairfax, VA 22030; 800-672-3888; <www.nra.org>
International Defensive Pistol Association, 2232 County
  Road 719, Berryville, AR 72616; 870-545-3886;
  <www.idpa.com>
U.S. Practical Shooting Association (affiliated with the
  International Practical Shooting Confederation), P.O.
  Box 811, Sedro Woolley, WA 98284; 360-855-2245;
  <www.uspsa.org>

VIDEO TRAINING

Advanced Interactive Systems, 665 Andover Park West,
  Seattle, WA 98188; 800-441-4487;
  <www.ais-sim.com>

HANDLOADING EQUIPMENT

Dillon Precision Products, Inc., 8009 East Dillon's
  Way, Scottsdale, AZ 85260; 800-223-4570;
  <www.dillonprecision.com>
Hornady Manufacturing Co., P.O. Box 1848, Grand Island,
  NE 68802; 800-338-3220; <www.hornady.com>

Lee Precision, Inc., 4275 Highway U, Hartford, WI 53027;
   262-673-3075; <www.leeprecision.com>
Lyman Products Corp., 475 Smith Street, Middletown, CT
   06457; 800-225-9626; <www.lymanproducts.com>
RCBS, 605 Oro Dam Boulevard, Oroville, CA 95965; 800-
   533-5000; <www.rcbs.com>

CLEANING PRODUCTS

Bushnell Outdoor Products, 9200 Cody, Overland Park, KS
   66214; 800-423-3537; <www.hoppes.com>
Break-Free, Inc.,13386 International Parkway, Jacksonville,
   FL 32218; 800-433-2909; <www.break-free.com>

Chapter Thirteen

STATE CONCEALED-HANDGUN CARRY LAWS

In the three-and-a-half years since this manual was last updated, two more states—Kansas and Nebraska—have passed shall-issue or right-to-carry concealed-weapons laws allowing almost any law-abiding adult to acquire a license or permit to carry a concealed handgun. This leaves only two states—Illinois and Wisconsin—without any provision for civilians to carry concealed handguns in public for protection.

In 1997, the Kansas Legislature first passed a concealed-weapons bill which was vetoed by then Governor Bill Graves (R). A second try died in the senate in 1999. The legislature passed another concealed-carry bill in 2004 only to have it vetoed, this time by Governor Kathleen Sebelius (D). In March 2006 the legislature again passed the bill, and Sebelius again vetoed it. But this time the lawmakers had enough votes to override the governor's veto, and the bill became law. Kansans started applying for concealed-weapon licenses July 1, and the state started issuing them January 1, 2007. Much of the credit goes to Senator Phil Journey (R), a lawyer and former president of the Kansas State Rifle Association, and Leavenworth Representative Candy Ruff (D), who looks at concealed-carry as a women's issue.

A similar decade-long fight took place in Nebraska. The first concealed-carry bill was introduced in 1996, but it wasn't until 2006 that it got through the Nebraska Legislature successfully. Governor Dave Heineman (R) signed the bill into law on April 5, 2006. The Nebraska State Patrol started issuing licenses in January 2007. However, by August only 2,109 licenses had been issued compared with 8,958 in Kansas.

There has been a steady progression of concealed-carry licenses or permits issued in most of these other thirty-six states that make getting one relatively easy, although often not inexpensive. Typical were North Carolina, which went from 61,000 licenses in 2004 to 95,000 in 2007, and Pennsylvania, from 602,000 to 668,000.

When Hurricane Katrina roared ashore in August 2005, it devastated New Orleans and coastal Mississippi. Local gun owners felt the aftershocks. In Mississippi between 2004 and 2007, concealed-carry permits almost tripled, increasing to about 47,500 from 16,700. The surge in permits was mainly due to the hurricane, according to Lt. James Gann of the Mississippi Department of Public Safety. During the insecurity that followed Katrina, Mississippi residents along the Gulf Coast felt the need to be able to defend themselves.

This increase in licenses was not matched, however, in Louisiana. With the exception of Nebraska, which started issuing licenses only at the beginning of 2007, Louisiana has always had the lowest percentage of license holders of all the shall-issue states. There appear to be several reasons for this. Applicants for concealed-handgun licenses may be charged as much as $150 if they have not lived in the state for at least fifteen years. You can buy a lot of jambalaya for $150. Louisiana is an open-carry state that regards a person's vehicle as an extension of their abode, which means you can keep a loaded gun concealed in your car or pickup without a license. As more people carry in their vehicles than do on their persons, fewer residents feel the need for a permit in the Pelican State. Also thousands of residents fled the state during and after Katrina, and many of them have not returned. Those who have settled outside the state will not be renewing their licenses. Louisiana has seen a modest increase in permits, but nothing like the explosion that happened in Mississippi. In 2007, there were 14,084 licenses active, up from 13,032 in 2004.

Concealed-carry laws were on a roll in 2003 and early 2004. Five states passed shall-issue concealed-handgun laws. In addition, one state passed a so-called Vermont-style law, which enables adults to carry handguns openly or concealed without a license. Not able to prevent state legislatures from passing these laws, the anti-self-defense crowd has turned to the courts and has succeeded in tying up these laws for a time, though not permanently.

Colorado passed a shall-issue law that went into effect May 18, 2003. Despite failed court challenges by the City of Denver, by the end of 2006, Colorado sheriffs had issued more than 28,000 licenses. In April 1999 the Colorado Legislature was about to consider a right-to-carry-concealed law when two students at Columbine High School in a Denver suburb gunned down a dozen of their fellow students and a teacher. In the aftermath of the shooting, amid the shrill cries of the anti-self-defense politicians and activists, the concealed-carry bill was withdrawn. This produced what I call the Columbine Hump, when no right-to-carry legislation was passed by a state legislature for two years. However, in 2001, the chilling effect of the Columbine massacre eased when legislatures in Michigan and New Mexico passed concealed-carry laws. By mid 2007 nearly 150,000 licenses had been issued in Michigan.

Unfortunately, the then-mayor of Albuquerque challenged the New Mexico law in court, and the state's Supreme Court ruled it unconstitutional. The whole process was repeated in 2003 when the legislature passed another concealed-carry law, which was signed by Governor Bill Richardson (D). Again, the new law was challenged and was put on hold until the Supreme Court heard the case once more. On January 5, 2004, the court handed New Mexicans a win for citizen safety by declaring the law constitutional. By August 2007, the New Mexico Department of Public Safety had issued more than 10,000 licenses.

In Minnesota Governor Tim Pawlenty (R) signed a shall-issue concealed-carry law on April 28, 2003. Sheriffs started accepting applications for licenses May 28 when the law went into effect.

However, the law, as in New Mexico, was challenged in the courts and ruled unconstitutional on a technicality. Legislators fixed the law in 2005, and by the end of August 2007 more than 48,000 Minnesotans had licenses to carry concealed.

The Missouri Legislature passed a concealed-carry law in May 2003 by large majorities in both house and senate. Governor Bob Holden (D) vetoed the law, but on September 11 the legislature overrode the veto. However, just before the law was due to go into effect October 11, it was challenged on constitutional grounds. The law was put on hold pending a decision by the Missouri Supreme Court. The court heard arguments in January 2004 and ruled on February 26 that the law was constitutional. St. Louis City and County were the last jurisdictions to start issuing licenses. They procrastinated until July 2005 before accepting applications.

While Missouri sheriffs had issued more than 36,000 licenses by mid 2007, many residents of the Show Me State are apparently still carrying on non-resident licenses from other states. Tim Oliver, secretary of the Missouri Sports Shooting Association and owner of Learn To Carry instruction, estimated that about ten thousand Missouri residents were carrying concealed on out-of-state licenses. Most of these people live in Kansas City and St. Louis where there was a lot of resistance to the concealed-carry law.

"They fought us for thirteen years; why give them money if they don't like you. If Wal-Mart doesn't like you, you go to Target," Oliver said.

The Ohio Legislature passed a concealed-carry law, which was reluctantly signed by Governor Bob Taft (R) in January 2004 after he insisted that journalists have access to the names of license holders. The law went into effect April 8, 2004. One of the more bizarre provisions of the law involved carrying a loaded handgun in a motor vehicle. Even with a concealed-handgun license, it was illegal to carry a loaded gun concealed in a vehicle unless it was locked up. The law stated that a license holder in Ohio had a choice when in a vehicle. He or she could either wear the gun in a holster "in plain sight," or it had to be locked in the glove compartment, or put in a "case that is in plain view and that is locked."

Fortunately, this weird requirement was fixed by the legislature in 2006. License holders in the Buckeye State can now carry their handguns concealed in their SUVs. No longer do license holders wear out their jackets putting them on and taking them off each time they exit or enter their vehicles. If they choose to carry in a purse or bag, it doesn't have to be locked, though it still has to be in plain sight.

In each of these states, the new right-to-carry-concealed laws were the work of years of lobbying by activists who believe in a citizen's right to self-defense. On the downside, the Wisconsin Legislature passed a concealed-carry law by large margins in 2004 and again in 2006, but each time Governor Jim Doyle (D) vetoed it, and legislators did not have quite the votes to override. So Wisconsin along with Illinois remain the only two states that have no provision for civilians to carry concealed handguns for protection.

Alaska passed a shall-issue concealed-carry law that went into effect January 1, 1995. However, in 2003, the legislature went a step further, passing a Vermont-style law that allows anyone twenty-one years or older, resident or visitor, to carry a handgun openly or concealed without a license or permit. The bill was introduced by Representative Eric Croft, a Democrat, in February 2003. Croft was working on tweaking the existing concealed-weapons law when he outlined the Vermont-style law.

"The more I looked at it, the more sense it made to me," Croft said.

He passed the bill around to other legislators, and they suggested he send it forward. By the time he introduced it into the forty-member House of Representatives, it had twenty-five sponsors. The bill passed the house and senate, and Governor Frank Murkowski (R) signed it into law on June 11, 2003. Croft says the success of the bill surprised him. He thought it would take several years to pass.

"I had no real expectation that it was going to pass in that session," he said.

Legislators kept the Alaska concealed-weapons permitting system in place so residents could take advantage of reciprocity agreements with other states. The new law has resulted in a decline in the number of active licenses in Alaska. Residents no longer need the license to carry concealed, so many have let their licenses lapse. In February 2004, there were 15,561 licenses but by August 2007 only 9,547 Alaskans were licensed.

As of late summer 2007, nearly four million people in thirty-eight states have licenses to carry concealed handguns. Thirty-nine states have "right-to-carry-concealed" laws regarding handguns. The additional state is Vermont, which requires no license or permit for anyone legally entitled to possess a handgun to carry it in the open or concealed.

Thirty-two of the thirty-eight right-to-carry-concealed states that issue licenses keep statewide tallies of currently valid licenses. Those states account for more than 3.5 million license holders. In these states, licenses have been issued to an average of about 2 percent of residents. Extrapolating to the six states that keep no statewide figures, an estimated 3.98 million people in the thirty-eight states had licenses by late summer 2007. This is an increase of about 630,000 license holders or nearly 20 percent since I last conducted this survey in early 2004.

Several states, such as Florida, New Hampshire, and Utah, issue licenses to non-residents. This means that some people may have licenses in more than one state. Others may not have licenses in their own state because they are more difficult or impossible to obtain. For example, a significant number of Arizona's three thousand non-resident licenses are issued to residents of California, where licenses are harder to get. More than 2,700 of Connecticut's 8,500 non-resident licenses are issued to New York residents. In calculating the total numbers of license holders, I have included non-resident licenses.

The four million or so license holders comprise only a small fraction of the U.S. adults that criminology professor Gary Kleck estimates carry guns for self defense outside their own homes. The Florida State University professor has conducted several surveys on the self-defense use of guns. In his National Self Defense Survey, conducted in 1993, Kleck estimated 8.8 percent of the adult population, or about seventeen million people at that time, carried guns for protection on their persons or in a vehicle. This estimate is more than four times the average 2 percent that hold concealed-carry licenses in right-to-carry-concealed states. Of the adults surveyed, 3.7 percent, or nationally an estimated seven million, carried on their persons. The survey results were reported in Kleck's book, *Targeting Guns: Firearms and Their Control.* Kleck concludes that issuing concealed-carry licenses does not necessarily increase the number of guns on the street by 2 percent, but in many cases just makes legal what people have been doing illegally all along.

"The big unknown is you really don't know how much carrying increases. You just know how many permit holders there are," Kleck said.

A trend that has accelerated in the last few years is that more states are honoring licenses or permits from other states. Alaska, Arizona, South Dakota, and Tennessee have joined Idaho, Indiana, Kentucky, Michigan, Missouri, Oklahoma, and Utah in honoring any valid concealed-handgun license issued by any state. In the last three years, Texas has put reciprocity on a fast track. In the first eight years of concealed carry in the state, the Department of Public Safety negotiated eight reciprocity agreements with other states. Unsatisfied with such progress, in 2003 legislators transferred responsibility for negotiating agreements to the state Attorney General's Office. Between April 2004 and the fall of 2007, the Attorney General has negotiated twenty more reciprocal agreements and has made unilateral proclamations to honor licenses from a further twelve states. The latter are mostly states like California and New York that are very unlikely to grant reciprocity to Texas license holders.

Many states, such as Alabama, Colorado, and Wyoming will honor licenses only from states that recognize their licenses. Others, like Connecticut and Maine, honor no licenses but their own, though they will issue permits to non-residents.

M ost of the states that have passed concealed-carry laws in the late 1980s and 1990s, such as Florida and Texas, stipulate that anybody who meets certain criteria, such as being twenty-one years old, sane, and having no criminal record, SHALL be issued a license. Some states, such as Alabama and Connecticut, give varying degrees of discretion to issuing authorities, but most law-abiding adult residents in those states can get a license.

Florida is generally accepted to have taken the lead in passing the new wave of what have become known as "shall-issue" laws that has swept the country. Some states have had a tradition of allowing their law-abiding citizens to carry handguns for self defense. For example, since 1961 Washington State has had a non-discretionary concealed-carry law, which stipulates that sheriffs and police chiefs "shall issue" concealed-carry licenses, providing applicants qualify. However, Florida is generally accepted as starting the trend when it passed its non-discretionary statute in 1987. Other states followed. Some states, like Arizona and Kentucky, previously had an open-carry law but no provision for civilians to carry handguns concealed. Others, like Montana, had regulated the wearing of arms for decades, but permits were issued at the discretion of authorities. Yet others, such as Texas, had no previous provision for civilians to wear handguns in public at all.

The blood bath predicted by the gun-control advocates has not come to pass in any of the states that have passed shall-issue concealed-carry laws. Quite the contrary, licensed handgun carriers seem to be particularly law-abiding. Engineer Bill Sturdevant, of Navasota, Texas, compared arrest rates for Texas license holders with the general population of Texas residents twenty-one years and older. He used Texas Department of Public Safety statistics from 1996 through 2000—the first five years the Texas concealed-handgun law was in effect. Sturdevant found that people in the general population of Texas residents twenty-one years and older were five times more likely to be arrested for a violent crime than were license holders. Residents were also thirteen times as likely to be arrested for a non-violent crime as license holders.

In states with shall-issue laws, not everyone gets a permit. The proportion of residents who go to the trouble of acquiring concealed-carry licenses varies by state. In many states with relatively new shall-issue laws, such as Kansas and Nebraska, less than 1 percent of the population is licensed. Pennsylvania issues the most licenses, with more than 668,000 as of April 2007, and has the highest rates, with more than 5 percent of its population licensed.

As Gary Kleck notes, many people undoubtedly carry guns illegally, as they have always done. These people include not just habitual criminals, but otherwise law-abiding citizens, many of them women, who for a variety of reasons do not wish to go through the licensing process. Some feel that by applying for a concealed-carry license, they are admitting to the government that they own firearms. Should the government decide to confiscate weapons, as has happened in Britain, Australia, and California, they will be first to be visited by police. They believe registration, of people or weapons, is the first step to confiscation. Others believe the Second Amendment in the Bill of Rights gives them the right to keep and bear arms already, and they don't need any government approval or license to carry firearms.

Cost is probably a more important factor in who gets licensed to carry concealed handguns. The charge for licenses varies by state, from South Dakota where the fee is $10 for four years to Texas where a five-year license costs $140. In addition, the cost is higher when the price of a mandatory training course is thrown in. In Texas the mandatory training course seems to vary between $50 and $200. Judging by the South Dakota and Texas experiences, it is likely that the costs of expensive license and training programs are deterrents to carrying legally. If a husband and wife have to spend more than $500 for licenses and training programs, only the wealthy and the dedicated are going to afford it.

Suzanna Gratia Hupp (R), whose parents were murdered in the Killeen shooting in 1991, says the Texas concealed-handgun law is a big step in the right direction. However, she criticizes it for its cost. She says the inner-city poor—mostly blacks and Hispanics—who live in the highest crime areas can't afford licenses. They are the ones who need them the most.

"I think our permitting system is discriminatory at best and racist at worst," Hupp says. "At the very least, we should get rid of the fees."

Hupp, who was a representative in the Texas Legislature, likens the cost of the license to the poll tax. For the first half of the twentieth century, Texans had to pay a poll tax for registering to vote. This effectively kept most blacks and Hispanics from voting.

"They are taxing me to be able to exercise a right, and I think that is fundamentally wrong," she says.

Alaska legislator Eric Croft (D) agrees with her. In October 2004, he was keynote speaker at a banquet in Phoenix to celebrate ten years of concealed carry in Arizona. Croft said the tenth anniversary of concealed carry was a milestone in the progress of right to carry and was worthy of celebration.

"But I was brought down all the way from Alaska really to ask you nice people one simple question: why is it that we should have to get a government permit to exercise a constitutional right?"

When he was promoting his bill to allow concealed carry without a permit, Croft was told repeatedly that permits and licenses were required for driving a motor vehicle and for building a house. Why should concealed carry be any different.

"I would have to say, very slowly so they understood, because this is a constitutional right," Croft said.

In almost every state that has passed a concealed-carry law that requires a permit or license, government authorities regard the document giving civilians the ability to carry a concealed handgun legally as a privilege, not a right.

There is less interest in concealed-handgun licenses where it is already legal to carry a loaded gun in your car or pickup. For example, in New Mexico a vehicle is regarded as an extension of a person's home. Many people who get licenses do not intend to wear or carry the gun on their persons. They just want to carry it in their vehicles for emergencies. This is confirmed in Gary Kleck's survey of all gun carriers, legal and illegal. He

A group of applicants for Texas concealed-handgun licenses going through the qualification course.

found more than half carried only in their vehicles. Most of these people will see little advantage in getting a license in New Mexico or Louisiana. In neighboring Texas, it had never been legal to carry a loaded gun in your vehicle unless you qualified as a "traveler." Consequently, one Texan out of a hundred has a license, compared with one person in three hundred in Louisiana. This law was changed by the legislature in 2005 and reinforced in 2007 to define a traveler as almost anyone in a vehicle.

Between January 1, 2002, and October 31, 2006, the Texas Department of Public Safety issued 303,383 concealed-handgun licenses. This figure includes initial licenses and renewals. It also means that some license holders were counted twice, since for most of this period the license was good for four years. However, it does give a good demographic look at Texas license holders by race, gender, and age. While most people cannot get a license until they are twenty-one, since 2004 members of the military and veterans can qualify for licenses at eighteen years. Twenty-five people have qualified under this rule.

From twenty-one years, when 3,481 applicants were issued licenses, the number of license holders by age increased steadily to a peak of 8,822 at the age of fifty-six. From fifty-seven onward, the numbers decline fairly steadily into the nineties age group. Fifty-three applicants aged ninety to ninety-five were issued licenses, and one person obtained a license at age ninety-eight. Almost three-quarters —74 percent—of license holders were older than forty. By gender, only about 18 percent were women. The majority—89 percent—listed their race as white. For some reason, in a state with a large Hispanic population, there is no Hispanic category. They are apparently lumped in with whites. So in Texas the profile of a typical concealed-handgun-license holder is a white or Hispanic man, aged forty through seventy—not your high-crime age group.

In Florida, 75 percent of license holders are over the age of thirty-five, but only 15 percent of those with licenses are women. Florida does not provide a breakdown by race.

Between October 1987 and August 2007, Florida issued 1,274,367 concealed-weapons licenses and has revoked 3,311 for crimes committed while the holders were licensed. Only 162 of those crimes, however, involved the use of a firearm.

Even among those who are licensed to carry, most do not pack their guns all the time. In hot climates, guns are harder to hide in skimpy clothing. Unless you are used to carrying a gun, it may make you feel awkward and embarrassed, so many people will end up keeping the gun at home or in the car.

The eleven states that currently prevent most law-abiding citizens from carrying concealed handguns for protection include those that contain our largest cities with the highest violent crime rates: New York, Chicago, and Los Angeles. They fall into two categories: those that prohibit civilians from carrying guns at all and those where permits are issued at the discretion of the authorities.

Discretionary states are: California, Delaware, Hawaii, Iowa, Maryland, Massachusetts, New Jersey, New York, and Rhode Island. In these states, residents usually have to show a "need," which apparently does not include self-protection, or they have to be politically well connected. Sometimes, those public figures who have acquired carry permits have been strong advocates of gun control or prohibition. The former publisher of the New York Times, Arthur Ochs Sulzberger, whose paper exhibits a strong anti-gun stance, is one. U.S. Senator Diane Feinstein (D) of California, who has consistently supported gun-control legislation, is another.

In some discretionary states, such as California and New York, there is little consistency. Permits may be relatively easy to get in some counties or cities and impossible to get in others. It depends on the attitude of the local authorities. In Chico, California, one man told me, "The sheriff is all for it (concealed-carry) but the police chief is against it. The sheriff has said, 'if you get turned down by the police chief, come and see me.'"

It appears concealed-handgun licenses are much harder to acquire in the large cities. It is almost impossible for an ordinary citizen to get a concealed-handgun permit in Los Angeles or New York City—cities where residents need them most.

States with an outright ban on civilians carrying concealed handguns are Illinois and Wisconsin.

In states with relatively new shall-issue laws, a shaking-down period follows passage of the statute. For example, in Texas and many other states, employers and all private-property owners have the right to ban firearms from their premises. This affects customers and employees.

"If you can tell somebody they can't eat at your diner because they have no shoes or no shirt, then you have the right to tell them they can't come in there with a concealed weapon," says Texas Land Commissioner Jerry Patterson (R), one of the authors of the Texas concealed-handgun law. "It may be a stupid policy, but private-property owners have the right to make that policy."

Before the concealed-handgun law took effect, a boom occurred in the sign-making business in Texas. Restaurants, video stores, shopping malls, city governments, and public transportation bodies rushed to erect signs prohibiting licensed gun carriers from packing protection on their premises. Most of these signs have disappeared. As customers complained, managers realized the signs were bad for business and that the concealed-carry law was not a threat to public safety.

In 2003 a group of churches in Minnesota banded together to fight their new shall-issue law. It seems that they do not trust their parishioners.

Businesses and employers prohibiting guns on their premises are not a major problem for Texas customers. The business has to be correctly signed for its prohibition to have legal standing, and very few are. If the business is correctly signed, you have two legal options: you can leave your gun in your car, or you can take your business elsewhere.

If, however, you are an employee, things are different. Many employers—particularly in large businesses—prohibit their workers from carrying firearms. If you are caught transgressing the ban, you can be fired. This is no help to the nurse or store clerk who works late and has to cross a darkened parking lot to get to her car. Former Senator Patterson and Texas Representative Ron Wilson (D) acknowledge this is a problem not solved by the legislation.

Some companies even forbid their employees from keeping firearms locked in their privately owned vehicles parked on company property. Oklahoma tried to fix this after several employees of Weyerhaeuser Corporation were fired in 2002 when firearms were found in their vehicles during a search for drugs. The legislature overwhelmingly passed a law that stipulated that no company could prevent its employees from leaving firearms in their locked private vehicles. Whirlpool and ConocoPhillips sued the state in federal court and got an injunction preventing the law from taking effect. Three years later, as the case meanders its way through federal court at a speed that makes an armadillo look like a highway patrol cruiser chasing a speeder, employees at work in Oklahoma have no legal protection for their tools of choice for self-defense.

The Texas law includes a long list of places—such as racetracks, polling places, schools, and bars—where carrying a handgun is specifically prohibited by the statute. While Patterson supports the right of a property or business owner to ban guns from his premises, he says the only other places where guns should not be carried legally are public schools, bars, and sporting events where alcohol is sold. Both legislators say the number of prohibited locations needs to be pared down.

Some public-transit corporations have tried to prevent permit holders from traveling armed on public buses. Patterson says any rules made by a transit company are just that: rules. They have no force of law. The transit companies cannot charge people with trespass because you can trespass only on real property, not vehicles.

"When the bad guys are aware of the rule that bus riders are unarmed, what are the bad guys going to do?" Patterson asks. "They're going to go to bus stops and start bumping off bus riders. So what we have created is a target area. Transit authorities have created a killing field for criminals."

Patterson and Wilson feel the Texas law is a good start but should be modified to shake the bugs out of it. The Texas concealed-handgun law was passed in 1995 and modified by the legislature in subsequent sessions. Some banned locations, such as hospitals and racetracks, were required to post signs; private property signs were required to have specific wording; driveways and parking lots were excluded from otherwise-banned locations; and alterations were made in mental-health requirements for license holders. Patterson said the changes were mostly improvements.

"It's better than it was when first passed. I still think there are some improvements to be made," he said.

This shakedown period is occurring in most states with relatively new shall-issue laws. Florida has amended its law more than once. The law there now requires that license applicants pass a shooting test. As mentioned earlier, Ohio has made improvements to its law.

In 1999 I interviewed David Kopel, research director of the Independence Institute and co-author of the research paper, "Shall Issue: The New Wave of Concealed Handgun Permit Laws." At the time he predicted more states would pass these laws, followed by a national concealed-handgun-carry system.

"I think it's going to continue to spread until it's the law in around forty states. At which point, I think the pressure to nationalize the issue will become overwhelming," Kopel said.

He foresaw shall-issue laws passing in Kansas, Colorado, New Mexico, Nebraska, and Missouri. He was right about all of them, though as of September 2007 there has been little progress on a federal reciprocity law.

FEDERAL LAW

Persons prohibited from possessing firearms

Federal law prohibits the following people from possessing firearms, which means they cannot legally acquire state concealed-handgun licenses.

- Anyone who is under indictment for, or who has been convicted of a felony.
- A fugitive from justice.
- Anyone who is an unlawful user of or is addicted to any controlled substance (drugs).
- Anyone judged by a court to be mentally defective or who has been committed to a mental institution.
- An illegal alien.
- A former U.S. citizen who has renounced his/her citizenship.
- Anyone who has been dishonorably discharged from the military.
- Anyone currently subject to a court order to prevent domestic violence or harassment.
- Anyone who has been convicted of a misdemeanor crime of domestic violence.

Travel by vehicle

A person traveling from one place where he or she may legally possess a firearm to another place where he or she may legally possess a firearm may transport the firearm in a vehicle under certain circumstances.

- The firearm must be unloaded.
- It must be locked in the trunk. If the vehicle doesn't have a trunk, the firearm should be locked in a container—not the

glove compartment or console—that is not readily accessible to the occupants of the vehicle.
- Ammunition should also be locked away.

This federal law is supposed to allow people to transport guns through states where possession or transportation of firearms would otherwise contravene state or local law. However, some states and municipalities have more onerous laws, so it is advisable to contact state and local authorities particularly where your concealed-carry license is not recognized.

Travel by commercial aircraft

The Transportation Security Administration has issued the following regulations for transporting firearms and ammunition.
- The firearm must be checked with the air carrier as luggage. Firearms are prohibited from carry-on luggage.
- The firearm must be declared orally or in writing in accordance with the air carrier's procedures.
- The firearm must be unloaded.
- The firearm must be carried in a hard-sided container.
- The container must be locked and only the passenger may retain the key or combination.
- All checked baggage is subject to inspection. If during the inspection process it is necessary to open the container, air carriers are required to locate the passenger, and the passenger must unlock the container for further inspection. The firearm may not be transported if the passenger cannot be located to unlock the container. If you are traveling with a firearm, pay close attention to airport pages and announcements. If requested, provide the cooperation necessary to inspect your firearm.
- Ammunition is also prohibited from carry-on luggage. Ammunition may not be carried loose. It must travel in the manufacturer's packaging or other packaging suitable for transport.

• Contact your air carrier for its specific procedures for traveling with firearms as they vary slightly from airline to airline. In particular, consult your carrier to determine ammunition quantity limitations or whether the ammunition must be packed separately from the firearm.

Further information

For further information about federal firearms laws contact your local office of the federal Bureau of Alcohol, Tobacco, Firearms, and Explosives.

In the tables presented following, the states classified as "right-to-carry-concealed" are listed along with some details of their laws and numbers of license holders. Most shall-issue states have web sites that contain concealed-carry laws and procedures. Where possible, I have included web-site addresses. The web sites vary considerably in the amount and quality of information they provide. One of the best is that of Florida's Department of Agriculture and Consumer Services. In addition to the usual reciprocity agreements with other states, statutes concerning concealed carry, and directions for getting a license, the web site has an excellent section on the use of deadly force in self defense.

NOTES:

• Almost all jurisdictions require a person with a concealed-carry license to carry it when packing the handgun and to produce it when requested by a law-enforcement officer. Where this is written into the law, I have included it under the heading of "Requirements."
• When a license holder is visiting a state that honors his or her license, the visitor is required to obey the concealed-carry laws of the state being visited.
• A felony is generally defined as a crime for which a person can be sentenced to more than one year in prison. A

misdemeanor is a crime for which a sentence of up to a year can be given.

- Most states will not issue carry licenses to persons who have been judged guilty of the juvenile equivalent of a felony.
- Most state laws include an appeal process if a license is denied or revoked.
- Federal law prohibits the carrying of firearms in federal facilities with the exception of some military bases, where the rules are at the discretion of the base commander.
- State population estimates by the U.S. Bureau of the Census, updated to July 1, 2006, have been used to calculate the percentage of a state's population with licenses.
- Some states, such as Florida, New Hampshire, and Utah, will issue licenses to non-residents. In the first table, I have used the number of licenses issued only to residents of that state where possible. Only a total figure was available for some states such as Pennsylvania, so I have used that number. However, in the calculations that follow the first table, I have included non-resident licenses.
- Some states will honor resident licenses from another state, but not non-resident permits. If you have a non-resident license, check that it will be honored where you intend to travel.
- Some states, like Texas, issue concealed-handgun licenses; others, like Florida, issue concealed-weapons licenses that allow the holder to carry other weapons such as knives or billy clubs. As we are concerned in this book with concealed handguns, I have not differentiated between the two types of license.
- Some states call their concealed-carry document a "license," while others refer to it as a "permit." I have used the two words indiscriminately to mean the same thing.

WARNING:

The following information was derived principally from the government departments that issue or administer the licenses. It was current at time of writing, but has been condensed and abbreviated. The information presented here is only a general guide. Any person who wishes to carry a concealed handgun should read and understand federal law relating to ownership and possession of handguns and the state laws affecting concealed-carry licenses, and understand, as well, the circumstances in which someone is justified in using deadly or lethal force.

In the reciprocity tables and the entries in each state's law summary, U.S. Postal Service two-letter abbreviations, as follows, are used for the names of the states.

Alabama	AL	Montana	MT
Alaska	AK	Nebraska	NE
Arkansas	AR	Nevada	NV
Arizona	AZ	New Hampshire	NH
California	CA	New Jersey	NJ
Colorado	CO	New Mexico	NM
Connecticut	CT	New York	NY
Delaware	DE	North Carolina	NC
Florida	FL	North Dakota	ND
Georgia	GA	Ohio	OH
Hawaii	HI	Oklahoma	OK
Idaho	ID	Oregon	OR
Illinois	IL	Pennsylvania	PA
Indiana	IN	Rhode Island	RI
Iowa	IA	South Carolina	SC
Kansas	KS	South Dakota	SD
Kentucky	KY	Tennessee	TN
Louisiana	LA	Texas	TX
Maine	ME	Utah	UT
Maryland	MD	Vermont	VT
Massachusetts	MA	Virginia	VA
Michigan	MI	Washington	WA
Minnesota	MN	West Virginia	WV
Mississippi	MS	Wisconsin	WI
Missouri	MO	Wyoming	WY

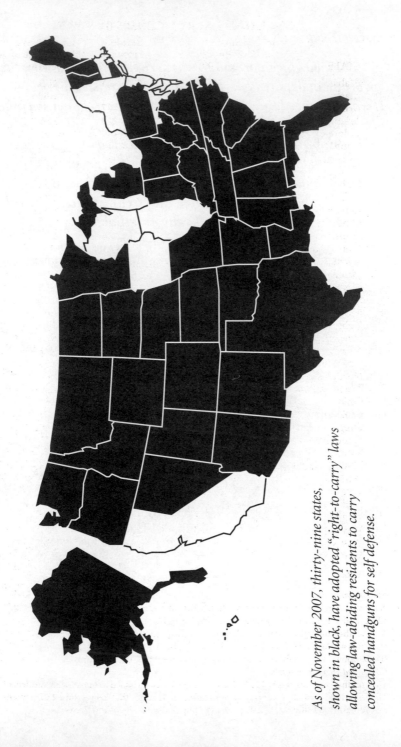

As of November 2007, thirty-nine states, shown in black, have adopted "right-to-carry" laws allowing law-abiding residents to carry concealed handguns for self defense.

CONCEALED-CARRY LICENSES BY STATE

STATE	State Population (x 1,000)	Resident Licenses, Mid-2007	Licenses as a Percentage of Population
Alabama	4,599	N/A	N/A
Alaska	670	9547	1.42
Arizona	6,166	95,447	1.55
Arkansas	2,811	54,919	1.95
Colorado	4,753	28,454	0.60
Connecticut	3,505	124,670	3.55
Florida	18,090	399,064	2.21
Georgia	9,364	N/A	N/A
Idaho	1,466	48,364	3.30
Indiana	6,314	274,263	4.34
Kansas	2,764	8,958	0.32
Kentucky	4,206	95,638	2.27
Louisiana	4,288	14,084	0.32
Maine	1,322	N/A	N/A
Michigan	10,096	148,751	1.47
Minnesota	5,167	48,396	0.94
Mississippi	2,911	47,500	1.63
Missouri	5,843	36,105	0.62
Montana	945	15,336	1.62
Nebraska	1,768	2,109	0.12
Nevada	2,496	N/A	N/A
New Hampshire	1,315	N/A	N/A
New Mexico	1,955	10,566	0.54
North Carolina	8,857	95,502	1.08
North Dakota	636	8,364	1.32
Ohio	11,478	97,912	0.85
Oklahoma	3,579	57,540	1.61
Oregon	3,701	95,005	2.59
Pennsylvania	12,441	668,372	5.37
South Carolina	4,321	56,715	1.31
South Dakota	782	27,656	3.54
Tennessee	6,039	179,376	2.97
Texas	23,508	275,978	1.17
Utah	2,550	64,646	2.54
Virginia	7,643	146,874	1.92
Washington	6,396	236,975	3.71
West Virginia	1,818	N/A	N/A
Wyoming	515	11,977	2.33
Total	**197,078**	**3,473,984**	

State populations:
Note: Vermont is a right-to-carry-concealed state, but issues neither licenses nor permits.
32 states that keep total active license numbers: **176,164,000**
38 states that have right-to-carry and have issued licenses for more than six months: **197,078,000**
Six states without total license numbers, but with right-to-carry: **20,914,000**
(Population estimates for states as of July 1, 2006, from U.S. Census Bureau.)
Concealed-carry licenses:
32 states that keep totals: **3,562,051.** (Includes 88,965 licenses issued to out-of-state residents.)
All icense holders as a percentage of population in 32 states that keep totals: **2.02 percent**
Extrapolating for 38 states at 2.02 percent of population: **3.98 million licenses.**

CONCEALED-CARRY RECIPROCITY BY STATE—TABLE 1

STATE	OTHER STATE LICENSES HONORED
Alabama	AK, AZ, AR, CO, FL, GA, ID, IN, KY, LA, MI, MS, MO, NH, NC, ND, OK, SD, TN, TX, UT, WY
Alaska	All licenses
Arizona	All licenses
Arkansas	AL, AK, AZ, CO, DE, FL, ID, IN, KS, KY, LA, MI, MS, MO, MT, NC, ND, OK, PA, SC, SD, TN, TX, UT, VA, WV
Colorado	AL, AK, AZ, AR, DE, FL, GA, ID, IN, KS, KY, LA, MI, MS, MO, MT, NH, NM, NC, ND, OK, PA, SD, TN, TX, UT, WY
Connecticut	None
Delaware	AK, AZ, CO, FL, KY, MI, MO, NC, ND, OH, OK, TN, TX, UT
Florida	AL, AK, AZ, AR, CO, DE, GA, ID, IN, KS, KY, LA, MI, MS, MO, MT, NH, NM, NC, ND, OK, PA, SD, TN, TX, UT, VA, WV, WY
Georgia	AL, AK, CO, FL, ID, IN, KY, LA, MI, MS, MO, MT, NH, NC, OK, PA, SD, TN, TX, UT, WY
Idaho	All licenses
Indiana	All licenses
Kansas	AK, AZ, AR, CO, FL, HI, KY, LA, MI, MN, MO, NE, NV, NJ, NM, NC, OH, OK, SC, TN, TX, WV
Kentucky	All licenses
Louisiana	AL, AK, AZ, AR, CO, FL, GA, ID, IN, KS, KY, MI, MS, MO, MT, NH, NC, ND, OK, PA, SC, SD, TN, TX, UT, VA, WA, WY
Maine	None
Michigan	All licenses
Minnesota	AK, AR, KS, KY, LA, MI, MO, NV, NM, OH, OK, TN, TX, UT, WY
Mississippi	AL, AK, CO, FL, GA, KY, LA, MI, MT, NH, NC, OK, SD, TN, TX, UT, WA, WY
Missouri	All licenses

Montana	AK, AZ, AR, CA, CO, CT, FL, GA, ID, IN, IA, KS, KY, LA, MD, MA, MI, MN, MS, MO, NE, NV, NJ, NM, NY, NC, ND, OH, OK, OR, PA, SC, SD, TN, TX, UT, VA, WA, WV, WY
Nebraska	None
Nevada	AK, AR, KS, LA, MO, NE, TN, UT
New Hampshire	AL, AK, AZ, CO, FL, GA, ID, IN, KY, LA, MI, MS, MO, NC, ND, OK, PA, TN, UT, WY
New Mexico	AK, AZ, CO, DE, FL, KY, MI, MN, MO, MT, NC, ND, OH, OK, SC, TN, TX, UT, VA, WY
North Carolina	AL, AK, AZ, AR, CO, DE, FL, GA, ID, IN, KS, KY, MI, MS, MO, MT, NH, ND, OH, OK, PA, SC, SD, TN, TX, UT, VA, WA, WV
North Dakota	AL, AK, AZ, AR, CO, DE, FL, ID, IN, KY, LA, MI, MO, MT, NH, NM, NC, OK, SD, TN, TX, UT
Ohio	AK, AZ, DE, FL, ID, KY, MI, MO, NC, OK, SC, TN, UT, VA, WA, WV, WY
Oklahoma	All licenses
Oregon	None
Pennsylvania	AK, CO, FL, GA, ID, KY, LA, MI, MO, MT, NH, NC, ND, OK, SD, TN, TX, UT, VA, WV, WY
South Carolina	AK, AR, KS, LA, MI, MO, NC, OH, TN, TX, WY
South Dakota	All licenses
Tennessee	All licenses
Texas	AL, AK, AZ, AR, CA, CO, CT, DE, FL, GA, HI, ID, IN, IA, KS, KY, LA, MD, MA, MI, MS, MO, MT, NE, NV, NJ, NM, NY, NC, ND, OK, PA, RI, SC, SD, TN, UT, VA, WA, WY
Utah	All licenses
Vermont	No licenses issued or required
Virginia	AK, AZ, AR, FL, KY, LA, MI, MN, MO, MT, NM, NC, OH, OK, PA, SC, TN, TX, UT, WA, WV, WY
Washington	None
West Virginia	AR, FL, KY, NC, OH, PA, VA
Wyoming	AL, AK, AZ, CO, FL, GA, ID, IN, KY, LA, MI, MS, MT, NH, NM, OH, OK, PA, SC, SD, TN, TX, UT

CONCEALED-CARRY RECIPROCITY BY STATE—TABLE 2

STATE	OTHER STATES WHERE LICENSE IS HONORED
Alabama	AK, AZ, AR, CO, FL, GA, ID, IN, KY, LA, MI, MS, MO, NH, NC, ND, OK, SD, TN, TX, UT, VT, WY
Alaska	AL, AZ, AR, CO, DE, FL, GA, ID, IN, KS, KY, LA, MI, MN, MS, MO, MT, NV, NH, NM, NC, ND, OH, OK, PA, SC, SD, TN, TX, UT, VT, VA, WY
Arizona	AK, AR, CO, DE, FL, ID, IN, KS, KY, LA, MI, MO, MT, NH, NM, NC, ND, OH, OK, SD, TN, TX, UT, VT, VA, WY
Arkansas	AL, AK, AZ, CO, FL, ID, IN, KS, KY, LA, MI, MN, MO, MT, NV, NC, ND, OK, PA, SC, SD, TN, TX, UT, VT, VA, WV
California	AK, AZ, ID, IN, KY, MI, MO, MT, OK, SD, TN, TX, UT, VT
Colorado	AL, AK, AZ, AR, DE, FL, GA, ID, IN, KS, KY, LA, MI, MS, MO, MT, NH, NM, NC, ND, OK, PA, SD, TN, TX, UT, VT, WY
Connecticut	AK, AZ, ID, IN, KY, MI, MO, MT, OK, SD, TN, TX, UT, VT
Delaware	AK, AZ, CO, FL, ID, IN, KY, MI, MO, NM, NC, ND, OH, OK, SD, TN, TX, UT, VT
Florida	AL, AK, AZ, AR, CO, DE, GA, ID, IN, KS, KY, LA, MI, MS, MO, MT, NH, NM, NC, ND, OH, OK, PA, SD, TN, TX, UT, VT, VA, WV, WY
Georgia	AL, AK, AZ, CO, FL, ID, IN, KY, LA, MI, MS, MO, MT, NH, NC, OK, PA, SD, TN, TX, UT, VT, WY
Hawaii	AK, AZ, ID, IN, KS, KY, MI, MO, OK, SD, TN, TX, UT, VT
Idaho	AL, AK, AZ, AR, CO, FL, GA, IN, KY, LA, MI, MO, MT, NH, NC, ND, OH, OK, PA, SD, TN, TX, UT, VT, VA, WY
Indiana	AL, AK, AZ, AR, CO, FL, GA, ID, KY, LA, MI, MO, MT, NH, NC, ND, OK, SD, TN, TX, UT, VT, WY
Iowa	AK, AZ, ID, IN, KY, MI, MO, MT, OK, SD, TN, TX, UT, VT
Kansas	AK, AZ, CO, FL, ID, IN, KY, LA, MI, MN, MO, MT, NV, NC, OK, SC, SD, TN, TX, UT, VT
Kentucky	AL, AK, AZ, AR, CO, DE, FL, GA, ID, IN, KS, LA, MI, MN, MS, MO, MT, NH, NM, NC, ND, OH, OK, PA, SD, TN, TX, UT, VT, VA, WV, WY
Louisiana	AL, AK, AZ, AR, CO, FL, GA, ID, IN, KS, KY, MI, MN, MS, MO, MT, NV, NH, ND, OK, PA, SC, SD, TN, TX, UT, VT, VA, WA, WY
Maine	AK, AZ, ID, IN, KY, MI, MO, OK, SD, TN, UT, VT
Maryland	AK, AZ, ID, IN, KY, MI, MO, MT, OK, SD, TN, TX, UT, VT
Massachusetts	AK, AZ, ID, IN, KY, MI, MO, MT, OK, SD, TN, TX, UT, VT
Michigan	AL, AK, AZ, AR, CO, DE, FL, GA, ID, IN, KS, KY, LA, MN, MS, MO, MT, NH, NM, NC, ND, OH, OK, PA, SC, SD, TN, TX, UT, VT, VA, WY
Minnesota	AK, AZ, ID, IN, KS, KY, MI, MO, MT, NM, OK, SD, TN, UT, VT, VA
Mississippi	AL, AK, AZ, AR, CO, FL, GA, ID, IN, KY, LA, MI, MO, MT, NH, NC, OK, SD, TN, TX, UT, VT, WY

Missouri	AL, AK, AZ, AR, CO, DE, FL, GA, ID, IN, KS, KY, LA, MI, MN, MT, NV, NH, NM, NC, ND, OH, OK, PA, SC, SD, TN, TX, UT, VT, VA
Montana	AK, AZ, AR, CO, FL, GA, ID, IN, KY, LA, MI, MS, MO, NM, NC, ND, OK, PA, SD, TN, TX, UT, VT, VA, WY
Nebraska	AK, AZ, ID, IN, KS, KY, MI, MO, MT, NV, OK, SD, TN, TX, UT, VT
Nevada	AK, AZ, ID, IN, KS, KY, MI, MN, MO, MT, OK, SD, TN, TX, UT, VT
New Hampshire	AL, AK, AZ, CO, FL, GA, ID, IN, KY, LA, MI, MS, MO, NC, ND, OK, PA, SD, TN, UT, VT, WY
New Jersey	AK, AZ, ID, IN, KS, KY, MI, MO, MT, OK, SD, TN, TX, UT, VT
New Mexico	AK, AZ, CO, FL, ID, IN, KS, KY, MI, MN, MO, MT, ND, OK, SD, TN, TX, UT, VT, VA, WY
New York	AK, AZ, ID, IN, KY, MI, MO, MT, OK, SD, TN, TX, UT, VT
North Carolina	AL, AK, AZ, AR, CO, DE, FL, GA, ID, IN, KS, KY, LA, MI, MS, MO, MT, NH, NM, ND, OH, OK, PA, SC, SD, TN, TX, UT, VT, VA, WV, WY
North Dakota	AL, AK, AZ, AR, CO, DE, FL, ID, IN, KY, LA, MI, MO, MT, NH, NM, NC, OK, PA, SD, TN, TX, UT, VT, WY
Ohio	AK, AZ, DE, ID, IN, KS, KY, MI, MN, MO, MT, NM, NC, OK, SC, SD, TN, UT, VT, VA, WV, WY
Oklahoma	AL, AK, AZ, AR, CO, DE, FL, GA, ID, IN, KS, KY, LA, MI, MN, MS, MO, MT, NH, NM, NC, ND, OH, PA, SD, TN, TX, UT, VT, VA, WA, WY
Oregon	AK, AZ, ID, IN, KY, MI, MO, MT, OK, SD, TN, UT, VT
Pennsylvania	AK, AZ, AR, CO, FL, GA, ID, IN, KY, LA, MI, MO, MT, NH, NC, OK, SD, TN, TX, UT, VT, VA, WV, WY
Rhode Island	AK, AZ, ID, IN, KY, MI, MO, OK, SD, TN, TX, UT, VT
South Carolina	AK, AZ, AR, ID, IN, KS, KY, LA, MI, MO, MT, NM, NC, OH, OK, SD, TN, TX, UT, VT, VA, WY
South Dakota	AL, AK, AZ, AR, CO, FL, GA, ID, IN, KY, LA, MI, MS, MO, MT, NC, ND, OK, PA, TN, TX, UT, VT, WY
Tennessee	AL, AK, AZ, AR, CO, DE, FL, GA, ID, IN, KS, KY, LA, MI, MN, MS, MO, MT, NV, NH, NM, NC, ND, OH, OK, PA, SC, SD, TX, UT, VT, VA, WY
Texas	AL, AK, AZ, AR, CO, DE, FL, GA, ID, IN, KS, KY, LA, MI, MN, MS, MO, MT, NM, NC, ND, OK, PA, SC, SD, TN, UT, VT, VA, WY
Utah	AL, AK, AZ, AR, CO, DE, FL, GA, ID, IN, KY, LA, MI, MN, MS, MO, MT, NV, NH, NM, NC, ND, OH, OK, PA, SD, TN, TX, VT, VA, WA, WY
Virginia	AK, AZ, AR, FL, ID, IN, KY, LA, MI, MO, MT, NM, NC, OH, OK, PA, SD, TN, TX, UT, VT, WV
Washington	AK, AZ, ID, IN, KY, LA, MI, MS, MO, MT, NC, OH, OK, SD, TN, TX, UT, VT, VA
West Virginia	AK, AZ, AR, FL, ID, IN, KS, KY, MI, MO, MT, NC, OH, OK, PA, SD, TN, UT, VT, VA
Wyoming	AL, AK, AZ, CO, FL, GA, ID, IN, KY, LA, MI, MN, MS, MO, MT, NH, NM, NC, ND, OH, OK, PA, SC, SD, TN, TX, UT, VT, VA

ALABAMA

Effective date: Alabama has regulated firearms since the 1800s, and the law has been revised many times.

Administered by: Sheriff of each county.

License cost and duration: cost varies between $7.50 and $30, depending on the county, and is good for one year. For example, the cost of a license in Jefferson County, which includes Birmingham, is $7.50, while in Montgomery County and Mobile County the fee is $20.

Apply to: Sheriff of the county in which applicant resides. Non-residents planning to travel through or visit Alabama may get up-to-date information from the Alabama Department of Public Safety, Public Information/Education Unit, P.O. Box 1511, Montgomery, AL 36102-1511. Telephone: 334-242-4445. <www.dps.state.al.us> Gun laws and license reciprocity information can be found on the web site of the Alabama Attorney General at <www.ago.state.al.us> or through the office of the Attorney General, Alabama State House, 11 South Union Street, Third Floor, Montgomery, AL 36130. Telephone: 334-242-7300.

Qualifications: Qualified or unlimited licenses to carry a handgun concealed or in a vehicle are issued by the county sheriff, who has discretion to determine if the applicant is a suitable person; pass background check; resident of the state; 19 years or older, depending on sheriff; not convicted of committing or attempting to commit a crime of violence; not a drug addict or habitual drunkard; not of unsound mind.

Training course: Not required.

Prohibitions: Public demonstrations; school property.

Reciprocity: Alabama recognizes the licenses of any state that honors its licenses, provided the license holder is at least 21 years old. As of August 2007, these are: AK, AZ, AR, CO, FL, GA, ID, IN, KY, LA, MI, MS, MO, NH, NC, ND, OK, SD, TN (some limitations for Alabama residents who work in Tennessee), TX, UT, and WY. Visitors do not need licenses to carry concealed or openly in AK and VT. For the latest information, call, write, or check the Attorney General's web site.

Licenses in use: No statewide figures available.

ALASKA

In 2003 the Alaska Legislature passed a law that allows anyone 21 years or older who may legally carry a firearm to carry it concealed without having to obtain a permit. This applies to visitors as well as residents.

Effective date: January 1, 1995.

Administered by: Alaska Department of Public Safety.

License cost and duration: $99 for five years; renewal $25. The licensing system has been kept in operation so Alaskans can carry concealed in other states that honor their permits.

Apply to: Alaska Concealed Handgun Permit Program, 5700 East Tudor Road, Anchorage, AK 99507. Telephone: 907-269-0392. <www.dps.state.ak.us/PermitsLicensing/achp/>

Qualifications: Twenty-one years or older; not prohibited under state and federal law to own or possess a handgun; resident of state for at least 90 days; pass competency training course; not convicted in the last six years of two or more Class A misdemeanors; not ordered by a court in the last three years to complete an alcohol or substance abuse program.

Training course: Twelve hours instruction in law relating to firearms, use of deadly force, safe and responsible use of a handgun, self-defense principles; plus competency test for each action and maximum caliber licensee wishes to carry. No training required to renew license.

Carry prohibitions: Schools, school grounds or school buses; anywhere alcohol is sold for consumption on premises, except restaurants where the person carrying the firearm does not consume alcohol; licensed child-care facilities or assisted-living homes for the elderly or mentally or physically disabled; courthouses, courtrooms, or offices of the Alaska Court System; within domestic-violence or sexual-assault shelters that receive state funding; in private residences without permission; federal facilities; the secure areas of airports; within certain National Park areas; buildings or facilities that are posted to prohibit carrying concealed handguns.

Requirements: Immediately inform a peace officer if you are carrying a concealed handgun with or without a permit.

Reciprocity: Alaska recognizes valid concealed-handgun permits from all other states and jurisdictions. Alaska permits
are honored by AL, AZ, AR, CO, DE, FL, GA, ID, IN, KS, KY,
LA, MI, MS, MO, MT, NH, NM, NC, ND (license holder must
be 21 or older), OH, OK, PA, SC, SD, TN, TX, UT, VA, and
WY. Visitors to Vermmont do not need a license to carry in
the open or conealed. For latest information, call, write, or
check web site.
Active licenses: 9,547 as of August 17, 2007. Permits have
decreased from more than 15,000 in 2004 as they are no longer
needed to carry concealed.
License holders as a percentage of state population: 1.4.

ARIZONA

Effective date: July 18, 1994.
Administered by: Arizona Department of Public Safety.
License cost and duration: $65 for five years, if issued after
August 11, 2005, or for four years, if issued before that date;
renewals $65.
Apply to: Concealed Weapon Permit Unit, Arizona Department
of Public Safety, P.O. Box 6488, Phoenix, AZ 85005-6488.
Telephone: 602-256-6280. <www.dps.state.az.us/ccw>
Qualifications: Resident of Arizona or U.S. citizen; 21 years or
older; not under indictment or convicted of a felony; not mentally ill, found mentally incompetent or committed to mental institution; not unlawfully in the U.S.; completed an
approved training course; not prohibited by federal law
from possessing firearms; pass criminal-record check.
Training course: At least eight hours of instruction; law relating to firearms; use of deadly force; safety; weapon care and
maintenance; shooting techniques; mental conditioning; judg-
mental shooting; written test and range test.
Carry prohibitions: Places that sell alcohol for on-premises consumption, including restaurants but not hotel rooms;
polling places on election day; grounds of correctional
facilities; school grounds; nuclear and hydroelectric-generating
stations; federal buildings; military installations; Indian
reservations; game preserves; national parks; secure areas of
airports; where prohibited by federal, state, and local law;

buildings, including businesses and government buildings where signs are posted prohibiting weapons; private property without consent of the owner.

Requirements: Upon request by a peace officer, the license holder, if carrying a concealed weapon, shall present the license to the officer for inspection.

Reciprocity: Arizona honors all licenses from other jurisdictions, provided the license holder is 21 years or older. Arizona licenses are honored by AK, AR, CO, DE, FL, ID, IN, KS, KY, LA, MI, MO, MT, NH, MN, NC, ND, OH, OK, SD, TN, TX, UT, VA, AND WY. Visitors do not need licenses to carry concealed or openly in AK and VT. For latest information, call, write, or check web site.

Active licenses: 95,447 as of August 30, 2007; however, an additional 3,221 were issued to out-of-state residents.

License holders as a percentage of state population: 1.55.

ARKANSAS

Effective date: July 28, 1995.

Administered by: Arkansas State Police.

License cost and duration: $144 for five years; renewals $55.

Apply to: Arkansas State Police, Conceded Handgun Section, #1 Sate Police Plaza Drive, Little Rock, AR 72209. Telephone 501-618-8600.

Qualifications: Resident of the state for at least one year; U.S. citizen; 21 years or older; pass criminal-record check, no felony convictions; eligible to possess a handgun under federal and state law; no mental or physical infirmity that would preclude safe handgun handling; not threatened or attempted suicide; not a chronic abuser of alcohol or drugs; not a fugitive from justice; not judged mentally incompetent or committed to a mental institution; not dishonorably discharged from the military; never renounced U.S. citizenship; signed oath of allegiance to U.S. and Arkansas constitutions; passed training course. Violent misdemeanor conviction in past five years may be grounds for denial of license. Two types of license are issued. With a restricted license, the holder may not carry a semi-automatic handgun. Any type of legal handgun may be carried with an unrestricted license.

Training course: Five hours minimum; handguns and ammunition; fundamentals; self defense and the law; a range test.
Carry prohibitions: Law-enforcement or prison facilities;
government meeting places; polling places; courthouses or
courtrooms; public parks; athletic events; establishments where
alcohol is sold for consumption on-premises, except restaurants; schools or colleges; airport terminals; churches or other
places of worship; posted businesses; private homes without permission; while participating in parades or demonstrations; where prohibited by federal law.
Requirements:A license holder who is carrying a firearm is
required to produce the license if asked by a police officer.
Reciprocity: Arkansas has reciprocal agreements with AL,
AK, AZ, CO, FL, ID, IN, KS, KY, LA, MI, MS, MO, MT, NC,
ND, OK, PA, SC, SD, TN, TX, UT, VA, and WV. Visitors do
not need licenses to carry concealed or openly in AK and VT.
For latest information, call, write, or check web site.
Active licenses: 54,919 as of August 20, 2007.
License holders as a percentage of state population: 1.95.

COLORADO

On March 18, 2003, Governor Bill Owens signed into law a bill
that made it considerably easier for law-abiding Colorado
residents to get concealed-handgun permits. He also signed
a bill that will standardize concealed-carry laws throughout
the state.
Effective date: May 18, 2003.
Administered by: County sheriffs. For more information,
contact local county sheriff or, particularly for visitors to the
state, the Colorado Bureau of Investigation, 690 Kipling Street,
Denver, CO 80215. Telephone: 303-239-4235.
<www.cbi.state.co.us>
License cost and duration: A fee not to exceed $100 to the
sheriff plus $52.50 to the Colorado Bureau of Investigation
for a state and federal criminal record check; the license is valid
for five years. Renewal not to exceed $63, provided applicant
has had his or her fingerprints checked previously by CBI.
Apply to: Sheriff in county of residence.

Qualifications: Legal resident of Colorado; 21 years of age or older; is eligible to possess a firearm under state and federal law; has not been convicted of perjury as a result of information supplied or omitted on the application form for a concealed-handgun permit; does not chronically and habitually use alcohol to a state of impairment; is not an unlawful user of or is addicted to illegal drugs; is not subject to a restraining order at the time of application; demonstrates competence with a handgun. A sheriff may deny a permit if he or she reasonably believes, based on documented previous behavior, that the applicant is likely to present a danger to self or others if the permit is issued.

Training course: Any one of several approved training courses or other documentary evidence of competency with a handgun, such as military training or shooting competition.

Carry prohibitions: Anywhere that would violate state or federal law; on the property of public schools, unless the handgun is in a vehicle; an exception is made for undeveloped school property that is used for hunting or other shooting sports; inside a public building where people are screened electronically for possession of weapons. Private property owners or tenants. Private employers or business entities have the right to exclude concealed handguns from their premises.

Requirements: Permit holders carrying concealed handguns are required to present their permits and photo identification to a police officer on demand.

Reciprocity: Colorado recognizes the concealed-carry licenses of residents over the age of 21 from any state that recognizes its licenses. These states are AL, AK, AZ, AR, DE, FL, GA, ID, IN, KS, KY, LA, MI, MS, MO, MT, NH, NM, NC, ND, OK, PA, SD, TN, TX, UT, and WY. It does not honor non-resident permits. For an up-to-date list of reciprocity states, check with the Colorado Bureau of Investigation web site <www.cbi.state.co.us> Visitors do not need licenses to carry concealed or openly in AK and VT.

Active licenses: From 2003 to December 31, 2006, Colorado sheriffs issued 28,902 permits and revoked 448 for an approximate total of 28,454 licenses active. (This does not include

people who have died, but it does include those who have moved out of state.)
License holders as a percentage of state population: 0.60.

CONNECTICUT

Connecticut issues pistol permits that allow holders discretion to carry handguns concealed or in the open. The permit law took effect sometime prior to 1977. Changes in the law in 1994 made some license holders ineligible, and their licenses were revoked.

Administered by: Connecticut State Police.

License cost and duration: $35 for five years; renewals $35.

Apply to: Connecticut State Police, Special Licensing and Firearms Unit, 1111 Country Club Road, P.O. Box 2794, Middletown, CT 06457-9294. Telephone: 860-685-8494. <www.state.ct.us/dps/SLFU/index.html> click on Pistol Permits. License application forms can be picked up at any police station. A Connecticut resident applying for a state permit must first obtain a temporary state permit valid for 60 days through local police department or first selectman. This costs $35, plus $24 for an FBI fingerprint and record check. Once a local permit is issued, application can be made to the Connecticut State Police for the five-year permit at a cost of $35. Out-of-state residents should apply directly to the State Police, who will issue the five-year permit. Non-residents require a valid license from another state or a letter from their local chief of police or sheriff stating that the applicant has passed a criminal record check.

Qualifications: Twenty-one years or older; a legal resident of the U.S.; pass a criminal-record check; have no felony convictions or outstanding charges; no convictions or outstanding charges for any of 11 misdemeanors, mostly involving violence or the threat of violence; not have been discharged in preceding 20 years after having been found not guilty of a crime by reason of mental disease or defect; not been confined in previous 12 months by court order for mental illness; not subject to a restraining or protective order as a result of use, attempted use, or threatened use of physical force against another person; not currently subject to firearms seizure; not renounced U.S. citizenship; not dishonorably discharged from the military. There should be no evidence that the applicant is an "unsuitable person" or that he or she intends to use a handgun unlawfully.

Training course: An approved course of at least eight hours on safety and use of handguns taught by a certified government or private instructor.

Carry prohibitions: Places where "mature judgment" dictates that no handguns should be carried, such as bars or other places where alcohol is being consumed; in stressful situations such as arguments; after consuming alcohol or illegal drugs; in buildings housing the general assembly or any of its committees, or the offices of any of its members, officers, or employees; state and federal government buildings; federal property; residential or commercial property that is posted with signs prohibiting handguns.

Reciprocity: Connecticut does not honor out-of-state concealed-carry licenses; however, the state will issue licenses to residents of other states. Connecticut licenses are honored by AK, AZ, ID, IN, KY, MI, MO, MT, OK, SD, TN, TX, and UT. Visitors do not need licenses to carry concealed or openly in AK and VT.

Active licenses: 124,670 residential licenses as of September 6, 2007, plus 8,582 licenses issued to nonresidents for a total of 133,252.

Residential license holders as a percentage of state population: 3.55.

FLORIDA

Effective date: October 1, 1987.

Administered by: Florida Department of Agriculture & Consumer Services.

License cost and duration: $117 for five years; renewal $65.

Apply to: Florida Department of Agriculture and Consumer Services, Division of Licensing, P.O. Box 6687, Tallahassee, FL 32314-6687. Telephone 850-488-5381.

Qualifications: Legal resident of the U.S. (does not have to reside in Florida; 21 years or older; pass criminal record check; never convicted of a felony unless firearms rights have been restored; not convicted of violent or drug misdemeanor within last three years; not have adjudication withheld or sentence suspended on felony or misdemeanor of domestic violence unless three years have elapsed since probation or other conditions of the court have been fulfilled; not currently under injunction restraining applicant from committing acts of domestic violence or acts of repeated violence; not a chronic abuser of drugs or alcohol; not convicted of two or more drinking and driving offenses in the previous three years; not judged mentally incompetent or committed to a mental institution in last five years; no physical infirmity that would prevent safe handgun handling; complete a firearm training course; not renounced U.S. citizenship; not dishonorably discharged from armed forces; not fugitive from justice.

Training course: Various, including hunter training, NRA; must include a range course.

Carry prohibitions: Any "place of nuisance," which includes places of illegal gambling or prostitution; law enforcement or detention facilities; courthouses or courtrooms; polling places; meetings of the governing bodies of counties, public school districts, municipalities, or special districts; any meetings of the legislature or any of its committees; school, college, or professional athletic events; schools, colleges, or educational facilities; bars or places primarily used for the sale and consumption of alcohol; airports; where it is against federal law.

Reciprocity: Florida recognizes licenses from any state that honors its concealed weapons licenses, provided the license holder is 21 years or older. These states are: AL, AK, AZ, AR, CO, DE, GA, ID, IN, KS, KY, LA, MI, MS, MO, MT, NH, NM, NC, ND, OK, PA, SD, TN, TX, UT, VA, WV, and WY. Visitors do not need licenses to carry concealed or openly in AK and VT. For latest information call, write, or check web site.

Active licenses: 399,064 issued to Florida residents as of July 31, 2007; plus non-Florida residents 45,974, for a total of 445,038.

License holders as a percentage of state population: 2.21.

GEORGIA

Effective date: Current law in 1968, but became more stringently interpreted as non-discretionary in 1989.

Administered by: Local probate courts.

License cost and duration: Cost varies according to county, but is about $50 for five years, renewals about the same. For example, Fulton County, which includes Atlanta, charges $44.41 for a license and $44.41 for a renewal.

Apply to: The probate court in county of residence. For out-of-state inquiries, contact: Georgia Department of Public Safety, Legal Services Division, P.O. Box 1456, Atlanta, GA 30371-2303. Telephone: 404-624-7423. Georgia Attorney General's Office has up to date information on reciprocity with other states. The office is located at 40 Capital Square, SW, Atlanta, GA 30334-1300. Telephone: 404-656-3300.

<www.state.ga.us/ago/> Georgia law relating to carrying concealed firearms can be found at <www.legis.state.ga.us/> click on Georgia Code and search under Firearms. The relevant laws are in Title 16, Chapter 11, Sections 126 to 130.

Qualifications: Pass criminal-record check; not prohibited under federal law from possessing a firearm; 21 years or older; not a fugitive from justice; not currently charged with a felony, forcible misdemeanor, or weapons violation; not having been convicted of a felony unless pardoned; if convicted of a forcible misdemeanor, free from supervision for at least five years; if convicted of a weapons violation, free from supervision for at least three years; no drug convictions; not hospitalized for mental or alcohol/drug treatment in last five years.

Training course: Not required.

Carry prohibitions: Public gatherings such as athletic or sporting events; churches or church functions; political rallies or functions; publicly owned or operated buildings; establishments selling alcohol for consumption on-premises; on the premises of nuclear-power facilities; within school-safety zones, at school functions or on school property. "Schools" refers to any educational facilities, including universities, colleges, technical, and vocational schools.

Reciprocity: Georgia has reciprocal agreements with AL, AK, CO, FL, ID, IN, KY, LA, MI, MS, MO, MT, NH, NC, OK, PA, SD, TN, TX, UT, and WY. In addition, Arizona honors GA licenses. Visitors do not need licenses to carry concealed or openly in AK and VT. For latest information, call, write, or check web site of the Georgia Attorney General at <www.state.ga.us/ago/> under Media Advisories.

Active licenses: No statewide figures are kept.

IDAHO

Effective date: Non-discretionary system adopted in 1990.

Administered by: County sheriffs.

License cost and duration: $20, plus some administrative costs (in Ada County, administrative costs are $36, for a total of $56); license lasts for five years; renewal $12 plus (in Ada County $5) administrative costs.

Apply to: Sheriff in county of residence. The Idaho Attorney General's Office has a list of frequently asked questions and answers about the concealed-weapons law at <http://www2.state.id.us/ag/> The office is at 700 West State Street, P.O. Box 83720, Boise, ID 83720-0010. Telephone: 208-334-2400. Ada County Sheriff's Office in Boise can answer questions for out-of-state license holders planning to visit Idaho. Contact: Ada County Sheriff's Office, Attention: Concealed Weapons, 7200 Barrister Drive, Boise, ID 83704. Telephone: 208-577-3112.

Qualifications: Legal resident of the U.S.; 21 years or older, but a sheriff has discretion to issue license to an applicant between 18 and 21; eligible to possess a firearm under federal and state law; not charged with, or convicted of, a felony; not a fugitive from justice; not an unlawful user or addict of drugs; not judged lacking mental capacity, mentally ill, gravely disabled, or incapacitated; not dishonorably discharged from the military; not judged guilty of a violent misdemeanor unless three years have elapsed since disposition or pardon; not subject of a withheld judgment that would disqualify; has not renounced U.S. citizenship; not awaiting trial, appeal or sentencing for a crime that would disqualify; not the subject of a protective order.

Training course: A sheriff may require proof of familiarity with a firearm by completion of any of a wide variety of training courses or other means.

Carry prohibitions: Courthouses; juvenile detention facilities or jails; adult correctional facilities; prisons; jails; public or private schools, or school buses; the Idaho State Capitol Mall. Other federal, state, or local governmental entities may restrict carrying weapons on their premises. Permit holders may not carry while under the influence of alcohol or drugs.

Reciprocity: Idaho honors any valid concealed-carry license issued in another state. Idaho licenses are honored by AL, AK, AZ, AR, CO, FL, GA, IN, KY, LA, MI, MO, MT, NH, NC, ND, OH, OK, PA, SD, TN, TX, UT, VA, and WY. Visitors do not need licenses to carry concealed or openly in AK and VT.

Active licenses: 48,364 as of August 22, 2007.

License holders as a percentage of state population: 3.30.

INDIANA

Effective date: 1935.

Administered by: Superintendent of the Indiana State Police.

License cost and duration: Indiana issues qualified licenses for hunting or target shooting and unlimited licenses for protection of life and property. An unlimited license, issued for four years, costs $40, or for the lifetime of the applicant, $125. Cost of a lifetime license for a person who has a four-year license is $100.

Apply to: Chief of police or county sheriff where applicant resides; if applicant is non-resident in Indiana but has a regular place of business or employment in the state, apply to sheriff in county of employment. A non-resident may not be issued a lifetime license. For non-resident inquiries, call or write to: Indiana State Police, Firearms Section, 100 North Senate Avenue, Room 302, Indianapolis, IN 46204. Telephone: 317-232-8264. Concealed-handgun laws can be found at: <www.state.in.us/legislative/ic/code/title35/ar47/>

Qualifications: Has a proper reason for carrying a handgun (includes protection of life and property); is of good character and reputation; is a proper person to be licensed; is a

U.S. citizen, or if not a U.S. citizen, is allowed to carry a firearm under federal law; 18 years or older; not convicted of a felony; is not under 23 years if previously adjudicated a delinquent child for an act that would be a felony if committed by an adult; not convicted for resisting law enforcement in last five years; not convicted of domestic battery; no unresolved indictments for a Class A or B felony or a violent felony; not an alcohol or drug abuser; not prone to violence or emotionally unstable conduct; not mentally incompetent.

Training course: Not required.

Carry prohibitions: School property, school functions, or school buses.

Reciprocity: Indiana recognizes concealed-handgun licenses from all other states. Indiana licenses are honored by AL, AK, AZ, AR,CO, FL, GA, ID, KY, LA, MI, MO, MT, NH, NC, ND, OK, SD, TN, TX, UT, and WY. Visitors do not need licenses to carry concealed or openly in AK and VT.

Active unlimited licenses: 274,263 as of August 29, 2007.

License holders as a percentage of state population: 4.34.

KANSAS

Effective date: January 1, 2007.

Administered by: Kansas Attorney General's office and local sheriffs.

License cost and duration: $150 for four years; renewal $100.

Apply to: Local sheriff in county of residence. For more information contact: Concealed Carry Handgun Unit, Office of the Attorney General, 120 SW Tenth Avenue, Topeka, KS 66612. Telephone: 785-291-3765. <www.ksag.org>

Qualifications: Resident of Kansas for at least six months, at least 21 years of age; does not suffer from a physical infirmity which prevents safe handling of a handgun; not convicted or placed on diversion for a felony or the juvenile equivalent of a felony; not convicted or placed on diversion in five years preceding application for a misdemeanor involving various offences, including drugs and domestic violence; not currently charged with an offence that would make applicant ineligible for a license if convicted; has not been ordered by a court to receive treatment for mental illness, alcohol or drug dependency unless treatment completed more than five years prior to application; desires a legal means to carry a concealed weapon for self defense; completed an approved safety and training course; not judged disabled for obtaining a guardian or conservator, unless capacity restored three or more years prior to application; has not been dishonorably discharged from the military; is a U.S. citizen; is not subject to a restraining order; is not in contempt of court in a child-support proceeding; passes a criminal background check.

Training course: Eight-hour approved training course that includes safety and storage of handguns; instruction in the laws concerning concealed carry and the use of deadly force; a range course.

Carry prohibitions: Buildings with signs prohibiting the carrying of handguns; any police, sheriff, or highway patrol station; any detention facility, prison, or jail; any courthouse or courtroom; any polling place on election day; any meeting of local government; on the state fair grounds; any state office building; any athletic event not involving firearms sponsored by schools or colleges; any professional athletic event not involving firearms; any drinking establishment, but not including restaurants; any school, college, or university; any place where carrying firearms is prohibited by state or federal law; any child exchange or visitation center; any mental-health center or hospital; any city hall; any public library; any day-care home, preschool, or childcare center; any church or temple; federal lands and facilities; casinos; race tracks; state parks if posted; places defined as "common nuisances" where illegal activities relating to gambling, prostitution, obscenity, illegal drugs, alcohol, tobacco, criminal street gangs, or pyrotechnics occur. Tribal lands are independently governed and state law does not apply. It is illegal to carry a handgun while under the influence of alcohol or drugs. Except for federal property, parking lots cannot be posted.

Requirements: When stopped by a law enforcement officer and asked if the license holder is armed or has a concealed-carry license, the license holder is required to produce the license.

Reciprocity: Kansas honors concealed-carry licenses from the following states, provided the license holder is a resident of that state: AK, AZ, AR, CO, FL, HI, KY, LA, MI, MN, MO, NE, NV, NJ, NM, NC, OH, OK, SC, TN, TX, and WV. Kansas licenses are recognized in AK, AZ, AR, CO, FL, ID, IN, KY, LA, MI, MN, MO, MT, NC, OK, SC, SD, TN, TX, and UT. Visitors do not need licenses to carry concealed or openly in AK or VT. For latest information call, write, or check web site.

Active licenses: 8,958 as of August 1, 2007.

License holders as a percentage of state population: 0.32.

KENTUCKY

Effective date: October 1, 1996.

Administered by: Kentucky State Police.

License cost and duration: $60 for five years; renewals $60.

Apply to: Local sheriff in county of residence. For information contact: Kentucky State Police, Information Services, 1250 Louisville Road, Frankfort, KY 40601. Telephone: 502-227-8700. <www.kentuckystatepolice.org/conceal.htm>

Qualifications: Be a U.S. citizen; resident of the state for at least six months; 21 years or older; eligible to possess a firearm under state and federal law; not convicted of or under indictment for a felony; not be a fugitive from justice; not an unlawful user of or addicted to any controlled substance; not been judged a mental defective or committed to a mental institution; not discharged from the military under dishonorable conditions; not subject to a domestic violence order or emergency protective order; not convicted of a misdemeanor of domestic violence; not been committed to a drug treatment facility or convicted of a misdemeanor relating to illegal drugs in the last three years; not have two or more convictions for operating a vehicle while impaired by alcohol or drugs in the previous three years; not been committed as an alcoholic within the last three years; not owe a year or more in child support; have complied with any subpoena or warrant relating to child support or paternity; not convicted of misdemeanor assault in the fourth degree or of terroristic threatening within previous three years; complete firearms training and safety course.

Training course: An approved firearms-training and safety course that includes instruction in handgun marksmanship principles, handgun safety and cleaning, laws relating to firearms and use of deadly force, and a range course of 20 rounds at a silhouette target at seven yards.

Carry prohibitions: Police stations or sheriffs' offices; detention facilities, prisons, or jails; courthouses or courtrooms; meetings of the governing bodies of counties, municipalities, or special districts; meetings of the General Assembly or its committees; anywhere alcohol is served by the drink, except for restaurants that make more income from the sale of food; schools, child-care facilities, day-care centers, or certified family-child-care homes; secure areas of airports; places where carrying firearms is prohibited by federal law. Employers, managers, and property owners have the right to prohibit the carrying of firearms on their property.

Reciprocity: Kentucky honors all valid concealed-carry licenses issued in other states. Kentucky licenses are recognized by AL, AK, AZ, AR, CO, DE, FL, GA, ID, IN, KS, LA, MI, MN, MS, MO, MT, NH, NM, NC, ND, OH, OK, PA, SD, TN, TX, UT, VA, WV, and WY. Visitors do not need licenses to carry concealed or openly in AK and VT.

Active licenses: 95,638 as of August 27, 2007.

License holders as a percentage of state population: 2.27.

LOUISIANA

Effective date: September 20, 1996.

Administered by: Louisiana Department of Public Safety and Corrections.

License cost and duration: $100 for four years or $50 for two years. Renewals: $100 for four years or $50 for two years. Senior citizens aged 65 or older pay half fees for initial license and renewals. Applicants who have not lived in the state for 15 years may be charged an additional $50 for a criminal record check.

Apply to: Louisiana State Police, Concealed Handgun Permit Section, P.O. Box 66375, Baton Rouge, LA 70896. Telephone 225-925-4867. <www.lsp.org/handguns.html>

Qualifications: Legal resident of the state for at least six months; 21 years or older; pass approved handgun safety and training course or other evidence of handgun competence such as proof of military or law-enforcement academy small-arms training or possession of a current local concealed-carry permit; not suffering from mental or physical infirmity that prevents safe handgun handling; pass criminal-record check; not convicted of a felony; not committed to an institution for abuse of a controlled dangerous substance or guilty of or charged with a misdemeanor relating to the abuse of a controlled substance in preceding five years; not a chronic abuser of alcohol; not guilty of a violent misdemeanor unless five years have elapsed since court-imposed conditions fulfilled; not guilty of or charged with any crime of violence or crime punishable by one year or more of imprisonment; not a fugitive from justice; not an addict or unlawful user of marijuana, depressants, stimulants, or narcotics; not judged mentally deficient or committed to a mental institution; not having a history of engaging in violent behavior; not discharged from the military under other than honorable conditions; eligible to possess a firearm under federal law.

Training course: One of several approved handgun safety and training courses. The Department of Public Safety and Corrections course includes: one hour instruction on handgun nomenclature and safe-handling procedures; one hour on ammunition knowledge and fundamentals of pistol shooting; one hour on handgun-shooting positions; three hours on the use of deadly force and relevant laws; one hour on child-access prevention; two hours of range shooting and proper handgun-cleaning procedures, including 12 rounds and a safe reload at each of 6, 10, and 15 feet.

Carry prohibitions: Any facilities, buildings, locations, zones, or areas in which firearms are banned by local, state, or federal law; any law-enforcement offices, stations, or buildings; detention facilities, prisons, or jails; courthouses or court-

rooms; polling places; meeting places of governing authorities of political subdivisions; state Capitol building; secure
areas of airports; churches, synagogues, mosques, or similar places of worship; government-permitted parades or demonstrations; any part of establishments licensed to sell alcohol
for consumption on the premises; any school "firearm-free
zones"; private residences, unless the permittee first receives
permission; any other properties or premises where access
by those possessing concealed handguns is restricted by
the property owner, lessee, or custodian. May not carry
while under the influence of alcohol or drugs.

Requirements: Permit holder must produce the license when
requested by a police officer. When approached by a police officer in an official capacity, the permit holder must inform the
officer that he or she is armed and submit to a pat-down search.

Reciprocity: Louisiana has reciprocal agreements with AL,
AK, AZ, AR, CO, FL, GA, ID, IN, KS, KY, MI, MS, MO, MT,
NH, NC, ND, OK, PA, SC, SD, TN, TX, UT, VA, WA, and WY.
In addition MN honors Louisiana licenses. Visitors do not
need licenses to carry concealed or openly in AK and VT.

Active licenses: 14,084 as of August 28, 2007.

License holders as a percentage of state population: 0.32.

MAINE

Effective date: Concealed-carry law took effect: prior to 1977,
but current law passed in 1989, with amendments in 1991
and 1993.

Administered by: Maine State Police in 244 small towns and
unorganized territories and police departments in larger towns
and cities.

License cost and duration: $35 for four years; $20 to renew; non-
residential, $60, issued by Maine State Police.

Apply to: Local police department or Maine State Police,
Gaming & Weapons Section, 164 State House Station,
Augusta, ME 04333-0164. Telephone: 207-624-7210.
<http://www.state.me.us/dps/msp/> click on Licenses &
Permits, then click on Weapons Permits.

Qualifications: A legal resident of the U.S.; 18 years or older; of
good moral character; pass criminal-record check; not prohibited

from possessing firearms under state or federal law; not convicted of or currently charged with a felony; not convicted of
or currently charged with a misdemeanor involving use of a
dangerous weapon against another person; not subject of a
restraining order regarding harassing, stalking, or threatening
in a domestic situation; not a fugitive from justice; not a drug
abuser; not mentally unstable or incapacitated; not found
not guilty of a felony by means of mental disease or defect; not
dishonorably discharged from the military in the last five
years; not convicted in past five years of possession of a
firearm on premises licensed for liquor consumption.

Training course: Applicants are required to demonstrate a
knowledge of handgun safety by taking a course in last five years
or by having received basic firearms training in the military.

Carry prohibitions: Schools, colleges, and other educational facilities; wildlife sanctuaries; at labor disputes; places licensed
for on-premises consumption of liquor; in the Capitol area,
including the legislature and state offices; courthouses; and
on federal property.

Requirements: A license holder carrying a concealed handgun
is required to display the license on request of a law enforcement officer.

Reciprocity: Maine has no agreements for concealed-carry license
reciprocity with other states. However, as of September
2007 the Maine Attorney General's Office was researching
the possibility of negotiating reciprocity with other states.
At this time the state will not recognize out-of-state licenses,
but it will issue Maine licenses to qualified applicants living
in other states. Other states that honor Maine licenses are AK,
AZ, ID, IN, KY, MI, MO, OK, SD, TN, and UT. Visitors do
not need licenses to carry concealed or openly in AK and VT.

Active licenses: No statewide figures are kept.

MICHIGAN

Effective date: July 1, 2001.

Administered by: Michigan county gun boards and Michigan
State Police.

License cost and duration: Initial license is $105 and is valid
for four years plus the number of days to applicant's next birthday; renewals are $105 for five years.

Apply to: Applications are available from local sheriffs, police
departments, or county clerks. Completed applications
should be filed with county clerks. Licenses are issued by county
gun boards. For more information, contact the Michigan State
Police Headquarters, 714 South Harrison Road, East Lansing,
MI 48823; telephone 517-332-5518.

<www.michigan.gov/msp/> click on Licensing & Permits.

Qualifications: At least 21 years old; U.S. citizen or legal resident; resident in Michigan for at least six months; completed
safety-training course; not subject to an order or disposition
involving mental health, legal incapacitation, involuntary hospitalization, or found not guilty by reason of insanity; not
subject to a conditional bond release where firearm possession
is prohibited; not subject to a personal protection order; not
a felon in possession of a firearm; never convicted of a
felony; no felony charge pending; not been dishonorably discharged from the U.S. armed forces; not convicted of any of
17 misdemeanors, many of them involving firearms or violence, in the eight years preceding application; not convicted
of any one of 25 other misdemeanors for three years prior
to application; not found not guilty but mentally ill or
acquitted by reason of insanity; never committed due to mental illness; not currently diagnosed with mental illness; not
under a court order for legal incapacity.

Training course: Program certified by national or state firearms-
training organization and includes safe storage, handling, and
use of a handgun; ammunition knowledge and fundamentals of pistol shooting; shooting positions; firearms
law including civil liability; avoiding criminal attack and controlling a violent confrontation; concealed-handgun laws.
At least eight hours of instruction, including three hours of
range time with a minimum of 30 rounds fired.

Carry prohibitions: Schools or school property, except in a vehicle for a parent dropping off or picking up a child; public or
private day-care centers, child-caring or placing agencies; sports
arenas or stadiums; taverns where the primary source of income

is from alcohol sold by the glass for consumption on the premises; property or facilities owned by churches or other places of worship, unless specifically permitted by presiding officials; entertainment facilities with seating capacity of more than 2,500; hospitals; dormitories, or classrooms of community colleges, colleges, or universities; casinos; courtrooms, offices, or other spaces used for official court business or by judicial employees. May not carry while under the influence of alcohol or drugs. Parking lots of the above "pistol-free zones" are not considered part of these zones.

Requirements: If stopped by a police officer, a license holder is required immediately to inform the officer that he or she is armed or that there is a firearm in the vehicle.

Reciprocity: Michigan will recognize valid concealed-pistol permits from all other states. Michigan concealed-pistol permits are recognized in AL, AK, AZ, AR, CO, DE, FL, GA, ID, IN, KS, KY, LA, MN, MS, MO, MT, NH, NM, NC, ND, OH, OK, PA, SC, SD, TN, TX, UT, VA, and WY. Visitors do not need licenses to carry concealed or openly in AK and VT.

Active licenses: 148,751 as of August 1, 2007.

License holders as a percentage of state population: 1.47

MINNESOTA

Effective date: Handgun-carry law was reenacted on May 25, 2005; previous law took effect May 28, 2003, but was ruled unconstitutional on July 13, 2004. A license holder under the Personal Protection Act may carry a handgun in the open or concealed.

Administered by: County sheriffs. For more information, contact your local county sheriff or any sheriff for non-residents. Some information, including reciprocity agreements with other states, can be found through the Minnesota Department of Public Safety, Bureau of Criminal Apprehension, 1430 Maryland Avenue East, St. Paul, MN 55106. Telephone 651-793-7000. <www.dps.state.mn.us>

License cost and duration: A fee not to exceed $100 for a first license or $75 for a renewal; the license is valid for five years.

Apply to: Sheriff in county of residence.

Qualifications: Has received training in the safe use of a pistol; 21 years of age or older; is a citizen or legal resident of the U.S.; is eligible to possess a firearm under state and federal law; is not listed in the state's criminal gang investigative database; passes a criminal record check.

Training course: Completion of an approved training course that includes the fundamentals of pistol use; a range course; the legal aspects of carrying and using a pistol in self defense; restrictions on the use of deadly force.

Carry prohibitions: On the property of schools; child-care centers when children are present; on school buses; where it is against state or federal law, including the state legislature, courthouses, airports, federal property, prisons, and jails. Private-property owners or tenants, private employers or business entities have the right to prohibit concealed handguns from their premises, but not from parking facilities.

Requirements: Upon request of a peace officer, a permit holder must disclose to the officer whether or not the permit holder is carrying a firearm.

Reciprocity: Minnesota honors concealed-carry licenses from AK, AR, KS, KY, LA, MI, MO, NM, NV, OH, OK, TN, TX, UT, and WY. The following states recognize Minnesota concealed-carry licenses: AK, AZ, ID, IN, KS, KY, MI, MO, MT, NM, OK, SD, TN, UT, and VA. Visitors do not need licenses to carry concealed or openly in AK and VT.

Active licenses: 48,,396 residential licenses as of August 31, 2007 plus 393 issued to out-of-state residents, a total of 48,789.

Residential license holders as a percentage of state population: 0.94

MISSISSIPPI

Effective date: July 1, 1991.

Administered by: Mississippi Department of Public Safety.

License cost and duration: $127 for four years; renewal $77.

Apply to: Mississippi Department of Public Safety, Firearm Permits Unit, P.O. Box 958, Jackson, MS 39205. Telephone: 601-987-1586. <www.dps.state.ms.us> click on Firearm Permits Unit. Application forms are available at any one of nine substations of the Mississippi Highway Patrol.

Qualifications: Resident of the state for 12 months; 21 years or
older; not suffering from a physical infirmity preventing safe
handling of a handgun; pass a criminal-record check; not convicted of a felony; not a habitual illegal drug or alcohol abuser
in last three years; has not been judged mentally incompetent or committed to a mental institution or has waited five
years since restoration of competency; has not been voluntarily
or involuntarily committed to a mental institute or treatment
facility unless in possession of a certificate from a psychiatrist that states the applicant has not suffered from disability for five years; has not been judged guilty of a felony where
sentence suspended or withheld unless three years have
elapsed since fulfillment of court conditions; not a fugitive
from justice; not disqualified from possessing a firearm
under federal law. License may be denied for conviction of
violent misdemeanor if three years have not elapsed since
completion of conditions set by the court.

Training course: Not required.

Carry prohibitions: Any "place of nuisance," which is defined
as a brothel; law-enforcement facilities; prisons, jails, or
detention facilities; courthouses or courtrooms; polling
places; meeting places of any governmental entity, including the legislature or its committees; public parks; school,
college, or professional athletic events; bars where alcohol
is served; schools, colleges, or universities; passenger terminals
of airports; churches or places of worship; places where
carrying handguns is prohibited by federal law; parades or
demonstrations; premises where signs prohibiting firearms
are posted by the management.

Requirements: A license holder must display the license and proper
identification upon demand of a law enforcement officer.

Reciprocity: Mississippi has reciprocity agreements with AL,
AK, CO, FL, GA, KY, LA, MI, MT, NH, NC, OK, SD, TN, TX,
UT, WA, and WY. In addition, Mississippi concealed-carry
licenses are recognized in AZ, AR, ID, IN, and MO. For
latest information, call, write, or check web site. Visitors do
not need licenses to carry concealed or openly in AK and VT.

Active licenses: approximately 47,500 as of August 29, 2007.

License holders as a percentage of state population: 1.63.

MISSOURI

Effective date: February 26, 2004.

Administered by: County sheriffs. For more information, contact your local county sheriff or any sheriff for non-residents. For reciprocity information, check with the Missouri Attorney General's Office, Supreme Court Building, 207 West High Street, P.O. Box 899, Jefferson City, MO 65102. Telephone 573-751-3321. <www.ago.mo.gov> click on Law Enforcement, then click on Concealed Carry Reciprocity.

License cost and duration: A fee not to exceed $100 for a first license or $50 for a renewal; the license is valid for three years. The license takes the form of an endorsement on the applicant's driver's license or on a separate non-driver's license. Most applicants opt for the separate license.

Apply to: Sheriff in county of residence.

Qualifications: Has received training in the safe use of a pistol; 23 years of age or older; is a U.S. citizen and has been a resident of Missouri for at least six months, or is a member of the armed forces stationed in the state, or is the spouse of such a member; has not been convicted of a felony or a misdemeanor involving certain weapons violations; has not been convicted of a violent misdemeanor within five years of application; has not been convicted of two or more misdemeanors of driving under the influence of alcohol or drugs, or possession or abuse of drugs within five years of application; is not a fugitive from justice or charged with a felony or misdemeanor involving certain weapons violations; has not been discharged dishonorably from the military; has not engaged in a documented pattern of behavior that causes the sheriff to believe the applicant presents a danger to himself or others; has not been adjudged mentally incompetent within the preceding five years or has not been committed to a mental health facility; is not the respondent of a full order of protection still in effect; passes a criminal record check.

Training course: A training course of at least eight hours conducted by a certified instructor to include safety and handling of revolvers and semi-automatics, principles of marksmanship, care and cleaning, safe storage, laws related to concealed carry and the justifiable use of force, and a live-fire exercise.

Carry prohibitions: Any law enforcement facility; within 25 feet of polling places on election day; any adult or juvenile detention facility, prison, or jail; courthouses, courtrooms, or court offices; any meeting of the governing body of a unit of local government or meeting of the General Assembly or any of its committees; any government or private premises posted as prohibiting concealed weapons; any establishment licensed to dispense "intoxicating liquor or non-intoxicating beer" for consumption on the premises, but not including restaurants capable of serving at least 50 persons provided they make more than 51 percent of their revenue from the sale of food; the secure areas of airports; anywhere carrying a firearm is prohibited by federal law; any school or facility of higher education; any child-care facility; any riverboat gambling operation; any gated area of an amusement park; any church or place of worship without consent of the minister; any sports arena or stadium with a seating capacity of 5,000 or more; any hospital. It is legal to leave a handgun in a vehicle when visiting most of the above locations, provided it is not brandished.

Reciprocity: Missouri recognizes any concealed-weapons license or permit issued by any other state or political subdivision of another state. Missouri license endorsements are honored by AL, AK, AZ, AR, CO, DE, FL, GA, ID, IN, KS, KY, LA, MI, MN, MT, NH, NM, NC, ND, OH, OK, PA, SC, SD, TN, TX, UT, and VA. Visitors do not need licenses to carry concealed or openly in AK and VT.

Active licenses: 36,105 as of August 3, 2007.

License holders as a percentage of state population: 0.62.

MONTANA

Effective date: Montana has regulated carrying of concealed weapons since 1919; the law was changed to be non-discretionary in 1991.

Administered by: County sheriffs.

License cost and duration: $50 for four years; renewal $25.

Apply to: Sheriff of county in which applicant resides. For more information, contact: Montana Department of Justice, P.O. Box 201401, Helena, MT 59620. Telephone: 406-444-2026. click on Law Enforcement, then on Concealed Weapons.

Qualifications: Resident of the state for six months, a U.S. citizen; 18 years or older; has a Montana driver's license or other state-issued photo identification; eligible under state and federal law to possess a firearm; no unresolved felony charges; no felony or violent-crime conviction; no conviction for carrying concealed under the influence or in a prohibited place in last five years; no warrant for arrest; not judged an unlawful abuser of drugs or alcohol and under state supervision; not judged mentally ill, defective, or disabled; not dishonorably discharged from the military.

Training course: No particular course, but applicant must demonstrate competency by completing firearms, hunter-safety, or similar course.

Carry prohibitions: Buildings leased or owned by state, federal, or local governments; banks or other financial institutions; schools; rooms where alcohol is sold, dispensed, or consumed on the premises. Local governments can regulate the wearing of firearms at public assemblies, public buildings, and parks. It is illegal to carry while intoxicated.

Reciprocity: Montana honors concealed-carry licenses from all states that require a criminal-record check before issuing licenses. These are AK, AZ, AR, CA, CO, CT, FL, GA, ID, IN, IA, KS, KY, LA, MD, MA, MI, MN, MS, MO, NB, NV, NJ, NM, NY, NC, ND, OH, OK, OR, PA, SC, SD, TN, TX, UT, VA, WA, WV, and WY. Montana licenses are recognized by AK, AZ, AR, CO, FL, GA, ID, IN, KY, LA, MI, MS, MO, NM, NC, ND, OK, PA, SD, TN, TX, UT, VA, and WY. Visitors do not need licenses to carry concealed or openly in AK and VT. For latest information, call, write, or check web site.

Active licenses: 15,336 as of August 29, 2007.

License holders as a percentage of state population: 1.62.

NEBRASKA

Concealed-carry law took effect: January 3, 2007.

Administered by: Nebraska State Patrol.

License cost and duration: $100 for five years; renewal $50.

Apply to: Nebraska State Patrol at the Criminal Identification Division in Lincoln or at any troop area headquarters outside Lincoln. For more information contact: Criminal Identification Division, 233 South Tenth Street, Suite 101, Lincoln, NE 68508. Telephone: 402-471-4545.
<www.nsp.state.ne.us>

Applicant qualifications: Be at least 21 years old; not prohibited from buying or possessing a handgun under federal law; possess eyesight required for a Class O operator's driver's license; not convicted of a felony; not currently judged mentally incompetent or mentally ill and dangerous in the past 10 years; resident of Nebraska for at least 180 days; had no violations relating to firearms or drugs in the past 10 years; not be on parole, probation, house arrest, or work release for any offense; be a U.S. citizen; pass approved training course; pass criminal background check.

Training course: Conducted by an approved instructor that includes ways to avoid criminal attack, defuse or control a violent confrontation; safe handling of handguns and ammunition; safe-storage practices, including practices to prevent injury to children; shooting fundamentals; knowledge of laws affecting purchase, ownership, transportation, and possession of handguns; knowledge of laws pertaining to use of deadly force; a range-qualification course of 30 rounds; a written test of 30 questions.

Places license holders may not carry: Any law-enforcement station or office; any detention facility, prison, or jail; courtroom or building containing a courtroom; polling place during an election; meeting of the governing body of a county, public-school district, municipality, or other political subdivision; meeting of the legislature or any of its committees; financial institutions, professional, semi-professional, or collegiate athletic events; schools, school grounds, school-owned vehicles, school-sponsored activities, or athletic events; colleges or universities; places of worship; hospitals, emergency rooms, or trauma centers; political rallies or fund raisers; establishment having a liquor license which derives more than half of its income from the sale of alcohol; any place where carrying a firearm is prohibited by state or federal law. Business owners, employers, and ordinary citizens have the right to prohibit concealed handguns in their premises or vehicles by posting conspicuous signs or by verbal notification. However, private businesses cannot exclude handguns from their parking lots.

Requirements: A permit holder carrying a concealed handgun who is officially contacted by a peace officer or emergency-services personnel must immediately inform them of the handgun, unless physically unable to do so.

Reciprocity: There is no provision in the current law for honoring other states' licenses. Other states that recognize Nebraska licenses are AK, AZ, ID, IN, KS, KY, MI, MO, MT, OK, SD, TN, TX, and UT. Visitors do not need licenses to carry concealed or openly in AK and VT. For latest information, call, write, or check web site.

Active licenses: 2,109 as of August 30, 2007.

License holders as a percentage of state population: 0.12.

NEVADA

Effective date: October 1, 1995.

Administered by: Local county sheriffs.

License cost and duration: Up to $105 for five years; renewal $70. Nevada issues licenses to out-of-state residents at the same cost as for residents, but the license is good for three years.

Apply to: Local sheriff's office in county of residence. Licenses are issued by the Las Vegas Metropolitan Police Department for Clark County residents and for out-of-state residents who passed the required training course in that county. Information is available through LVMPD, CCW Detail, 5880 Cameron Street, Las Vegas, NV 89118. Telephone: 702-828-3996. <www.lvmpd.com> click on Permits, then click on Concealed Firearms Permits.

Qualifications: Resident of the county of application or out-of-state resident; 21 years or older; demonstrated competence by passing a training course; pass a criminal record check; no outstanding warrant for arrest; not convicted of a felony; not convicted of a violent misdemeanor in last three years; not convicted of a crime involving domestic violence or stalking; not subject to a restraining or protective order to prevent domestic violence; not on probation or parole; not been subject in the last five years to any conditions set by a court in lieu of a felony conviction; not judicially declared incompetent or insane; not admitted to a mental health facility in last five years; not an abuser of alcohol or drugs; no pending criminal charges; eligible to possess firearms under state and federal law.

Training course: Any approved training course that includes instruction in the use of the handguns to be carried, in Nevada laws governing the proper use of firearms, and including a 30-round range test. The make, model, and caliber of any gun to be carried must be listed on the permit, and the applicant has to qualify with each gun.

Carry prohibitions: Law-enforcement facilities; prisons, jails, or detention facilities; courthouses or courtrooms; schools, colleges, or other educational facilities; any buildings owned or occupied by any level of government; any other places prohibited by state or federal law; public buildings with metal detectors at each public entrance or that are posted as prohibiting the carrying of firearms on premises; public buildings on the property of a public airport.

Requirements: A permit holder carrying a concealed handgun is required to display the permit and proper identification on the request of a peace officer.

Reciprocity: Nevada honors concealed-handgun licenses from AK, AR, KS, LA, MO, NB, TN, and UT. Nevada licenses are recognized by AK, AZ, ID, IN, KS, KY, MI, MN, MO, MT, OK, SD, TN, TX, and UT.

Active licenses: Statewide figures not kept.

NEW HAMPSHIRE

Effective date: Prior to 1977.

Administered by: Local police departments, mayors, and selectmen for residents; New Hampshire State Police for non-residents.

License cost and duration: License costs $10 and expires on applicant's birthday no less than four years after the date of issue. Non-residents $20 for four years, provided they have a concealed-carry license in their own state. For Vermont residents a letter of approval from their local police chief is required.

Apply to: Local police department. For more information, contact: New Hampshire State Police, Permits and Licensing Unit, Room 106, 10 Hazen Drive, Concord, NH 03305. Telephone: 603-271-3575. <www.nh.gov/safety/nhsp> click on Permits and Licensing. New Hampshire firearms laws can be found at <www.state.nh.us/government/laws.html> check under Title 12, Public Safety and Welfare, click on Chapter 159, Pistols and Revolvers.

Qualifications: A suitable person; 18 years or older; not convicted of a misdemeanor of domestic violence; no pending charges; not a drug abuser; not confined for mental disorder; eligible to possess firearms under state and federal law.

Training course: Not required.

Carry prohibitions: Courtrooms or areas used by courts; schools; where posted with signs prohibiting the carrying of handguns; where prohibited by state or federal law.

Reciprocity: New Hampshire has reciprocity agreements with AL, AK, AZ, CO, FL, GA, ID, IN, KY, LA, MI, MS, MO, NC, ND, OK, PA, TN, UT, and WY. New Hampshire honors only licenses issued to residents of the issuing state. In addition, New Hampshire licenses are honored by SD. Visitors do not need licenses to carry concealed or openly in AK and VT.

Licenses currently in use: No statewide figures kept.

NEW MEXICO

Effective date: January 5, 2004.

Administered by: New Mexico Department of Public Safety.

License cost and duration: $100 for four years; renewal $75. There is a requalification requirement of two hours after two years.

For the most up to date information, contact the New Mexico Department of Public Safety, Concealed Handgun Licensing Unit, 6301 Indian School Road N.E., Suite 310, Albuquerque, New Mexico 87110. Telephone: 505-841-8053. <www.dps.nm.org>

Qualifications: U.S. citizen; New Mexico resident or member of the armed forces stationed in New Mexico; 21 years or older; not a fugitive from justice; not convicted of a felony; not under indictment for a felony; not prohibited by federal or state law from possessing a firearm; not been adjudicated mentally incompetent or committed to a mental institution; not addicted to alcohol or controlled substances; completed an approved training course; not convicted of a misdemeanor offense involving a crime of violence within 10 years of making application; not convicted of a misdemeanor of possession or abuse of a controlled substance within 10 years of making application; not convicted of driving under the influence of alcohol or drugs within five years of making application; not convicted of a misdemeanor of family violence.

Training course: Fifteen hours of instruction to include safe handling of handguns; safe storage and child safety; shooting fundamentals; a range test with the category and caliber of handgun to be carried, with minimum caliber being .32; developing and maintaining handgun shooting skills; laws pertaining to use and possession of handguns; avoiding criminal attack and controlling a violent confrontation; nonviolent dispute resolution.

Carry prohibitions: Where it would violate federal or state law; on the premises of a school or pre-school; on tribal land without authorization; in a courthouse or court facility; on private property if posted or notified verbally not to carry.

Reciprocity: New Mexico recognizes licenses from AK, AZ, CO, DE, FL, KY, MI, MN, MO, MT, NC, ND, OH, OK, SC, TN, TX, UT, VA, and WY. New Mexico licenses are honored by AK, AZ, CO, FL, ID, IN, KS, KY, MI, MN, MO, MT, ND, OK, SD, TN, TX, UT, VA, and WY. Visitors do not need licenses to carry concealed or openly in AK and VT.

Active licenses: 10,566 as of August 14, 2007.
License holders as a percentage of state population: 0.54.

NORTH CAROLINA

Effective date: December 1, 1995.
Administered by: Local county sheriffs.
License cost and duration: $90 for five years; renewal $75.
Apply to: Sheriff in county of residence. For more information, contact: Office of the Attorney General, North Carolina Department of Justice, 9001 Mail Service Center, Raleigh, NC 27699-9001. Telephone: 919-716-6400. <www.ncdog.com> click on Crime and Law Enforcement, then Concealed Handguns.
Qualifications: Resident of the state for at least 30 days; U.S. citizen; 21 years or older; eligible under state and federal law to possess a handgun; does not suffer from mental or physical infirmity preventing safe gun handling; completed a firearms training and safety course; not found guilty of a felony or some misdemeanors, even if awarded a suspended sentence or prayer for judgment; no unresolved charges of a felony; not a fugitive from justice; not convicted of impaired driving in last three years; not an addict or user of illegal drugs; not dishonorably discharged from the military; not ruled lacking mental capacity or mentally ill.
Training course: Firearms training and safety course required.
Carry prohibitions: Law-enforcement or correctional facilities; any offices or buildings occupied by state or federal employees; financial institutions; any premises posted as prohibiting firearms by person in control of the premises; educational property; areas of assemblies, parades, funerals, picket lines, and demonstrations; where alcohol is sold and consumed; state-occupied property; state or federal courthouse; legislative buildings; any local government buildings, premises, or parks, if the local government has posted signs prohibiting firearms; in schools or on school grounds. It is illegal to carry when under the influence of alcohol or drugs.
Requirements: Permit holders must carry the permit and valid identification with them when carrying a concealed handgun. If approached or addressed by a law enforcement

officer, they are required to disclose the permit and that they are carrying a gun.

Reciprocity: North Carolina has reciprocal agreements with AL, AK, AZ, AR, CO, DE, FL, GA, ID, IN, KS, KY, MI, MS, MO, MT, NH, ND, OH, OK, PA, SC, SD, TN, TX, UT, VA, WA, and WV. In addition North Carolina licenses are honored in LA. Visitors do not need licenses to carry concealed or openly in AK and VT.

Active licenses: 95,502 as of September 12, 2007.

License holders as a percentage of state population: 1.08.

NORTH DAKOTA

Effective date: Prior to 1977, but current law passed in 1985.

Administered by: Office of Attorney General, Bureau of Criminal Investigation.

License cost and duration: $25 for three years; renewal $25. Licenses are issued to non-residents.

Apply to: Your local law enforcement agency. After local background check is completed, the application will be sent on to the North Dakota Bureau of Criminal Investigation. Non-residents should apply directly to the Bureau of Criminal Investigation. For more information contact the Bureau of Criminal Investigation, Attention: Firearms Permits, P.O. Box 1054, Bismarck, ND 58502-1054. Telephone: 701-328-5500. <www.ag.state.nd.us/> click on Bureau of Criminal Investigation, then Concealed Weapons Permits.

Qualifications: Pass criminal record check; not convicted of a felony involving violence or intimidation in the last 10 years; not convicted of a felony that did not involve violence or intimidation in the last five years; not convicted of a Class A misdemeanor involving violence or intimidation while armed with a firearm or other deadly weapon in the last five years; approval of sheriff or police chief; 18 years or older; no history of mental illness in last three years; not prohibited under federal law from possessing firearms; pass written test.

Training course: To cost no more than $25. Firearm safety and operation; law regarding the license and use of deadly force; open book test of 10 true or false questions.

Carry prohibitions: Licensed liquor establishments; gaming sites; athletic and sporting events; schools and school functions; churches and church functions; political rallies or events; musical concerts; public parks and public buildings; public gatherings.

Requirements: License holder who is armed must show the license to a law-enforcement officer on demand.

Reciprocity: North Dakota has reciprocal agreements with AL, AK, AZ, AR, CO, DE, FL, ID, IN, KY, LA, MI, MO, MT, NH, NM, NC, OK, SD, TN, TX, and UT. In addition, AK, AZ, CO, FL, and TX recognize the North Dakota license only if the holder is at least 21 years old. Also, CO, FL, and TX recognize the license only if the holder is a North Dakota resident. In addition, North Dakota licenses are honored in PA. Visitors do not need licenses to carry concealed or openly in AK and VT.

Active Licenses: 8,364 as of August 30, 2007.

License holders as a percentage of state population: 1.32.

OHIO

Concealed-carry law took effect: April 8, 2004.

Administered by: County Sheriffs.

License cost and duration: The license lasts for four years; it may not cost more than $45 unless the applicant has been an Ohio resident for less than five years and an FBI criminal record check is required. The cost of the FBI check is added to the license cost. Renewal $45. Sheriffs may issue temporary emergency licenses if applicants are in imminent danger.

Apply to: The sheriff in the county where you reside or the sheriff of an adjacent county. For more information, contact the Ohio Attorney General's Office, State Office Tower, 30 East Broad Street, 17th Floor, Columbus, OH 43215. Telephone: 614-466-4320.

Qualifications: Pass criminal record check and mental competency check; a legal resident of the U.S.; resident of the state for at least 45 days and resident of the county or adjacent county for at least 30 days; at least 21 years old; not a fugitive from justice; not under indictment or convicted of a felony; not under indictment, charged with, or convicted of a drug offense; not under indictment, charged with, or convicted of a misdemeanor involving violence in the last three years; not under indictment, charged with, or convicted of resisting arrest in the past 10 years; not under indictment or charged with assault or negligent assault; not convicted of assault or negligent assault twice or more in the last five years; not been convicted of assaulting a peace officer; not been adjudicated a mental defective or mental incompetent, or committed to a mental institution, or found by a court to require involuntary hospitalization for mental illness; not currently subject to a protection order; not prohibited under federal law from possessing firearms; pass training course within last six years.

Training course: Ten hours classroom instruction plus two hours range training by an approved trainer. Applicants receive a government pamphlet covering firearms law, dispute resolution, and use of deadly force. Other course topics include safe handgun and ammunition handling, storage, and shooting.

Carry prohibitions: Rooms or open-air arenas licensed to dispense liquor; school safety zones, school buildings, or school functions; courthouses or buildings containing courts; law-enforcement facilities; prisons, jails, or detention facilities; airport passenger terminals; public or private colleges, universities, or institutes of higher learning, unless locked in a vehicle; churches, synagogues, mosques, or other places of worship; child-day-care homes and centers; commercial aircraft; any buildings or parts of buildings owned or leased by the state or any political subdivision of the state; any place where handguns are prohibited by federal law. Private owners and employers may prohibit concealed handguns on their property or in their vehicles. Public or private premises that prohibit concealed handguns must be posted with signs. It is illegal to carry a concealed handgun while under the influence of alcohol or a drug of abuse.

Requirements: When carrying a handgun in a vehicle, a license holder has a choice. He or she can wear the gun in a holster; put it into a closed case, bag, or box in plain sight; lock it in the glove compartment; or lock it in a case. When stopped by a law-enforcement officer, the license holder is required to keep both hands in plain sight and to have no contact with the handgun unless otherwise instructed by the officer.

Reciprocity: Ohio has reciprocity agreements with AK, AZ, DE, ID, KY, MI, MO, NC, OK, SC, TN, UT, VA, WA, WV, and WY. Check attorney general's web site for latest information. Other states that recognize Ohio licenses are IN, KS, MN, MT, and SD. Visitors do not need licenses to carry concealed or openly in AK and VT.

Active licenses: 97,912 as of June 30, 2007.

License holders as a percentage of state population: 0.85.

OKLAHOMA

Effective date: January 1, 1996.

Administered by: Oklahoma State Bureau of Investigation.

License cost and duration: $100 for five years, plus a fingerprinting fee paid to the local sheriff not to exceed $25; renewal $85.

Apply to: Oklahoma State Bureau of Investigation, Self-Defense Act Licensing Unit, 6600 North Harvey, Oklahoma City, OK 73116. Telephone: 800-207-6724 or 405-848-6724. <www.osbi.state.ok.us/> click on Self-Defense Act. Take completed applications to local sheriff.

Qualifications: U.S. citizen and current legal resident of Oklahoma; at least 21 years of age; complete training course; not convicted of a felony in any jurisdiction; not judged incompetent; not convicted of any of five misdemeanors relating to assault and battery, stalking, domestic abuse or illegal drugs; not attempted suicide or otherwise indicated mental instability within the previous 10 years; not currently undergoing treatment for mental illness; not a habitual criminal; not ineligible under state or federal law to possess a pistol; not subject to an outstanding felony warrant; as a juvenile, not adjudicated as delinquent for a felony-grade offense in the last 10 years. A further list of conditions precludes residents from applying for a license for a specified period of time, usually three years.

Training course: An eight-hour course from an approved instructor for a fee not to exceed $60. Course to include pistol handling, safety and storage; dynamics of ammunition and firing; methods and positions for firing a pistol; laws relating to concealed carry and use of appropriate force; a practice shooting session; no weapon of a caliber larger than .45 may be used. License holder may not carry a semi-automatic unless training course was completed with a semi-automatic.

Carry prohibitions: Bars or establishments where the sale and consumption of alcohol on the premises is the primary business; structures, buildings, or office space owned or leased by any city, town, county, state, or federal government authority for the purpose of doing business with the public; meetings of city, town, county, state, or federal officials, school board members, or other elected or appointed officials; prisons, jails, or detention facilities; elementary, secondary, vocational-technical schools, colleges, or universities; public or private school buses; sports arenas during professional sporting events; places where parimutuel betting is authorized. Business owners, property owners, and employers have the right to control the possession of weapons on their premises, but cannot prevent license-holders from transporting or storing firearms in a locked vehicle in any designated parking lot or area. It is illegal to carry while under the influence of alcohol or drugs.

Requirements: License holders must carry handguns concealed and have their licenses with them while armed. They have a positive duty to immediately disclose to a peace officer that they are carrying a handgun when approached by the officer.

Reciprocity: Oklahoma recognizes any valid concealed-carry weapons permit or license issued by another state. In addition, the following states honor Oklahoma concealed-carry licenses: AL, AK, AZ, AR, CO, DE, FL, GA, ID, IN, KS, KY, LA, MI, MN, MS, MO, MT, NH, NM, NC, ND, OH, PA, SD, TN, TX, UT, VA, WA, and WY. Visitors do not need licenses to carry concealed or openly in AK and VT.

Active licenses: 57,540 as of July 17, 2007.

License holders as a percentage of state population: 1.61.

OREGON

Effective date: Non-discretionary law adopted in 1990.

Administered by: County sheriffs.

License cost and duration: $65 for four years; renewal $50.

Apply to: Sheriff in county of residence. For more information contact your local sheriff's office or the Oregon State Police, Firearms Unit, 3772 Portland Road NE, Salem, OR 97303. Telephone 503-378-3070. <www.leg.state.or.us/ors/166.html> relevant statutes are from 166.291 to 166.297.

Qualifications: U.S. citizen or legal resident alien in the county of application, who has declared in writing to the Citizenship and Immigration Services intent to acquire citizenship; 21 years or older; has a principal residence in the county of application; has no outstanding arrest warrants; is not free on any form of pretrial release; demonstrates competence with handgun; not convicted of a felony; not convicted of a misdemeanor within last four years; not committed to state mental-health division; not found mentally ill or prohibited from possessing a firearm as a result of that illness; not convicted of a misdemeanor of domestic violence.

Training course: Any of various handgun safety courses, or demonstrates competency through organized shooting competition or military service.

Carry prohibitions: Courtrooms, jury rooms, judge's chambers, or adjacent areas; federal buildings and facilities; national parks; airport property; Indian reservations without written permission; public or private property where firearms are prohibited by posted signs.

Reciprocity: Oregon does not honor out-of-state concealed-handgun licenses. States that recognize Oregon licenses are AK, AZ, ID, IN, KY, MI, MO, MT, OK, SD, TN, and UT. Visitors do not need licenses to carry concealed or openly in AK and VT.

Active licenses: 96,005 as of September 4, 2007.

License holders as a percentage of state population: 2.59.

PENNSYLVANIA

Effective date: Pennsylvania changed from discretionary issue of permits to "shall-issue" in 1989 except for Philadelphia; most recent change in the law, effective October 11, 1995, eased restrictions on residents of Philadelphia.

Administered by: County Sheriffs (except in Philadelphia, where the police department issues the licenses) and the Pennsylvania State Police.

License cost and duration: $19 for five years. However, some sheriffs add fees that can more than double the cost.

Apply to: Local sheriff where applicant resides or police department in Philadelphia. For more information, contact: Pennsylvania State Police, Firearms Unit, 1800 Elmerton Avenue, Harrisburg, PA 17110. Telephone: 717-783-5598. For reciprocity, contact Pennsylvania Office of Attorney General, Office of Legislative Affairs, 16th Floor, Strawberry Square, Harrisburg, PA 17120. Telephone: 717-783-3085. <www.attorneygeneral.gov/> click on Crime, click on Firearms. Out-of-state residents who have concealed-handgun licenses from their state of residence may apply for a Pennsylvania license to any sheriff's office.

Qualifications: Of good character and reputation; 21 years or older; legal resident of the U.S.; not charged or convicted of a felony or crime of violence; of sound mind and never committed to a mental institution; not been convicted of a drug offense; not an illegal drug user or habitual drunkard; not dishonorably discharged from the military; not a fugitive from justice; not prevented from possessing a firearm by state or federal law.

Training course: Not required.

Carry prohibitions: Schools; school buses; educational establishments; state parks; courthouses where posted; federal property. In addition, game laws include some restrictions.

Reciprocity: Pennsylvania has written reciprocity agreements with AK, FL, GA, KY, MI, MO, NH, NC, OK, SD, TN, TX, VA, WV, and WY. Pennsylvania has informal reciprocity agreements with CO, ID, LA, MT, ND, and UT. In addition the following states honor Pennsylvania licenses: AZ, AR, ID, IN, MI, MT, OK, and UT. Visitors do not need licenses to carry concealed or openly in AK and VT.

Active licenses: 668,372 as of April 27, 2007.

License holders as a percentage of state population: 5.37.

SOUTH CAROLINA

Effective date: August 24, 1996.

Administered by: South Carolina Law Enforcement Division.

License cost and duration: $50 for four years; renewal $50.

Apply to: Pick up application forms at any sheriff's office, then mail the completed application to South Carolina Law Enforcement Division, Attention: Regulatory Department, P.O. Box 21398, Columbia, SC 29221-1398. Telephone 803-896-7014.

Qualifications: A legal resident of the U.S.; resident of the state for at least 90 days; 21 years or older; pass an approved training course; pass a criminal record check; not prohibited by federal, state, or local law from possessing a firearm; have a "favorable background." A resident of another state who owns real property in South Carolina may apply for a South Carolina license.

Training course: Minimum eight-hour course to include instruction in law relating to handguns and the use of deadly force; handgun use and safety; proper storage, with emphasis on preventing injury to children; range course.

Carry prohibitions: Law enforcement offices or facilities; prisons, jails, or detention facilities or offices; courthouses or courtrooms; polling places on election days; offices or meetings of governing bodies of counties, public school districts, municipalities, or special-purpose districts; school or college athletic events; day-care or preschool facilities; wherever prohibited by federal law; churches or other established religious sanctuaries; hospitals, medical clinics, doctors' offices, or other medical facilities. Public and private employers may prohibit their employees from carrying firearms at work. Private businesses and property owners may prohibit carrying firearms on their property by posting signs: "No Concealable Weapons Allowed." License holders must have express permission to carry concealed handguns into private residences.

Requirements: A license holder who is carrying a concealed handgun is required to present the license to a law-enforcement officer if the officer asks for identification or for the holder's driver's license.

Reciprocity: South Carolina has reciprocity agreements with AK, AR, KS, LA, MI, MO, NC, OH, TN, TX, and WY. In addition, South Carolina licenses are honored in AZ, ID, IN, KY, MT, NM, OK, SD, UT, and VA. Visitors do not need licenses to carry concealed or openly in AK and VT.

Licenses currently in use: 56,715 as of September 5, 2007. About 56 of those were issued to South Carolina property owners who live out of state.

License holders as a percentage of state population: 1.31.

SOUTH DAKOTA

Effective date: Prior to 1977 with most recent amendments in 1995.

Administered by: Local sheriffs and the South Dakota Secretary of State's Office.

License cost and duration: $10 for four years.

Apply to: Sheriff of the county in which applicant resides. For more information, contact: South Dakota Secretary of State's Office, 500 East Capitol Avenue, Pierre, SD 57501-5070. Telephone: 605-773-3537. <www.sdsos.gov/> click on Administrative Services, then on Concealed Pistol Permits.

Qualifications: Resident of the county or municipality where applying for at least 30 days; U.S. citizen; 18 years or older; neither pleaded guilty to, pleaded nolo contendere to, nor been convicted of a felony or crime of violence; not habitually in an intoxicated or drugged condition; has no history of violence; not found in last 10 years to be a danger to self or others; not currently judged mentally incompetent; no weapons or drug violations in the past five years; not a fugitive from justice.

Training course: Not required.

Carry prohibitions: Licensed establishments that derive more than half their income from the sale of alcohol; county courthouses, elementary and secondary schools.

Reciprocity: South Dakota recognizes any valid concealed-handgun permit from another state that is not issued to a South Dakota resident. This includes non-resident licenses from such states as AZ, FL, and UT. It has reciprocity agreements with AL, AK, AZ, CO, FL, GA, ID, IN, KY, LA, MI, MS, MO, MT, NC, ND, OK, PA, TN, TX, UT, and WY. The South Dakota resident must be at least 21 years old for the license to be honored in AK, CO, GA, KY, MI, NC, TN, UT, WV, and WY. In addition South Dakota concealed-handgun licenses are honored in AR. Visitors do not need licenses to carry concealed or openly in AK and VT.

Active licenses: 27,656 as of September 5, 2007.

License holders as a percentage of state population: 3.54.

TENNESSEE

Effective date: A non-discretionary system was adopted in 1994 administered by local sheriffs; the law was amended to give administration to the state, effective October 1, 1996.

Administered by: Tennessee Department of Safety.

License cost and duration: $115 for four years; renewal fee $50.

Apply to: Local drivers' license office. For more information, contact: Handgun Carry Permit Office, Tennessee Department of Safety, 1150 Foster Avenue, Nashville, TN 37243-1000. Telephone: 615 251-8590. <www.state.tn.us/safety/handguns.html>

Qualifications: Legal resident of Tennessee; 21 years or older; not prohibited from possessing a firearm under state or federal law; not convicted of a felony; not currently charged with a felony; not currently subject of a protection order that prohibits applicant from possessing or carrying a firearm; not a fugitive from justice; not addicted to alcohol or drugs; has not been hospitalized for mental illness, alcohol, or drug problems in last 10 years; not judged mentally ill and/or had a conservator appointed by a court by reason of a mental defect; not been found by a court in the last seven years to pose an immediate substantial likelihood of serious harm because of mental illness; not convicted of a misdemeanor of domestic violence; not receiving social security benefits by reason of alcohol or drug dependence or mental disability; not convicted of stalking; not convicted of driving under the influence of an intoxicant twice or more in the last 10 years and no such convictions in the last five years; not renounced U.S. citizenship; not dishonorably discharged from armed forces; pass approved training course.

Training course: Approved course involving classroom and range work.

Carry prohibitions: Anywhere alcohol is sold or served for consumption on premises; during judicial proceedings; public parks, playgrounds, civic centers, and other recreational buildings and grounds; schools, school buses, school property, public or private educational facilities including colleges and universities, unless the handgun remains in a vehicle; churches; where prohibited by individuals, corporations, businesses, or local, state, or federal government entities on their premises when posted or announced.

Reciprocity: Tennessee honors all licenses from other states. It has reciprocal agreements with AK, AZ, AR, FL, GA, KY, LA, MI, MS, NH, OH, PA, NC, SC, SD, TX, VA, and WY. In addition, Tennessee licenses are honored in AL, CO, DE, ID, IN, KS, MN, MO, MT, NM, ND, OK, and UT. For the latest information, call, write, or check web site. Visitors do not need licenses to carry concealed or openly in AK and VT.

Licenses currently in use: 179,356 as of May 8, 2007.

License holders as a percentage of state population: 2.97.

TEXAS

Effective date: January 1, 1996.

Administered by: Texas Department of Public Safety.

License cost and duration: $140 for four years ($70 for senior citizens and indigents); renewal $70 ($35 for senior citizens).

Apply to: Concealed Handgun Licensing Section, Texas Department of Public Safety, P.O. Box 4143, Austin, TX 78765-4143. Telephone: 512-424-7293/4. <www.txdps.state.tx.us/> click on Online Services—Concealed Handgun.

Qualifications: Pass criminal record check—not convicted of, or currently charged with, a felony or with a Class A or B misdemeanor in last five years; not a fugitive from justice; 21 years or older; legal resident of Texas; not chemically dependent or of unsound mind—capable of exercising sound judgement with respect to the proper use and storage of a handgun; not delinquent in paying child support, taxes, or student loan; not currently under a spousal protective or restraining order; qualified under state and federal law to possess a handgun; pass training course.

Training course: Ten to 15 hours of classroom and range instruction covering laws relating to weapons and use of deadly force; handgun use, proficiency, and safety; nonviolent dispute resolution; storage practices particularly regarding child safety; 50-round proficiency test with semi-automatic or revolver of minimum .32 caliber. Applicants who qualify with a semi-auto may carry either action, but those who qualify with a revolver may carry a revolver only.

Carry prohibitions: The premises or buses of schools or educational institutes; polling places; courtrooms or court offices; racetracks; secured areas of airports; correctional facilities; within 1,000 feet of a place of execution on execution day; businesses that derive 51 percent or more of their revenue from the sale of alcohol for on-premises consumption; at high-school, collegiate, or professional sporting events. Provided they are properly signed, hospitals, nursing homes, amusement parks, churches, or places of worship, meetings of governmental entities, and private businesses. Premises do not include parking areas or driveways. It is illegal to carry while intoxicated.

Reciprocity: Texas has reciprocal agreements or effective reciprocity with AL, AK, AZ, AR, CO, DE, FL, GA, ID, IN, KS, KY, LA, MI, MS, MO, MT, NM, NC, ND, OK, PA, SC, SD, TN, UT, VA, and WY. In addition, Texas licenses are honored in MN. Texas recognizes concealed-handgun licenses from CA, CT, HI, IA, MD, MA, NB, NV, NJ, NY, and RI. For the latest information, call, write or check web site. Visitors do not need licenses to carry concealed or openly in AK and VT.

Active licenses: 276,876 as of July 17, 2007.

License holders as a percentage of state population: 1.18.

UTAH

Effective date: May 1, 1995.

Administered by: Department of Public Safety.

License cost and duration: $65.25 for five years; renewal $10. Utah will issue licenses to non-residents.

Apply to: Utah Department of Public Safety, Bureau of Criminal Identification, 3888 West 5400 South, Salt Lake City, UT 84118. Telephone: 801-965-4445. <www.bci.utah.gov/CFP/CFPHome.html> click on Concealed Firearms Permit.

Qualifications: Pass criminal record check—not convicted of a felony or crime involving violence, domestic violence, alcohol, narcotics, moral turpitude; 21 years or older; legal resident of the U.S.; not judged mentally incompetent; pass a firearms familiarity course.

Training course: Handling and safety of firearms; laws concerning use of deadly force, self defense; transportation and concealment of firearms.

Carry prohibitions: Secure areas of airports and federal-government property. Any secure areas in which firearms are prohibited and that are posted. This includes courthouses, courtrooms, mental-health, and correctional facilities. Churches and places of worship if notice is given. Private residences if notice is given. Private businesses may post signs prohibiting firearms, but it is not a criminal offence to ignore them. It is illegal to carry a handgun while intoxicated (standard is 0.08), but there is nothing to prevent a license holder from entering a bar with a concealed handgun.

Requirements: If stopped by a police officer, a permit holder is required to inform the officer that he or she has a permit and is carrying a firearm.

Reciprocity: Utah will honor any permit which has been issued by another state or county. Utah has formal reciprocity with AL, AK, CO, FL, GA, LA, MS, NH, NC, ND, OH, SD, TX, and WA. In addition Utah licenses are recognized by AZ, AR, DE, ID, IN, KY, MI, MN, MO, MT, NM, OK, PA, TN, VA, and WY. For latest information, call, write, or check web site. Visitors do not need licenses to carry concealed or openly in AK and VT.

Active licenses: 64,646 residential as of August 31, 2007, plus 28,347 non-residential licenses for a total of 92,993.

Residential license holders as a percentage of state population: 2.54.

VERMONT

Vermont allows its residents and visitors to carry handguns for protection in the open or concealed without a permit or license. However, some of the larger cities have local ordinances regulating the use and carrying of loaded and/or concealed handguns in their jurisdictions. For more information, contact Vermont State Police Headquarters, 103 South Main Street, Waterbury, VT 05671-2101. Telephone 802-244-8775. <www.dps.state.vt.us/> or the Vermont Attorney General's Office, 109 State Street, Montpelier, VT 05609. Telephone: 802-828-3171. <www.atg.state.vt.us/> Residents must be 16 years or older to possess a firearm unless they have permission from parent or guardian.

Places where firearms may not be carried: On the premises or grounds of state institutions, courthouses, and schools.

VIRGINIA

Effective date: 1988 with amendments July 1, 1995.

Administered by: Virginia State Police and local circuit courts.

License cost and duration: Not to exceed $50 for five years; renewal $50.

Apply to: Clerk of local circuit court of county or city in which applicant resides. For more information, contact: Virginia State Police, Firearms Transaction Center, P.O. Box 85608, Richmond, VA 23285-5608. Telephone: 804-674-2292. <www.vsp.state.va.us/> click on Firearms/Concealed Handguns.

Qualifications: Pass criminal record check; 21 years or older; eligible under state and federal law to possess a handgun; not released from commitment to a mental institution within five years; not had mental competency restored in last five years; not subject to a restraining or protective order; not convicted of two misdemeanors within last five years if one was a Class 1 misdemeanor; not an unlawful user or distributor of illegal drugs; not a habitual drunkard; a legal resident of the U.S.; not having been dishonorably discharged from the military; not a fugitive from justice; not facing a pending charge or conviction for a felony or, within the last three years, a violent misdemeanor; not convicted of a drug charge in the last three years and no such charge pending; not convicted of stalking and no such charge pending; not received mental-health or substance-abuse treatment in a residential setting in past five years.

Training course: Circuit court may require proof that applicant has demonstrated competence with a handgun by completion of one of several firearms safety and training courses or proof of similar training through shooting competition or military service.

Carry prohibitions: Businesses or special events for which licenses have been granted by the Virginia Alcoholic Beverage Control Board to serve alcohol for on-premises consumption; private property where posted or prohibited by the owner; places of religious worship; courthouses; school property; airports. May not carry while under the influence of alcohol or illegal drugs.

Requirements: A permit holder carrying a concealed handgun shall display the permit and government-issued identification on demand of a law-enforcement officer.

Reciprocity: Virginia has formal or informal reciprocity agreements with AK, AZ, AR, FL, KY, LA, MI, MO, MT, NM, NC, OH, OK, PA, TN, TX, UT, and WV. FL and WV do not recognize Virginia non-resident permits. Virginia also honors licenses from MN, SC, WA, and WY. In addition, Virginia licenses are honored in SD. Visitors do not need licenses to carry concealed or openly in AK and VT.

Active licenses: 146,874 as of August 5, 2007. In addition, 1,550 licenses are issued to non-residents of Virginia for a total of 148,424.

Residential license holders as a percentage of state population: 1.92.

WASHINGTON

Effective date: The law changed from discretionary issue of permits to "shall-issue" in 1961; the most recent changes went into effect June 6, 1996.

Administered by: State of Washington, Department of Licensing, Firearms Program, P.O. Box 9649, Olympia, WA 98507-9649. Telephone: 360-664-6616.
<www.wa.gov/dol/bpd/firfront.htm>

License cost and duration: $55.25 for five years; renewal $32.

Apply to: Local sheriff or police chief in incorporated areas, otherwise local sheriff. A non-resident may apply to any police chief or sheriff.

Qualifications: Twenty-one years or older; U.S. citizen or possessor of an alien firearms license from the Department of Licensing; eligible to possess a handgun under state and federal law; pass criminal record check; no convictions or unresolved charges for felonies or domestic violence misdemeanors; not subject to a court order or injunction regarding firearms; never committed to mental institution; no mental conditions that would prevent the applicant from being licensed.

Training course: Not required.

Carry prohibitions: Schools, school vehicles, and facilities being used by schools; law-enforcement facilities; courts; jails; mental institutions; bars.

Reciprocity: Washington has reciprocity agreements with LA, MI, MS, NC, OH, OK, and UT. In addition, Washington licenses are honored by the following states: AK, AZ, ID, IN, KY, MO, MT, SD, TN, TX, and VA. Visitors do not need licenses to carry concealed or openly in AK and VT.

Active licenses: 236,975 as of September 5, 2007.

License holders as a percentage of state population: 3.71.

WEST VIRGINIA

Effective date: Non-discretionary law adopted in 1989; latest amendments effective 1998.

Administered by: Local county sheriffs.

License cost and duration: $75 for five years.

Apply to: Sheriff of county of residence. For more information, contact your local sheriff or the West Virginia State Police, Legal Division, 725 Jefferson Road South, Charleston, WV 25309. Telephone: 304-746-2100. Reciprocity information at <www.wvstatepolice.com> click on Legal Division, then Frequently Asked Questions.

Qualifications: Legal resident of West Virginia; 21 years or older; not addicted to or an illegal user of alcohol or drugs; not convicted of a felony, an act of domestic violence, or an act of violence involving the misuse of a deadly weapon; no unresolved criminal charges pending; not currently serving a sentence of confinement, parole, probation, or other court-ordered supervision due to a charge of domestic violence; not subject to a restraining order as a result of a domestic-violence act; never judged mentally incompetent; not dishonorably discharged from the military; physically and mentally competent to carry and shoot a handgun; qualified to shoot and handle firearms by having completed one of various firearms safety and training courses; qualified under federal and state law to possess firearms.

Training course: Any one of various firearms safety and training courses is required.

Carry prohibitions: Police station or sheriff's office; detention facility, prison, or jail; courthouses, courtrooms, or court proceedings; federal property; school premises or school buses; restricted areas of airports; anywhere carrying a firearm is prohibited by federal law; any private property where the carrying of firearms is posted or prohibited.

Reciprocity: West Virginia has reciprocity with AR, FL, KY, NC, OH, PA, and VA. However, it will honor licenses of residents of those states only. In addition, a West Virginia concealed-carry license is honored in AK, AZ, AR, FL, ID, IN, KS, KY, MI, MO, MT, NC, OH, OK, PA, SD, TN, UT, and VA. Visitors do not need licenses to carry concealed or openly in Alaska and Vermont.

Licenses currently in use: statewide figures not available.

WYOMING

Effective date: October 1, 1994.

Administered by: Attorney General, Division of Criminal Investigation.

License cost and duration: $74 for five years; renewal $50.

Apply to: Local county sheriff. For more information, contact: Wyoming Division of Criminal Investigation, Attn: Concealed Firearms Permits, 316 West 22nd Street, Cheyenne, WY 82002. Telephone: 307-777-7181. <attorneygeneral.state.wy.us/dci/>

Qualifications: Pass criminal record check—no felony or drug convictions; 21 years or older; resident of Wyoming for at least six months; does not suffer from a physical infirmity that would preclude safe handgun handling; not a chronic abuser of alcohol; has not been judged incompetent or committed to a mental institution; demonstrate familiarity with firearm; eligible to possess firearms under federal and state law. Violent misdemeanor convictions in last three years may be grounds for denial of license.

Training course: Various.

Carry prohibitions: Law enforcement facilities; detention facilities or jails; courtrooms; meetings of governmental or legislative entities; school, college, or professional athletic events; bars; churches or places of worship; schools or college facilities; anywhere carrying firearms is prohibited by state or federal law.

Reciprocity: Wyoming honors licenses from states that recognize its licenses, provided the licenses are valid statewide, and the state has laws similar to Wyoming's. These are AL, AK, AZ, CO, FL, GA, ID, IN, KY, LA, MI, MS, MT, NH, NM, OH, OK, PA, SC, SD, TN, TX, and UT. In addition Wyoming licenses are honored in MO. Visitors do not need licenses to carry concealed or openly in AK and VT.

Active licenses: 11,977 as of August 31, 2007.

License holders as a percentage of state population: 2.33.

AFTERWORD

Now that you have reached the end of this book, you should have a good idea of the rights and responsibilities of carrying a handgun. Stay out of trouble when you can, but stay in practice for when you can't. Live up to the responsibilities and guard the rights of keeping and bearing arms.

We live in a society where social order is breaking down and the number of violent crimes in which guns, particularly handguns, are used is very high. However, guns are not the cause of violent crime. Both Switzerland and Israel have well-armed civilian populations yet suffer little violent crime. Terrorism in Israel is a separate issue.

Unfortunately, it is all too easy for politicians to blame our high crime rate on inanimate objects—guns—rather than address more complex problems, such as the breakdown of the family, kids without adequate supervision or education, or violent video games, movies, and television. Politicians looking for something to ban are aided and abetted by members of the news media, most of whom know little about guns and are afraid of them.

I have been a handgun shooter and enthusiast for more than four decades. When I grew up in England, it was possible, but difficult, to own and shoot a handgun or rifle. When I migrated to Canada in the 1960s there were few restrictions on owning rifles and shotguns. There was more red tape to owning a handgun, but it was still possible. For a time in the late-1960s I lived in Australia and found a similar situation there.

Recently I have been appalled to see how restricted gun ownership and particularly handgun ownership has become in those countries. In 1996, a lunatic armed with legally-owned handguns gunned down a group of school kids in Scotland. In a knee-jerk response the government outlawed handguns. As a result, all handguns owned by law-abiding British civilians have been confiscated. Only the military and police have handguns in a country where the police used to pride themselves on being unarmed. Britain's Olympic pistol competitors have to practice in other countries. Armed robberies in London have reached epidemic proportions.

Also in 1996, another mental case opened fire with a semi-automatic rifle on a crowd of tourists in Tasmania. Using the excuse that it will cut down violent crime, the Australian government banned all semi-automatic rifles and all semi-automatic and pump-action shotguns. Since the ban, violent crime has skyrocketed. In Canada, the government has spent a billion dollars trying to set up a bureaucracy to register all seven million long guns in the country. Handguns are already registered and strictly controlled. The next step, of course, will be confiscation.

Here in the United States most of us are still able to enjoy the possession of arms, provided we don't live in one of the country's three largest and most dangerous cities—New York, Chicago, or Los Angeles. We are even making headway in many states in the battle to bear arms for self defense. But it will take only one massacre of the Killeen type by a licensed handgun carrier to turn the tide. We cannot afford to give the news media any cause for legitimate criticism. Therefore, I urge you to act responsibly, not just to preserve your right to bear arms, but so others may continue to enjoy the rights envisaged by the founding fathers. I also urge you to join the National Rifle Association, without which I am sure we would have lost those rights already.

Finally, may you never have to use your gun in self defense, but if you do I hope you will acquit yourself well. If you become involved in an armed confrontation, and if you found the information in this book of help or hindrance, please let me know.

GLOSSARY

auto-loader, auto-loading pistol. *See* semi-automatic.

ball. Usually used to refer to military ammunition loaded with round-nosed bullets.

barrel. Tube attached to a handgun through which the bullet passes when fired from the cartridge.

belly band. A belt about four inches wide, usually made of elastic and nylon, that is worn under a shirt above the waist band and contains a built-in holster.

bullet. Projectile fired by a handgun or rifle.

butt. Where the gun is gripped. The lower part of the frame to which the stocks are attached.

caliber. Measurement in decimal fractions of an inch or millimeters of the internal diameter of a gun barrel.

cartridge. A piece of ammunition consisting of a case, primer, powder, and bullet.

case, casing. The cylinder-shaped container with one closed end into which primer, powder, and bullet are inserted to form a cartridge or round of ammunition.

centerfire. Refers to a gun that fires a cartridge containing a primer in the center of the base of the cartridge case.

chamber. Cylinder into which a cartridge is put. A semi-automatic pistol contains one chamber that forms the rear end of the barrel. A revolver contains several chambers arranged in a circle in the cylinder.

clip. Sometimes used inaccurately as a synonym for magazine.

crane. The yoke that attaches a revolver's cylinder to its frame.

cross draw. A way of carrying a handgun in a belt holster on the side of the body opposite the shooting hand. A right-handed shooter would carry a cross-draw holster on the left side of his belt. Drawing from a cross-draw holster requires the shooting arm to cross the chest to reach the holstered gun.

cylinder. A metal cylinder set in the frame of a revolver in which several chambers are drilled to contain cartridges.

cylinder latch. The latch, usually located on the left side of the frame, that holds a revolver cylinder closed.

double action. Originally a term that indicated a handgun could be fired in two ways: by cocking the hammer manually and squeezing the trigger or by a long, heavy pull on the trigger that cocks the hammer and lets it fall. It has come to mean shooting a handgun using the long, self-cocking pull and to refer to handguns designed to be fired in this way.

double stack. Describes a magazine for a semi-automatic pistol that staggers the rounds in it so it can hold more ammunition for a given length. It is wider than a single stack magazine.

draw. The process of taking a handgun from a holster and bringing it into a firing position.

ejection port. A slot machined into the slide of a semi-automatic pistol through which the fired case is ejected from the gun.

firing pin. A pin that when rapped by the hammer hits the primer, which ignites the powder and fires the bullet. Some revolvers have the firing pin attached to the hammer, others are spring loaded in the frame. Semi-automatics usually have the firing pin set in the slide.

frame. The body of a handgun, to which all other parts are attached.

front sight. Used in conjunction with the rear sight to aim a handgun, it is usually located on the muzzle-end of the barrel or slide. Can be ramp or post shaped, or in older guns even semi-circular.

grain. A measure used to describe the weight of a bullet or the powder in a cartridge. There are seven thousand grains in a pound.

grip. The position of the hands in holding a handgun. Has also come to be used to describe the butt or part of the gun that is gripped.

grip safety. A safety lever in the butt which is depressed when the gun is gripped correctly.

grips. Has come to be used as a synonym for stocks.

hammer. A moving part of a handgun's action that is tripped by the trigger and drives the firing pin into the primer, firing the cartridge.

handgun. A gun designed to be fired with one hand. Most modern self-defense handguns are revolvers or semi-automatics.

hip draw. To draw a handgun from a holster located on the belt in the area of the hip on the side of the shooting hand. The holster holds the gun butt to the rear.

hollow point. A bullet that has a cavity in its front end designed to make it expand when it hits flesh.

holster. A pouch, usually made of leather, molded plastic, or woven nylon, designed to hold a handgun being worn on the person.

magazine. A narrow box that contains cartridges and usually fits into the butt of a semi-automatic. It contains a follower and a spring.

magazine well. The slot in the butt of a semi-automatic into which the magazine is inserted.

misfire. When the firing pin hits the primer of a cartridge but the round fails to fire. Can be caused by a weak firing pin spring or defective primer.

muzzle. The end of a gun barrel where the bullet emerges when the gun is fired.

powder. The propellant which provides the energy to drive the bullet out of the barrel and to the target.

primer. A small metal cap in the base of a cartridge that contains the detonating compound that ignites the powder.

rack. To pull the slide of a semi-automatic back and let it go. Used in loading, unloading, and clearing malfunctions.

rear sight. Used in conjunction with front sight to aim the handgun, it is usually located on the rear end of the slide or frame. It usually takes the form of a rectangular-shaped notch between horizontal shoulders.

recoil. The kick experienced by a shooter when the weapon fires.

revolver. A multiple-shot handgun that carries usually five or six cartridges in a revolving cylinder.

rimfire. A cartridge or weapon that fires a cartridge with the detonating compound inside the rim of the case.

rifling. The twisting grooves cut in the barrel of a gun designed to put a spin on the bullet to make it more stable in flight.

round. A cartridge.

safety. A small lever that prevents a gun being fired.

semi-automatic, semi-auto. Short for semi-automatic or self-loading pistol. Fires one shot for each pull of the trigger. Uses energy from the fired cartridge to eject the spent case and recharge the chamber with a fresh round from the magazine.

semi-wadcutter. A bullet with a truncated-cone-shaped nose.

single action. A handgun that can be fired only after the hammer is cocked manually.

single stack. Describes a magazine for a semi-automatic pistol that holds the rounds one on top of another rather than staggered. It is narrower than a double stack magazine and holds fewer rounds for a given length.

slide. The top part of a semi-automatic that usually contains the barrel and on which the sights are mounted.

snubby. A short barreled revolver, usually in .38 Special or .357 Magnum caliber.

speedloader. A device used for reloading a double-action revolver. It holds five or six rounds in a cylindrical pattern.

stopping power. The ability of a cartridge to stop an adversary. It is an imprecise calculation that takes into account bullet shape, weight, and speed.

stovepipe. A malfunction in a semi-automatic in which a fired cartridge case is not ejected but gets stuck vertically in the ejection port and resembles a stovepipe.

strong hand. The hand you normally shoot with when shooting one handed; the right hand of a right-handed shooter.

trigger. The lever that fires the gun, usually pressed by the forefinger.

trigger guard. A partial hoop of metal attached to the frame that prevents the trigger from being pulled inadvertently.

weak hand. The supporting hand. Opposite of strong hand; left hand of a right-handed shooter.

wadcutter. A flat-nosed bullet with a sharp shoulder designed to cut clean holes in a paper target.

yoke. Another name for crane. It is the yoke that holds the cylinder of a revolver to the frame.

BIBLIOGRAPHY

Applegate, Col. Rex. *Kill or Get Killed: Riot Control Techniques, Manhandling, and Close Combat for Police and the Military.* Harrisburg, Penn.: Stackpole, 1961.

Askins, Col. Charles. *The Pistol Shooter's Book.* Harrisburg, Penn.: The Stackpole Company, 1961.

Awerbuck, Louis. *Tactical Reality: An Uncommon Look at Common-Sense Firearms Training and Tactics.* Boulder, Colo.: Paladin Press, 1999.

Ayoob, Massad F. *In the Gravest Extreme, the Role of the Firearm in Personal Protection.* Concord, N.H.: Police Bookshelf, 1980.

_____. *StressFire, Gunfighting for Police: Advanced Tactics and Techniques, vol. 1.* Concord, N.H.: Police Bookshelf, 1984.

_____. *The Truth about Self-Protection.* New York: Bantam Books, 1983.

Bloodworth, Trey, and Mike Raley. *Hidden in Plain Sight: A Practical Guide to Concealed Handgun Carry.* Chapel Hill, N.C.: Professional Press, 1995.

Bovard, James. *Terrorism and Tyranny: Trampling Freedom, Justice, and Peace to Rid the World of Evil.* New York: Palgrave Macmillan, 2003.

Cassidy, William L. *Quick or Dead.* Boulder, Colo.: Paladin Press, 1993.

Cirillo, Jim. *Guns, Bullets, and Gunfights: Lessons and Tales from a Modern-Day Gunfighter.* Boulder, Colo.: Paladin Press, 1996.

Cooper, Jeff. *Principles of Personal Defense.* Boulder, Colo.: Paladin Press, 1989.

_____. *To Ride, Shoot Straight and Speak the Truth.* Paulden, Ariz.: Gunsite Press, 1990.

Cramer, Clayton E., and David B. Kopel. *"Shall Issue": The New Wave of Concealed Handgun Permit Laws.* Golden, Colo.: Independence Institute, 1994.

Enos, Brian. *Practical Shooting: Beyond Fundamentals.* Clifton, Colo.: Zediker Publishing, 1990.

Fairbairn, Capt. William E., and Capt. Eric A. Sykes. *Shooting to Live, with the One Hand Gun.* Boulder, Colo.: Paladin Press, 1987.

Farnam, John S. *The Farnam Method of Defensive Handgunning.* Boulder, Colo.:DTI Publications, 2005.

Gaylord, Chic. *Handgunner's Guide.* New York: Hastings House, 1960.

Givens, Tom. *Fighting Smarter: A Practical Guide for Surviving Violent Confrontation.* Memphis, Tenn.: Rangemaster, 2000.

Grossman, Lt. Col. Dave. *On Killing: The Psychological Cost of Learning to Kill in War and Society.* New York: Little, Brown and Company, 1995.

Grossman, Lt. Col. Dave, Gloria DeGaetano. *Stop Teaching Our Kids to Kill: A Call to Action Against TV, Movie & Video Game Violence.* New York: Crown Publishers, 1999.

Hayes, Gila. *Effective Defense,* 2d ed. Seattle: Wash.: The Firearms Academy of Seattle, 2000.

Jenkins, John H., and H. Gordon Frost. *"I'm Frank Hamer": The Life of a Texas Peace Officer.* Austin and New York: Pemberton Press, 1968.

Jordan, William H. *No Second Place Winner.* N.p., 1965.

Keith, Elmer. *Sixguns by Keith.* Harrisburg, Penn.: The Stackpole Company, 1961.

Kleck, Gary. *Targeting Guns: Firearms and Their Control.* New York: Aldine de Gruyter, 1997.

_____, and Don B. Kates. *Armed: New Perspectives on Gun Control.* Amherst, N.Y.: Prometheus Books, 2001.

Kopel, David B. *The Samurai, the Mountie, and the Cowboy: Should America Adopt the Gun Controls of Other Democracies?* Buffalo, N.Y.: Prometheus Books, 1992.

Lake, Stuart N. *Wyatt Earp: Frontier Marshal.* Boston and New York: Houghton Mifflin, 1931.

LaPierre, Wayne. *Guns, Crime and Freedom.* Washington: Regnery Publishing, 1994.

Lott, John R., Jr. *The Bias against Guns: Why Almost Everything You've Heard about Gun Control Is Wrong.* Washington: Regnery Publishing, 2003.

_____. *More Guns, Less Crime: Understanding Crime and Gun Control Laws.* Chicago: University of Chicago Press, 1998.

Lovette, Ed. *The Snubby Revolver: The ECQ, Backup, and Concealed Carry Standard.* Boulder, Colo.: Paladin Press, 2007.

Lovette, Ed, Dave Spaulding. *Defensive Living: Preserving Your Personal Safety Through Awareness, Attitude & Armed Action.* New York: Looseleaf Law Publications, 2005.

McGivern, Ed. *Fast and Fancy Revolver Shooting and Police Training.* Chicago: Follett, 1938.

O'Connor, Jack, Roy Dunlap, Alex Kerr, and Jeff Cooper. *Complete Book of Shooting: Rifles, Shotguns, Handguns.* New York: Harper & Row, 1965.

Plaxco, J. Michael. *Shooting from Within.* Clifton, Colo., Zediker Publishing, 1991.

Quigley, Paxton. *Armed & Female.* New York: E. P. Dutton, 1989.

Rauch, Walt. *Real-World Survival: What Has Worked For Me.* Lafayette Hill, Penn.: Rauch & Company, 1998.

Rosa, Joseph G. *They Called Him Wild Bill: The Life and Adventures of James Butler Hickok.* Norman, Okla.: University of Oklahoma Press, 1974.

Siddle, Bruce K. *Sharpening the Warrior's Edge.* Millstadt, Ill.: PPCT Research Publications, 1995.

Stanford, Andy. *Fight at Night: Tools, Techniques, Tactics, and Training for Combat in Low Light and Darkness.* Boulder, Colo.: Paladin Press, 1999.

_____. *Surgical Speed Shooting: How to Achieve High-Speed Marksmanship in a Gunfight.* Boulder, Colo.: Paladin Press, 2001.

Taylor, Chuck. *The Complete Book of Combat Handgunning.* Boulder, Colo.: Paladin Press, 1982.

Taylor, John "Pondoro." *African Rifles & Cartridges.* Georgetown, S.C.: Thomas G. Samworth, 1948.

INDEX

Red Lake Indian Reservation high
   school, 23
Reid, Richard, 74
reloading, 214, 281, 283-293, 336,
   405
   empty, for revolver, 288-292
   empty, for semi-automatic,
   284-286
   tactical, for revolver, 292-293
   tactical, for semi-automatic,
   286-288
reloading equipment. See handloading equipment
Reno, Janet, 23, 88
Response Options, 15-17, 37
retention draw. See draw, from a
   holster
revolvers, 148-161
   versus semi-automatics, 178-
   181
Rhode Island, 437, 451
Ridge, Tom, 79 80
right-to-carry laws, 112, 425- 438
Riley, Warren, 44
road rage, 136
Roberts, Charles Carl, 23-24
Rodriguez, Albert, 315
Roosevelt, Theodore, 136
Rorke's Drift, battle of, 333-334
Ross, Todd, 10
Ruff, Candy, 102-104, 425
Ruger. See Sturm, Ruger & Co.
Ruggerio, Kevin, 211-212
Rupp, Tim, 224
Ryker, Jake, 17-22, 24, 25
Ryker, Robert, 19-22, 25
safety and handling, 211-219
safety precautions, 120-129, 207-
   208, 213-229
safety rules, 213-218, 337
school shootings, 1-37

teaching students to fight
   back, 15-17
Schumer, Charles, 115
Second Amendment Foundation,
   44-45
Second Amendment to the
   Constitution, 24, 26, 44, 109-
   110, 433, 370
Seecamp, L. W., Co., 170, 182
   semi-automatics, 170-172, 203
Selleck, Tom, 25
semi-automatic pistols, 161-181
September 11, 2001, 70-75, 77, 78
"shall-issue" laws, 105-118, 425- 438
shooting. See handgun shooting
shooting organizations, 423
shooting positions
   kneeling, 281
   one handed, 243, 244
   prone, 281-283
   standing, 239-244
   supine, 282-283
shooting schools and courses, 408-
   417
Shreveport, 46-56
Siddle, Bruce, 240, 303-304, 330
SIG Sauer, Inc., 182
   semi-automatics, 164, 166-
   168, 180, 203
sight alignment and sight picture,
   233, 244-247, 264, 274, 301-
   305
sights, 247-258
   fiber-optic, 247
   laser, 251-258
   tritium, 248, 250-251
   XS Express, 247-249, 268
single action. See revolvers, semi-
   automatic pistols
Smith, Clint, 102, 120, 263, 267, 273,
   275, 283-284, 301, 316, 336,
   360, 393, 397, 416-417, 418

Give the Gift of Knowledge
to Yourself or Someone Else

CALL TOLL-FREE AND ORDER NOW

 1-888-700-4333

Please have your card ready.

Orders by mail: **Privateer Publications**, P.O. Box 29427, San Antonio, TX 78229. Make checks and money orders payable to: **Privateer Publications**.

Please send _____ copies of ***The Concealed Handgun Manual*** at $22.95 each, plus $5 each for shipping and handling. Texas residents add $1.89 each sales tax.

Please send _____ copies of ***Thank God I Had a Gun*** at $19.95 each, plus $5 each for shipping and handling. Texas residents add $1.65 each for sales tax.

Name: _____

Organization: _____

Address: _____

City, State, ZIP: _____

Phone: _____email: _____

Total enclosed or authorized to be charged: $ _____

Card # _____ Exp. Date: _____

Three digit check # on signature panel: _____

Signature: _____

I understand that I may return any books for a full refund for any reason, no questions asked. Please phone 210-308-8191 for information on quantity discounts.

Visit our web site for more information at:
www.privateerpublications.com

Give the Gift of Knowledge
to Yourself or Someone Else

CALL TOLL-FREE AND ORDER NOW

 1-888-700-4333
Please have your card ready.

Orders by mail: **Privateer Publications**, P.O. Box 29427, San Antonio, TX 78229. Make checks and money orders payable to: **Privateer Publications**.

Please send _____ copies of *The Concealed Handgun Manual* at $22.95 each, plus $5 each for shipping and handling. Texas residents add $1.89 each sales tax.

Please send _____ copies of *Thank God I Had a Gun* at $19.95 each, plus $5 each for shipping and handling. Texas residents add $1.65 each for sales tax.

Name: _____
Organization: _____
Address: _____
City, State, ZIP: _____
Phone: _____email: _____
Total enclosed or authorized to be charged: $ _____
Card # _____ Exp. Date: _____
Three digit check # on signature panel: _____
Signature: _____

I understand that I may return any books for a full refund for any reason, no questions asked. Please phone 210-308-8191 for information on quantity discounts.

'isit our web site for more information at:
  vw.**privateerpublications.com**